Interventions: New Studies in Medieval Culture

ETHAN KNAPP, SERIES EDITOR

Form and Reform

Reading across the Fifteenth Century

EDITED BY
SHANNON GAYK AND
KATHLEEN TONRY

THE OHIO STATE UNIVERSITY PRESS · COLUMBUS

Copyright © 2011 by The Ohio State University.
All rights reserved.

Library of Congress Cataloging-in-Publication Data
Form and reform : reading across the fifteenth century / edited by Shannon Gayk and Kathleen Tonry.
    p. cm. — (Interventions: new studies in medieval culture)
Includes bibliographical references and index.
ISBN-13: 978-0-8142-1163-2 (cloth : alk. paper)
ISBN-10: 0-8142-1163-1 (cloth : alk. paper)
ISBN-13: 978-0-8142-9264-8 (cd)
  1. English literature—Middle English, 1100–1500—History and criticism. 2. Literary form—History—To 1500. I. Gayk, Shannon Noelle. II. Tonry, Kathleen Ann. III. Series: Interventions : new studies in medieval culture.
PR293.F67 2011
820.9'002—dc22
                        2010053790

This book is available in the following editions:
Cloth (ISBN 978-0-8142-1163-2)
CD-ROM (ISBN 978-0-8142-9264-8)
Paper (ISBN: 978-0-8142-5633-6)
Cover design by Laurence Nozik
Type set in Times New Roman

contents

List of Illustrations   vii
List of Abbreviations   ix
Acknowledgments   xi

Introduction: The "Sotil Fourmes" of the Fifteenth Century
    KATHLEEN TONRY   1

PART 1. THE MATERIALS OF FORM

1   Forms of Reading in the Book of Brome
    JESSICA BRANTLEY   19

2   The Style of Humanist Latin Letters at the University of Oxford: On Thomas Chaundler and the *Epistolae Academicae Oxon.* (*Registrum F*)
    ANDREW COLE   40

PART 2. FORMS OF DEVOTION

3   Osbern Bokenham's "englische boke": Re-forming Holy Women
    KAREN A. WINSTEAD   67

4   "Ete this book": Literary Consumption and Poetic Invention in John Capgrave's *Life of Saint Katherine*
    SHANNON GAYK   88

5   Jesus' Voice: Dialogue and Late-Medieval Readers
    REBECCA KRUG   110

PART 3. REFORMING SKELTON

6   Conception Is a Blessing: Marian Devotion, Heresy, and the Literary in Skelton's *A Replycacion*
    ROBERT J. MEYER-LEE   133

7 Useless Mouths: Reformist Poetics in Audelay and Skelton
   MISHTOONI BOSE   159

8 Killing Authors: Skelton's Dreadful *Bowge of Courte*
   JAMES SIMPSON   180

Bibliography   197
Contributors   213
Index   215

list of illustrations

CHAPTER 1

Figure 1.1. New Haven, Yale University, Beinecke Library MS 365 [Book of Brome], f. 19v. Atypical layout with stage directions integrated into speech. 24

Figure 1.2. New Haven, Yale University, Beinecke Library MS 365 [Book of Brome], f. 2v. Poem on fortune-telling with dice. 26

Figure 1.3. New Haven, Yale University, Beinecke Library MS 365 [Book of Brome], f. 14v. Final page of *Adrian and Epotys* with devotional emblem. 27

Figure 1.4. New Haven, Yale University, Beinecke Library MS 365 [Book of Brome], f. 15r. First page of *Abraham and Isaac*. 30

Figure 1.5. New Haven, Yale University, Beinecke Library MS 365 [Book of Brome], f. 1r. "Man in merthe hath meser in mynd." 32

CHAPTER 2

Figure 2.1. Oxford University Archives NEP/supra/Reg F [Registrum F], f. 65r 45

CHAPTER 6

Figure 6.1. San Marino, Calif., Huntington Library: Skelton's *A Replycacion* (printed by Richard Pynson, 1528), STC 22609, A1v. Reproduced by permission of The Huntington Library, San Marino, California. 144

Figure 6.2. San Marino, Calif., Huntington Library: Skelton's *A Replycacion* (printed by Richard Pynson, 1528), STC 22609, A2v. Reproduced by permission of The Huntington Library, San Marino, California. 145

List of Illustrations

Figure 6.3. San Marino, Calif., Huntington Library: Skelton's *A Replycacion* (printed by Richard Pynson, 1528), STC 22609, B2v. Reproduced by permission of The Huntington Library, San Marino, California. 153

Figure 6.4. San Marino, Calif., Huntington Library: Skelton's *A Replycacion* (printed by Richard Pynson, 1528), STC 22609, A1r. Reproduced by permission of The Huntington Library, San Marino, California. 156

list of abbreviations

EETS	*Early English Text Society*
e.s.	Extra Series
o.s.	Original Series
s.s.	Special Series
MED	*Middle English Dictionary*
OED	*Oxford English Dictionary*
PL	*Patrologia Latina*
STC	A. W. Pollard and G. R. Redgrave, *A Short Title Catalogue of Books Printed in England, Scotland, and Ireland, and of English Books Printed Abroad, 1475–1640*, ed. W. A. Jackson, F. S. Ferguson, and Katherine F. Pantzer, 2nd ed., 3 vols. (London, Bibliographical Society, 1976–91).

acknowledgments

This volume began, as many books do, with some casual but excited conversation; this particular one started after a typically witty and provocative paper at Kalamazoo by Steven Justice on new formalism. That the conversation has been extended and deepened, both over time and among so many of our colleagues, deserves at the very least this written record.

Our casual talk found its first formal platform in a series of three panels entitled "At the End of the Fifteenth Century," delivered at the International Congress of Medieval Studies held at Kalamazoo. We are grateful to Steven Justice for his role as a remarkable respondent to those sessions. In addition to the contributors with essays in this volume, Amy Appleford, Lisa Cooper, Vincent Gillespie, and Susan Phillips all presented papers that moved our conversations forward and contributed to this volume in ways that are enmeshed in the notes, critical contexts, and scope of these essays.

As a collaborative project, this volume also benefited from the collegiality of both the editors' institutions. At the University of Connecticut, we would like to thank C. David Benson, Frederick M. Biggs, Robert Hasenfratz and, although only honorary medievalists, Brian and Mary Lynch. At Indiana University we are especially grateful for the guidance of Patricia Clare Ingham. And while medievalists are famously collegial folk, the support and encouragement of Nicholas Watson and Daniel Wakelin deserve special mention. Finally, the influence and inspiration of our teacher, Maura Nolan, is everywhere in this volume. As a mentor, she has a talent for challenging her students to reform their thinking until the best ideas take form.

Acknowledgments

The editors at The Ohio State University Press, Malcolm Litchfield and Ethan Knapp, were supportive of and expertly guided this project from its earliest stages. We are also grateful to the press's two anonymous readers, who contributed so many excellent comments to each of the essays. Our final thanks go to our contributors, for not only their fine essays, but also for their willingness to engage creatively with the theme of this collection.

introduction

The "Sotil Fourmes" of the Fifteenth Century

KATHLEEN TONRY

I.

>   Logiciens deliyte in argumentys
>   Philosophers in vertuous lyuynge
>   And legistres folowynge the ententys
>   Greatly reioyse in lucre and wynnynge
>   Phesiciens trauayle for getinge
>   And of poetys this the sotil fourme
>   By newe Invencion thynges to transfourme.[1]
>   —John Lydgate, *Fall of Princes* (c. 1431–38)

This stanza from the third book of *Fall of Princes* appears as John Lydgate launches a defense for the value of poetic work alongside other intellectual professions, including logicians, philosophers, lawyers, and physicians. Until the last couplet the argument of these lines is obvious, even pedestrian: practitioners of various professions pursue predictable goals, or simply monetary gain. At the level of syntax, the stanza sets up a repeating pattern where subjects are linked to the present tense of a simple verb: logicians "deliyte," as do philosophers; lawyers "reioyse"; physicians "trauayle." Yet in those last two lines the verb is deferred to the very end, where it occurs in the more complicated form of a tran-

---

1. *Fall of Princes*, 4 vols. ed. Henry Bergen, EETS, e.s. 122 (Oxford: Oxford University Press, 1924–27; rpt.1967): 3.3815–21. This stanza occurs as part of a longer argument against construing poetic work as idleness, which Lydgate imports largely from Boccaccio.

sitive infinitive, "to transfourme," which demands that the reader return not to the "poetys," but rather to the more unexpected "sotil fourme" as the new governing agent of the couplet.

Lydgate's adjectival "sotil" indicates that which is exceptionally artful, skilled, or gracefully wrought;[2] it is precisely this emphasis on the artfulness of poetic form that invites attention to Lydgate's own exploration of form through a close reading of syntax, diction, and rhyme. And it is the emergence of form as an active agent, yoked and then transmuted by rhyme into the verb "transform," that recasts poetic work not just as a specific kind of writing but as a language constantly in motion, animated by its consistent interaction with and reshaping of the "thynges" of the world. In turn, Lydgate's "poetys"—here removed by syntax from the linear alignments of those other professions with their singular goals—both produce and are produced by the ongoing work of this "sotil fourme" of language.

Lydgate is an apt spokesman for a perspective on form that demonstrates both the familiarity and dissonance of a late-medieval poetic in relation to the critical strategies of literary studies. On the one hand, the uneven, disruptive, and sometimes awkward formal features of a stanza like the one above recall the long centuries of scholarly skepticism about Lydgate, centuries during which the field's most prominent scholars each succeeded to a rather merry tradition of scolding Lydgate for writing such verse.[3] The work of Lydgate has provided a kind of proving ground for formalist critiques of the fifteenth century, most of which are full-throated in their pessimism, while also attesting to the persistence of formalism itself in medieval scholarship.[4]

Yet on the other hand, that same stanza's articulation of form aligns surprisingly well with current critical directions, which emphasize the creative, energetic capacities of form at work within a generously configured aesthetic field: in short, form matters now, and it matters to histories material, discursive, and literary in the ways that it seems to have mattered for Lydgate as the very engine of "newe Invencion" itself. This replacement of formalism with an attention to form has been embraced in recent medieval scholarship, especially at the chronologically

---

2. MED, s.v. "sotil" especially 2c.

3. A representative sample of formalist readings of Lydgate include: Thomas Warton, *The History of English Poetry from the Twelfth to the Close of the Sixteenth Century*, ed. W. Carew Hazlott (London: Reeves and Turner, 1871; orig. pub. 1774–1781); C. S. Lewis, *English Literature in the Sixteenth Century Excluding Drama* (Oxford: Clarendon Press, 1954); and Derek Pearsall, *John Lydgate* (London: Routledge and Kegan Paul, 1970) and, more recently, as editor of *Chaucer to Spenser: An Anthology of Writings in English, 1375–1575* (Oxford: Blackwell, 1999). For overviews of critical (and mostly formalist) hostility to Lydgate, see Phillipa Hardman, "Lydgate's Uneasy Syntax," in *John Lydgate: Poetry, Culture, and Lancastrian England*, ed. Larry Scanlon and James Simpson (Notre Dame: University of Notre Dame Press, 2006): 12–35.

4. See Seth Lerer, "The Endurance of Formalism in Middle English Studies," *Literature Compass* 1 (2003): 1–15.

early and late parts of the field, but not without its own push-pull in relation to the broader disciplinary conversation, and not without Lydgate.

Medievalists' recent explorations of form clearly align with what Susan Wolfson has termed "activist" investments."[5] These investments draw deeply on Marxist—and more specifically, Adornean—theories about the relation between aesthetics and the historical/cultural horizon; here "form" emerges as a dynamic force, a participant in the processes of history in ways that are, as Stephen Cohen has noted, "productive rather than merely reflective."[6] The priority of form in this mode of analysis is one that relies on the movements of history in dialectical engagement with the work of form, each in transformative tension with the other. Thus Maura Nolan argues, in her study of Lydgate, "that form—meaning those conventions through which experience is rendered legible and lent a significance that transcends the local (particular times and places)—constitutes the only genuinely historical category of analysis for the cultural critic, that it is only through grasping how form works in culture that we may come to understand the historicity of the past."[7] The work of form, then, relies on the work of the reader in detecting tensions and competing interpretations (what Adorno terms "contradictions"), and in this too, medieval scholarship and early poetic texts find fruitful alliance. D. Vance Smith, for example, demonstrates the ways in which medieval poets anticipated complex and intricate readings as these were "part of the communal experience of educated reading in the English Middle Ages, a reading for form that proceeded out of a common discipline and that ultimately formed the community of readers."[8] We have already seen this anticipation of a sophisticated readership in action: the stanza opening this essay offers itself up to close reading through the slight waver in its syntactic structure, a feature that pays back such attention by imaginatively reconfiguring the poetic arena in which such readerly work takes place.

But the medievalist turn to form also strikes a note of challenge. Christopher Cannon, whose work has pioneered the new emphasis on form especially in analyses of early Middle English texts, insists that "while English literature in all periods might benefit from such careful attention to form, this method is also *uniquely* valuable for the understanding of Middle English."[9] As Cannon traces

---

5. Susan Wolfson, "Introduction," in *Reading for Form*, ed. Susan Wolfson and Marshall Brown (Seattle and London: University of Washington Press, 2006): 3–24; see esp. 6. Carol Levinson has recently put the term "activist formalism" to more central use in her useful overview of the "new formalism" in "What Is New Formalism?" *PMLA* 122.2 (2007): 558–69.

6. Stephen Cohen, "Between Form and Culture: New Historicism and the Promise of Historical Formalism," in *Renaissance Literature and Its Formal Engagements*, ed. Mark David Rasmussen (New York: Palgrave, 2002): 17–41, see esp. 23. Also cited by Levinson, 563.

7. Maura Nolan, *John Lydgate and the Making of Public Culture* (Cambridge: Cambridge University Press, 2004): 28.

8. D. Vance Smith, "Medieval *Forma:* The Logic of the Work," in *Reading for Form*, 79.

9. Christopher Cannon, "Form," in *Oxford Twenty-First Century Approaches to Literature: Middle*

back this singularity to the historical conditions of early texts, his subsequent readings imply that medieval literature provides a uniquely historicized accounting of form that carries with it genuinely new structuring dynamics between immaterial and material, between the literary and what he elsewhere terms the "grounds" of literature. Smith similarly works through a medieval interest in form (or more accurately, *forma*) that details the close exploration and ultimate reconciliation of the *forma tractandi* and *forma tractatus* as modes of thinking through the work of a text.[10] These scholars, among others, situate medieval literature as a powerfully innovative corpus that offers up to the attentive reader often surprising configurations of the "literary" and the "thynges" of history, as discovered in the scrolling narrative of images embroidered on a tapestry, in the early-fourteenth-century experimentations with propositional language, and in fifteenth-century mummings.[11]

These interventions in the early part of our collective literary history not only insist on historicizing concepts of form, but also present alternative modalities of form that are crucial in emphasizing the often submerged pressures of medieval literature at work upon our literary histories. Close attention to the specific forms of individual medieval texts—in many cases, the sole extant copies—is a critique-in-practice of the notion that "new formalism" is, at its core, the recuperation of the "promises of new historicism," as several authors of Renaissance-oriented essay collections have put it.[12] Instead, the uniqueness *and* the diversity of medieval literary forms suggests that the experimental, innovative energy of medieval poetics continues to work upon our literary histories in ways not always visible nor even traceable but nevertheless deeply influential.

The renewed critical attention to form has revealed, particularly in Lydgate

---

English, ed. Paul Strohm (Oxford: Oxford University Press, 2007): 178; italics mine.

10. D. Vance Smith, "Medieval *Forma:* The Logic of the Work," 66–79.

11. These examples are from work by Christopher Cannon in *The Grounds of English Literature* (Oxford: Oxford University Press, 2004), as well as D. Vance Smith and Maura Nolan, as cited above.

12. Carol Levinson notes this tendency in her PMLA overview—see especially her summary of the "mixed bag" of new formalism (562). The claim on new formalism by early modern scholars is staked out quite boldly: see Stephen Cohen, "Between Form and Culture" (17–41), as well as Rasmussen's introductory essay, "New Formalisms?" (1–14) and Richard Strier, "How Formalism Became a Dirty Word and Why We Can't Do Without It" (207–15, esp. 213), all in *Renaissance Literature and Its Formal Engagements.* The pursuit of a "new formalism" out of the ashes of the new historicism—and as particularly germane to Renaissance studies and texts—is also writ large in the title and scope of the volume *Shakespeare and Historical Formalism,* ed. Stephen Cohen (Aldershot, UK: Ashgate, 2007). We should be wary of such a recovery unattended by skepticism, especially one that doesn't revisit the periodizing premises of much new historicist work. David Matthews, for instance, reminds us that early modernists remain "quite comfortable" with the new historicist thesis about self-awareness, a comfort and familiarity that helps explain why the traffic between medieval and early modern studies tends to run in one chronological direction (that is, forward). See David Matthews, "The Medieval Invasion of Early Modern England," *New Medieval Literatures* 10 (2008): 223–44. The distinctions made here between this Renaissance-centered recuperation and the recent medievalist turn to form seeks to avoid a recuperation of form that leaves intact the historical story of rupture, change and medieval difference.

scholarship, a rift between understandings of form as an aesthetic criterion or as a deeply historical expression. Lydgate's own prominence in discussions of the fifteenth century reveals the tensions between competing formalisms. Derek Pearsall, for example, situates Lydgate as an index to the "exhaustions" and "self-contradictions" of the fifteenth century, underscoring as evidence the ways that Lydgate's "verbosity, the inflation of his diction, the uneasiness of his syntax, and the unevenness of his metre are obstacles to pleasure."[13] As Larry Scanlon and James Simpson demonstrate in a joint essay, this kind of "aesthetic hostility" is typical of Lydgate scholarship and has defined Lydgate's place in literary history for over a century, while also (in the way of formalism) situating him as a synecdochal key to a whole fifteenth-century poetic: Lydgate is often the dreadful flag-bearer for a dreadful century in literary history.[14] The first full-length monograph on Lydgate after Pearsall's study, Maura Nolan's *John Lydgate and the Making of Public Culture,* begins a recuperation of Lydgate's critical status precisely through re-historicizing his use of different literary forms. Nolan foregrounds the category of the literary, yet because she situates form and history as part of an integral dynamic, her study also organically moves into a revision of the political narratives (especially Lancastrianism) most frequently used to frame the fifteenth century. Nolan thus avers formal*ism* in favor of a more dynamic picture of form at work through and with its specific historical horizons.

It is James Simpson's work on the literary history of the fifteenth century that reveals most broadly both the productive entanglements of form with history, and Lydgate's central role as the subject of pioneering studies in the fifteenth century. In his landmark *Reform and Cultural Revolution,* Simpson argues forcefully for a Lydgate who represents what he terms a "reformist" culture, one in which the discursive responses to change are registered by an emphasis on continuities, the strategies of *bricolage* and accretion, and features that disallow cultural monopoly while emphasizing complexity, dispersal, and juxtaposition—all features and strategies that recognize, in short, historicity.[15] This strong revision of the historical discourse used to describe the "medieval" presents a capacious, plural context upon which the forms of literature work, and from which Simpson launches his own account of literary forms over the years 1350–1550. Although certainly not formalist, Simpson's resituated literary history everywhere emphasizes the literary play of forms at the structural and stylistic level, and their cultural work

---

13. Derek Pearsall, *From Chaucer to Spenser,* 343.
14. See Larry Scanlon and James Simpson, "Introduction," *John Lydgate: Poetry, Culture and Lancastrian England* (Notre Dame: University of Notre Dame Press, 2006): 1–11. See also Scanlon's essay in the same volume, "Lydgate's Poetics: Laureation and Domesticity in the *Temple of Glass,*" 61–97, as well as the analysis offered by James Simpson in the first chapter of *The Oxford English Literary History, Volume 2: 1350–1547; Reform and Cultural Revolution,* general editor Jonathan Bate (Oxford: Oxford University Press, 2002): 34–67.
15. Simpson, esp. 35–38 and 62.

within the reformist/revolutionary historical modes that underwrite them.[16] It is a recuperation of Lydgate that begins undoing formalist processes precisely by recapturing a sense of form as it engages with history.

And so it is John Lydgate who has become the field's critical touchstone, the spur to a large-scale reevaluation of both aesthetics and history that has pulled the fifteenth century into the foreground of medieval literary scholarship. Few studies on the literature of the fifteenth century can proceed without acknowledging the role of Lydgate in provoking and producing that period's current critical topos—form and reform—terms that describe not merely static poles but an unusually supple integration of both aesthetic and historical horizons. One effect of the emphasis on Lydgate has been a corresponding scholarly output weighted toward the reassessment of single authors writing in the first part of that century, locating the most detailed representations of the 1400s through the texts, writers, and contexts of its early decades.[17]

Yet although the fifteenth century has been recuperated through representations and studies of Lydgate, Lydgate himself died before its midway point, and the decades of his greatest productivity had little in common with the cascade of dramatic, tumultuous events and changes that marked the middle and later 1400s. His death in 1449 occurred a tick before the printing press made its appearance in Mainz, Germany; by 1500, Lydgate's work had appeared in twenty-four editions from the various presses of a native English industry. The year 1450 also saw Jack Cade's rebellion in Kent, just one event in a series of political oscillations that included the beginning of what we now call the Wars of the Roses in 1455, the brief and awkward Readeption of Henry VI, Richard III's usurpation, and the ascension of the Tudors. The span of the medieval now marches well past the Battle of Bosworth, of course; John Watts noted over a decade ago that the "hegemony of 1485 has been well and truly broken," replaced by the thicker and more complex

---

16. See especially 62–67 for the careful construction of the move from a "reformist" cultural context into a wide-ranging discussion of literary form.

17. These include: Nolan, *John Lydgate and the Making of Public Culture* (2005); Lisa H. Cooper and Andrea Denny-Brown, eds., *Lydgate Matters: Poetry and Material Culture in the Fifteenth Century* (New York: Palgrave, 2007); Scanlon and Simpson, eds., *John Lydgate: Poetry, Culture, and Lancastrian England*; Ethan Knapp, *The Bureaucratic Muse: Thomas Hoccleve and the Literature of Late Medieval England* (State Park, PA: Pennsylvania State University Press, 2001); Nicholas Perkins, *Hoccleve's 'Regiment of Princes': Counsel and Constraint* (Cambridge: D. S. Brewer, 2001); Nigel Mortimer, *John Lydgate's Fall of Princes: Narrative Tragedy in Its Literary and Political Contexts* (Oxford: Oxford University Press, 2005). Lydgate's revival and the resulting move into the fifteenth century is due to several important earlier works, among them Seth Lerer's *Chaucer and His Readers: Imagining the Author in Late-Medieval England* (Princeton: Princeton University Press, 1993); Larry Scanlon's *Narrative, Authority and Power* (Cambridge: Cambridge University Press, 1994); and Paul Strohm's *England's Empty Throne* (New Haven: Yale University Press, 1998). It is also true, of course, that several recent studies—especially those tracing specific genres, manuscript and print contexts, and religious writing—move beyond a Lydgatean context. See Matthews, "Early Medieval Invasion," for a detailed overview and analysis.

watershed of the 1530s.[18] This elongation of the late medieval, however, leaves an even greater gap between the critically excavated early 1400s and the Reformation, a gap figured as an odd aporia around figures closest to the Reformation events. Influential *literati* working right at the cusp of the period, like John Rastell, Alexander Barclay, Henry Medwall and Stephen Hawes, remain critical ciphers.[19]

Even apart from these figures, whose very nearness to the concurrent discursive, theological, and historiographical ruptures of the Reformation might logically bracket their consideration, there is a substantial corpus of literature produced between the death of Lydgate and the Reformation—or even, to narrow the scope, between the middle and end of that century. Reginald Pecock was forced to recant his writings in 1457, but other religious writers, among them John Capgrave, Osbern Bokenham, and Henry Bradshaw, made important contributions that reflected the period's considerable intellectual investments around religious writing. Those decades, too, span the careers of William Caxton, Thomas Malory, William Worcester, and George Ashby, and demonstrate a thriving interest in the genre of romance (*Ipomedon*, for instance, was translated at different points in the latter years of the century into prose, stanzaic verse, and couplet versions). They also saw the production of manuscript records of the cycle plays, as well as the Robin Hood story cycles and the plays *Mankind* and *Everyman*. Lydgate stands at the beginning of a very, very long century, one marked by more questions than answers about aesthetic and historical continuity. Indeed, this long century is often uneasily compressed, not only into its first quarter, but into narratives that expect it either to anticipate the early modern or regressively turn back to the fourteenth century.

And so this volume now moves, if not entirely past Lydgate, at least beyond a Lydgatean fifteenth century. Shifting our perspective away from the early years of the century offers an alternative reading of the middle and late 1400s that discloses disruptions and contradictions among a diverse group of authors and texts. John Skelton, the Book of Brome, and the *Fifteen Oes* all find their places here within what we hope is a provocatively untidy fifteenth century. This cultivated untidiness refuses the responsibilities of an overview or survey—although often present in the scope of individual chapters, missing here are extended discussions about print, romances, alliterative forms, political verse, or lyrics. As a whole, rather, this volume suggests a fifteenth century available through a series of nodal points—several rather than all of which are represented here.

---

18. John Watts, "Introduction: History, the Fifteenth Century and the Renaissance," in *The End of the Middle Ages? England in the Fifteenth and Sixteenth Centuries*, ed. John Watts (Goucestershire, UK: Sutton Publishing, 1998): 17.

19. Important discussions of these writers have been included in recent monographs, among them Robert Meyer-Lee, *Poets and Power from Chaucer to Wyatt* (Cambridge: Cambridge University Press, 2007) and Daniel Wakelin, *Humanism, Reading and English Literature, 1430–1530* (Oxford: Oxford University Press, 2007).

Introduction

This volume also offers a distinct approach to the pressures of periodization, looking neither to the past, towards a coherent narrative defining the century, nor forward to the Reformation. Several recent studies in late-medieval poetics press back against periodizing discourses by tracing continuities and finding points of connection, tradition and similarity that undo the artificial break instantiated by the revolutionary discourses of the 1530s; this book is a meant to be a strong ally to that broader work.[20] Concentrating on the work just prior to the Reformation, however, is another kind of challenge to periodicity. These essays lend more specific texture to the years directly before the Reformation, but do so with attention focused on local formal innovations that emerge—if only temporarily—free from narratives that arc toward an historiographical break. Together these chapters resist patterns and trajectories, privileging instead the many and diverse "sotil fourmes" at work across the fifteenth century.

II.

Form and Reform developed out of a series of three panels at the International Medieval Congress in 2007. The original title of that thread—"At the End of the Fifteenth Century"—grew into an exploration of the century that often did not span the last decades of the century but instead yielded a far richer and more interestingly extended sense of a century that took up points both earlier and later than we had expected. We gratefully took our cue from our original panelists as we shaped this volume: while extending the critical chronology of work in the fifteenth century, the chapters traverse the full length of the century with an emphasis on the middle and later years—a move that these essays together imply is both essential and essentially complicating for current claims about that century's role in literary history.

The book is divided into three sections that read the categories of form and reform against different horizons: the first section reminds us of the various ways that the material text might revise our understanding of form; the following section revisits devotional writing within and beyond the context of reform; and the final section offers a series of perspectives on the work of John Skelton that each challenge and test notions of the fifteenth century in literary history. While these three sections are meant to foreground particular interests, this is also a project that has grown into a book through conversation and dialogue—at Kalamazoo, through individual correspondences, and with the broader field. Those conversa-

---

20. See Matthews, "The Medieval Invasion of Early Modern England," for a comprehensive overview of this more recent work.

tions have left their traces in the several themes that tie these chapters together across the texts and approaches under consideration, and we would like to draw out four of these in brief.

Nearly all these chapters seem to be in tacit agreement with the argument advanced by Susan Wolfson (among others) for a thick, necessary link between close reading and a renewed attention to form. In these recent discipline-wide discussions, the Althusserian framework within which ideology emerges as form, and reading as a mode of production, has been tweaked, a little, to emphasize instead the more nimble ways reading *discloses* the ongoing work of form; reading thus participates in the interactionality of form, rather than simply revealing its ideological matrix.[21]

Reading across the fifteenth century emerges here not just as a practice with refreshed disciplinary privilege but as an historical category that is complex and diverse in its own right. "Reading" is often at work on multiple levels in these chapters: Brantley argues for an intertextual interpretive framework made possible by the material form of the book in conjunction with the material traces of that book's readers; Cole corrects a longstanding critical misreading of a manuscript with close readings of first the script and then the genre of the letters found within that book; Gayk reveals fresh connections between reading and the processes of composition within the work of John Capgrave; and Simpson argues for an ethics of reading informing the fictive audience represented within Skelton's *Bowge of Courte,* as well as the poem's readers. These chapters also discover everywhere the close attention to form and nuanced reading that comprised the shared expectations of writers and readers in the 1400s—Krug demonstrates how dialogues in Jesus' voice make available to readers a range of imaginative postures in relation to clerical and institutional authority, while Winstead traces the emergence of an "intellectual liberalism" in Osbern Bokenham that relies on an optimism and faith in the intellectual engagement of his lay readership. "Reading across the fifteenth century," in short, is offered here as a subtitle and an important subtext in this volume.

Crucial to this collection, too, is a confidence in the capacity of form to return us to questions of institutional and literary authority which move beyond identifying patterns of resistance or subversion. Until recently, the literary history of the fifteenth century was written as a series of authoritative pressures working to produce a general cultural submissiveness—of Lydgate to Chaucer, of dissenters to ecclesiastical orthodoxy, of court poets to the Lancastrians. The resulting literary landscape was derivative, infantilized, or simply an adumbration of broader institutional powers. There have been plenty of correctives to this framework over the

---

21. See Wolfson, *Reading for Form,* and Levinson, "What is New Formalism?," esp. 560 on the agency of the artwork. Also see Ellen Rooney, "Form and Contentment," in *Reading for Form,* 45–47.

last decade and perhaps especially within the last five years; again, this volume is part of that work. These chapters, however, are most interested in the complicated interactions between various, and sometimes competing, modes and histories of authority. For example, both Meyer-Lee and Bose explore—albeit with different conclusions—the pressure of the ecclesiastical and political arenas on the literary forms taken up by Skelton. The play of ecclesiastical authority within the literary is reconfigured in the chapters by Winstead, Krug, and Gayk, who each offer models of writers appropriating and renewing ecclesiastical authority rather than dissenting from it. And the institutionality of literary authority itself is raised as a question rather than an assumption by Andrew Cole, who draws important connections between Latin humanism in England and the native intellectual currents that gave rise to a sense of the institutional place imagined for English poetry.

Traveling across these chapters is also a practice, a kindred approach to the texts of the fifteenth century, which suggests a further dimension to our title terms of form and reform. Both terms spread beyond the expected parameters of their use in current disciplinary discourse: form refers in these pages to the several levels of structure, style, genre and syntax, but our contributors also press beyond those textual features to insist on form as part of our consideration of the orthographical, the codicological, the reader's trace, the image on the page, the metaphorical valences of language and books, the reforming of manuscript texts into print. Similarly "reform" points the way to reforming currents of orthodoxy, as well as to the alternately conservative and reforming practices of hagiographic and other devotional genres, and the intellectual currents of both reform and conservatism present in Oxford. Just as form and reform are terms that do not map comfortably onto the conceptual categories of text and context, the texts under consideration here—largely absent from or marginal to critical canons, like the *Fifteen Oes,* the Brome Abraham and Isaac play, the Oxford petitionary forms recorded in Registrum F, and Skelton's "Ware the Hauke"—provoke a deliberate uneasiness that is useful, we suggest, in reimagining a century just emerging from the margins of periodizing discourses.

Our first section, "The Materials of Form," is an argument in practice that an attention to form is not opposed to an interest in material culture; rather, as Douglas Bruster elsewhere reminds us, form itself might be most accurately understood as potentially material, materially produced, and/or materially productive.[22] Indeed, nearly all of the essays in this volume invoke or rely upon a reading of material form: Meyer-Lee and Simpson both read their arguments through printed editions of Skelton's work; the discovery of the Abbottsford manuscript enables Winstead's astute reading of differences between that and the

---

22. Douglas Bruster, "The Materiality of Shakespearean Form," in *Shakespeare and Historical Formalism,* 31–48.

earlier Arundel collection of *vitae;* and Gayk takes up the provocative alimentary metaphors of books consumed. We start the volume with two essays in particular that help foreground the role that material forms—compilations, books, and other material artifacts—play in fifteenth-century literary culture.

Jessica Brantley reads the specific material context of the Abraham and Isaac play in the commonplace manuscript known as the *Book of Brome,* framing a provocative analysis of the rubrications within the play against a broader argument about that text's physical and interpretive relationship to its manuscript context. She identifies a "typological imaginary" accessible through the visual presentation of the play, a presentation shaped by readerly traces (mostly rubrications) that reveal a consistent engagement with the interpretive practices of typology, not only in the play but across several of the texts in the Brome manuscript. The performance of the Brome Abraham and Isaac, as Brantley puts it, is one that can be most productively understood as the "performance of interpretation" that foregrounds the role of the reader.

Andrew Cole's essay focuses on the administrative letters in Registrum F housed in the University Archives of Oxford (edited as the *Epistolae academicae Oxon.*). In his fresh investigation of the epistles, Cole ultimately challenges several of the key assumptions about humanism in England, primarily that it was an imported, impoverished, and neglected movement. His provocative two-fold reading of form takes into account the material letterforms of Chaundler's script and the petitionary form of the letters in the *registra.* His reading of these forms together builds a layered, specific argument about one book that branches out to think about affiliations with early-century and vernacular petitionary poetry, as well as resituates the petitionary genre as one that contains within itself the periodizing rhetoric of rebirth.

Considerations of religious writing in the fifteenth century have most frequently been posed against the context of orthodoxy and dissent, a historical backdrop that has seemed more urgent and, in many cases, more dramatic than the role this kind of writing may have played in its literary milieu. The essays in this second section, "Devotional Forms," work to rebalance the conversation, suggesting that devotional writing of this period engaged with a variety of reformist (and conserving) traditions precisely through aesthetic innovation and experiment. Through close readings that emphasize genre, metaphor, and reading traditions, these chapters question what we thought we knew about the politics of hagiography, about the use of dialogue, about sweetness and the forms of devotional expression.

Karen Winstead offers a critical reappraisal of Osbern Bokenham in the wake of the Abbotsford manuscript discovery, identified as Bokenham's lost *Legenda Aurea* by Simon Horobin in 2005. Moving between the Abbotsford saints' lives and the *vitae* contained in the Arundel manuscript, Winstead establishes a new chronology as well as a new framework for understanding Bokenham's engagement with the genre of hagiography. Three of the Abbotsford legends—those of Apollonia, Barbara, and Winifred—provide grounds for tracing Bokenham's move toward an intellectual liberalism, a liberalism at once bold and experimental as it emerges through legends that treat the full intellectual range of women as scholars, students, teachers, and, most surprisingly, preachers. Winstead argues that Bokenham's more mature, experimental use of hagiography reveals his optimistic reassessment of learning and reading as a singularly creative response to conservative ecclesiastical pressures surrounding the issue of lay religious instruction.

The vital energies of a lay readership also play a part in Gayk's essay on Capgrave's *Life of Saint Katherine*. Gayk offers a persuasive reading of what she terms Capgrave's "aesthetic of sweetness," ultimately suggesting that religious writing offers a corrective to our privileging of the more secular "aureate sweetness" that has long been considered the hallmark of fifteenth-century stylistics. Beginning with the alimentary metaphors that undergird Capgrave's prologue to the *Life*—where a priest dreams of quite literally consuming a book, binding and all—Gayk moves outward to trace Capgrave's own careful, sustained interest in a series of interlinking connections between hiddenness and plain-speaking, composition and reading, form and meaning. By moving through the multilayered metaphorics of what it means to read (and write) sweet words, Gayk demonstrates how Capgrave's acute awareness of "sweet" forms discloses writing as a joint production between reader and writer: Capgrave's *Life* is a text unafraid to articulate at once a concern with readerly receptivity as well as the hard "hermeneutic labor" reading requires.

Krug's chapter is the second in our collection to find critical traction in the performative aspects of texts meant to be read instead of staged—in this instance, scripted dialogues of Jesus' voice. This understudied but important genre is common in texts across the later medieval literary corpus, as Krug reminds us, and she reads three examples composed largely for a female devotional audience: Margaret Beaufort's *Imitation of Christ,* the Fifteen *Oes,* and Margery Kempe's *Book*. Krug finds that dialogues open up a fictive, experiential space in which readers reexperience and potentially reexpress inscribed, authoritative language. These dialogues, however, cannot be read easily as part of a generalized narrative of empowerment or individuality; instead, Krug is careful to demonstrate the quite different relationships figured between readers and clerical/ecclesiastical authority embedded across these texts. The readerly dynamics made possible by these dialogues, though, suggest that writers engaged with this devotional form to signal a discrete mode of piety. Krug's identification and initial analysis of this genre also continues to remind us that in religious as well as literary registers, the work of form and the work of reading were interdependent experiences.

By concluding with a group of essays in conversation about Skelton, this volume's third and final section offers an alternative ending to the literary history of the fifteenth century—one that reads one of the most troublesome poets in the English canon against the provocations of form and reform as they work in the earlier chapters of this collection. Skelton traditionally serves as a watershed figure demarcating the medieval from Renaissance periods, but in this section he is a specifically fifteenth-century poet. What that means, however, is productively contested: Meyer-Lee argues for a distinct fifteenth-century literary culture, bookended by Lydgate and Skelton, which traces a trajectory of aureate poetics; Bose, on the other hand, proposes a more "Langlandian" echo that plays through the work of John Audelay before it ends in the dissolution and fragmentation of Skelton's polyvocal verse; and Simpson explores the end of the Middle Ages, at least figuratively, in the "dreadful" death of the author as imagined in the *Bowge of Courte*. Among these competing claims on Skelton, though, is a shared interest in Skelton as a figure neither exemplary nor anomalous, but rather of a piece with the fifteenth-century appetite for innovation and experimentation, and thus well within the circumference of this volume's interests.

Meyer-Lee brings us to the eve of the Reformation in his consideration of John Skelton's A *Replycacion against Certayne Yong Scolers Abjured of Late,* which appeared from Pynson's press in 1528. Looking back to Lydgate's *Life of Our Lady* (1422) as a strong influence for Skelton's poem, Meyer-Lee argues that what may first appear to be Skelton's highly idiosyncratic *Replycacion* unfolds as a strikingly similar project to Lydgate's, only one at once more witty and blunt, and, in a sense, turned inside out: if the *Life* is an orthodox Marian devotion that modulates at times into a defense of poetry and, more subtly, a polemic against early-fifteenth-century Lollardy, the *Replycacion* is a satiric attack on early sixteenth-century Lollard-like heresy that marshals both Marian orthodoxy and a defense of poetry to its cause. And yet this difference is, in an important respect, decisive: in the *Life,* the literary emerges metaphorically and its relation to political power is indirect; in contrast, while the defense of poetry in the *Replycacion* is explicit, learned, and impassioned, the literary itself devolves into, as Skelton puts it, "a privilege granted by the king." This manifest royal instrumentality siphons off the hieratic aura upon which the poem's claim for the literary depends, thereby marking the boundary of a characteristically fifteenth-century articulation of the literary and signifying one of the ways that we might say that the fifteenth century, considered as a distinct literary culture, ends.

The challenge of thinking any specific endpoint through Skelton is addressed in a different register by Bose, who emphasizes Skelton's clerical status as she traces a narrative of competing tensions and paradoxes in the long tradition of the priest-poet through the fifteenth century. Beginning with a reflection on the clerical poet as *bouche inutile,* the "useless mouth," Bose explores the reformist context of Skelton's work as one which makes explicit the contact between ecclesiastical and literary cultures, and thus the constant tension in the priest-poet's situation between his "empowering vocation and his prophetic compulsions." Bose's path to Skelton thus leads not through Lydgate (or Chaucer) but through the "clerical" writers, Langland and Audelay. Traced along this path, the macaronic, polyvocal, and linguistically fragmented language of Skelton's satires call into question the capacity of poetry to "do theology." While the questions at the heart of Bose's reading of Skelton are those posed by *Piers Plowman*—"What is poetry good for?" and "Can and should clerks be poets?"—the answers that Skelton formulates are, of course, quite different from Langland's own: in this volume's second consideration of the *Replycacion,* Bose reads Skelton as he "playfully guys the annihilation of institutions and hierarchies in order that it might come into being." Bose's reading thus offers a literary history that draws to a close through a loss of the poet's ecclesiastical role.

Skelton's inheritance and then dispersal of literary forms is taken up again in this collection's final essay by James Simpson, who offers a close reading of the *Bowge of Courte* that situates Skelton as a poet who makes visible the dynamics of his moment from within the complex codes of his political and historical horizons, rather than being coded by them. The formal qualities of the poem—the noninteractive soliloquies of Drede's interlocutors, the semantic limits of the allegorical figures themselves—reveal the terrifying "alienating quality of the non-communication" and produce the paranoia of the poet-narrator himself. Yet Simpson moves beyond a consideration of the narrator in this poem to implicate the reader as well, suggesting that for Skelton the categories of reader and author are mutually constitutive. It is a relationship that Simpson argues must be construed, finally, as an ethical one. And by positing ethics here, Simpson forcefully reaffirms authorial intention, suggesting that acts of reading are decisions taken by readers, "not something ineradicably there 'in' the text," and that these decisions are choices "which bring an author into being." It is only through this conscious acknowledgement of and turn toward the author that we might register the extraordinary ways Skelton finds to say "I cannot say anything." Skelton, perhaps, both invites and refuses the idea of an "end" to the fifteenth century at all.

ALTHOUGH THIS volume was spurred by a chronological gap in our literary history, these essays nevertheless remain coy about mapping a full, or fully coherent, fifteenth century. The reassessments here prefer instead to highlight the local—the instance, the edition, the manuscript, the letter—and thus form and reform are terms that emerge as points of particularity. Yet the particular carries with it a distinct energy that consistently teases and troubles the place of the fifteenth century within straitening, periodizing narratives. As Skelton might put it, the sum of the parts creates an "effecte energiall," encouraging us to see the volume's guiding terms as active participles, describing the continual processes of forming and reforming throughout the later fifteenth century.[23]

---

23. My thanks to Shannon Gayk and Daniel Wakelin for their helpful comments on this essay.

part 1

THE MATERIALS OF FORM

1

Forms of Reading in the Book of Brome

JESSICA BRANTLEY

The late-fifteenth-century Book of Brome—so-called because it was found at Brome Hall, in Suffolk—is best known for the Abraham and Isaac play it contains.[1] Located early in the book (New Haven, CT, Yale University, Beinecke Library MS 365, ff. 15r–22r), this stand-alone pageant gives memorable weight and shape to the deep emotions of a story told many times, in many ways, throughout the Middle Ages.[2] In its 465 lines, the Brome play dramatizes the unthinkable sacrifice demanded of Abraham with particular expressive force, concentrating on such details as the initial love and trust between father and son, the father's extended agony at the necessity of obeying God's cruel command, and the boy's continual thoughts of his mother, which move from a wish that she could intervene ("Now I wold to God my moder were her on þis hyll! / Sche woold knele for me on both hyre kneys / To save my lyffe," 175–77) to a wish that she be protected entirely from any knowledge of the event ("But, good fader, tell ȝe my moder nothyng, / Sey þat I am in another cuntré dwellyng," 205–06).[3] Even after God's angel appears to provide an alternative animal for sacrifice, Isaac quite reasonably continues to suspect his father's intentions towards him:

---

1. For their helpful reactions to these ideas in early versions, I wish to thank audiences at the New Chaucer Society, the Michigan Medieval Seminar, and the University of Virginia Medieval Colloquium. Special thanks to James Simpson, Peggy McCracken, Catherine Sanok, and Gabriel Haley.

2. All of the extant cycles include plays on the subject, and there exists another free-standing version: the Northampton Abraham and Isaac (Dublin, Trinity College MS 432). Unlike the Norwich Grocers' Play and the Newcastle Noah's Ark, neither the Brome nor the Northampton play can be plausibly connected to a lost cycle.

3. All quotation of the Brome play, unless otherwise indicated, is drawn from *Early English Drama: An Anthology*, ed. John C. Coldewey (New York and London: Garland, 1993).

he offers to "stowppe down lowe" to blow on the sacrificial fire, but first has to ask, "ȝe wyll not kyll me with ȝowre sword, I trowe?" (378). The play concludes with a speech from a "Doctor," who summarizes the "good lernyng" to be drawn from "thys solom story" (436).

Questions of form have dominated discussion of the Brome play. Although it is an independent dramatic piece, it shares especially close verbal patterns with the version of the Abraham and Isaac story found in the Chester cycle. But critics have been unable to determine conclusively whether both plays descend from a common source, Brome precedes Chester, or Chester precedes Brome.[4] The argument about priority proceeds according to formalist criteria for assessing relative literary value. The fundamental question is whether one assumes that those constructing a second text from an original are more likely to improve or debase it: one might argue either that the better play must be the earliest version (that is, any imitation could only be derivative) or that it must be the final word (any initial draft must be incompletely realized). In either case, the judgment turns upon whether one deems Brome or Chester to be the better play, a decision that has come down to determining whether metrical skill (as demonstrated by Chester) is more or less important to a dramatic poem than characterization (the strength of Brome). Ultimately, then, these questions about priority and comparative literary value rest on weighing the importance of form—both quantifiable features such as metrical structures, and also the kinds of literary effects that a formalist criticism such as close reading is so well suited to reveal.

Although the relationship with Chester has thus far been the main question in critical discussion of the Brome play, it is not a question—barring unanticipated discoveries in the archive—that is likely to be very productive in the future. The connections that can be traced (or imagined) through literary forms too often ignore salient differences in material form that promise greater insight. Whereas the Chester play exists in a handful of manuscripts, some of which preserve a fully imagined dramatic cycle, the Brome version is found only within one household book, where it is the singular play.[5] Instead of pursuing the relationship between analogous texts through patterns of repetition and rhyme, I am interested in thinking about the formal properties of the Brome play through the appearance

---

4. See, e.g., Alexander R. Hohlfeld, "Two Old English Mystery Plays on the Subject of Abraham's Sacrifice," *Modern Language Notes* 5.4 (1890): 111–19; Carrie A. Harper, "A Comparison between the Brome and Chester Plays of Abraham and Isaac," in *Studies in English and Comparative Literature by Former and Present Students at Radcliffe College, presented to Agnes Irwin, Dean of Radcliffe College, 1894–1909*, Radcliffe College Monographs 15 (Boston and London: Ginn, 1910); Margaret Dancy Fort, "The Metres of the Brome and Chester Abraham and Isaac Plays," *PMLA* 41.1 (1926): 832–39; and especially J. Burke Severs, "The Relationship between the Brome and Chester Plays of Abraham and Isaac," *Modern Philology* 42.3 (1945): 137–51.

5. For the manuscripts of Chester, see R. M. Lumiansky and David Mills, eds., *The Chester Mystery Cycle*, 2 vols., EETS s.s. 3 and 9 (London: Oxford University Press, 1974, 1986).

of its words on the page: the text's physical relationship to its own manuscript context. For the play's connections to other playtexts prove less revealing than its place within the strange miscellany. The physical form of the Brome *Abraham and Isaac* can provide perspective on what the text means, and especially on the ways in which its literary forms were read. As Christopher Cannon has observed, "'Form' (as both concept and term) always allows analysis to build a bridge between the immaterial and the material: 'form' is necessarily the 'werk' seen in terms of the 'thoughte' behind it, the brute physicality of some thing as it is rooted in the realm of ideas conceived in the mind."[6] In particular, I will argue that the mysterious patterns of rubrication that appear in the Brome play join "brute physicality" to "the realm of ideas," for they can be understood along with other scribal decoration in the miscellany to reveal a practice of reading, rather than (as has sometimes been suggested) a practice of performance. Illuminating methods of literary interpretation rather than practices of histrionic declamation, the highlighted words constitute a "reading" of the text that shows the importance of reading itself to our understanding of it.[7]

The dramatic text sorts uncomfortably with the book's other miscellaneous contents, which include both nondramatic poems and practical writings such as model legal documents, recipes, tax lists, and accounts.[8] The manuscript was written, probably in a gentry household, by at least two hands over a period of years in the late fifteenth century.[9] Many of the more businesslike items were entered between 1499 and 1508 by the second of these hands, which can be identified as that of Robert Melton of Stuston. Perhaps, then, the miscellaneity of the book arises in part from its different scribes and registers their changing

---

6. Christopher Cannon, "Form," in Paul Strohm, ed., *Oxford Twenty-First Century Approaches to Literature: Middle English* (Oxford: Oxford University Press, 2007), 177–90, at 178. See also D. Vance Smith "Medieval *Forma*," in *Reading For Form,* ed. Susan J. Wolfson and Marshall Brown (Seattle, WA: University of Washington Press, 2006), 66–79, who notes that for medieval readers "'form' usually denoted the material shape of a text, including orthographic practice: in *Piers Plowman,* one figure complains about the 'newe clerkes' who cannot 'versifye faire ne formaliche enditen, / Ne naught oon among an hundred that an auctour kan construwe' (XV.373–75)."

7. Susan Wolfson and Marshall Brown have observed that in the wake of a purely formalist literary criticism, attention to form has lately implied attention to practices of reading ("Introduction," *Reading for Form,* 14).

8. For descriptions of the manuscript, see Norman Davis, "The Brome Hall Commonplace Book," *Theatre Notebook* 24 (1969–70): 84–86; Stanley J. Kahrl, "The Brome Hall Commonplace Book," *Theatre Notebook* 22 (1968): 157–61; Thomas E. Marston, "The Book of Brome," *Yale University Library Gazette* 41.4 (1967): 141–45; and *Non-Cycle Plays and Fragments,* ed. Norman Davis, EETS s.s. 1 (London and New York: Oxford University Press, 1970). See also the Beinecke Library Catalogue entry (http://brblnet.library.yale.edu/pre1600ms/docs/pre1600.ms365.htm); and the full set of digital images the library has made available (http://beinecke.library.yale.edu/dl_crosscollex/ SetsSearchExecXC.asp?srchtype=ITEM).

9. The manuscript is usually dated to the last quarter of the fifteenth century on the basis of handwriting and paper, whose watermarks suggest that it was manufactured on the Continent around 1465–75. Although some leaves have been cut out, the omissions do not seem to affect any of the text.

intentions for how it should be used. However, the anonymous first scribe himself included a range of matter in the book. Although he was the one who copied the literary items of greatest interest—including the play—he also copied model legal documents showing the proper forms of private charters and bonds, such as "a grant of a pigeon-cote, with reversions to second and third grantees, if the first and second grantees respectively die without heirs" or "a bond for the payment of £10 on demand."[10] He also copied ciphers and antifeminist puzzles. The more literary pieces include: a poem on fortune-telling by dice ("Have your desire"); *The Fifteen Signs of Doomsday;* the catechetical dialogue *Adrian and Epotys;* the purgatorial journey *Owein Miles;* a *Life of St. Margaret;* a carol of the Annunciation; part of Lydgate's *Pageant of Knowledge;* verses adapted from Chaucer's *Lak of Stedfastnesse;* and a number of shorter lyrics including "Man in merthe hath meser in mynd," "The hart lovyt þe wood," "Fyrst arysse erly," "I stond as styll as ony ston," and "Lux ys leyd a downe."

Even leaving aside Melton's sixteenth-century accounts, the variety of these pieces is puzzling: they represent traditions both devotional and secular; poetic and prosaic; anonymous and authorized; dramatic, lyric, and hagiographic. A certain practicality is common to most of the selections, in the sense that the book includes a number of how-to texts: how to tell your fortune by dice, how to know if doomsday is approaching, how to give away your pigeon-cote. Even the anonymous dialogue *Adrian and Epotys* and Lydgate's *Pageant of Knowledge* share a basic concern with imparting essential moral information; these texts do not offer complicated theologies, but practical instruction in the faith: how to be a Christian. The book thus concentrates on "the objective things of religion" and generally reveals "the strongly utilitarian reading practices of many gentry households."[11] A text as self-consciously artful as the play of Abraham and Isaac—and critics generally agree that this is the most successfully realized dramatic version of that story—might seem out of place in a practical book such as this. But another way of linking the wide range of genres represented in the Brome miscellany is to understand their practicality as reflecting a common

---

10. The documents are so characterized in *A Commonplace Book of the Fifteenth Century, Containing a Religious Play and Poetry, Legal Forms, and Local Accounts,* Lucy Toulmin Smith, ed. (London: Trübner and Co., 1886), 132. For a discussion of the scribal evidence, see *Non-Cycle Plays,* Davis ed.: "The documents are surely later than the poems, but the hand is not appreciably different and the interval cannot have been very long" (lxii). Moreover, poems copied by the first scribe appear both before and after the documents, so it would seem that the main reason to distinguish them is their genre.

11. For the first quotation, see Eamon Duffy, *The Stripping of the Altars* (New Haven, CT: Yale University Press, 1992), 75; and for the second, Nicola MacDonald, "Fragments of *(Have your) Desire:* Brome Women at Play," in *Medieval Domesticity: Home, Housing, and Household in Medieval England* (Cambridge: Cambridge University Press, 2008), 232–58; at 236. For considerations of the manuscript in the context of other household miscellanies, see Duffy, *Stripping of the Altars,* 68–77; and Julia Boffey and John J. Thompson, "Anthologies and Miscellanies," in *Book Production and Publishing in Britain, 1375–1475* (Cambridge: Cambridge University Press, 1989), 279–315.

formalist concern: texts offering the proper templates for legal documents, or ways to interpret patterns thrown in dice, derive their interest directly from the reproduction or analysis of structures of meaning—structures that, I will argue, are equally important to the Brome *Abraham and Isaac*.[12] The contents of this book matter for our understanding of the play, not for their thematic or topical resonances with it, but for their complicated generic and formal ones.

The inclusion of the Abraham and Isaac play with so many nondramatic texts in the Book of Brome suggests that—whatever its performance history extrinsic to this volume—at some point someone thought it worth reading.[13] It is the only dramatic text in a manuscript otherwise unconcerned with the theater, and for this reason it is hard to imagine that it was copied primarily for the purpose of reenactment.[14] And in its appearance, as well as in the company it keeps, the Brome *Abraham and Isaac* presents itself as a medieval play for reading. The basic *ordinatio* of the play suggests readers rather than spectators, for it differs in some significant ways from the standard visual conventions of fifteenth-century drama.[15] Most often in plays of this period, speakers' names are found in the right margin, set off by lines that separate each part from the others (e.g., BL MS Add. 35290 [York Register]). Stage directions, as well, are usually separated from the text to be read, distinguished by some combination of linguistic difference (they are often in Latin) and visual difference (they are often in larger display scripts, and even rubricated). In the Brome play, by contrast, the characters' names are placed to the left of their speeches, replicating the layout of a dialogue, rather than a staged play (f. 19v; Fig. 1.1).

The stage directions are written within the playtext, seemingly a part of the characters' speeches: on this folio, the words "Here Abraham layd a cloth over Ysaacys face, thus seyyng" form the beginning of the patriarch's second speech. This placement of the words would perhaps confuse an actor trying to make sense of his spoken part, but would pose no particular problem to a reader who needs visual descriptions of the characters' actions as well as their words, to provide a sense of the drama.

---

12. For a consideration of the dicing poem in the context of divination, see W. L. Braeckman, "Fortune-Telling by the Casting of Dice: A Middle English Poem and Its Background," *Studia Neophilologica* 52 (1980): 3–29.

13. The performance history of the play is not definitively known. For records of dramatic activity near Stuston, see Kahrl, "Brome Hall Commonplace Book," 161. Lucy Toulmin-Smith, *A Commonplace Book of the Fifteenth Century*, 47, notes that religious plays were performed in East Anglia at Wymondham, Manningtree, and Cambridge.

14. The Book of Brome has what Boffey and Thompson call a "sectional structure," making it possible to imagine that parts of it once traveled independently. The contents of the book were "finally and irrevocably fixed" early in its life, however, by Robert Melton, the second of the main scribes. See Boffey and Thompson, "Anthologies and Miscellanies," 293–94.

15. On the difficulties of identifying medieval plays from written records alone, see Carol Symes, "The Appearance of Early Vernacular Plays: Forms, Functions, and the Future of Medieval Theater," *Speculum* 77 (2002): 778–831.

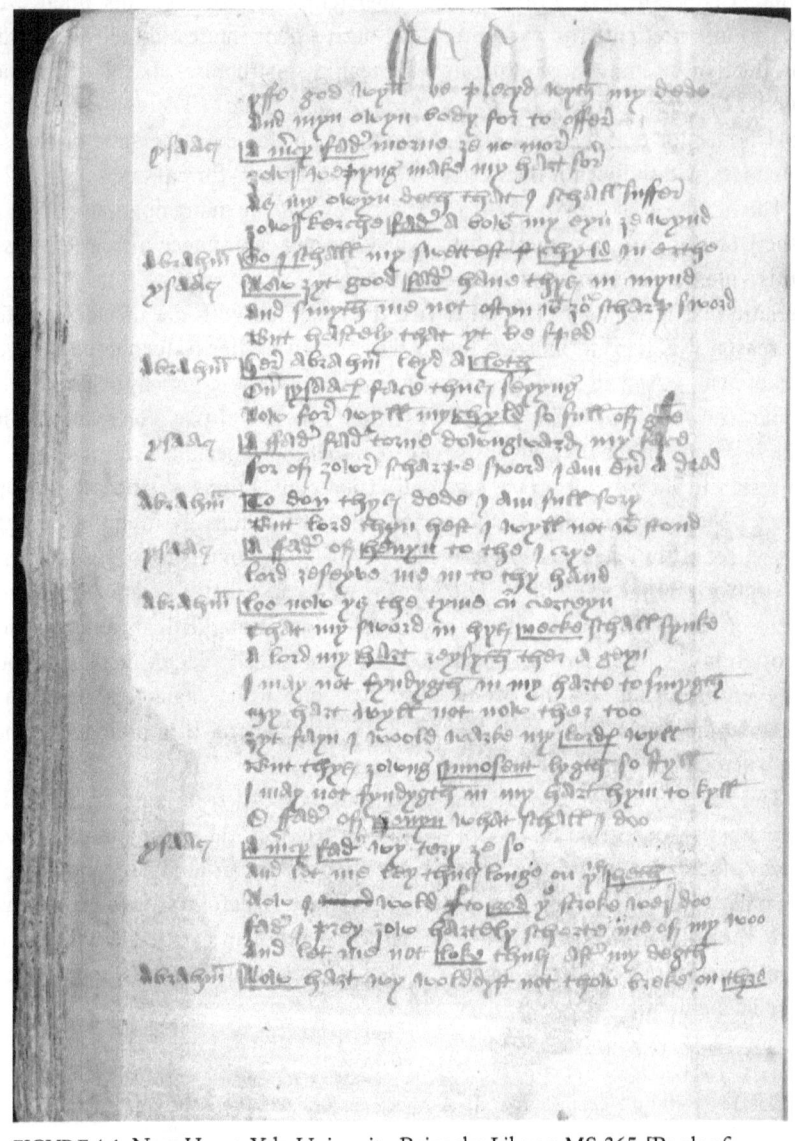

FIGURE 1.1. New Haven, Yale University, Beinecke Library MS 365 [Book of Brome], f. 19v. Atypical layout with stage directions integrated into speech.

The line between reading and performance in late medieval culture is, of course, complicated and ultimately fine. As Joyce Coleman has shown, reading aloud to an audience from a book—praelection—was a very common practice even in the late Middle Ages, making such a reader very nearly an actor, and his audience very nearly spectators. It is possible—even probable—that the Brome Abraham and Isaac play, along with other texts in the miscellaneous manuscript, were read aloud in this way. But in a study of the miscellany's antifeminist ciphers, Ian Johnson notes a wide variety of ways in which they might have been used:

> The Brome Ciphers have varied potential for exhibition/concealment in their reception and circulation; they can be enjoyed homosocially away from women (perhaps with the added fuel of communal drinking), or shown to them to annoy them. Easy to find quite near the beginning of the miscellany, they could be read as private graffiti eminently reusable for sniggering *consolacioun, meditacioun,* or *recreacioun*.[16]

None of these imagined contexts for reading the ciphers has to do with histrionic reenactment, or even praelection—these are not texts that lend themselves particularly to aural reception. (This is even more obviously true of the accounts and legal documents.)[17] But the balance Johnson describes between exhibition and concealment, between recreation and meditation, is pertinent to the play as well.[18] Given its codicological context, this copy of the play is more likely to have been read—either in private or aloud—than to have served as an instrumental, throwaway script.[19] And so, though it undoubtedly relies on the memory or prospective fantasy of actors embodying roles and speaking lines aloud—that is to say, on a performance that has nothing to do with a book—this play also has a life on the page.

---

16. Ian Johnson, "Xpmbn: The Gendered Ciphers of the Book of Brome and the Limits of Misogyny," *Women: A Cultural Review* 18.2 (2007): 145–61, at 156.

17. The dramatic or undramatic appearance of a piece is no certain proof of its uses, of course. Cf. the Macro MS (Washington DC, Folger Shakespeare Library MS V.a.354), a collection of texts clearly marked as plays that were also probably privately read.

18. Nicola MacDonald identifies the antifeminist verses as part of a "fully-fledged ludic programme" in the Brome manuscript ("Fragments," 242). She does not include the Brome play among the manuscript's ludic texts, but I would argue that some modes of reading encouraged by the games are relevant, also, to the *ludus* of *Abraham and Isaac*.

19. According to Kahrl, "In this context it becomes immediately apparent that these texts, all of a decidedly devotional cast, were collected for purposes of meditation. It is thus extremely unlikely that the text of the play of Abraham and Isaac as we have it in the Brome manuscript was copied out for someone intending to stage the play" (Kahrl, "Brome Hall Commonplace Book," 159). See also Rosemary Woolf: "Furthermore, whilst there is nothing in the text to suggest that they were not composed for performance on the stage, it is possible that they were copied for private reading, since they seem to be preserved on equal terms with other kinds of poetry, some religious, some secular" (*The English Mystery Plays* [Berkeley and Los Angeles: University of California Press, 1972], 153).

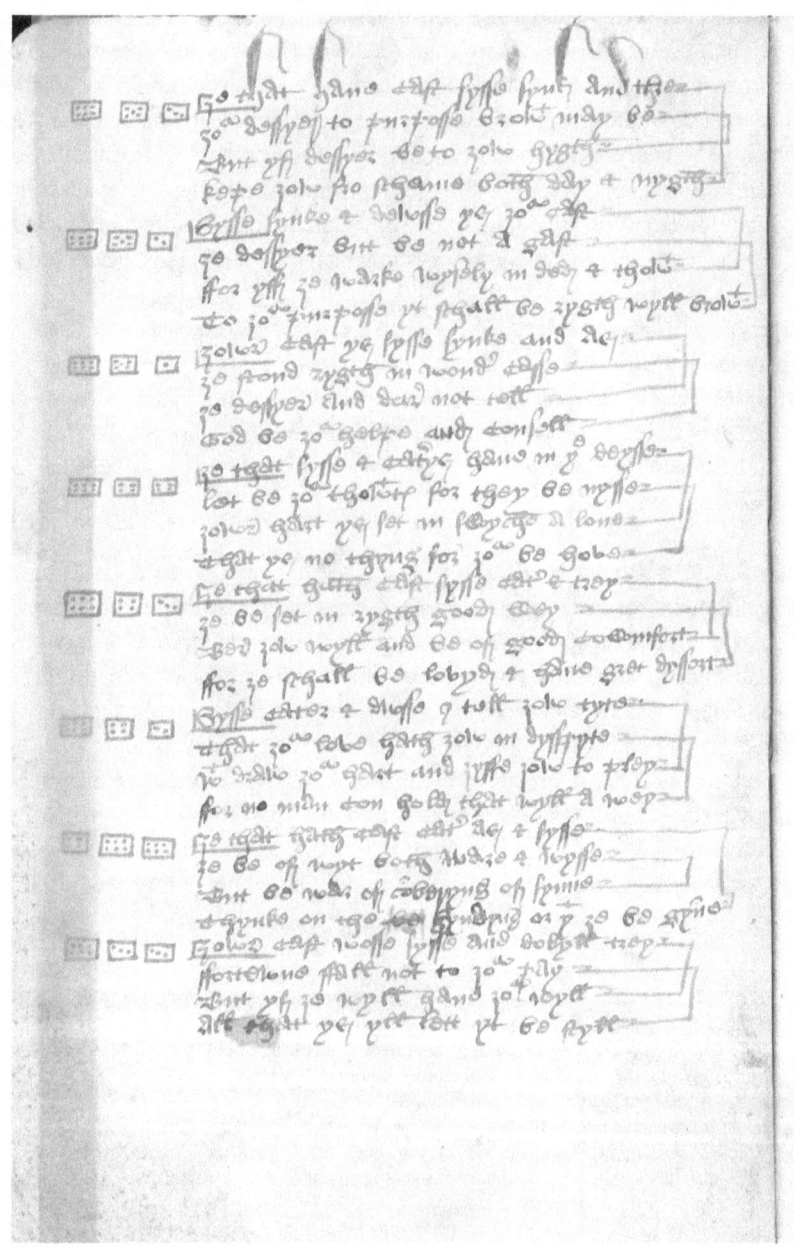

FIGURE 1.2. New Haven, Yale University, Beinecke Library MS 365 [Book of Brome], f. 2v. Poem on fortune-telling with dice.

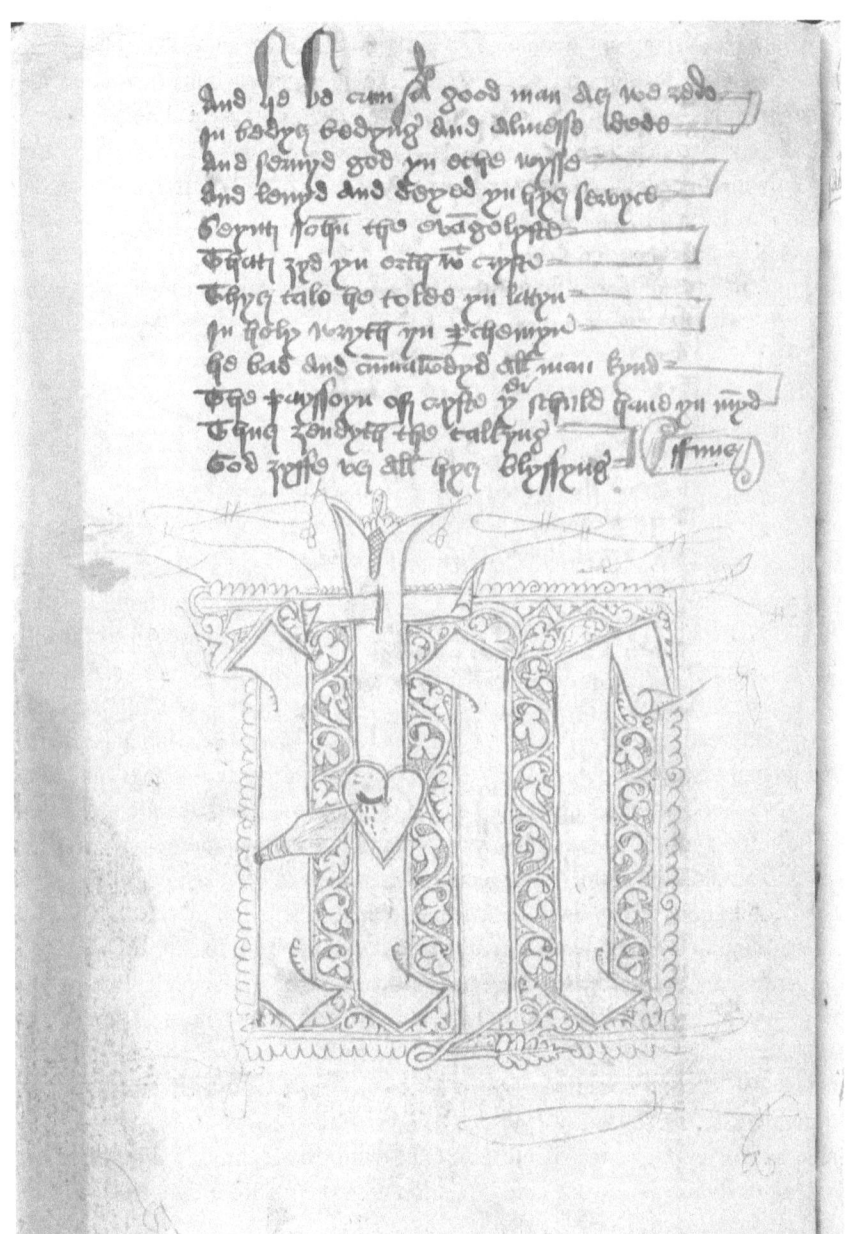

FIGURE 1.3. New Haven, Yale University, Beinecke Library MS 365 [Book of Brome], f. 14v. Final page of *Adrian and Epotys* with devotional emblem.

The point is confirmed by the fact that some of the items in the manuscript are illustrated with diagrams that mandate individual visual reading. The ciphers and puzzles studied by Johnson, for example, include some layouts that could only be significant to someone looking at the page, such as brackets showing rhymes, and large, rubricated titles: "Take iii claterars . . . " (f. 1v). The poem on fortune-telling with dice includes marginal images to organize and reinforce its message (f.2v; Fig. 1.2).

Moreover, at the end of the dialogue of *Adrian and Epotys,* there is an elaborate devotional emblem in the form of the Holy Monogram (ihc) with a bleeding heart (f. 14v; Fig 1.3). The poem concludes:

He [St. John] bad and commanded all man kynd
The payssoyn of cryste þei schuld haue yn mynd
Thus ȝendeth the talkyng
God ȝeffe vs all hys blyssyng.

With the end of the dialogue—of "the talkyng"—the reader is led into a silent visual space where he can be helped to fulfill the familiar injunction: the spear wounding the bleeding heart, which is crucified on the crossed ascender of the letter "h," compels him to have the passion of Christ in mind as he looks at the page.

I have argued in another context for a pervasive practice of performative devotional reading in the fifteenth century—that is, private reading animated by textual and visual allusions to the conditions of performance.[20] The Brome commonplace book provides a good example of how these cross-generic affiliations work in the period, for it combines drama and meditational devotion, plays and lyrics, diagrams and emblems, pageants and snippets of Chaucer, coming as close as any other book in the English tradition to the profusion of performative imagetexts found in the Carthusian miscellany that was the basis for my argument.[21] If the genres of the other texts in the Book of Brome affect our understanding of this play's meaning—they were privately read, and it, too, must be considered to have an unperformed, "literary" existence—its clear affiliations with dramatic performance also affect the reading of them. One could note the miscellany's inclusion of dialogue in the case of *Adrian and Epotys:* dialogue as a genre, though never intended for performance, is closely allied with drama through the differential voicing of its words. Or one could mention the excerpts from Lydgate's *Pageant*

---

20. Jessica Brantley, *Reading in the Wilderness: Private Devotion and Public Performance in Late Medieval England* (Chicago: University of Chicago Press, 2007).

21. BL MS Additional 37049. A similar collection of devotional and dramatic material, though largely unillustrated, can be found in the commonplace book of Robert Reynes (Oxford, Bodleian Library MS Tanner 407). For discussion of this and other household commonplace books, see Boffey and Thompson, "Anthologies and Miscellanies," esp. 291–303; and Duffy, *Stripping of the Altars* 68–77.

of Knowledge, a text that takes advantage of the visual and dramatic resonances of that word (*pageant*) to offer an imagined spectacle of allegorical characters speaking their moral mottos. Traces of performance lurk in these nondramatic texts, just as marks of reading suffuse the more obviously performative ones.

But continuing to think through this codicological context to the play itself: How do the interactions we can see here between reading and performance influence our understanding of this text's meaning and the ways in which it was understood by its first readers to mean? If it *was* privately read in this performative vein, *how* was it privately read?

Some answers to these questions are suggested by the physical layout of the page, for, like the other texts in the Book of Brome, the play has been presented in some ways that would signify only to a reader who was looking at the manuscript (f. 15r; Fig. 1.4).

The most striking feature to notice is the variety of rubrication: the display script and flourishes in the first line, the red touches in the initial letters of each line, as well as the brackets that indicate patterns of rhyme (although the brackets appear only on this first page).[22] There are less decorative elements (such as correction marked in red; e.g., ll. 19, 21) as well as more decorative elements (such as line-fillers; e.g., f. 18v). Most intriguingly, various words in the Brome play have been underlined in red in an inexplicable pattern. As Norman Davis explains in his edition of the text:

> The principle on which these are chosen is not apparent. Some of them are obviously important, especially names and designations of relationship such as *wyffe* 7, *chyld* 12, *Fader* 14, *son* 15, all of which are underlined almost every time they occur; but also marked are *lyvelod* 4, *erth* 6, *creaturys* 8, *sacryfyce* 39, 42, *offryng* 49, *best* 52, *hyll* 56, *lyffe* 81, *blood* 97, *fagot* 116, *handys* 120, *harte* 121, *backe* 130, and many others equally miscellaneous. Some of them are perhaps important enough to merit special emphasis, but it is not clear that they are more so than other words that are not underlined.[23]

Although the rubrication seems to be part of the manuscript's original design, it is probably scribal rather than authorial. Some readers have offered up the idea of performance as an explanation for these underlined words: John Coldewey, for example, has suggested that perhaps "the underlining acted as cues or as mnemonic devices for actors, for an overseer of the play, or for an early reader."[24]

---

22. For similar decoration in a dramatic manuscript, see the ornate capitals in the Towneley Plays (San Marino, Huntington Library MS HM 1).

23. *Non-Cycle Plays,* lxii. See also *Non-Cycle Plays and the Winchester Dialogues,* ed. Norman Davis, Leeds Texts and Monographs, Medieval Drama Facsimiles 5 (Leeds: School of English, 1979), 50.

24. *Early English Drama,* 136.

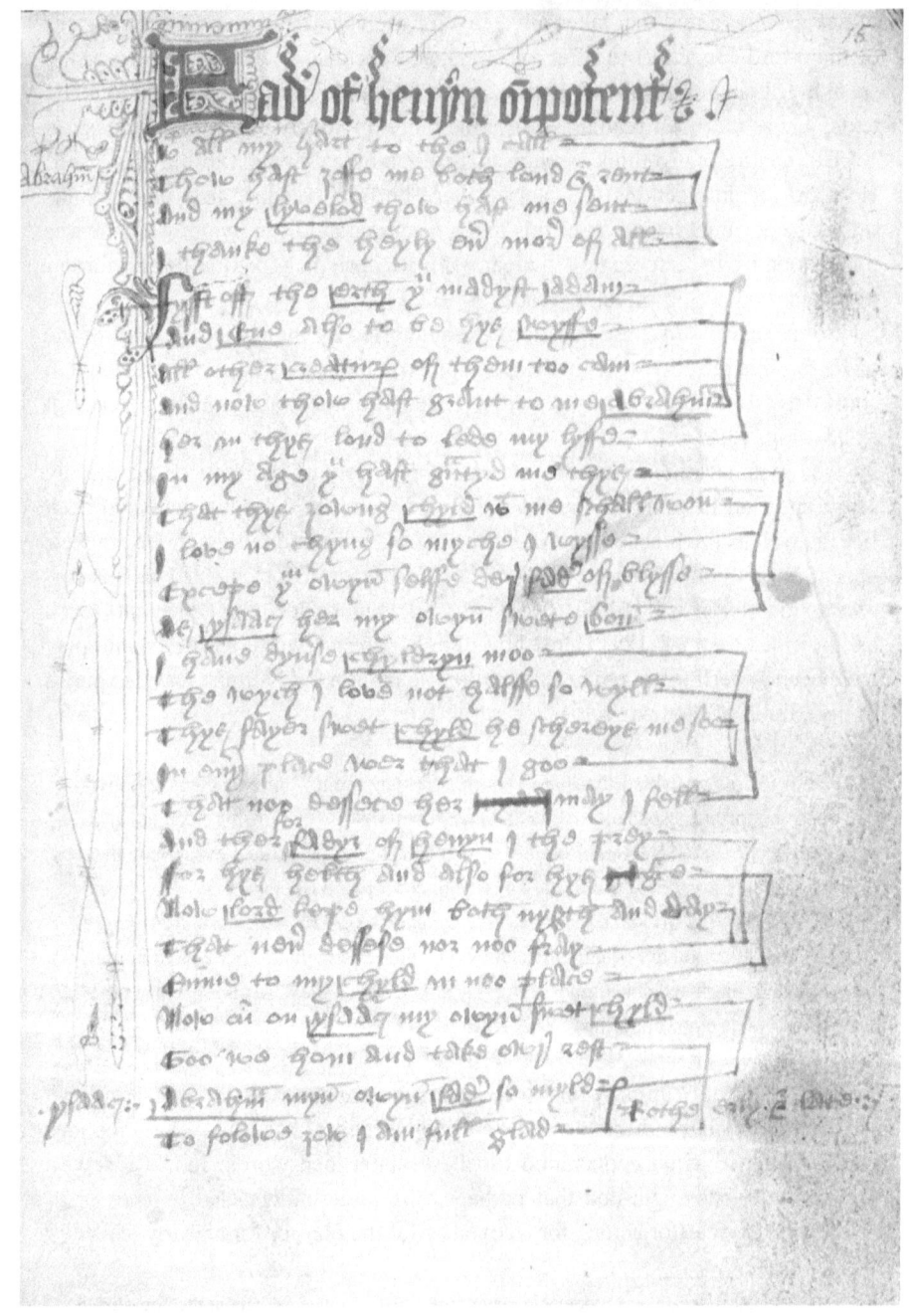

FIGURE 1.4. New Haven, Yale University, Beinecke Library MS 365 [Book of Brome], f. 15r. First page of *Abraham and Isaac*.

Given the layout and the miscellaneous context of this particular copy of the text, it seems most pertinent to explore the last of Coldewey's suggestions and to ask about the relevance of the rubrication to practices of reading.

The most striking piece of evidence against a simple performance context for these emphasized words is the fact that they are not unique to the Abraham and Isaac play. The scribe includes such rubrication in many of the texts he transcribes—both those with performative elements and those without. But lest we conclude that the scribe routinely picks out formal divisions in every text, there are a few texts not treated in this way: The short carol that begins "Nowell! Nowell! Nowell!" contains no rubrication at all (f. 79v), and *The Fifteen Signs of Doomsday* contains no underlining (f. 23r). As in the Abraham and Isaac play, some rubrication serves merely to emphasize the formal structure of these poems: to highlight the first words of each stanza, for example, or the first letter of each line. But in this poem in praise of moderation (Fig. 1.5; f. 1r), you can see that some words—many important, but some less so—are underlined in an inconclusive pattern that seems to have to do with interpretation: reasonably significant words such as *meser, suffer, sufferance, vertuys,* and *grace,* join with *hast* and *much* and *thynges*—for which the rationale in context is much less obvious.

As a principle, names are quite commonly emphasized; in the fragmentary *Life of St. Margaret,* the only three words underlined are names: *Olybryus* twice, and *Margaret* once.[25] And although it appears that the scribe has more completely rubricated the poems in the beginning of the manuscript—the barest ones are towards the end—this rule is not absolute: the *Life of St. Margaret* (with underlined names) comes after *The Fifteen Signs of Doomsday* (with no rubrication at all other than the first line). While the choice to rubricate appears to be a significant one, it is not reserved uniquely for clearly performative pieces. In general the rubrication found outside of the Abraham and Isaac play is as mysterious as the rubrication within it.

Outside of the Book of Brome, rubrication for emphasis appears in other non-dramatic texts: the B-version of *Piers Plowman,* for example, is often treated in this way. Linguistic difference in this macaronic poem is often signaled by some kind of visual emphasis on its Latin quotations, either underlining or writing in red ink. Less routinely, but still quite frequently, scribes of *Piers Plowman* B call attention to other words or brief phrases: some emphasis of this kind can be found in twelve of the B-version manuscripts, and it is prominent in four.[26] The styles

---

25. For *Olybryus,* see f. 40v, and for *Margaret,* f. 41r. *Margaret* is underlined at the moment when the king asks the saint her name and she replies, so the emphasis here perhaps indicates that the name is pronounced as direct speech within the narrative, as well as marking the significance of the revelation.

26. For a detailed discussion of the emphasized words, see C. David Benson and Lynne S. Blanchfield, *The Manuscripts of* Piers Plowman: *The B-Version* (Cambridge: D. S. Brewer, 1997), 17–20. The four most heavily rubricated manuscripts are Cambridge, University Library, MS Dd.i.17 (C); Cambridge, University Library, MS Ll.iv.14 (C2); Oxford, Corpus Christi College, MS 201 (F); and

FIGURE 1.5. New Haven, Yale University, Beinecke Library MS 365 [Book of Brome], f. 1r. "Man in merthe hath meser in mynd."

of emphasis include "underlining, boxing, highlighting, or actually writing the words in red," and it is possible in some cases that different methods signify varying levels of importance.[27] These words or phrases show some general similarities to the ones marked in Brome, for they include proper names (*Piers, Meed*), titles (*vitaillers, erchedekenes*), place names (*Gallilee*), and technical terms (*contra, ergo*) that would all seem to call for some differentiation from the regular course of the text. Some of the words and phrases marked in *Piers Plowman*, however, seem to C. David Benson "unimportant, and thus questionable": *sche is assoilled, residue, south, namliche, bakbyte, skoorne, skoolde, sklawndres, places, in, awhte.*[28]

How might the rubrication in *Piers Plowman* help to explain the practices of the Brome scribe? Some of the marks call attention to the largest structures of the poem—new speakers or textual divisions—thus helping readers to find their way more easily around a famously complicated text. Others emphasize formal features of the poetry: the rubricator of Oxford, Corpus Christi College, MS 201 is interested in alliteration, for example, marking alliterating nouns, but also—more surprisingly—verbs. This scribe also routinely underscores *quod*, sometimes even adding that word to the text, as well as the names of speakers. He emphasizes, then, the plurality of voices in the poem, and implicitly identifies its genre as "dialogue"—a word used to describe *Piers Plowman* in some manuscripts, though not in this one. The primary generic analogue, however, is not dialogic but historical. Although this sort of emphasis also appears in some Lydgate manuscripts and in a few copies of the *Canterbury Tales,* it appears most commonly in historical prose: the prose *Brut,* chronicles of London, Mandeville's *Travels,* and even the Winchester Malory. Cambridge University Library MS Dd.i.17 binds together a marked copy of *Piers* with Latin historical works marked for reading in a similar way, suggesting that perhaps the socially conscious alliterative verse of *Piers Plowman* was occasionally mistaken for historical prose. In spite of their general "opacity," Benson finds interpretative interest in the highlighted words, which suggest one reader's perspective on important characters and lively, dialogic passages.[29] Whatever the explanation of any particular scribe's interests, the alternative patterns of emphasis in *Piers Plowman* suggest that such marking is not authorial but interpretative. Even within a single manuscript the marking is rarely consistent, seeming to reflect the varying intensities of the process of reading, rather than a carefully planned and formal layout, conscientiously executed.

In the Brome *Abraham and Isaac,* the scribe's meaningful rubrication includes words that are important, either structurally (they are the first in the line), or categor-

---

Cambridge, Newnham College, MS 4 [Yates-Thompson MS] (Y). I rely on Benson's "Introduction" for much of the discussion following.

27. Benson and Blanchfield, *Manuscripts of* Piers Plowman, 17.
28. Benson and Blanchfield, *Manuscripts of* Piers Plowman, 19.
29. Benson and Blanchfield, *Manuscripts of* Piers Plowman, 18.

ically (they are proper names), or dramatically (and there is some overlap—names, for example, could be emphasized when declaimed). But there remain words that do not seem to fit into any of these categories, the sort of words that Davis finds self-evidently unimportant, and that Benson finds questionable. It would be hard to imagine a performance, or even a praelection, that would pause over or emphasize them all. I cannot conclusively explain the meaning of all of these marks wherever they appear in the Book of Brome, but I want to suggest that the underlined words in the play point in part towards an *interpretation* of it, an interpretation that could of course be communicated by any performance, but one that is equally relevant to, and that I think arises from, the practice of reading in solitude.

In the case of this play, nearly all of the underlined words can be interpreted typologically. Words such as *sacrifice, hill, beste, blood,* and *faggot,* for example, may not seem important of themselves, but they point towards the elements of the Abraham and Isaac story that have the most memorable correspondences with the familiar interpretation of the story as a type of Christ's passion.[30] Critics including Rosemary Woolf and V. A. Kolve have shown in detail that the Abraham and Isaac story is the "*locus classicus* of typological interpretation in the cycles": easily dramatized for its obvious human pathos, but also for its figural relevance to the story of Christ's redemptive sacrifice.[31] As the Expositor points out at the end of the Chester Abraham and Isaac play (and remember the strong connection between Chester and Brome):

> This deed ye see done here in this place,
> in example of Jesus done it was,
> that for to win Mankind grace
> was sacrificed on the rood.
>
> By Abraham I may understand
> The Father of Heaven that can fond
> with his Son's blood to break that bond
> the Devil had brought us to.
> By Isaac understand I may
> Jesus that was obedient ay,
> his Father's will to work always,
> and death to underfo.[32]

---

30. I thank Christopher Grobe for first suggesting this idea to me, and for sparking my interest in the Book of Brome.

31. Thomas Rendall, "Visual Typology in the Abraham and Isaac Plays," *Modern Philology* 81.3 (1984): 221–32, at 223. See Rosemary Woolf, "The Effect of Typology on the Mediaeval Plays of Abraham and Isaac," *Speculum* 32.4 (1957): 805–25; V. A. Kolve, *The Play Called Corpus Christi* (Stanford: Stanford University Press, 1966), 70–75; and Woolf, *English Mystery Plays*, 145–53.

32. *The Chester Mystery Cycle: A New Edition with Modernised Spelling*, ed. David Mills (East

Thus the play posits both Abraham as a figure for God and Isaac as a figure for Christ. That the Brome play does not make the typological associations of its narrative as explicit does not mean that they were not operative for its audience; the "typological imaginary," as Kathleen Biddick describes the medieval Christian fantasy of the New Law superseding the Old, was so powerful in this context that it is difficult to imagine what contemporary reader would not have understood the Abraham and Isaac story in this way.[33] In fact, the rubricated words could themselves serve as a visual version of the kind of interpretative gesture that Chester provides verbally.

Though it does not itself form part of a dramatic cycle, the play is nonetheless aware of its place in the figural patterns of biblical history; its cyclical aesthetic emerges through the repetitive structure of the marked words.[34] The most commonly emphasized words are all essential to the idea of the typological correspondence between the two narratives: *Abraham, father, child, son, Lord, heaven*. Moreover, the rubricator underlines *sacrifice* and *offering* nearly every time they appear. The Brome play's insistence on Isaac's carrying the wood on his back for the sacrificial fire (i.e., the wood of the cross) or its choice to dwell so long on the sheep who turns up "among the brerys" (i.e., wearing a crown of thorns) just in time to provide a sacrificial animal, echo Tertullian's influential readings of the story as figure.[35] The rubricator's repeated emphasis on the *hill* on which the offering is to be made, the *cloth* with which Abraham wipes Isaac's face, the *sword* in the father's *hand* that so frightens the son, the unlucky *scheepe* or *best* that happens along, even the *fruit* of Abraham's loins that is *multiplied* like *stars* in the sky, create mental images that encourage a typological reading. The hill is only important insofar as it prefigures Calvary; the quick beast only insofar as it prefigures Christ; the stars remind us of this story's implications for the future of Abraham's descendants. The Brome rubricator did not capitalize on every occasion for a typological interpretation—but if his readings were not consistently skilled, they are nonetheless *readings*. It seems clear that he sought to emphasize, for himself or for others, this particular meaning of the play. Thus his presentation of the text offers, to quote Kolve, "further evidence that 'figuration' as a concept was a part of the medieval dramatist's [or at least the medieval reader's] understanding of his material."[36]

Lansing, MI: Colleagues Press, 1992), 81 (Play 4, ll. 465–76).

33. Kathleen Biddick, *The Typological Imaginary: Circumcision, Technology, History* (Philadelphia: University of Pennsylvania Press, 2003).

34. For a modern reading of the Brome play that emphasizes the repetition of the word "heart," see C. F. Burgess, "Art and Artistry in the *Brome Miracle Play of Abraham and Isaac*," *Cithara* 1 (1962): 37–42. But although "heart" is underlined twice (ll. 35, 121), it is not one of the words most often chosen for emphasis by the contemporary rubricator.

35. Kolve, *Play Called Corpus Christi*, 73–74.

36. *Play Called Corpus Christi*, 70–71.

Edgar Schell argues that the Brome *Abraham and Isaac* is more thoroughly typological than any other dramatic treatment of the story. He notes verbal echoes of the Passion narrative, such as Isaac's proud promise that "aȝens my Lordys wyll / I wyll neuer groche, lowd nor styll" (190–91). Such precise echoes reinforce more general Christological themes, such as Isaac's concern in death for the benefit of others. And visual tableaux, such as Isaac carrying the wood on his back for the sacrifice, or submitting calmly to his binding on the altar, superimpose one narrative upon the other imagistically. As Schell explains, "[t]he figure on the altar is Isaac, of course, but with a concentrated power of assertion unique among the biblical plays, Brome has made the image of Christ approaching his own sacrifice almost equally vivid."[37] Many readers of medieval drama have seen that typology often works its analogies through visual means: dramatic tableaux and memorial images that make clear that Isaac's carrying of the wood mirrors (and the visual metaphor here is not quite dead) Christ's carrying of the cross.[38] But this is not the only way in which typological meanings can be envisioned, as the Brome miscellany shows. The devotional emblem we saw at the end of *Adrian and Epotys* helps the reader of *Abraham and Isaac* to a typological interpretation, for it directly precedes the start of the play (ff. 14v–15r). With a linguistic emblem—the holy monogram—rather than a crucifixion-tableau, the visual form of the manuscript opening thus puts the reader in "mind of Christ's Passion" just before embarking on the story that prefigures it. The bloody spear wounding the heart helps that reader to imagine the death prefigured by Abraham's terrifying sword, and the extremity of Christ's—or Isaac's—sacrifice.

If the narrative of the play, its rubricator's emphases, and its codicological context offer a spur to the "typological imaginary," the final words of the text perhaps offer a corrective. The play concludes with an epilogue spoken by a "Doctor," a direct address to the audience that asks them to reflect upon the kinds of moral lessons the narrative enjoins. The Brome Doctor calls on parents who have lost children not to grieve overmuch, reminded by Abraham's willingness to sacrifice his son that the most important thing is obedience to God. Woolf links this epilogue to *Pearl*, calling both "occasional."[39] As the product of a historically specific occasion, the Brome epilogue might be antitypological: instead of mak-

---

37. Edgar Schell, "Fulfilling the Law in the Brome Abraham and Isaac," *Leeds Studies in English* 25 (1994): 149–58, at 155–56.

38. Thomas Rendall, "Visual Typology in the Abraham and Isaac Plays," *Modern Philology* 81.3 (1984): 221–32.

39. Woolf, *English Mystery Plays*, 153: "Unlike a typological exposition, this moral is disconcertingly constrictive, and from the purely literary point of view even more infelicitous than the fairly common moral that the play demonstrates how children should be obedient to their parents. The Brome *moralitas* turns the play into a complement to *The Pearl*, and it is possible that these parallel studies in rebelliousness and obedient acquiescence in loss may have been occasional works, the occasion being some bereavement, which of necessity can no longer be identified."

ing the story of Abraham and Isaac resonate with sacred time, the Brome Doctor brings the biblical narrative firmly into the contemporary human present of its audience. As David Mills has thoroughly demonstrated, however, the moral to parents to show patience in the face of adversity was a traditional one.[40] Neither can the story be understood simply as exemplary, for the Doctor acknowledges that a sacrifice comparable to Abraham's could never be expected of the members of his audience:

> Trowe ye, sorys, and God sent an angell
> And commaundyd yow yowre chyld to slayn,
> Be youre trowthe ys ther ony of yow
> That eyther wold [groche] or stryve therageyn?
> How thynk ye now, sorys, therby?
> I trow there be thre ore a fowr or moo . . . (443–48)

The very distance between Abraham's experience and the Brome reader's experience, however, reinforces the likelihood of a typological reading. If Abraham's sacrifice of Isaac is both inspiring and incomprehensible, so is God the Father's sacrifice of Christ. By just so much as Abraham's sacrifice exceeds any normally patient human parent, so does Christ's sacrifice exceed Abraham's.

The typological understanding of medieval drama long ago rescued the plays from critical oblivion, both elevating the texts as literary objects and recovering the possibilities of these plays for visual stagecraft. In so doing, typological critics argued that figural interpretations—often thought a kind of allegory—should enrich readings based on the drama of individual characterization or the pathos of human situations. Christ should be just as visible as Isaac, when the boy rests on the sacrificial altar. As Auerbach so clearly saw, the historicity of the figure is crucially important, for neither Isaac nor Christ loses the particularity of his own story as an effect of the figural relation between them.[41] It is the balance between individual history and sacred image, the way each dimension informs the other, that creates the power of the figural in the plays. Typological meaning and narrative pathos (what we could call contemporary resonance, or even history) are the same thing, in this view, for the realism of the play's characterization of both the child and the father serves to show how deeply felt Christ's passion should be. While acknowledging the affecting human story, the play uses typological means to show that Abraham's compassion for Isaac is the same as his obedience to God—that in both cases the law is fulfilled through love.

---

40. David Mills, "The Doctor's Epilogue to the Brome Abraham and Isaac: A Possible Analogue," *Leeds Studies in English* 11 (1980): 105–10.

41. Erich Auerbach, "Figura," in *Scenes from the Drama of European Literature* (Minneapolis, MN: University of Minnesota Press, 1984), 11–76.

Recent critical voices have found more complications to inhere in these connections of figure and history. Biddick's understanding of the typological imaginary, for example, takes Auerbach's insistence on history to its logical conclusion, to ask what historical effects such a mode of thinking necessarily had. The status of each figure firmly within history reveals the inherent reversibility of typological thinking ("the shattering threat of typological reversibility") against which the teleological narrative must establish itself: as she writes, "[w]ithout the fantasy of supersession the figure of the Christian is always possibly the truth of the Jew."[42] Or, in the case of Abraham and Isaac, without the fantasy of supersession the figure of the resurrected Christ is possibly the truth of the frightened human child. Allen J. Frantzen identifies similar problems with sacrificial logic, arguing that the Brome play in particular questions the reassuring Christian fantasy. In his view, the ultimately "antisacrificial" play undermines the consolations of typology by hinting at "the futility and social cost of sacrifice."[43]

Intriguingly, Biddick positions the inscription of this historical problem in the layout of medieval books, rather than in the theatrical performance of plays. She finds the typological imaginary incised, for example, into the *mise-en-page* of the *Glossa Ordinaria*, a familiar schoolbook that in turn inscribes it in the hearts and the minds of those who learn habits of thought from their experience of such material texts.[44] The static layout of the page and gloss manifests the rewriting of the Old Law by the New, and makes the supersession of one narrative by the other, rather than the biblical text itself, the center of its meaning. "Typology and graphic technology are thus closely bound," Biddick argues, and are "historically constitutive of each other."[45] Typological reading in the Book of Brome, too, is such a matter of seeing an interpretation laid out in the physical form of the page, a layering of Christ's story on top of Isaac's—or a picking of Christ's story out of Isaac's—that no medieval Christian reader could do without. Here the vision of the concrete page itself rather than of the figures it superimposes in the abstract leads a reader to a figural interpretation. Interestingly, Benson notes that the annotations in *Piers Plowman* manuscripts frequently highlight Old and New Testament names, suggesting that typological thinking is similarly inscribed upon that poem.[46] The evidence of such layouts and rubrications and underlinings concerns *reading* in a typological manner: not

---

42. Biddick, *Typological Imaginary,* 6.

43. Allen J. Frantzen, "Tears for Abraham: The Chester Play of Abraham and Isaac and Antisacrifice in Works by Wilfred Owen, Benjamin Britten, and Derek Jarman," *Journal of Medieval and Early Modern Studies* 31.3 (2001): 445–76, at 447.

44. Biddick, *Typological Imaginary,* 12–20, and Fig. 1.

45. Biddick, *Typological Imaginary,* 12.

46. Benson and Blanchfield, *Manuscripts of* Piers Plowman, 19, write that both Old and New Testament names are frequently rubricated in Cambridge University Library MS Dd.i.17 and Cambridge University Library MS Ll.iv.14.

speeches declaimed or the interpretation of stage-pictures, but the visual effects of words on a manuscript page.

The intersections here between typological interpretation and histories of reading return us to questions about the Brome play that have surrounded its criticism: namely, the Chester problem. J. B. Severs, arguing strongly for Chester as a corrupt version of Brome, uses the question of textual inheritance to think through various possibilities for textual transmission. He imagines the actual creation of the text as partaking of the circumstances of performance: "To be sure, there are signs of imperfection caused by written transmission, and errors of this kind are undoubtedly present; but much more numerous are the errors suggesting inaccurate memory." But further he supposes: "The sort of corruptness in which Chester abounds suggests an author-compiler, well-acquainted with the play [i.e., Brome] from having frequently heard or read it, attempting to reconstruct it from memory."[47] He here opens up the possibility that the Chester author was not only hearing but frequently reading the play. An alternative mode of transmission, then, would be the memory of seeing a written page, rather than memory of seeing a performance. And the memory of seeing these particular pages—though of course it could never be certain that the author of Chester saw the Book of Brome—inscribe the memory of typological interpretation, as well as the memory of the narrative itself.

I began with a pun based on bringing reading as interpretation together with reading as decoding ("a *reading* of the Brome play that shows the importance of *reading* itself"). What I have hoped to explore here is both aspects of the word: the ways in which the rubricator's marks reveal a practice of private reading that performs a typological interpretation of the text. Instead of seeing the performance of medieval drama as typological, we might think of typological reading as itself performative.[48] Of course, any performance is also always an interpretation, and so every performance is therefore also a kind of reading—in so many ways, the two practices are deeply and densely connected. But the Brome rubrication is more about reading itself—about the performance of interpretation—than simply about the ways in which ideas can be put forth in theatrical or extrinsic spectacle. The typological reading of the story of Abraham and Isaac is attested in multiple ways throughout medieval culture, both embodied by actors and inscribed on books. But this fifteenth-century instance of it is a reminder that the forms of medieval plays were read (both decoded and interpreted) as well as performed, and that late-medieval dramatic texts have a material existence we should not wish away in our search for the elusive conditions of performance.

---

47. Both quotations are from Severs, "Brome and Chester Plays," 151.
48. For this insight I am grateful to Helen Solterer.

2

The Style of Humanist Latin Letters at the University of Oxford

On Thomas Chaundler and the *Epistolae Academicae Oxon. (Registrum F)*

ANDREW COLE

We youre humble oratours . . .

What was once said of English poetry of the fifteenth century—that it was just so much dull prattle—was also until recently a common description of humanist Latin literature of the same period. One might think of Joseph Ritson's infamous characterization of Lydgate as that "voluminous, prosaic and driving monk" when reading scholarly descriptions of humanist writing: a "poetic production . . . [of] . . . little merit" here, "a dreary performance" there, and—most of all—Roberto Weiss's repeated assertions that "During the first quarter of the fifteenth century there prevailed . . . a taste for writing Latin in an extremely flowery and 'euphistic' style. This fashion was more a symptom of decadence than novelty."[1] While it remains to be seen whether humanist texts will catch on in the way Hoccleve and Lydgate have in the last fifteen years, scholars such as David Rundle and Daniel Wakelin have made real advances in

---

1. Doris Enright-Clark Shoukri, ed., *Liber apologeticus de omni statu humanae naturae* (New York: Modern Humanities Research Council in conjunction with Renaissance Society of America, 1974), 34n42; Arthur F. Leach, *The Schools of Medieval England* (London: Methuen, 1915), 248; Roberto Weiss, *Humanism in England during the Fifteenth Century*, 3rd ed. (Oxford: Basil Blackwell, 1967), 28. For other disparaging claims about English humanism, see the comments cited by Elizabeth Cox Wright, "Continuity in XV Century English Humanism," *PMLA* 51 (1936): 370–76; here, 370–71.

the study of humanist writing, showing the seriousness, interest, and style of a collection of classicizing works that can no longer be dismissed in the manner of Weiss, who famously raises up humanist writing in England only to knock it back down in disparaging statement after disparaging statement about its paltry quality in comparison to continental examples.[2] For my part, I'll join the critical conversation about humanism in England by examining a work about which it can be said, by its own editor no less, that "the entire artlessness of the whole production is beyond question."[3] That work is the letter book, Registrum F, in the Oxford University Archives (shelf mark NEP/supra/Reg F), now known by the title of the modern (though now old) edition, *Epistolae academicae Oxon.* But the purported artlessness of this "whole" gives in turn special prominence to real moments of scribal intelligence and a humanist style of a special, referential, and rhetorical kind.

The letters in Registrum F were entered between the years 1421 and 1498 and record communications and transactions between successive chancellors of Oxford and various heads of state and church—kings, dukes, earls, archbishops and bishops alike. I will look at "letters" in Registrum F in two senses of the term: letterforms as scribal style, and letters or epistles as historical documents with powerful rhetorical and petitionary attributes. The first sort of letter concerns a single epistle written by Thomas Chaundler, an extremely well-connected man with humanist interests and an administrator of considerable influence at the University of Oxford, having served as its chancellor for some years, among other occupations.[4] Written in 1443, and dated 23 October, this letter is said to exhibit a mix of letterforms, an attempt by Chaundler—not entirely wholehearted—to

---

2. See David Rundle, "Of Republics and Tyrants: aspects of quattrocento humanist writings and their reception in England, c. 1400–c. 1460" (D.Phil. thesis, University of Oxford, 1997) and "On the Difference between Virtue and Weiss: Humanist Texts in England during the Fifteenth Century," *Courts, Counties, and the Capital in the Later Middle Ages*, ed. Diana E. S. Dunn, The Fifteenth Century Series, 4 (Stroud, Eng.: Sutton, 1996), 181–203, as well as Daniel Wakelin, *Humanism, Reading, and English Literature 1430–1530* (Oxford: Oxford University Press, 2007). See also Susanne Saygin, *Humphrey, Duke of Gloucester (1390–1447) and the Italian Humanists* (Leiden: Brill, 2002) and Alessandra Petrina, *Cultural Politics in Fifteenth-Century England: The Case of Humphrey, Duke of Gloucester* (Leiden: Brill, 2004).

3. *Epistolae Academicae Oxon. (Registrum F)*, 2 vols., ed. Henry Anstey (Oxford: Oxford Historical Society, 1898), 1.xiv. In this essay, I focus mainly on the materials edited in volume one; here, I am only scratching the surface of what's important and interesting about this item. The epigraph is from *Epistolae*, 1.336. On the flyleaves of Registrum F are several trials of the expression, "Vestri oratores studiosissimi," which is used in the letters variously (as in 2.361 [signed by the scribe John Farley], and 2.362).

4. Thomas Chaundler graduated New College, Oxford in 1455 as a doctor of theology, after which point he became chancellor of Oxford (1457–61 and 1472–79). He also served two stints as Warden, first of Winchester College (1450) and then New College (1454–75). He was also once chaplain of Edward IV, and had as his patron both the enormously powerful Bishop William Wykeham and Bishop Thomas Bekynton. For more biographical details, see Jeremy Catto's entry, "Chaundler, Thomas," in *Oxford Dictionary of National Biography*, ed. H. C. G. Matthew and Brian Harrison, 60 vols. (Oxford University Press, 2004), 11.268–69.

include modern continental humanist script within Latin cursive (in which so much fifteenth-century theology was hashed out).[5] I set out to uncover some of Chaundler's intentions in producing a hybrid script that stands out among other entries in the Register and that, through a conscientious aesthetics of the page, imaginatively relocates or indeed "delivers" the letter to another institutional context across the channel. Here, I construe script as both a mode of address and as a phenomenological practice that invites a certain study of appearances, whereby Chaundler's aberrant style appears to frame an intention and send a message, directing local attention towards the objects and practices of the institution to which the letter itself is directed and where certain hybrid scribal styles are fostered: the Roman curia. My discussion of this single letter may seem pedantic in its close reading of paleographical and codicological details, but this precision is justified: the letter is something of a canonical text (or canonical hand) within modern scholarly studies of humanism.

The second part of this discussion turns from a literal consideration of letters to letters in the generic and rhetorical sense. Considering the letters in Registrum F *in toto*, I explore how they express and inform a certain history of humanism (or lack thereof) at the University of Oxford. The letters, that is, all strike a similar chord in complaining about Oxford as overrun with poverty and suffering from a lack of books. Some scholars have viewed these letters as "documents" or historical reportage, from Weiss to current histories of the University of Oxford. I argue here, however, that we must appreciate the petitionary rhetoric of these letters and the great extent to which their authors used this language to give meaning and shape to the humanist interests of their patrons, who were usually willing to donate but needed to hear reasons to do so, including Duke Humphrey, the "humanissimus princeps [the most humane prince]."[6] The letters, written by several chancellors and proctors, are diverse in content but consistent enough in their rhetorical features to limn an "Oxford school" of letter writing—a disciplined and at points repetitious method for communicating with certain influential patrons using humanist terminologies and postures. In fact, as will become clear below, these letters define humanism through their practice, exhibiting the fusion of administrative language with classical references.[7]

---

5. The letter appears in ibid., 1.223, and its photo is included in *Duke Humfrey and English Humanism in the Fifteenth Century: Catalogue of an Exhibition held in the Bodleian Library, Oxford* (Oxford: Bodleian Library, 1970), plate iii [back of book].

6. *Epistolae*, 1.255. Guarino da Verona used the same phrase to describe Leonello d'Este, marquis of Ferrara and Duke of Modena; see Marianne Pade, *The Reception of Plutarch's Lives in Fifteenth-Century Italy*, 2 vols. (Copenhagen: Museum Tusculanum Press, University of Copenhagen, 2007), 1.250.

7. Martin Camargo, "If You Can't Join Them, Beat Them; or, When Grammar Met Business Writing (in Fifteenth-Century Oxford)," *Letter-Writing Manuals and Instruction from Antiquity to the Present* (Columbia: University of South Carolina Press, 2007), 67–87, richly documents an essential background to what I discuss here, assessing the inclusion of letter writing within grammatical training at the

This double focus on letters and letterforms allows me to describe some of the achievements of early humanist documents. I conclude with some reflections on the significance of Latin petitions to vernacular verse and Middle English studies more generally, demonstrating that a literary history of the fifteenth century must both account for Latin literary production and for its influence on English poetry.[8]

THOMAS CHAUNDLER:
THE SCRIBAL AESTHETICS OF A LETTER BOOK

> *On the whole there are sufficient disturbing causes or defective arrangements to fully account for the bad spelling, bad writing, bad grammar, and mutilated documents, which, if they surprise, will not be without amusement to any one who has a taste for this kind of study.*[9]

Weiss was right to say that Thomas Chaundler, sometime chancellor of the University of Oxford, was "one of the principal pioneers of early humanism" but he then goes on to say (wrongly) that "his attempts at writing like a classicist met with mediocre success" and that his "literary remains are not very interesting."[10] Weiss elaborates:

> Although his aim was to write like a humanist, he was not able to perceive the fundamental difference between the scholastic and modern outlooks, and his attempts at being "Ciceronian" proved far from successful. His efforts to give a humane character to some of his writings, and his use of neo-classical and ancient texts while pursuing typically scholastic studies, indicate clearly his conception of modern learning merely as a means by which the old learning could be improved.[11]

After so many critiques of periodization, let alone of Weiss, it would now be facile to pounce on these confident statements about the clear distinction between medieval and modern practices, although some recent work on humanism continues to perpetuate myths about the Middle Ages; for example, one scholar has spoken of "the relapse into medievalism" on the question of the reception of Plato

---

university (see 68–69, 72–74, 78).

8. I am grateful for my interlocutors. Maura Nolan offered incisive feedback early on, and Andrew Galloway and David Rundle gave it a once-over late in the day. The readers for OSU Press supplied helpful ideas for revision that I was glad to implement, and the fantastic audience at the Cambridge medieval seminar (26 May 2010) helped me with the finishing touches. I thank Daniel Wakelin for the invitation to speak and his generous sharing of ideas. Finally, the Bodleian Library, University of Oxford, kindly granted permission to consult their resources and publish a photograph of Registrum F (shelfmark NEP/supra/Reg F).

9. *Epistolae*, xiv.

10. *Humanism in England*, 135.

11. Ibid., 136.

in the fifteenth century.¹² Rather than critiquing Weiss and others, however, I have found it more productive to investigate what in Chaundler's work gives the impression that he puts modernity in the service of the medieval, the humanistic in the service of the scholastic.¹³ Indeed, there is perhaps no better emblem of Chaundler's purported mix of medieval and modern modes than a certain letter he wrote in 1443 to three men residing at the Papal Curia—Andrew Holes, Richard Caunton, and one W. Symond (about whom I can as yet find no good information). This letter is preserved in Registrum F at fol. 65r, and in it Chaundler urges the recipients to commend to Pope Eugene IV the current chancellor of Oxford, Henry Sever, so that the Pope himself can in turn commend Sever to the English king, Henry VI. The recipients, in essence, are asked to butter up the pope in preparation for his receipt of the commendation itself (fol. 65r–65v)—written by Chaundler on behalf of the congregation (see below).¹⁴ The letter reads very much like a modern letter of recommendation, lauding the "eruditissimo et gravissimo viro" in the first, the "clarum et excellentem virum" in the second.¹⁵

None of this content is particularly relevant to incipient humanism in England—no Ciceronian references or other classical authorities. The humanist relevance, instead, is betrayed in the script of the first letter, which seems to confirm Weiss' assessment of Chaundler's "attempts at writing like a classicist;" the Bodleian exhibition catalogue itself, which offers a description and plate of this letter, echoes Weiss in labeling the missive "Thomas Chaundler's attempts at humanistic script."¹⁶ The word "attempts," in both cases, is a gentle way of characterizing Chaundler's seemingly amateurish and poorly executed humanistic script: heavily inked, stylized letterforms, whereby features of the Latin cursive, especially ascenders and descenders, are exaggerated and the aspect is often deliberately upright (see Fig. 2.1).

To be crudely periodizing about the script of this example, the letter forms for e, a (in some of its accentuated ascenders), o, v, x, g, and p (in its audaciously sloping descender) seem modern, while forms for d, i, h, b, r ("Octobris" [line 20] but not "tempore" [line 10]) are medieval, along with the standard Latin abbreviations for "-n-"/"-m-," "-us," "-er," "con-," "-um," "-que," which of course are

---

12. See the third chapter of Sears Reynolds Jayne's *Plato in Renaissance England* (Dordrecht: Kluwer Academic Publishers, 1995), 22–59.

13. For an assessment of Chaundler's literary humanism, see my "Heresy and Humanism," *Twenty-First Century Approaches to Literature: Middle English*, ed. Paul Strohm (Oxford: Oxford University Press, 2007), 421–37; here, 427–33.

14. Virginia Davis suggests that Sever "plainly stood high in the king's favour, for on 11 October 1440, in his charter of incorporation, Henry VI appointed him to be the first provost of the new royal foundation of Eton College, a post he held until 1442. He may have left the king's service in some disfavour, however"—hence, requiring the letter of commendation, which apparently worked: Sever was made the king's almoner (*Oxford Dictionary of National Biography*, 49.818).

15. See *Epistolae*, 1.223 and 225.

16. *Duke Humfrey and English Humanism in the Fifteenth Century*, 19.

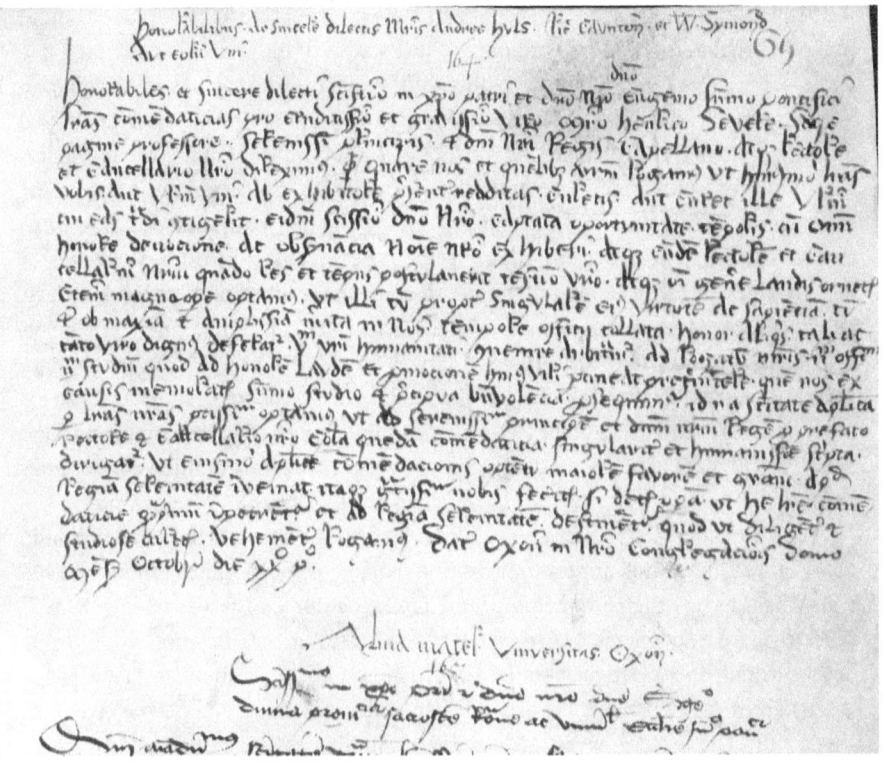

FIGURE 2.1. Oxford University Archives NEP/supra/Reg F [Registrum F], f. 65r

found in early modern printed books containing Latin. Yet one man's modernity is another's Middle Ages. For the new *littera humanistica* (including all the hands that can go by this name) is not new or even classical; it revives the more legible Carolingian miniscule of the eighth century in which a bibliophilic Italian humanist might have read many classical works, not even realizing they were medieval copies to begin with.[17]

To understand the significance of Chaundler's letter to the history of humanism, however, is to appreciate properly its context and, more generally, the purposes and peculiarities of Registrum F. In other words, I am regarding the "whole" mentioned at the outset so as to get a better idea of the unique instances that merit our attention. To begin with, this register is on parchment, a somewhat unusual medium in view of other Oxford registers from the early- and mid-fifteenth century, such as Register Aa (the Register of Congregations) and Register

---

17. Technically, then, humanistic scripts are a revival of a revival, the Carolingian renaissance. See Albert Derolez, *The Palaeography of Gothic Manuscript Books: From the Twelfth to the Early Sixteenth Century* (Cambridge: Cambridge University Press, 2003), as well as his earlier *Codicologie des manuscrits en écriture humanistique sur parchemin*, 2 vols. (Turnhout: Brepols, 1984).

Aaa (the Registrum Cancellari), both of whose pages are paper. Indeed, these two other registers were both unbound—just stacks of loose sheets contained in a chest—for a significant amount of time until they suffered serious misfortune: in February of 1544, their sheets were torn, trampled upon, or otherwise destroyed during a notorious burglary in the old Congregation house that broke up the university chests containing these and other documents, valuables, and money. The silver lining of this tale can be seen in an analogy. What John Leland is to English monastic books and libraries, Brian Twyne, the seventeenth-century Keeper of the Archives, is to these administrative documents at Oxford: after the burglary, he reassembled the two registers in what must have been a real hermeneutic labor, and they remain in that form today.[18] Given that Registrum F is on parchment, one could suppose that this book was particularly treasured, considered to be more valuable than these other two items and thus committed to permanence and handled with care. But even a quick glance suggests that this opinion cannot fully hold.

Like the other two registers, Registrum F seems to have started as an unbound item. The earlier folios appear to have first existed as loose sheets or maybe even a booklet that was then cropped to fit the present volume as it was taking shape.[19] After these earlier pages, the register begins to even out, but not without one oddity, which starts between fols. 11 and 12, and becomes more frequent in the latter half of the register: there are nineteen stubs indicating that pages have been sliced out. That's verging on an inordinate number. Most of these folios were excised while the book was already bound, but—strangely enough—there is no discernible loss of text, with continuity within an entry preserved across the stubs, across the extraction, sometimes across multiple stubs. Several folios, themselves never removed, bear the wounds or slices from the excision of adjacent pages.[20]

---

18. See *The Register of Congregation, 1448–1463*, ed. W. A. Pantin and W. T. Mitchell (Oxford: Clarendon Press, 1972), xi, xviii–xix.

19. For instance, the letter on 1v (item 5) goes too far into the gutter to have been written in a volume bound with this many folios. Likewise, the text on 21v; see also 4v, 10r, 17v, 22v, 25v, 26v, 27v—after which the entries do not go nearly so far toward the gutter. Possibly, these early loose sheets or booklet pages were made into the first quire for the larger book we now have, as evident from cropping. For example, the letter on folio 2r, dated 1423 (item 6), was cropped, chopping off words at the end of each line, but a medieval hand replaced the cropped letters near the gutter of each subsequent line. Seeing as these additions are in the same hand as the note at the end of the entry, "Nota quod Universitas non consuevit vocare bacallarios Magistros," which refers to a matter addressed on fol. 39v (item 107) whereby in 1435 bachelors are clamoring to be called masters, we can suppose that this initial cropping and binding transpired at least twelve years later, in the serial gathering of quires or booklets. It is, in other words, a medieval patch job.

20. The stubs are located between the folios listed here; the italics signal a folio that has been damaged by the extractions: fols. 11–12 (one stub), 83–84 (one stub), 136–*37* (one stub, belonging to the former bifolium containing 137, only slightly scored); 143–44 (one stub), 161–*62* (five stubs), 163–64 (one stub), 169–70 (two stubs), *174–75* (two stubs), *179*–80 (one stub), 187–*88* (two stubs), *191–92* (two stubs).

Why were these pages removed from a book meant to preserve entries? One possibility is that poorly copied letters were discarded—though that notion begs the question since many entries, as Anstey notes, are sloppily or mistakenly written. It is likely, however, that the folios were removed after the time the loose sheets were collected into a book and joined with booklets of blank pages. Under these conditions, sheets that were blank and farther on in the book were removed for some official purpose, seeing as they were at a safe distance from pages where entries were recorded. That blank extracts were used for other purposes is consistent with the general practice (as seen in the two other registers), in which loose sheets were often preferred for recording business in locales around Oxford where those transactions actually transpired.

Yet what goes out must go back in: some sheets have been added to the register,[21] while others may have been extracted and then reinserted.[22] This process at points perpetrates the codicological folly of setting the hairside of a folio against the flesh side—whatever it took to wedge a document or series of documents into the correct place and sequence.[23] It is indeed strange to think of a formulary or register as a parchment farm, or a book whose boundaries are so permeable that items leave only to return.[24] All of this extraction and insertion runs against the common sense regarding literary book production or booklet assembly for miscellanies, in which repeated and injurious excision simply does not happen because it cannot practically happen during a single scribal stint or production coordinated simultaneously among two or more scribes, except in cases where things go wrong and sheets become disarranged within a booklet, as

---

21. Folio 112, with ruled margins, is an insertion, glued and wrapped around folios 113–16, with its edge visible on 116v at the gutter (this edge is rough, unlike the cleanly sliced edges instanced in the other stubs in this book). It is blank on the recto side, and on its verso are two entries in their entirety, items 241 and 242, in the hand of John Farley. By way of note, all blank pages in Registrum F are recto sides.

22. As for these extractions and reinsertions, the clearest case is folios 94 and 95, which were removed and then reglued into place on a scrap with Latin cursive, thus proving that this was done rather contemporaneously. The original attachments or stubs are visible between folios 93 and 94. Could these have been removed to serve as exemplars for another book—removed, so that the entire book would not have to be lent out? Conversely, could they have been removed so that the items could be copied from another source and then set back in? Folios 94 and 95 contain items 215 through to the indenture ("Hec indentura . . . ," which is completed on 96r).

23. Folios 159 and 160 comprise a bifolium that seems to have been inserted—namely because these pages interrupt the intervals of flesh side facing flesh side, hair side facing hair side. There is also stitching between these two pages. The interruption begins after 158v (hair side), where 159r (flesh side) is inserted, then: 159v (hair side), 160r (hair side), 160v (flesh side), 161r (hair side), 161v (flesh side), at which point the proper pattern resumes but with the first of five stubs, the recto of which is the flesh side. This first stub belongs to folio 157.

24. There is also a spell of achronology between folios 110r and 113r, in which the dates jump from 1460 to 1467–71 (110v–112v) back to 1460. It is hard to make heads or tails of the etiology of this disorder; but it can be noted that it all is contained within one quire of five bifolia (fols. 109–119), not counting an inserted loose sheet (fol. 112), as discussed in note 21. For an example of how chronology has to be ignored by scribes seeking pages to record entries, see *Register of Congregation*, xviii.

in the case of the Trinity Gower (Cambridge, Trinity College MS R.3.2) examined by Doyle and Parkes in their famous article of 1978.[25]

Registrum F is not only codicologically peculiar but paleographically so, as the epigraph from Anstey avers. Some letters are just better written than others, much more slowly and carefully copied in a competently lineated way.[26] Some material was more hastily or sloppily written than others, and often in available blank spaces (see, for instance, fol. 37r and 62v, the second memorandum). Some letters end abruptly, mid-sentence, and some exhibit corrections and cross outs. Yet even this situation is rather normal for a book that unfolds over time and is used for many purposes. Take, for instance, William Swan's letterbook—Oxford, Bodleian Library, Arch. Selden B. 23, also paper.[27] Swan's letterbook is relevant as a contemporary example because the man himself was papal secretary under Pope Gregory VII at the Council of Constance—a council important not only for church reforms but also as a meeting ground for persons with interests in humanism.[28] In view of his job, we should expect great things of his letterbook. Yet what stands out, markedly, upon inspection of this item is that Swan (often in his own

---

25. A. I. Doyle and M. B. Parkes, "The Production of copies of the *Canterbury Tales* and the *Confessio Amantis* in the early Fifteenth Century," *Medieval Scribes, Manuscripts and Libraries: Essays presented to N.R. Ker*, ed. M. B. Parkes and Andrew G. Watson (London: Scolar Press, 1978), 163–203.

26. On the matter of scribal identification: there is an odd hand on folio 19v (item 57, from 1431) that bends downward as it heads toward the gutter. The text, however, on folio 20r turns downward as well, but toward the edge of the page (not the gutter). The writing in the same hand rights itself on folio 20r, with "Noverint universi." I believe this to be the wild and heavy hand of Thomas Gascoigne. It sufficiently matches the more judicious script in Oxford, St. John's College MS 17, fol. 111v [col. b], where he complains about a scribe's use of ampersand as an abbreviation for "et" (as in "&iam" for "etiam"), and it corresponds (sloping excepted) with his known handwriting in Lincoln College MS Lat. 54, 17v–18r and, more precisely (with the sloping), Oxford Bodleian Library, MS Lat.theo.e.33, fols, 39r–69v. Second, the entries on fol. 19v, 20r, and 41v of Registrum F bear Gascoigne's signature mark, "jesus: maria" or "jesus: maria: anna: orata" (fols. 20r and 41v), variations of which are in St. John's MS 17, fols. 95v, 103v, 105r, 109v, 111r–v, 114r and 115r–v, and Lincoln College MS Lat. 54, fols. 15v, 17v, 18r, 55r; MS Lat.theo.e.33, fols. 1r, 3r–6v, 10v, 30v, 34v, 36v–38v, 39v–69v. Cf. this mark in a different hand on fol. 75v of Registrum F ("ihs maria katerina," from 1446). Also perhaps by Gascoigne are entries on 29r (item 74, from 1433) and 41v (item 111, from 1436). The latter is a testimonial letter *for* Gascoigne, and that it is potentially by his own hand would not be unusual for a man who wrote his own obituary in a rather senescent looking script, complete with a marginal blank "___" to be filled in after he departs "ab hac vita" (MS Lat.theo.e.33, fol. 41r; the obit continues on 68v). The letter on 34r (item 91) and 66v (item 167) of Registrum F show a similar swerve but may not be by Gascoigne, as does the letter on 147r (item 319). What we have in Gascoigne is a scribe who does not always follow conventions within the register. On fol. 20r (item 57) and fol. 29r (item 74), he adds, at the end of each letter, descriptive material about the placement of addresses and valedictions in each letter, "infrascripcio littere" and "suprascricio littere," guiding the placement of the material (fol. 29r; Anstey takes this scribe's cue and silently relocates the address from the end to the beginning of the letter; see 1.96–97).

27. Another letterbook of Swan's is contained in the sundry collection that is London, British Library, MS Cotton Cleopatra C.iv.

28. On William Swan, see E. F. Jacob, "To and From the Court of Rome in the Early Fifteenth Century," *Studies in French Language and Mediaeval Literature: Presented to Professor Mildred K. Pope, by pupils, colleagues, and friends* (Freeport, NY: Books for Libraries Press, 1969), 161–82.

hand) corrects many of his own letters. One explanation for his activity is that Swan is fixing letters that were miscopied by the scribe he charged to record his outgoing communications. (Are there never any good copyists around?) But at points this explanation provokes disbelief, as more than a few of these corrections are not the kind with which modern editors are familiar: eye skips, spoonerisms, misspellings, grammatical mistakes, and so forth. Rather, Swan at various points replaces single words with phrases in what seem to be clarifications of expression, along with deletions of superfluous wording (41v–42r, 48v, 49r, 50r), and instances of rewrites (50v). Sometimes, he simply wished to change a verb's mood from "sit" to "est" (42v). Swan, in these instances at least, uses his formulary to compose letters.

Clearly, letterbooks are not always overly formal entities with strict rules for registering. Indeed, their messiness is what makes them attractive to the student of medieval culture interested in the workings of its institutions and authors. Often untidy productions, these volumes were living, evolving books that testify to cultures in the making and their modes of communication. In this light, it is clear that they are not always formularies in the technical sense of the term. Nor is Registrum F, as it contains only a few, brief examples of model letters (or *formae epistolarum*); fols. 70r–75v, for instance, contain relatively short models averaging 3–4 per folio side—which seems paltry in view of collections that contain upwards of 925 models.[29] Likewise, because Registrum F has few letters written *to* the university, it is not a register in the technical sense of recording receipts of documents and providing a full account of all communications with university officials. (The most famous receipts recorded in Registrum F are the donations of books by Duke Humphrey, more on whom below.[30]) At every level, then, Registrum F relieves itself of the obligation to be a stable, artistic object suitable for a museum. In such a book, where provisionality is the rule, Chaundler's letter can hardly be called a failed "attempt" at anything, much less an attempt to write a full-on *littera humanistica*. Chaundler, like all the other scribes contributing to Registrum F, knew full well that he was not writing his epistle for presentation as final copy. Whether the letter Chaundler actually sent to these men was written in a similar hand, we may never know, unless the original turns up at the Vatican.[31]

---

29. See Emil J. Polak, *Medieval and Renaissance Letter Treatises and Form Letters: A Census of Manuscripts found in Eastern Europe and the former U.S.S.R.* (Leiden: E. J. Brill, 1993), 6–7. This handlist is extremely valuable in communicating the variety of content in letter books. See also Polak's companion volume published by Brill in 1994: *Medieval and Renaissance Letter Treatises and Form Letters: A Census of Manuscripts found in part of Western Europe, Japan, and the United States of America*.

30. Folios 67v, 68r, 68v, are ruled for the list of books given to Oxford, yet the list of donated books on 52r–v, and 53r, is not ruled, and instead hand-drawn (i.e., imperfect) lines connect the title of the books, on the left, to the *secundo folio* designation on the right. The corresponding entry in the edition is at *Epistolae*, 1.177–84.

31. Why did Chaundler even make this entry? At the time of composition, he was junior proctor of the

Part 1, Chapter 2

We can, however, turn this problem around and offer a conclusion about how this letter functions *in its place* in Registrum F, how it "presents" itself, how it appears, within a book whose conventions emerge and change over time, through the accretion of entries. To arrive at an understanding of this function is to appreciate the aesthetics of the page in the register, and the governing decorum that often guides some of the scribes in recording entries. These scribes exhibit a great variation of practice, yet there is a prevailing sense that they seek appropriate places to register their texts, wanting not to follow too closely upon a previous entry—in one case, restarting the letter to allow for proper spacing[32]—or, as is sometimes the case, refusing to follow immediately after an entry and instead finding a fresh folio so that an entire page can be devoted to an important epistle.[33] Included within this aesthetics of the page is an interesting habit, which is seen far more frequently in the first half of the register than in the second, of offering *visually* pleasing salutations and valedictions, complete with skillful geometric patterns breaking off from the otiose strokes of stylized letterforms. Some letters for secular magnates, though by no means all,[34] receive a hearty helping of such stylization—which is, we must remember, not absolutely necessary as they are not original versions.[35] Here, then, flourish emerges as a kind of thinking about institutions, people, and places, insofar as it is a mode of reference, pointing both to recipients and their status, as well as to the very locations in which letters are read.[36] In a larger sense, then, style is an institution in which literary forms are

---

university (1444–45), and perhaps made the entry on the occasion of Sever's absence, or simply on his behalf (How odd would it be to commend yourself?!). Two proctors, one junior and one senior, served under the chancellor.

32. See fol. 12r, where a majuscule "S" is drawn but abandoned and restarted, lower and indented, to complete the word, "S[an]c[t]issi[m]o" [item 40], in an address to the pope.

33. See, for example, the spaces between fols. 10v and 11r (items 36 and 37), 38v to 39r (items 105 to 106), and 45v to 46r (items 124 to 125).

34. See fol. 48r (item 130) and 61r (item 153) addressed to the king; and fol 57v (item 148) to Duke Humphrey.

35. For instance, on fol. 36v, the letter to the Earl of Stafford may be the most elaborately and neatly done in the Registrum, especially the concluding "vestre dominaciones . . . ," which is followed by another letter with an even more grandly styled opening address to the Earl of Warwick, "Illustrissimo principi d[omi]no n[ost]ro comiti warwici" (fol. 36v). The second letter concludes on folio 37r, and near the bottom of that same folio begins a letter to the Archbishop of York, with a flourished address not matched by any of the other letters to ecclesiasts. These three letters are by the same scribe. On fol. 59v is a letter to Duke Humphrey placed on an entire folio side (item 152; *Epistolae*, 202, which I discuss below). There is a gesture towards stylistic formality, but nothing like the three letters discussed above. Likewise, the letters to Humphrey on fols. 59v and 75v (items 152 and 179) present some formal care. Incidentally, letters to high ecclesiasts do not typically receive these treatments, as in the case of the Archbishop of Canterbury (see fol. 28r [item 71] and 46r–v [item 125]), though letters to lower, albeit important, figures do display such flourishes, as on folio 84v (item 195b) to the Rector of Abchurch, London and, following, the letter to the dean of St. Paul's (item 196). See also the first English letter in the book to the executors of John Gedney on folio 85r (item 197). This letter sits alone on the page, and is written by the same scribe who had done items 195 and 196.

36. For another example of Chaundler's indexical or referential scribal habits, see my "Staging Advice in New College MS 288: On Thomas Chaundler and Thomas Bekynton," *After Arundel:*

scriptable before becoming even legible, writing before reading.[37] Letters are an opportunistically suitable genre with which to exhibit this kind of style, because it raises the idea of epistolary "address" from mere verbal salutation to total visual form.

Such an aesthetic—or indeed, a synaesthetic in its visual and verbal features—seems to inform Chaundler's own entry, which is visually and stylistically unique in Registrum F.[38] For no other scribe quite succeeds in offering a sustained example of a *fere-humanistica corsiva* in this register until some fifty years later.[39] The fact that he wrote in this manner seems rather audacious (fitting, I think, Chaundler's general demeanor) but no less aesthetically interesting because the style of his epistle—again, the hand exhibiting humanist with cursive features—is a mode of address in two ways. First, it speaks to local readers who are beholding in Registrum F an internationally directed letter. In fact, this is one of the few letters in the register, which contains upwards of 527 letters (a total not

---

Religious Writing in Fifteenth-Century England, ed. Vincent Gillespie and Kantik Ghosh (Turnhout: Brepols, 2011).

37. One possible (but to me unlikely) explanation is that this flourishing was done by a budding copyist intending to practice the art. Oxford, Bodleian Library, Ashmole MS 789, for instance, contains as its first item an interesting booklet of notarial exercises, offering examples of flourishing (see fol. 1r–3r), and sample flourished forms of each letter in the alphabet (fol. 3v–4r). However, the examples in the Ashmole manuscript are far more embellished than anything seen in Registrum F, whose examples seem less "practiced."

38. Anstey (*Epistolae*, xvii) notes that the volume becomes more modern in spelling and in Latin expression the more it proceeds, and the "old things" pass away. (He also acknowledges, as I do, that this is not a perfectly chronological volume; there are anachronistic interpolations from time to time.) Likewise, Weiss says that "Italian values" seems to have "brought an improvement in the style of the *Epistolae Academicae*, the prose of which during this period discloses an endeavour to write better Latin" (*Humanism in England*, 168; Weiss's footnote here reads, "Cf. the letters in the second volume of the *Epistolae Academicae*").

39. Granted, one can spot humanist influence here and there or, just as well, a simple change of scripts and scribes over the course of time. I cannot in the space here offer a deep study of all the hands in Registrum F, but items that stand out to my eye are: fol. 82r (item 192, dated 1449); 98r (item 220) with textura minims in places (lines 5–9); 108r (item 236), a clear secretary script that cuts off mid sentence; 111v–113r, 114r, 114v, 115v, all examples by John Farley (note, again, that 110v–112v contains entries chronologically out of order, from 1467–71); 118v, bottom, item 254, in what is likely John Farley's hand with humanist features; 119v, item 255, which exhibits a humanist aspect before reverting to cursive; 131v, middle item, "Universis sancte matris . . . ," which looks suspiciously like Chaundler's hand and falls within his second stint as chancellor; 133v, to Bishop William Wayneflete, with a very upright secretarial duct, also entered during Chaundler's stint as chancellor; 141v, starts out cursive but then in the last six lines beginning with "impediti ductos" turns quasi humanist, quasi secretary; 175v–176r, which contains three Latin texts and one English one (items 460, 461, 462); 176v (item 465, including the two acquittances); 181v (items 493 and 494 in a distinctive hand by "Burgeys"); 186r (items 510 and 511, also by "Burgeys"); 186v (items 512, 513[b] "Tertio . . . ," and 514, also by "Burgeys"). "Burgeys" does not sign all his entries, and I have not listed them all here, but items 488 (fol. 180v) and 493 (fol. 181v) of his seems to bear almost "italic" tendencies and these are from the years 1497 and 1498 respectively. Generally speaking, the hand changes significantly on fol. 107v (107r is a blank page), picking up with presumably a stint by John Farley, who signs his name "·J· ffarley" at the bottom of fol. 111v, followed by a blank page (112r), and then a neat cursive. Farley also signs his name in Greek on fol. 114v, 115v, 116v, among other places.

including testimonials and aquittances), addressed to persons outside of England, almost always the pope. This letter, however, goes to known humanists, especially Holes—an observation that brings us to the second mode of address: the letter's style suits its recipients, men at the Curia, which under Pope Eugene IV (1431–47) was actively sponsoring a *cancellaresca corsiva*,[40] a cursive chancery hand that the addressees themselves were expected to adopt in their communications. Chaundler's script may seem odd now in view of some abstracted notion or pseudo archetype of a "humanist" hand, but it would have signified to a contemporary English audience—perhaps because of its alienness and novelty—the context to which it was directed: the Curia and to persons with demonstrably humanist interests. Like the flourished titles in letters to prominent secular persons in Registrum F, then, this letter stylistically signals its importance, expressing learning, culture, style, and a keen sense of how genre and scribal hand not only suit but represent (as the Hegelian Vorstellung) an institutional context elsewhere. The letter never has to be delivered, never has to leave Registrum F, to get that humanist message across.

I would be remiss to conclude this analysis without remarking that Chaundler has a habit of using different hands for different purposes—a practice that is itself important in the history of humanist writing. For instance, immediately after his epistle there are two further entries that I am fairly certain are in his hand, but have yet to be identified as such, perhaps because they are in Latin cursive. Yet Chaundler's duct—most evident in his curiously written "p" (the lobe with a triangular top, and leftward descender) gives him away.[41] What we find here is one of several cases in which Chaundler writes in different scripts, sometimes within the same manuscript.[42] It is not entirely clear why Chaundler reverts to Latin cursive in Registrum F—though he likely does so to bring attention to his hybrid hand—but we can conclude that his general habit of switching hands is

---

40. See Anthony G. Petti, *English Literary Hands from Chaucer to Dryden* (London: Edward Arnold, 1977), 18.

41. These two letters were also sent across the channel—item 165 (fol. 65r), the commendation to the Pope (discussed above), and the next letter, item 166 (fol. 65v–66r), addressed to "ffrederico, Romanorum regi." I do not think that the words at the end of Chaundler's humanist epistle, "Alma mater Universitas Oxoniensis," included in Anstey (*Epistolae*, 1.224), are in his hand: it is written with a finer pen and is a more studied upright hand resembling the entries by Farley.

42. Chaundler's Latin glosses contrast markedly with the anglicana script of Walton's English Boethius in London, British Library, Harley MS 43, fols. 4r–29v; for his various signatures, see fols. 1v, 2r, 17r. Other examples of Chaundler's hand are London, British Library, Cotton Titus A.xxiv, fols. 2r–10v (with texts in anglicana in praise of Bishop William Wykeham) and 15r–63r (with the *collocutiones* and one of two *allocutiones* in anglicana); and fols. 11r–14r (a poem celebrating Bishop William Wykeham in a hybrid hand resembling in some particulars his hand in Registrum F). Chaundler also wrote colophons in clear secretary in Oxford, New College MS 288, according to M. R. James, *The Chaundler MSS* (London: J. B. Nichols and Sons, 1916), 29–30. My hypothesis, which will have to be set out at length elsewhere, is that Chaundler is also responsible for writing the English text of Walton's Boethius in Harley 43.

similar not only to the practices of contemporary humanists in England,[43] but also to those of later figures whose humanism and modernity are rarely challenged. For example, Sir Thomas More, "[i]n keeping with common practice in this period . . . seems to use secretary for his English writings and correspondence, and italic for Latin," as Malcolm Parkes observed long ago.[44] More's habit of using different hands for different circumstances is, as Parkes notes, common in early modern England.

For our purposes in evaluating Chaundler's significance, it is this habit, rather than individual features of the hand, that enables us to make comparisons between medieval and early modern writing. For we do not find this contrastive style in the practices of the contemporary vernacular and Latin scribes we usually deal with, beyond those aspects of *ordinatio* that call for capitals, uncials, and half-uncials to distinguish titles, chapters, and so forth. And granted, a scribe's hand may change on account of fatigue during a stint, or he may, for want of writing space, either produce smaller text or reduce the space between lines so that he need not carry on to another folio or booklet.[45] Paleographers have recently relied on this predictability or conventionality of a scribe's hand in the attempt to identify scribes and associate them with books previously thought to have been unconnected to them.[46] With Chaundler, however, we have something different, something new—a contrastive practice that tells us, in the end, how uniquely interesting, stylistically humanist, and contextually perceptive he and his contemporaries were. Further study of Chaundler's hand is in order, but suffice it to say

---

43. John Farley used distinct hands, as the range of examples show: Registrum F, New College 288 and likely Cambridge, Trinity College MS R.14.5, as well as his entries as university scribe in Registrum Aa, fols. 111v–28r (NEP/supra/Reg.Aa). Robert Flemmyng, nephew of the Bishop Richard Flemmyng (founder of Lincoln College, Oxford), exhibits a similar contrast of hands in Oxford, Lincoln College MS Lat. 43 (Cicero's *De Officiis*), writing in *fere-humanistica* but in secretary on the end pastedown signing his name (and declaring his scribal work on this book); see *Duke Humfrey and English Humanism in the Fifteenth Century*, 36–37, and plate xiii(a) in the back of the book. Greek glosses in Lincoln College MS Lat. 43 are on folios 18r, 21v, 25v, 32r, 49r (3x), 60v, and 107r, not all by the same hand. Likewise, in Oxford, Lincoln College MS Lat. 84, fols. 12r–59r, Flemmyng writes "partly in fere-humanistica" and "partly in a pointed gothic cursive (fol. 2–11v, 60–89, 249–end), with headings in his early humanistic hand" (ibid., 37) and, I would add, heavy glossing in cursive, fols. 12r–15v, with lighter glossing thereafter. "Fol. 90–240 were written by two Italian scribes in semi-humanistic script" (ibid.) and in double columns (fols. 90–276v).

44. M. B. Parkes, *English Cursive Book Hands, 1250–1500* (London: Scolar Press, 1979), 67. See also Petti, *English Literary Hands*, 16, and (in the case of Petrarch) Bernhard Bischoff, *Latin Paleography: Antiquity and the Middle Ages*, trans. Dáibhí Ó Cróinín and David Ganz (Cambridge: Cambridge University Press, 1990), 145–46.

45. Too much space is also a problem, as fol. 53v (item 143), 55v (final item), or, most strangely, 62v (final item) show, as the script slowly inflates almost after each line in an effort to reach the bottom of the page.

46. The most recently visible instance of this paleographical work is by Linne Mooney, "Chaucer's Scribe," *Speculum* 81 (2006): 97–138; "Some New Light on Thomas Hoccleve," *Studies in the Age of Chaucer* 29 (2007): 293–340; and the AHRC funded "Identification of the Scribes Responsible for Copying Major Works of Middle English Literature."

it is hard to imagine how one could ever conclude that he or his imaginatively skilled colleagues wrote from a "rigidly medieval standpoint" and were humanists *in deserto* among the "medievally minded theologians."[47]

"ONE CONTINUAL WAIL"; OR, AN OXFORD SCHOOL OF HUMANIST PETITIONS

> *We cannot feel our way in this darkness, but there is enough light to make us wonder not that the poverty was great, but that it was not even greater than these letters testify in one continual wail.*[48]

Registrum F screams of historicity, or at least wails about squalid conditions, if we are to take at face value its editor's words in this epigraph. Similarly, Roberto Weiss cites Registrum F numerous times in his book, *Humanism in England*, and regards it as an invaluable historical document—a practice that makes sense, since the edition itself was published by the Oxford Historical Society and bears a subtitle pitched especially to historians: "documents illustrative of academical life and studies at Oxford in the fifteenth century." Speaking of such "academical life," Weiss concludes:

> As a whole Oxford about 1450–60 was still fundamentally medieval. . . . The outward decadence of the University reflected the state of its learning. Endowment and books were grossly insufficient. Buildings were inadequate while colleges were practically closed corporations more anxious for their own welfare than for that of the University.[49]

Weiss, too, heard the wail. For in a footnote to these words, he references Registrum F, albeit in a cursory fashion *"Epistolae Academicae*, vols. I, II, passim."[50] To his credit, he (like Anstey) is indeed reading the content of the letters correctly, insofar as so many of them offer complaints about two things in particular: the scarcity of books and the decrepitude of buildings at Oxford. But he neglects to consider the generic horizons of such letters, their rhetorical purposes—their place at the end of a history of the *ars epistolandi* and their obvious commitment to the kind of rhetoric Augustine deplored in his *Confessions:* rhetoric as persuasion, the discursive art of moving the recipient or listener from one place (*locus*)

---

47. Weiss, *Humanism in England*, 134, and 100; see also 136.
48. Anstey, *Epistolae*, 1.xxiv.
49. *Humanism in England*, 131–32.
50. Ibid., 133n1 and n4.

to another by means of *amplificatio* and exaggeration.[51] A consideration of the rhetorical purposes of these letters, then, would seem to be important, not simply as a corrective to Weiss' assessments but also as a way of weighing in on both some recent characterizations of Oxford in the fifteenth century[52] and the more longstanding critical conversation about the character of fifteenth-century literary culture in England.

What the letters tell us about Oxford is simultaneously what they tell us about themselves, what their rhetorical qualities reveal. I am now talking about content, and as such, am compelled to read Registrum F as a narrative, to collect impressions about its content, and to identify which of its contents would seem to solicit an historical interpretation. Given that the Registrum is a book of 198 folios, any effort to draw a single conclusion about it would be a hazardous enterprise. Instead, I offer a single observation regarding the supposed decrepitude of Oxford's physical plant, which will demonstrate that the Registrum's Latin letters are discursively linked to petitionary rhetoric in general, including the kinds of "begging poems" we find in the work of Chaucer, Hoccleve, and Lydgate. For their part, the chancellors of the university, in speaking for themselves, on behalf of the congregation, or for both parties, write to such notable persons as the Archbishop of Canterbury, Duke Humphrey, the Earl of Warwick, and the Bishop of Winchester; their letters offer stories of material poverty jeopardizing study,[53] alongside observations about how a lack of money—resulting from the eradication of lecture fees—detracts from the education of students.[54] But no sooner do we conclude that these letters reflect on a dire state of affairs than we discover the chancellors commending Oxford scholars for various lucrative promotions, which are meant to indicate that this university produces the best scholars anyway, worthy of hire.[55] And back and forth the letters go, with grandiloquent

---

51. The Latinate practices of letter writing, of course, are an extension of the medieval discipline of rhetoric; epistolography adapts rhetorical practice to a variety of institutional environments both secular and religious; the *ars epistolandi*—a subset of the many arts of speaking, preaching, and writing—prescribes the standard missive forms from greeting to the valediction. For more on the *ars dictaminis*, which includes the *ars epistolandi*, see Martin Camargo, *Ars Dictaminis, Ars Dictandi* (Turnhout: Brepols, 1991).

52. Two opinions are germane here: Nicholas Watson's essay on censorship ("Censorship and Cultural Change in Late-Medieval England: Vernacular Theology, the Oxford Translation Debate, and Arundel's Constitutions of 1409," *Speculum* 70 [1995]: 822–64) shows that Archbishop Thomas Arundel sought to define the limits of orthodox theology at Oxford and settled the so-called "Oxford translation debate" concerning the problems of rendering the Vulgate into English, while Jeremy Catto's earlier contribution to the *History of Oxford University,* "Theology After Wycliffism," traces the rise of the supposed theological conservatism at Oxford from the 1430s, after the death of Arundel (J. I. Catto, and Ralph Evans, eds., *The History of the University of Oxford,* vol. 2 [Oxford: Clarendon Press, 1992], 263–80). Watson's corollary conclusion is that Arundel's efforts lead to a narrowing of "vernacular theology" in the fifteenth century—a view that has produced lively debate.

53. See *Epistolae,* 1.74–75; 83–89; also, 1.56–57; 57–58.

54. See ibid., 1.76–78.

55. See ibid., 1.9, 17–18, 39–40, 50–51, 91–92, 110–11; 111–12.

commendations followed by letters claiming that there are few students at the university, the streets are empty, and dereliction of infrastructure abounds.[56] All of these examples are rhetorically important and fundamentally petitionary; the logic that bad publicity is good publicity prevails. Cries about the terrible state of the university are prompts for patronage; laments about the lack of books are goads to get more. Even after the receipt of a large number of books, the discourse of impoverished learning continues to be in evidence and serves to show that what the university wants is what a given patron has, in abundance.[57]

Let's look at some examples more closely to examine how these petitions work. Few persons in fifteenth-century England received more petitions than Duke Humphrey of Gloucester—a not surprising claim given the duke's role in ensuring the growth of humanism at Oxford. Humphrey's hand in bringing Italian humanists to England has been well documented, and the correspondence between the duke and those figures, such as Pier Candido Decembrio and Pietro del Monte, is very well known. For their part, however, the writers in Registrum F partake of some of the more expected humanist laudations when speaking to Humphrey, heralding him as a military man of faith who loves learning and protects the university[58] and fashioning him as a classical and classically interested ruler—something of a Caesar[59] but also a Hector, Achilles, and Alexander.[60] This practice is consistent with those more celebrated letters of Pier and Pietro to Duke Humphrey, which associate classical learning with militarism[61]: as Humphrey replies to Decembrio using the royal "we," "whether we be at home or on a military campaign, never will these books leave our side."[62]

Indeed if the idea is to compare English with continental examples (always hastily assuming that the lines of influence proceed in one direction), then it is important to note that the Oxford letters are, stylistically, oranges to these oranges, offering easy matches to the more celebrated exchanges with the famed

---

56. See ibid., 1.186–87.
57. See ibid., 1.139 and 1.151; also 1.114–15 in light of 1.115–16.
58. See ibid., 1.61–62; 1.64–65.
59. See ibid., 1.178; 204; see also 1.53–54.
60. See ibid., 1.204. Comparing Humphrey to these persons, the letters thank him for introducing works by Cicero and Demosthenes, among others (1.241), to the university.
61. Such phrasing is characteristic in other humanist epistles. For comparison's sake: "quippe cum talis Cesar fuerit, talis Augustus, tales multi preclari viri quorum fama est immortalis [Of course such was Caesar at the time, such was Augustus, such were many excellent men whose fame is immortal]" (Alfonso Sammut, *Unfredo duca di Gloucester e gli umanisti italiani* [Padova: Antenore, 1980], 180). Saygin discusses a certain "Scipio/Caesar controversy between Poggio Bracciolini and Guarino da Verona" that Piero del Monte discussed and summarized in several texts addressed to Duke Humphrey; Caesar here is "portrayed . . . as an ambitious usurper" (*Humphrey, Duke of Gloucester*, 91). While Saygin does not assess the references to Caesar in Registrum F, I do not think that university officials would offer such an overt criticism of their patron.
62. Sammut, *Unfredo duca di Gloucester*, 187: "seu domi seu milite fuerimus eos nunquam a nostro latere discedere." All translations are mine; none exist for the items under investigation here.

Italians in their descriptions of the Duke. One letter from 1441 reads:

> This university of yours perhaps in the past stood out but in truth there was no learning. Without any growth, learning was unable to be sustained, books were lacking; of which now we have the most cherished in each treasury. And so if the Trojans through perpetual praises make known throughout the world their Hector, the Thessalians their Achilles, Macedonians their Alexander, and the Romans their Caesar, so too we Oxonians must make known our Humphrey through perpetual praises.[63]

It helps to know that the above remarks, and others like them,[64] are often grateful responses to the duke's generous donations of books to the university. Throughout their responses, the chancellors at Oxford offer highly formalized expressions that give meaning and focus to the duke's own humanistic interests. Not only do the letter writers make grandiose assertions about the duke in keeping with the humanist emphasis on individual fame[65]—"No one, however, among Christian princes is considered more celebrated by Greek and Italian authors, none more illustrious, none more renowned by the speech of many"[66]—but they also suggest that the activities that the duke himself supports at Oxford (namely, study) do the Italians themselves some good: "By means of the aforementioned study and vigilance, not only can others translate from Greek, but also by great contemplation your new works are forged in our language, not for us alone but even those most eloquent and learned men of Italy who toil!"[67]

Humanist assumptions—the very ones that would later altogether exclude England from some of the narratives of humanism on account of the kingdom's purported médiévalité—are fully evident in these Anglo-Latin letters. These are assumptions in evidence from Petrarch to Erasmus; the latter famously and nightmarishly finds himself in the world of Scotus before awakening from a dream to a dawning modernity.[68] Yet the *epistolae* offer more than just laments about a

---

63. *Epistolae*, 1.204: "Universitas istic antea fortasse exstitit, studium vero non. Sine quibus prefecto studium subsistere nequit, libri defuerunt; quos nunc omni thesauro preciosiores habemus. Si itaque Troyes suum Hectorem, Thessali Achillem, Macedones Alexandrum, Romani Cesarem in celum eternis laudibus efferant, nos Oxonienses nostrum Humfridum immortalibus laudibus efferre debemus."

64. See ibid., 1.107.

65. On humanism and fame, see Karl Enenkel, "In Search of Fame: Self-Representation in Neo-Latin Humanism," *Medieval and Renaissance Humanism*, 93–113.

66. *Epistolae*, 1.203: "Nullus enim inter princeps Christianos, apud Ytalos Grecosve scriptores celebrior, nullus clarior, nullus omnium ore personancior habetur."

67. Ibid.: "Quantis insuper lugubracionibus et vigiliis, non modo ut ceteri ex Grecis traducant, sed et contemplacioni magnitudinis vestra nova in nostrum linguam excudant opera, non nostrates solum sed ipsi etiam eloquentissimi et doctissimi de Italia viri insudaverunt!" Might this be a reference to the verse translation (by Thomas Norton?) of Palladius' *De agricultura?* On this text, see A. C. de la Mare, "Duke Humfrey's English Palladius (MS. Duke Humfrey d. 2)," *Bodleian Library Record* 12.1 (1985): 39–51.

68. See Bert Roest, "Rhetoric of Innovation and Recourse to Tradition in Humanist Pedagogical

previously darker, "medieval" age or a dreary indigent present; their use of classical references is not just window dressing. A letter from 1435 reads:

> Did not the once powerful Rome, while the study of sciences flourished in its senate, victoriously hold the entire globe, subjected to its imperium? Did not Greece, while within that country the study of the philosophers thrives, claim military honor and continuous triumph over their enemies, spreading their domain over the entire earth and every measure of the globe? Accordingly, with studies having been neglected, great decay of honor and glory is immediately known to have transpired here. Therefore on behalf of God the power of so great an invisible prince deigns to take action against new misfortunes of this kind, as that inimical infestation, the common people, is frightened by the power of the prince, just as the tracks of the lion frightens every single animal . . . ; so it is of your serenity, the university [lit., "female supplicant"], defended thus far by your most illustrious ancestor princes, under your protection nurtures in peace her sons in studies and virtues, for the church, the glory of the faith and kingdom, achievement and honor.[69]

What is of interest here is not simply the issuing of classical analogies in a letter to Humphrey—as if to suggest that the duke enjoys reading such references[70]—but also the fact that the university is almost indistinguishable from the classical empires the passage describes. Note not only the conflation of learning with empire—in what is a clear linking of the ideas of "studium" and "imperium," common in the motifs of *translatio studii et imperii*—but also the ease with which sentences about Rome and Greece are followed by those about Oxford. While thus addressing the topics involving the "translation of learning and rule," the letter itself persuasively enacts them by mapping the flow of cultural capital. After all, from the practical perspective, there is only one way for a duke or prince to live up to all this high talk of cultural *translatio*—namely, by donating or bequeathing books that fit rather exactly the description of "culture" crossing from one place to another, one language to another.

Discourse," *Medieval and Renaissance Humanism: Rhetoric, Representation and Reform*, ed. Stephen Gersh and Bert Roest (Leiden: Brill, 2003), 115–48, here, 122, 126–29.

69. *Epistolae*, 1.129: "Numquid Romana olim potestas, dum scienciarum studia in suo florebant senatu, totum orbem suo imperio victoriose tenebat subjectum? Numquid et illa Grecia, dum in ea philosophorum crevere studia, universe telluri omnique orbis climati spargendo sui cinguli [ms: singuli] militaris honorem, de suis hostibus continuum reportavit triumphum? In quibus, dissolutis studiis, non modicus marcor floridi honoris et victorie protenus esse legitur consecutus. . . . Igitur pro Deo exsurgere dignetur potencia tanti principis invincibilis, ad hujusmodi inauditorum malorum enervacionem, sic quod inimica infestacio plebeica paveat potenciam principis, sicut leonis vestigia pertimescunt animalia singula . . . ; ut vestre serenitatis oratrix sub proteccione vestra, sicut sub illustrissimorum principum vestrorum progenitorum hactenus communita, in pace lactet filios suos in scienciis et virtutibus, ad ecclesie, fidei et regni decorem, proficuum et honorem."

70. Indeed, he is not the only one to have read them. See *Epistolae*, 1.81 for similar expressions issued to the Duke of Bedford; and 1.122–23 to the Earl of Stafford.

No wonder, then, that countless letters describe the university as the ideal literate space to receive such cultural transmissions. It is called a "res publica"— a term Daniel Wakelin has discussed in relation to other texts, showing it to be a standard, even if quite polyvalent, humanist locution denoting the total public good or even the state (or realm).[71] Too numerous to count are the instances of this phrase in Registrum F, which describe, time and again, the university as a classically conceived "res publica" of book collecting and diligent scholarship.[72] So intense is this scholarship within the so-called "res publica" that it constitutes a local "renaissance" (or *renascencia*), thanks to Duke Humphrey, whose donations foster a "scienciarum renascencia florida [a burgeoning renewal of studies]," which "are reborn now among us by means of your pleasure in study especially, and which return to reason and illustriously revive the vineyard at our university to produce more than the accustomed abundant fruits."[73]

With all this talk of "res publica" and renaissance in early fifteenth-century (i.e., "medieval") Oxford, it should come as no surprise to learn that the *epistolae* often exhibit the characteristic forms of humanist periodization when they promote the interests of the university for the sake of the "now" and the future (*futuris temporibus*)—for the pursuit of donations and promises of more. One letter to Humphrey, dated 1439, reads:

> However at an earlier time and before your most gracious arrival, which without a shred of doubt proceeds from on high, our university was doubtless like a lifeless corpse, a lamp without light, a spring without water and a world without a sun; and now your most benign inspiration brought the body to life, a lamp with the most bright light, and that radiance at no time can be extinguished, a spring with living water surging toward minds to be consoled in study, and a world with the most splendid sun, which certainly not at any time would suffer an eclipse of studies, illuminating minds.[74]

---

71. See, for instance, *Epistolae*, 1.12, 149, 151, 247, 253, 263, 277, 288, 292, 296, 300, 324. On the significance of this term as it is used in other humanist works in England, see Wakelin, *Humanism, Reading, and English Literature*, 20–21 (for initial discussion), and many references thereafter, esp. 115–18, 122–23.

72. See *Epistolae*, 2.455, 476, 510, 532, 534, 535, 536, 539, 542, 543, 544, 546, 547, 548, 560, 562, 565, 566, 568, 570, 571, 573, 574, 575, 576, 578, 579, 580, 581 (by Chaundler), 582, 587, 588, 589, 592, 593, 598, 600, 607, 614, 615, 645, 656, 664, 665, 680, 681.

73. *Epistolae*, 1.152: "nunc apud nos vestri desiderii contemplacione precipue renascuntur, in mentes redeunt et in nostre Universitatis vinea clarissime reviviscunt, producture supra solitum germina fructuosa."

74. Ibid., 1.178: "Priori enim tempore et ante ipsam graciosissimam visitacionem vestram, quam haut dubium est ab alto processisse, Universitas nostra sine dubio fuerat velut corpus exanime, lucerna sine lumine, fons sine aqua et mundus sine sole; que jam benignissima inspiracione vestra corpus vitale effecta est, lucerna clarissimo lumine, et quod nunquam extinguetur irradians, fons aquis vivificis ad studencium animos consolandos exhuberans, et mundus splendidissimo sole, qui utique haud unquam patietur eclipsim studiorum, mentes illustrans." See also 1.309–10.

Here, again, is the material that truly makes Oxford seem stuck in its own "dark ages," as "lucerna sine lumine" before its own forthcoming enlightenment, "lucerna clarissimo lumine, et quod nunquam extinguetur irradians." It is a compelling image—the double figuration of the suffusion of light as the infusion of learning—and it reminds us that these medievalizing images are a kind of distinction making that serves the purposes of modernization, in the small "m" sense of the term: maintaining and acquiring resources as a way of preparing for the future of an institution, a future no farther away than tomorrow. The letter writers, then, periodize for the sake of a petition, and in some fundamental sense to petition is to periodize or, at the very least, to point to the passage of institutional time and to mark one's place in time. In this respect, and ironically perhaps, humanist ideas always contain their opposite—those elements, tendencies, ideas, and authorities that are thought to stand for the old, the archaic, the medieval, the past. It is often the case that in humanist language, the present is not sufficient and is in so many ways experienced as already the past. And from a practical perspective, why should it be otherwise?

Of course, gifts, in that classic formulation by Marcel Mauss, are not only about the recipient, the giver, or the so-called "thought that counts." Rather, it's about a relation that goes to the heart of another cliché—to boot, an inverted one: "what's yours is mine"[75]:

> And certainly so many monuments are abandoned, you supply, among us very excellent and expensive volumes destined for future times in perpetuity, and although the tongues of men falter, such monuments never conceal the fame of the glories of the prince. Also whence Julius Caesar, with the world having been conquered would have been seen to have conducted himself exceedingly insufficiently, lest he had a Roman library built; even if the fame of their name and power through the length of time should happen to fall from the minds of men, yet for themselves in books and parchment such fame should always freshly persist.[76]

Oxford, in other words, will make the duke famous by keeping and reading his books. It did. And the fame was certainly mutual.

Understanding these letters as exercises in rhetoric with the clear goal of

---

75. Marcel Mauss, *The Gift: The Form and Reason for Exchange in Archaic Societies,* trans. W. D. Halls, with a foreword by Mary Douglas (New York: W. W. Norton, 1990).

76. *Epistolae,* 1.178: "Que sane monumenta relicta sunt tot, supple, preclara ac preciosa volumina apud nos perpetuis futuris temporibus expectare debencia, que etsi lingue hominum defecerunt, tanti tamque gloriosi principis famam nunquam abscondent. Unde et Julius Cesar orbe subacto parum nimis sese egisse visus est, nisi et bibliothecam Rome construeret; ut si nominis viriumque suarum famam per temporis longitudinem ab hominum mentibus labi contingeret, ipsis tamen libris et membraneis recens semper perduret."

inspiring patronage prevents a fundamental error in the writing of history: believing that everything a medieval text "reports" is literally true or, even better, deciding in advance quite how it is true, what makes it a document or something else. Of course, this is not a new idea and is not meant to be (though there is still a lingering literalism in our field in the reading of chronicles). At any rate, assumptions about Oxford as decrepit and poverty-stricken must be bolstered by further evidence from account books or other financial records. The potentially more interesting historical point involves rhetoric and petition: officials conducted an aggressive campaign to acquire assistance and were not by any means the passive party in the exchanges with Humphrey, eager recipients of any and all attention.[77] Humphrey was a powerful patron, but he was not the only one by any means, and often some of the letters seem to perfect petitionary strategies by first trying them on one secular official before moving to the next. The writers had no qualms about repeating themselves and recycling expressions to stick with what works—a repetition that reveals a disciplined approach to the rhetoric of epistolography, handed down from one chancellor to another to such an extent that one detects what I am calling an "Oxford school" of letter writing—a protocol for communicating with outside authorities that saw little internal deviation and (just as importantly) no significant overlap with any other sorts of administrative letters outside of Oxford I have seen.

Who writes within this school? Who are Thomas Chase (1426), Gilbert Kymer (1431), Thomas Bouchier (1433), John Norton (1439), William Grey (1440), Richard Rodeham (1440), Henry Sever (1442), and Thomas Chaundler (1457, 1472)? They were the various chancellors of the university, but they were also humanists and can be dignified with the name, were we to accept a persuasive and well-known definition of humanism put forth by James Haskins: "Unlike modern political scientists or medieval scholastic philosophers, Renaissance humanists were not occupied with political theory as such. Professionally, humanists acted as teachers, diplomats, political propagandists, courtiers and bureaucrats."[78] Not all of these criteria apply to the chancellors of Oxford, certainly not the title of courtier—though, as I have discussed elsewhere, Chaundler exhibits a courtly sensibility in his other works[79]—but they are definitely "teachers" and "bureaucrats" and "rhetors" of sorts. The point to make here for what is literally a "working definition" of humanism is that these figures do not fit the usual mold whereby there is a distinction between, on the

---

77. Saygin, *Humphrey, Duke of Gloucester,* suggests that Humphrey needed Oxford in terms of bolstering his political authority.
78. James Haskins, "Humanism and the Origins of Modern Political Thought," *Cambridge Companion to Renaissance Humanism,* 118–41; here, 118.
79. Cole, "Staging Advice in New College MS 288," *After Arundel.*

one hand, "professional" activities as this or that bureaucrat and, on the other hand, humanist endeavors enjoyed away from the job when there's enough *otium* to look for books previously lost to time or write *belles lettres*—what Weiss has called "learned leisure."[80] For much of what I have discussed here is included in the very job description of chancellor.

LETTERS FROM THE FIFTEENTH CENTURY

I would like to make three points, in conclusion. First, any history of Anglo-Latin literature should be pushed much later into the fifteenth century and beyond the bracket of time considered in A. G. Rigg's indispensable study, *A History of Anglo-Latin Literature 1066–1422,* which stops right when humanism in England seems to be gaining momentum.[81] This essay is obviously not an attempt to offer such a thorough study as Rigg's, but it can be remarked that the supposed break between medieval and humanist Latin (or neo-Latin) that Rigg accepts in his history follows quite closely Weiss's assessments about fifteenth-century humanism. For instance, authors such as John Seward and Thomas Walsingham "start a trend towards classicism which remained unbroken until 'humanism' and 'Neo-Latin' came into its own. Latin was becoming an object of study rather than a casually used tool; this signals the beginning of its retreat into the schoolroom."[82] But it also signals, I suggest, the advance of Latin literature into classicizing forms of expression and instrumental applications unseen just a few decades before.

As for a kind of literary historical approach that is desirable, I suggest that these letters can be situated in the local history of humanist letter writing in England but not in a way that either fixates on one particular correspondence as the primary exhibit, such as that between Decembrio and Duke Humphrey, or assumes that the letters of any given visitor to England are the most influential, even if we know that (for instance) the letters of Poggio Bracciolini were collected in formularies, what is now London, British Library, Cotton Tiberius B.VI and Cambridge, Jesus College MS 63; similarly, it is often observed that letters

---

80. See *Humanism in England,* 33; see also 74.
81. A. G. Rigg, *A History of Anglo-Latin Literature, 1066–1422* (Cambridge: Cambridge University Press, 1992). David R. Carlson's *English Humanist Books: Writers and Patrons, Manuscript and Print, 1475–1525* (Toronto: University of Toronto Press, 1993), continues the investigations for the latter half of the fifteenth century.
82. Rigg, *A History of Anglo-Latin Literature,* 302. Rigg also rightly identifies epistolography, as well as prose in general, as an important site of investigation; see 310. On his reluctant exclusion of letters, see 7. Even though Rigg did not undertake to discuss humanist Anglo-Latin literature, one can find discussion of some important items in his fine book, such as Bishop Thomas Bekynton's anthology, Oxford, Bodleian Library, Additional A.44, which is chock full of the genres of Latin literature (see 152–53). For a necessary reappraisal of Walsingham, see James G. Clark, *A Monastic Renaissance at St. Albans: Thomas Walsingham and His Circle, c. 1350–1440* (Oxford: Clarendon Press, 2004).

by Decembrio were collected by Thomas Bekynton in his formulary *cum* diary, Oxford, Bodleian Library MS Ashmole 789. It is likely that these exchanges, viewed together with Registrum F, will tell us more about epistolography at Oxford and the emergence of new conventions than, arguably, looking at how certain rhetorical and epistolary texts new to England such as *De Inventione, Rhetorica ad Herennium,* or *De Oratore* influenced the Oxford style, as exhibited in the Register. We may well find, in other words, that such conventions emerge out of the practicalities of letter writing and communicating with other authors over an extended exchange, rather than from the prescriptive texts in the classical and medieval traditions (which assumes a unidirectional model of literary influence, from the Ciceronian greats to the medieval examples).

Second, an investigation of these letters has implications for our understanding of the relationship between vernacular and Latin literary practices. These letters assume postures of dullness to an extent greater than the fifteenth-century vernacular poets studied by David Lawton in his landmark essay on the period.[83] Lawton showed how English poets, using their own particular language of petition, called themselves dull, poor, and wretched, and critics from Ritson to Lewis took that language of dullness at face value and reiterated it as a value judgment about fifteenth-century poetry. The same, I would say, goes for these letters, and other kinds of humanist writing (largely in Latin): we would want, in other words, to hear the "one continuous wail" as it was meant to be heard—which sounds like an unfashionable claim but when dealing with rhetoric and certain kinds of formalized prose in petitionary circumstances, it may emerge as an acceptable position.

Third, and finally, there are questions about language and its institutional setting. These letters give us some insight into what is fully possible with petitionary rhetoric, enabling us to see that its expressions are not circumscribed only by parliamentary address or even by libels shaped by the legal apparatus.[84] The horizons of vernacular petitions themselves, what is sayable and not sayable in that language, and for what possible reasons, are indeed broad. But are the horizons of expectation for vernacular petitions limited by institutional settings in the same way Latin petitions usually are?[85] Is the voice of a vernacular petition

---

83. David Lawton, "Dullness and the Fifteenth Century," *English Literary History* 54 (1987): 761–99.

84. On petitions presented to parliament, see Gwilym Dodd, *Justice and Grace: Private Petitioning and the English Parliament in the Late Middle Ages* (Oxford: Oxford University Press, 2007). Petitions from universities are not covered here; the final chapter, "Writing and Presenting Private Petitions," 279–316 (esp. 297–303) should give literary critics a feel for the form. Matthew Giancarlo's *Parliament and Literature in Late Medieval England* (Cambridge: Cambridge University Press, 2007), links parliamentary and literary discourses; see chapter six especially, 209–54, and Wendy Scase's *Literature and Complaint in England, 1272–1553* (Oxford: Oxford University Press, 2007) traces the emergence of vernacular plaint in the light of judicial inventions beginning in the reign of Edward III especially.

85. It cannot be forgotten that there are vernacular letters in Registrum F addressed to various secular

that of an epistle, rather than a plea or complaint?[86] Are vernacular petitions a form of self-fashioning (of author and patron) or something else? Such questions can be posed knowing that, for the most part, the practice of petition is a Latin (and Anglo-French) phenomenon, and that the English versions we witness offer testimony to some form of institutionalization of vernacular verse, a sense of institutional place imagined within English poetry: in order to become a petitioner, one must first imagine oneself as part of an institution. In other words, even though petitioners construct themselves as humble outsiders, their petitions are grounded upon a presumption of institutional legitimacy and insider status. True outsiders cannot speak to power. Only those who can speak from positions of institutional legibility can address figures of authority and expect to achieve their goals. English petitions—and most English verse—depend upon forms of institutional authority in the fifteenth century, and it is the recognition of that dependence that will provide answers to many of our questions about humanism and the origins of certain English literary traditions. Such a recognition will also point the way forward to the sixteenth century and forge important links between medieval and Renaissance poetry, illuminating continuities where we would not think to find any.

---

persons (*Epistolae*, 1.259, 260–62, 319–20, 322, 323–24, 326–27, 336, 338) and even parliament (see ibid., 1.184, 293), and even one of the Latin letters, cited above, refers to vernacular literary production ("your new works are forged in our language").

86. My question here goes in the other direction from Scase's suggestion that petitionary complaint represents an *ars dictaminis* unto itself (see *Literature and Complaint*, 172), which seems true by Scase's persuasive account. I only mean to draw attention to the strong epistolary features of petitionary discourse and advance letters as a viable genre in which such discourse is expressed.

part 2

FORMS OF DEVOTION

3

Osbern Bokenham's "englische boke"

Re-forming Holy Women

KAREN A. WINSTEAD

The Austin friar Osbern Bokenham is well known to medievalists as the author of thirteen verse lives of female saints composed during the 1440s.[1] Bokenham's literary career apparently began in 1443, when his fellow friar Thomas Burgh talked him into writing an English life of St. Margaret. Other lives quickly followed, many likewise intended for his East Anglian friends and acquaintances—a "St. Anne" for the Denstons, a "St. Dorothy" for the Hunts, a "St. Katherine" for Katherines Howard and Denston, a "St. Agatha" for Agatha Flegge, a "St. Elizabeth" for Elizabeth Vere—and sundry others apparently meant for nobody in particular. By 1445 Bokenham had become something of a local celebrity. At a Twelfth Night party hosted by Isobel Bourchier, Countess of Eu, he boasted (by his own account) of the "dyuers legendys . . . of hooly wummen" that he had written to date: "as of" Saints Anne, Margaret, Dorothy, Faith, Christine, Agnes, and Ursula (5038–5044). The Countess forthwith requested a life of her own favorite saint, Mary Magdalene. In 1447, Burgh had thirteen of Bokenham's verse lives copied into a manuscript, which he intended to give to a local convent. Burgh's anthology survives (London, British Library, MS Arundel 327) and is known to modern readers by the title that the Early English Text Society gave its edition, *The Legends of Holy Women*.[2] Until recently, that anthology

---

1. *Bokenham's Legendys of Hooly Wummen*, ed. Mary S. Serjeantson, EETS.o.s. 206 (1938; reprint, New York: Kraus, 1971). Line references to this edition will be cited parenthetically.
2. For more on Arundel 327, see A. S. G. Edwards, "The Transmission and Audience of Osbern Bokenham's *Legendys of Hooly Wumen*," in *Late Medieval Religious Texts and Their Transmission*, ed. Alastair Minnis (Cambridge, UK: Brewer, 1994), 157–67. Sheila Delany discusses Bokenham's literary milieu in *Impolitic Bodies: Poetry, Saints, and Society in Fifteenth-Century England: The Work*

was all that we knew of Bokenham's hagiography—except that it wasn't, in fact, all of Bokenham's hagiography, for he alludes in his *Mappula Angliae,* a geographical treatise, to "the englische boke the whiche y haue compiled of legenda aurea and of oþer famous legendes at the instaunce of my specialle frendis."[3]

In 2005 that "englische boke," long presumed lost, turned up in Abbotsford, Scotland, amid the substantial personal library that Sir Walter Scott had bequeathed to his fellows of the Scottish bar, the Faculty of Advocates. Simon Horobin identified the manuscript as Bokenham's and as a translation, with added legends, of Jacobus de Voragine's influential thirteenth-century Latin legendary, the *Legenda aurea.*[4] Like the *Legenda aurea,* it consists of chapters on the saints and on major Church festivals, all arranged according to the liturgical calendar. Sadly, it is incomplete, missing a few pages from the beginning and a substantial number from the end, as well as some middle leaves. The losses at each end are especially regrettable because they have cost us whatever general prologue and epilogue Bokenham may have written. The manuscript breaks off towards the end of the Winifred legend, so lives of saints whose feast days fall after November 3 are missing.

Despite surface appearances, Bokenham's legendary is no straightforward translation of Jacobus. Most obviously, its mixture of prose and verse sets it apart from any other translation of the *Legenda aurea* I know of. Seventeen of the lives are in verse, including nine already known to us from Burgh's compilation: those of Agnes, Agatha, Dorothy, Margaret, Mary Magdalene, Christine, Faith, Lucy, and Ursula. (The remaining four lives in the Arundel manuscript are of saints—Anne, Katherine of Alexandria, Cecilia, and Elizabeth—whose feasts fall after November 3, and their legends, too, probably formed part of the intact Abbotsford legendary.) The "new" verse lives are of Barbara, Vincent, Apollonia, Mary of Egypt, Paul the Hermit, Ambrose, Audrey, and Winifred. It appears that, when Bokenham undertook his *Legenda aurea* translation project, probably sometime in the 1450s or early 1460s, he simply incorporated the verse lives that he had already written on his own initiative or at the request of patrons.

The discovery of the Abbotsford manuscript, Horobin writes, "transforms our understanding of Bokenham's life and work and compels a complete reassessment of his place in fifteenth-century literary history."[5] The Bokenham who

---

of Osbern Bokenham (Oxford: Oxford University Press, 1998), 3–28.

3. "Mappula Angliae, von Osbern Bokenham," ed. Carl Horstmann, *Englische Studien* 10 (1997): 1–34, at 6.

4. Simon Horobin, "The Angle of Oblivioun: A Lost Medieval Manuscript Discovered in Walter Scott's Collection," *Times Literary Supplement,* 11 November 2005, 12–13. For a more detailed discussion of the manuscript, see Horobin, "A Manuscript Found in Abbotsford House and the Lost Legendary of Osbern Bokenham," *English Manuscript Studies, 1100–1700* 14 (2007): 132–64.

5. "Politics, Patronage, and Piety in the Work of Osbern Bokenham," *Speculum* 82 (2007): 932–49, at 934.

emerges from the Abbotsford collection, he observes, is a cosmopolitan figure, with broad-ranging interests, whose hagiography appeals to the socially conservative values of a mixed audience of men and women, religious and lay.

While I generally agree with that assessment, I will argue here that the Abbotsford collection also reveals an intellectual liberalism that is not evident in the legends of the Arundel manuscript. In the Arundel lives, Bokenham shows little interest in Christian education or intellectual life; if anything, he evinces wariness about the effectiveness of teaching and preaching—especially when it is based on reasoned argumentation. That wariness, I will argue, is most evident in his lives of Katherine of Alexandria, renowned for her learning, and of Mary Magdalene, renowned for her preaching. It sets him apart from hagiographers of his day who were using saints' lives to champion education as the best way to combat heresy and to promote a staunch and vigorous orthodoxy. Those hagiographers included his fellow religious writers John Capgrave and John Lydgate, whose work he knew and professed to admire.[6] In fact, to judge from the lives comprising the Arundel manuscript, one might suspect Bokenham of being aligned with reactionaries within the Church, who discouraged theologizing in the vernacular and, in the wake of Archbishop Arundel's 1409 Constitutions, promoted what Rita Copeland has called "a systematized pedagogy of infantilization, an 'education' structured around conserving ignorance."[7]

By contrast, we find among the holy women in the Abbotsford collection female preachers, scholars, and readers of scripture. In his verse life of Apollonia, Bokenham goes out of his way to celebrate an eloquent *and effective* female preacher. While Bokenham is vague about exactly what lay men and women should be taught of their faith, he strongly favors preaching, and in several of his lives, most emphatically in his life of Barbara, he celebrates an intellectualized Christianity based on knowledge and reason. Read together, the Arundel and Abbotsford collections illuminate a conscientious, orthodox thinker grappling with complex issues pertaining to Christian education and reform that were much debated during the middle of the fifteenth century, notably in the writings of Reginald Pecock.

---

6. On the reformist impulses within fifteenth-century hagiography, see James Simpson, *Reform and Cultural Revolution, The Oxford English Literary History,* Vol. 2: 1350–1547 (Oxford: Oxford University Press, 2002), 383–457; and Karen A. Winstead, *John Capgrave's Fifteenth Century* (Philadelphia: University of Pennsylvania Press, 2007).

7. Rita Copeland, *Pedagogy, Intellectuals, and Dissent in the Later Middle Ages: Lollardy and Ideas of Learning* (Cambridge, UK: Cambridge University Press, 2001), 123. On the repercussions of the Constitutions on vernacular religious literature, see also Nicholas Watson's controversial and pathbreaking "Censorship and Cultural Change in Late-Medieval England: Vernacular Theology, the Oxford Translation Debate, and Arundel's Constitutions of 1409," *Speculum* 70 (1995): 822–64.

ARUNDEL 327: ARGUING IN VAIN

Sometime after Isobel Bourchier's Twelfth Night party, Bokenham turned his attention to the "Mary Magdalene" he had promised his hostess. Mary Magdalene enjoyed an enormous popularity in Bokenham's day and was widely revered as a penitent and contemplative beloved of Christ.[8] But the Countess of Eu expressed "synguler deuocyoun" for Mary in a more controversial role, namely, "of apostyls þe apostyllesse" (5066, 5068).

Mary had been known as *apostolorum apostola* since the twelfth century. The designation derived from the gospel account that she relayed Christ's Resurrection to the Twelve. Her designation as *apostola*, Katherine Jansen hypothesizes, was probably an offshoot of the eleventh-century *vita apostolica*, which represented her as a missionary to Gaul.[9] Mary's reputation as an apostle was widely spread in sermons, liturgy, and hagiography by clerics who had no interest in presenting her as a paragon for actual women. The proprietors of Mary's supposed relics at Vézelay, whence the *vita apostolica* issued, were eager to promote their sanctuary as a pilgrimage destination; the friars found Mary a useful "paradigm for fashioning mendicant identity."[10]

Yet the celebration of a preaching woman was bound to spark controversy. Jansen writes, "Just at the time that the image of the apostolic Magdalen became a commonplace in the preachers' homiletic vocabulary, a debate emerged—not coincidentally—that turned on the question of whether or not women were allowed to preach."[11] The answer was a resounding "no." Women lacked the training and education to preach; the necessary skills were beyond them; their beauty rather than their eloquence would captivate auditors and lead them into temptation. Preaching female saints, such as Mary Magdalene and Katherine of Alexandria, were special cases, extraordinary women who, authorized and guided by the Holy Spirit, preached, *ex necessitate*, during extraordinary times—if what they did could be called preaching at all. Indeed, many clergymen were uncomfortable with even female saints preaching. Vincent de Beauvais argued that Mary retired from preaching when she learned that St. Paul did not approve![12]

---

8. On Mary Magdalene's cult, see Katherine Ludwig Jansen, *The Making of the Magdalen: Preaching and Popular Devotion in the Later Middle Ages* (Princeton, NJ: Princeton University Press, 2000); and Theresa Coletti, *Mary Magdalene and the Drama of Saints: Theater, Gender, and Religion in Late Medieval England* (Philadelphia: University of Pennsylvania Press, 2004).

9. Jansen, *Making of the Magdalen*, 62.

10. Ibid., 50.

11. Ibid., 54. See also Alcuin Blamires, "Women and Preaching in Medieval Orthodoxy, Heresy, and Saints' Lives," *Viator* 26 (1995): 135–52; Alastair Minnis, *Fallible Authors: Chaucer's Pardoner and Wife of Bath* (Philadelphia: University of Pennsylvania Press, 2008); and Coletti, *Mary Magdalene and the Drama of Saints*, 127–50.

12. Jansen, *Making of the Magdalen*, 66.

It would hardly be surprising if Bokenham did not relish the prospect of celebrating a female apostle. His penchant was for re-creating traditional saints to emphasize attitudes and behaviors that would be appropriate for contemporary women.[13] His Anne is a "wyf ful couenable" (1636), his Elizabeth a "merour" for "alle wyuys" (5047).[14] Even his virgin martyrs display a gentility that sets them apart from the strident viragoes popularized by Jacobus de Voragine and so many of his English adapters.

At various points during his narrative, Bokenham hints at a certain discomfort with his assignment. In his "prolocutorye," he makes it clear that he undertook the life only at the countess's "myhty comaundement" (5084). His prologue praises Mary's "outward penaunce & inward contemplacyoun" (5281) but says nothing of her apostolic accomplishments. Bokenham omits Jacobus's explanation (attributed to no less an authority than the Church Father Ambrose) of how Mary came to be called *apostolorum apostola*.[15] In fact, he only refers to Mary as such *after* her death: Maximin devoutly buries the body of the "apostelesse" (6293); the body of "thys holy apostelesse" was later moved to a shrine in Burgundy (6301); Bokenham prays to the "gloryous apostolesse" (6305). The very structure of the life suggests uneasiness: Bokenham ostentatiously divides his narrative into two parts, concluding the story of Mary the penitent follower of Christ by saying that it is "aftyr þe gospel" and announcing the remainder of the narrative as "lych as Ianuence [Jacobus] yt doth dyscry" (5731, 5734). He thus reminds readers that the story about the preaching saint is *not* in the Gospel but that it is in no way his invention; he also obliquely invites readers to compare the authority of Gospel and "Ianuence." Before proceeding "ferþer in þis matere," he indicates that he is weary of his task but that, with God's grace and Mary's goodwill, he will push himself to do what "I haue promyssyd" (5738–39). He thus iterates that telling the story of a female preacher was not his idea. Of course, this disclaiming of responsibility may be nothing but a screen; however, as noted above, the other female saints in the Arundel manuscript are more "feminine," and Bokenham's apparent discomfort with the *apostolesse* may be genuine.

Mary Magdalene's apostolic career begins following Christ's death, when pagans set her and a few other Christians adrift in a rudderless boat, which washes ashore at Marseilles. Mary and her companions are part of the apostolic mis-

---

13. Karen A. Winstead, *Virgin Martyrs: Legends of Sainthood in Late Medieval England* (Ithaca, NY: Cornell University Press, 1997), 112–46. For another view of Bokenham's exemplarity, see Catherine Sanok, *Her Life Historical: Exemplarity and Female Saints' Lives in Late Medieval England* (Philadelphia: University of Pennsylvania Press, 2007), 50–82.

14. On Bokenham's "Anne," see Gail McMurray Gibson, "Saint Anne and the Religion of Childbed: Some East Anglian Texts and Talismans," in *Interpreting Cultural Symbols: Saint Anne in Late Medieval Society*, ed. Kathleen Ashley and Pamela Sheingorn (Athens: University of Georgia Press, 1990), 95–110.

15. Jacobus de Voragine, *The Golden Legend: Readings on the Saints*, 2 vols., trans. William Granger Ryan (Princeton, New Jersey: Princeton University Press, 1993), vol. 1: 376.

sion to "sowe & teche" "Goddys wurdys" everywhere (5751). Seeing the locals flock to a pagan temple, Mary "hem reuokyd from hyr ydolatrye, / And prechyd hem cryst most stedefastlye" (5785–86). Her audience is impressed: "Alle þat hir herdyn awundryd were" (5787). But Bokenham notes that her "beute" as much as "þe swetnesse . . . of hyr eloquency" gave people "uery delectacyoun / Stylle to stondyn & here hyr predycacyoun" (5788, 5790, 5792–93).

Does Mary actually convert anybody with her preaching? Bokenham doesn't exactly say. Instead, he tells at length the story of her encounter with two of the temple-goers that she has "reuokyd," the prince of Marseilles and his wife. Mary detains the couple, who are visiting the temple to pray for a child, with "a long sermoun" (5806) about Christ. She "counselyd hem to leue þere superstycyoun" (5807)—but to no avail:

> But at þat tyme, þe soth to seyn,
> Maryis wurdys auaylyd no thyng,
> For as þei cam þei hom ageyn
> Wentyn, obstynate in here errour stondyng. (5808–11)[16]

Mary follows up her sermon by appearing to the couple in a dream, urging them to help the needy Christians in their domain, but she ultimately moves them to do so only in a subsequent dream and through threats: "bettyr it is to obeye / Than to fallyn in-to þe indignacyoun / Of hyr god, & myscheuously deye" (5879–81), the wife decides. After hearing Mary preach on a later occasion, the still-skeptical prince asks, "Trowyst þat þou defende may / The feyth wych þou techyst so besyly?" (5887–88). Mary responds: "Ya, þat I may . . . / Be dayly myraclys & by wytnesse I-wys / Of oure maystyr Petyr, wych at Room is" (5889–91).

Miracles are what it takes to convert the prince and his wife. When Mary mentions "dayly myraclys," the couple is immediately ready to bargain:

> Lo, we be redy in al þinge to obeye
> What-euere þou comaunde us to do,
> Vp-on a condycyoun þat we þe seye.
> That is to seyn, yt þou wylt preye
> Thy god to us þat a chyld be bore
> To been oure eyr; we ask no more. (5893–98)

When his wife conceives a child, thanks allegedly to Mary's prayers, the prince is "dysposyd fully for to beleue"—so long as Peter can in fact "preue" "Maryis

---

16. This reference to Mary's failure is wholly Bokenham's. Jacobus writes: "Magdalene preached Christ to him [the prince] and dissuaded him from sacrificing" (*Golden Legend* 1: 377).

doctryne" (5907, 5909). The prince spends two years with Peter "in lernyng of þe feyth dylygently" (6040), but what convinces him to accept baptism is the resurrection of his wife, who had died in childbirth en route to Rome, and the preservation of their baby, who spent two years alone with his mother's corpse on a desert island. The happy beneficiary of three miracles, the prince admits that Mary has "shewyd" "weel" that "grace fer passyth naturys power" (6086–87). He and his wife are baptized, raze the pagan temples, build churches, and appoint Mary's brother, Lazarus, as bishop. Bokenham shows nobody being converted through preaching alone, but he leaves no doubt about the efficacy of miracles. When Mary Magdalene and her company leave Marseilles, they "come to a cyte clepyd Aguens, / Wych, with myraclys shewyde plenteuously, / To cryst was conuertyd ryht redyly" (6146–48). As we will also see him doing in his lives of Katherine and of Cecilia, Bokenham contrasts what works with what doesn't.

Shortly after he had completed the Countess of Eu's "Mary Magdalene," Bokenham set about writing a life of Katherine for the "consolacyoun" and "conforte" of two other friends among the Suffolk gentry, Katherines Denston and Howard (6365–66). Katherine of Alexandria's popularity matched, if not exceeded, Mary Magdalene's.[17] Superbly educated in the Seven Liberal Arts, the legendary virgin martyr was famous for out-arguing fifty pagan philosophers and converting them all to Christianity. Bokenham had been perusing a "newly compylyd" (6357) rendering of Katherine's life by John Capgrave, his Augustinian confrere from the priory of King's Lynn, Norfolk. In its eight thousand lines of verse, Capgrave's *Katherine* is a passionate celebration of learning, both secular and theological, which uses the saint's life both to educate readers and to impress upon them the importance of education.[18] Capgrave devotes almost two hundred lines to Katherine's training in the Seven Liberal Arts.[19] He later shows her academic training to be instrumental in vanquishing the fifty philosophers: she wields their own methods of academic disputation and marshals their own authorities against them. In recounting her conversion by the hermit Adrian, Capgrave relays Adrian's detailed answers to Katherine's tough questions on such topics as the Trinity and the Virgin Birth.[20] Clerics of his day who considered

---

17. See Katherine J. Lewis, *The Cult of St Katherine of Alexandria in Late Medieval England* (Woodbridge, Suffolk: Boydell Press, 2000).

18. On Capgrave's religious politics, see Sarah James, "'Doctryne and Studie': Female Learning and Religious Debate in Capgrave's *Life of St. Katharine*," *Leeds Studies in English* 36 (2005): 275–302; Simpson, *Reform and Cultural Revolution*, 406–29; Sarah Stanbury, "Knighton's Lollards, Capgrave's *Katherine*, and Walter Hilton's 'Merk Ymage,'" in her *The Visual Object of Desire in Late Medieval England* (Philadelphia: University of Pennsylvania Press, 2008), 33–75; and Winstead, *John Capgrave's Fifteenth Century*.

19. John Capgrave, *The Life of Saint Katherine*, ed. Karen A. Winstead (Kalamazoo, MI: Medieval Institute, 1999), Book 1, lines 246–434.

20. I discuss Capgrave's expositions on the Trinity at greater length in "Hagiography After Arundel: Expounding the Trinity," in *After Arundel: Religious Writing in Fifteenth-Century England*, ed. Kantik

Middle English an inappropriate medium for discussing abstruse doctrines would have been shocked. Indeed, Capgrave concedes, "It is ful hard swech thingis forto ryme, / To utter pleynly in langage of oure nacion, / Swech straunge doutes that long to the Incarnacion," but that does not prevent him from reporting, in unprecedented detail, the various arguments, on both sides, about the Incarnation and other matters.[21]

Bokenham warns his readers that his own version of Katherine's life will be nothing like Capgrave's. They should in "no wyse" expect

> That I shuld telle hou [Katherine] fyrst began
> To be crystyne, & howe oon clepyd Adryan
> Hyr conuertyd & crystnyd in hyr youthe,
> For þat mater to me is ful vnkouthe. (6349–53)

Anyone interested in "alle þat" should consult Capgrave's book, with its "balaadys rymyd ful craftyly" (6360, 6359); Bokenham will recount "oonly þe passyoun" (6364).

Bokenham not only creates a shorter and simpler version of Katherine's life than Capgrave's but deemphasizes learning and reasoning even in comparison to much shorter Katherine legends, such as that in Jacobus's *Legenda aurea*, Bokenham's chief source. As Paul Price has pointed out, in recounting Katherine's debate with the philosophers, Bokenham expunges all reference to academic disputation from Jacobus's account.[22] Where Jacobus's Katherine cites pagan authorities and refutes her opponents' arguments "with clear and cogent reasoning,"[23] Bokenham's Katherine convinces them with a simple declaration of faith, a paraphrase of the Nicene Creed. As Price puts it, "Bokenham's text pointedly celebrates intellectual modesty within a female martyr most renowned for her intellectual greatness. . . . Notions of intellectual value are dethroned and their place is occupied by simple, common piety."[24]

What Price does not point out is that Katherine's resort to "simple, common piety" represents a *change* in strategy on her part—Bokenham is showing his readers not only that faith prevails but also that reason fails. Katherine initially relies on her intellectual prowess, boasting to the emperor Maxentius that she was "instruct in þe lore / Of þe seuene scyencys clepyd liberal" (6592–93). Though she modestly adds, "Yet by my kunnyng ryht not at al / I set" (6594), she marshals the full force of that "kunnyng" against Maxentius. "In crafty wyse,"

Ghosh and Vincent Gillespie (Turnhout, Belgium: Brepols, 2011).
21. *Life of Saint Katherine*, Book 4, lines 2194–96, 1317–2340.
22. Paul Price, "Trumping Chaucer: Bokenham's *Katherine*," *Chaucer Review* 36 (2001): 158–83.
23. *Golden Legend*, 2: 336.
24. Price, "Trumping Chaucer," 160.

she attacks the pantheon "By dyuers conclusyons . . . / by many sylogysmys & by many an argument" (6490–92). She exhorts Maxentius to follow "þe weye of resoun" (6480) that will prove the existence of a single god. Even when she resolves to speak plainly ("return to comown speche" [6499]), she argues like a *magister:* she "dylatyd" about the Incarnation "by many a resoun," and she "dysputyd" "mych thyng . . . prudently" (6531–33).

Maxentius marvels at her "greth eloquence" and "prudence" (6559, 6560). He even acknowledges her persuasiveness:

She multyplyith many an argument,
And alle þat she seyth, by poysye,
By rethoryk or ellys by phylosophye
She confermyth ryht marualously. (6692–95)

Nevertheless, he is not in fact persuaded. Her "longe peroracyoun" (6558) merely confuses him: "We myht not wel takyn your entent, / Ner clerly vndyr-stond what ye ment" (6565–66). As he sees it, Katherine is trying to "snarlyn" him with "treccherous sotylte," using "exaunnplys of phylosophye / To bryngyn us all to . . . folye" (6657–60). Therefore, he calls in "maystrys of gramer / And of rethoryk" who will be able to converse with her on her own terms (6667–68).

Would Katherine have persuaded these experts with the dilatations and syllogisms she used against the emperor? We can't know, of course, because she doesn't try. But Bokenham injects a doubt that, to my knowledge, is unprecedented in Katherine legends. Instead of making the conventional claim that that the superbly educated Katherine surpassed all scholars, he more modestly avers that she could hold her own against anyone: "Was no clerk founde in þat cuntre / What-euere he were or of what degre, / But þat she wyth hym coude comune" (6395–97).[25] Readers might infer that Katherine changes tack because simply "communing" with these scholars won't suffice and perhaps because her failure with the emperor has undermined her confidence in academic disputation. When she promises the philosophers that she will speak "pleynly . . . / Wyth-owte rethoryk, in wurdys bare / Of argumentatyf dysceptacyoun" (6761–63), she actually does so—and triumphs. The philosophers are left "as stylle as newe-shorn shepe" (6799).

As Price points out, it is most implausible that Katherine should convert "the fifty most intelligent pagan men in the world through what, for them, is an utterly

---

25. Jacobus de Voragine simply writes that Katherine "was fully instructed in all the liberal studies" (*Golden Legend* 2: 334), but the widely circulated "Vulgate" version of Katherine's life says: "Et quamuis multi, experiendi studio litterati, obiectis eam questionibus attemptassent, stultos se et idiotas recognoscentes eam sane insuperabilem reliquerunt"; "Passio S. Katerine," in *Seinte Katerine,* ed. S. R. T. O. d'Ardenne and E. J. Dobson, EETS s.s. 7 (Oxford: Oxford University Press, 1981), 148.

unmodified, disorientating and unargued-for statement of her belief."[26] This very implausibility underscores Bokenham's point, namely, that the philosophers are not convinced by *what* Katherine says (the emperor, after all, is as unmoved by her creed as by her syllogisms); instead, as an angel assures Katherine on the eve of the "debate," they are "ful conuertyd thorgh a specyal grace" (6737). The philosophers "kunne ne moun hyr doctryn geyn-sey" because it is "fulfyllyd wyth þe influence / Of goddys spyryth" (6820, 6815–16). Not surprisingly, Bokenham omits the long tribute to the eloquence and effectiveness of Katherine's reasoned preaching that concludes Jacobus de Voragine's *vita*.[27] For Bokenham, affect triumphs over intellect; faith prevails where reason fails; and conversion is effected by God's grace, not by human eloquence or wisdom.

Bokenham's life of Saint Cecilia iterates this message. Cecilia was less controversial as a teacher than Mary Magdalene or Katherine of Alexandria, proselytizing only family members (i.e., her husband and her brother-in-law) in the privacy of her home until persecution pushes her into the public arena. Yet Bokenham subtly undermines the effectiveness even of this private teaching. When Tiburtius asks how his newly converted brother, Valerian, knows that the pagan gods are "uery deuelys" (7741), Valerian replies, "An aungel of god þus dede me teche," adding that Tiburtius will in "no wyse" be able to see the angel until he is "puryfyid . . . / From þe fylth of fals ydolatrye" (7745–47). In other words, Tiburtius cannot be taught without first committing to Christianity. In Jacobus de Voragine's account, by contrast, Cecilia "showed him [Tiburtius] plainly that all idols were without feeling or speech" and converts him through a lesson on Christian doctrine: Cecilia "began to instruct him about the coming of the Son of God and his passion, and to show the many ways in which his passion was fitting."[28]

Whereas Jacobus's Cecilia is confident and effective, Bokenham's heroine flounders as a teacher. She promises to explain why Tiburtius should not fear to become a Christian—"Tyburce, to me / Take heed a whyle, & I the ensence / Wyth goddys grace shal a bettyr sentence" (7786–88)—but her lecture on the joys of heaven, the Incarnation, and the Trinity merely confuses him: "þis manere talkyng / Ageyn al resoun me semyth to be; / For nowe o god þou puttyst, anoþir tyme thre; / To wych thyng my wyt can not inclyne" (7812–15). Cecilia tries to "preue" the Trinity "naturally": "Substancyally sum thyng but oon to be, / And yet by resoun yt ys dystynct in thre" (7822–24). She then abandons her

---

26. Price, "Trumping Chaucer," 163.
27. "Catherine's eloquence was admirable: it was abundant when she preached, as we have seen in her preaching, and extremely convincing in her reasoning. . . . Her speech had the power to attract the hearer, as is clear in the instances of Porphyrius and the queen, whom the sweetness of her eloquence drew to the faith. She was skillful in convincing, as we see in her winning over the orators," *Golden Legend* 2: 340.
28. Ibid., 320–21.

appeal to reason and admits, "resoun here faylyth, & oonly feyth / Preuaylyth" (7841–42), exhorting Tiburtius to "forsake euydence / And to doctryne of scryptur yiuyth credence" (7845–46). She concludes by reminding him that he will see angels if he is "clensyd & puryfyid" (7877–78). When she mentions angels, he immediately agrees to be baptized.

In Bokenham's other Arundel legends, too, we rarely find saints convincing unbelievers through teaching or preaching the fundamentals of the Christian faith. Miracles, though, induce conversion. Saints may rail and reason against idol worship, but razing temples through their prayers is what convinces people that their "wordis" are "both sage & wyhse" (2803). Dorothy's ability to procure a basket of roses and apples in February immediately transforms a sneering onlooker into a "greth credybyl wytnesse" whose "deuouth prechyng" (presumably about the miracle he has just witnessed) converts an entire city (4953–56).

As Cecilia found with Tiburtius, promises also persuade. Though he knows nothing about Christianity, Ursula's suitor is "anoon . . . crystnyd" (3220) as soon as he learns that she will marry him if he converts. Cecilia gains converts by appealing directly to their self-interest:

> But now of you I aske a questyoun:
> For ych peny [if] ye receyue shuld moun
> At a market or a feyr an hool shylyng,
> As many as þedyr ye dede bryng,
> Wolde ye not spedyn you þedyr hastly?
> I trowe ye wold! (8079–84)

After she explains that her God actually will trade them "an hundyrd for oon" (8091), they immediately cry out, "Cryst þi lord ys god oonly!" (8094). Katherine of Alexandria promises the emperor's wife a better husband and the emperor's right-hand man a better lord in a richer kingdom; no further instruction is necessary (6949–89, 7185–90).

The legends comprising Arundel 327 show little interest in pastoral endeavors, much less in Christian intellectual life, and little interest in how the saints themselves became Christians. One might attribute Bokenham's lack of attention to teaching and learning to the gender of his subjects, and perhaps to the gender of his patrons. Undermining the accomplishments of a female preacher or scholar, such as Mary Magdalene or Katherine of Alexandria, or of a preachy wife like Cecilia, certainly works to make those saints more exemplary by contemporary standards of femininity. Bokenham wrote in a milieu rich in female religious enthusiasts.[29] Though he was certainly eager to please his female friends, he may

---

29. See, for example, Roberta Gilchrist and Marilyn Oliva, *Religious Women in Medieval East Anglia: History and Archaeology, c. 1100–1540* (Norwich: Centre of East Anglian Studies, University

also have been wary of women like Margery Kempe—or perhaps even Isobel Bourchier, who apparently preferred the adventures of a *apostolesse* to the tears of a penitent.

Yet the Arundel legends are by no means only about gender. Taken together, they bespeak a pessimism about the capacity of ordinary people—men as well as women—to reason and to understand their faith. They portray a humanity that must be wooed to Christ by spectacles and promises, or ravished by the Holy Spirit.

ABBOTSFORD PREACHERS, SCHOLARS, AND EDUCATORS

There are clear continuities between the legends assembled in Arundel 327 and those of the Abbotsford collection. Most obviously, as I mentioned earlier, legends found in the Arundel manuscript also appear in the Abbotsford anthology, albeit without their original references to patrons and dedicatees. Bokenham also manifests his ongoing interest in female holiness. Five of the eight "new" verse lives found in the Abbotsford collection feature women. Among Bokenham's prose lives, Augustine's mother, Monica, whose life had previously been told only as part of her son's life, receives a life of her own. Bokenham also translated for the first time into Middle English the lives of the virgin martyrs Martina and Priscilla and of Claire of Assisi, which were not included in Jacobus's *Legenda aurea*. In writing about both male and female saints in the Abbotsford collection, Bokenham displays the same attention to exemplary conduct and human emotions that he had in the legends of Arundel 327.[30] Indeed, his penchant for psychological realism and exemplarity is both more pronounced and more deftly executed in many of his Abbotsford lives.

The most surprising feature of the Abbotsford collection is that we find among his holy women so many students, scholars, and teachers—even preachers. If Bokenham subtly undermined the effectiveness of Mary's preaching, he did nothing of the kind with her sister Martha—in fact, he did the opposite. Jacobus had written that Martha and her rather large party of Christian missionaries "converted the local populace to the faith" and says of Martha merely that she "spoke eloquently and was gracious to all."[31] Bokenham attributes the conver-

---

of East Anglia, 1993); Joel T. Rosenthal, "Local Girls Do It Better: Women and Religion in Late Medieval East Anglia," in *Traditions and Transformations in Late Medieval England*, ed. Douglas Biggs, Sharon D. Michalove, and A. Compton Reeves (Leiden: Brill, 2002), 1–20; as well as Coletti, Sanok, and Winstead (cited above).

30. Horobin discusses the exemplarity of Bokenham's Abbotsford saints in "Politics," 935–38.
31. *Golden Legend* 2: 23.

sions to Martha alone, and he specifically describes her as preaching: "[She] convertyd to the feyth myche peple by hyre doctrine and techynge, for she was ful facunde and ful eloquent in spekynge and prechynge" (146r). One of her miracles is to resurrect a man who had fallen into a river as he was straining to hear her preach on the other side. Upon her death, her servant Marcella wrote her biography and carried on her mission: "Marcella, Marthys handmayden (whiche seyde to oure lord as ys wrytyn in the gospel of Luc these wurdys, 'Blyssyd be the wumbe that bare the and the brestys eek whiche yove the souken') wroot the lyf of hyre maisteresse. The whiche Marcelle aftyr hyre maisteresse deth went in to a cuntre or a cyte clepyd Salauonia and prechyd there cristys gospell" (146v).[32] Bokenham's identification of Marcella as the woman referred to in Luke 11.27–28 (an identification not in Jacobus's account) is intriguing: when Margery Kempe was accused of preaching, she was quoting those very verses from Luke to argue "þat þe Gospel ȝeuyth me leue to spekyn of God."[33]

Bokenham's life of Martha might make socially conservative readers squirm, but his own contribution is mostly not to tamper with his source. Truly astonishing is his verse life of Apollonia, for there the hagiographer whose trademark was exemplarity goes out of his way to represent his heroine as a social radical—not only an effective preacher but a rebellious daughter. The best-known (and most authentic) version of Apollonia's story, derived from Eusebius's *Ecclesiastical History* and widely circulated in the *Legenda aurea* and elsewhere, represents her as an elderly woman whose teeth are knocked out by pagan thugs; when her tormentors threaten to burn her alive, she leaps onto the pyre they have prepared for her. There is no suggestion that she has ever preached; in Jacobus's account, she doesn't even speak.

Bokenham's Apollonia is a beautiful, outspoken princess whose father, the King of Alexandria, persecutes her because she will not desist from preaching. In portraying the saint as a young beauty rather than the "wonderful old woman" celebrated by Eusebius, Bokenham must have been drawing on a continental source.[34] During the fourteenth century, narratives and images representing Apollonia as a princess flourished, though I have not found a source that shares Bokenham's particular concern with preaching.[35]

---

32. Perhaps nervous about preaching women, the anonymous translator of the 1438 *Gilte Legende* transforms Marcella into Marcel: "Marcell wrote the lyff of his maistresse and after went into Esclauoyne and ther he preched the gospel of Ihesu Crist," *Gilte Legende*, 2 vols., ed. Richard Hamer and Vida Russell, EETS o.s. 327–28 (London: Oxford University Press, 2006–7), 2: 517.

33. *The Book of Margery Kempe*, ed. Emily Hope Allen and Sanford Brown Meech, EETS o.s 212 (Oxford: Oxford University Press, 1940), 126. I will have more to say about this incident from the *Book of Margery Kempe* below.

34. Eusebius, *History of the Church*, trans. G. A. Williamson (New York: Penguin, 1965), 276.

35. For a discussion and an example of this continental mode of representing Apollonia, see Maurice Coens, "Une 'passio S. Apolloniae' inédite suivie d'un miracle en Bourgogne," *Analecta Bollandiana*

Part 2, Chapter 3

Education transforms Apollonia and sparks a father-daughter conflict. Both her parents were "educat" in the "foule ordure" of "ydolatrie," and made it their "busy cure" that Apollonia "shuld doo the same"; however, thanks to "goddis mercy," she was "preserued and kept by a special grace" (fol. 64). A revelation sends her to a hermit living outside the city, by whom she is "plenerly instruct in cristen guyse" and baptized. Upon returning to Alexandria, she immediately "prechid" Christ to be the only God, "even openly and in wordis pleyn." Perhaps as a rejoinder to those who claimed that beautiful women could not be effective preachers, Bokenham makes it clear that her preaching was a success: "moche people with hir doctryne / from ydols worship she did inclyne."

Apollonia's passion revolves around her father's failed attempts to stop her from preaching. Angry that she "prechid criste openly," he exhorts her, "from such langage thi tunge restreyn" (fol. 64). When she refuses, he summons forty scholars to "to peruerte" her "with her resons"; she converts them all (fol. 64v). Upon hearing her "preisyn so eloquently / Of hir lorde Ihesu the grete godenesse," he orders her teeth yanked out, a torture designed "principally . . . for that entent" that she should not be "so eloquent" "in prechyng . . . as she was whan she first bigan." His efforts are in vain:

> Thurgh goddis grace more parfitely
> She spak than bifore and more eloquently.
> And anoon forthwith turnyng hir speche
> Unto the peple there stondyng aboute
> Cristis feith boldely she gan hem teche. (fol. 64v)

Other uses of force are equally futile. Set on a pyre, "with grete stedfastnesse / She prechid the peple the high vertu / The mercy the grace and the godenesse / Of hir soueryn lorde god criste Ihesu" (fol. 65). Cast from a tower, she picks herself up, and begins "ageyn to prechyn" (fol. 65v). Once again, Apollonia does not preach in vain: "Moche peple thurgh help of grace divyne / She conuertid there by hir doctryne."

Bokenham's Apollonia is a radical departure from the more conventionally feminine heroines of Arundel 327. Preaching women were commonly stereotyped as agents of misrule and likely purveyors of heresy.[36] A common accusation against the Lollards—however unfair—was that they encouraged women to preach, thus flouting propriety and the strictures of St. Paul.[37] Margery Kempe,

---

70 (1952): 138–59.

36. See, for example, the discussions by Minnis and Blamires (cited above). There was ambivalence even about preaching female saints, such as Mary Magdalene, because their examples could be used to justify more active pastoral roles for actual women. See Jansen, *The Making of the Magdalen*, 265–77.

37. See, for example, "The Trial of Walter Brut (1391)," *Woman Defamed and Women Defended,*

brought before the Archbishop of York by clerics who "wot . . . wel þat sche hath a deuyl wyth-inne hir, for sche spekyth of þe Gospel," hastens to rebut the charge that she has been preaching: "As-swyþe a gret clerke browt forth a boke & leyd Seynt Powyl for hys party a-geyns hir þat no woman xulde prechyn. Sche, answeryng þerto, seyd, 'I preche not, ser, I come in no pulpytt. I vse but comownycacyon & good wordys.'"[38] Bokenham, though, does not shrink from using "preach" to describe what his heroines are doing; he never replaces Jacobus's "preach" with some innocuous formulation like "comownycacyon & good wordys."

Preaching is only one of various ways in which holy women of the Abbotsford anthology participate fully and vigorously in Christian pastoral and/or intellectual endeavors. Martina, for example, is "instruct in cristis feith perfitely from hir youthe and in the misteries of holy scripture sufficiently enfourmed" (fol. 30). Paula is expert in Hebrew and has a deep and sophisticated understanding of Scripture:

> Hooly writte, which she redde, she kept passyngly wele in hir mynde, and though she loued wele the story aftir the lettir as the grounde and the fundament of truthe yit she folowed alwey more the gostely undirstondyng as for moste singuler edificacion of the soule. "The tunge of Hebreu the which I," quoth Jerome, "with grete labour and busynesse of youthe lernyd and haue yit grete difficulte to kepyn, she lernyd anoon and coude reden in Hebreu psalmes and expressen hem withoute ony propirte of Latyn tunge." (fol. 50v)

Her daughter is similarly skilled. Monica's "reson" and "witte" were "so grete and so excellent" that Augustine solicited her opinion on doctrinal points (fol. 102). Bokenham quotes the Church Father as saying, "I provided and ordeyned that whan leyser and oportunyte haboundid that ony thyng of divinite shuld be communed and disputid that she shuld nat ben absent so grete excellence of witte and reson I fonde in hir communyng."

Even as Bokenham attests to women's pastoral and scholarly pursuits, he humanizes them and endows them with features appropriate to lay women of his day. Paula was an "an example to al the matrones of the cité . . . in al hir porte and gouernaunce" (fol. 50); her imitable virtues—her fasting, modest dress, medita-

---

ed. Alcuin Blamires (Oxford: Oxford University Press, 1992), 250–55; and Margaret Aston, "Lollard Women Priests?" in her *Lollards and Literacy in Late Medieval Religion* (London: Hambledon Press, 1984), 49–70. For a study of women's actual participation in Lollard communities, which was far less colorful than contemporary stereotypes projected, see Shannon McSheffrey, *Gender and Heresy: Women and Men in Lollard Communities, 1420–1530* (Philadelphia: University of Pennsylvania Press, 1995).

38. *Book of Margery Kempe*, 126.

tions, and days given to charity and good works—are closely described. Monica is an exemplary wife, mother, and friend, whose piety is very much in the fifteenth-century style: devotion to the Eucharist, tears of compassion, joy in contemplation.

Bokenham's most complex and fully realized female saint is also his greatest intellectual: Saint Barbara. Though the life breaks off before the account of her passion is complete, even the truncated version, at over seventeen hundred lines, is one of the longest and most complex saint's lives in Middle English hagiography. Bokenham's source was a Latin life by the Flemish Augustinian Jean de Wackerzeele, which was also the source of a Middle English prose life found in two late-fifteenth-century manuscripts of the 1438 *Gilte Legende*.[39] Bokeham's life of Barbara is similar to Capgrave's *Katherine* in its detailed development of the virgin martyr's life *before* her passion, with particular attention to her conversion, and in its emphasis on her education and intelligence; in these respects, indeed, it is practically an antithesis to Bokenham's *own* life of Katherine.

Bokenham immediately signals the importance of Christian education as a theme in his "Barbara" by describing the activities of Christian missionaries—Pope Urban's in Rome and Origen's in Alexandria—before zeroing in on Barbara. The daughter of pagans, Barbara is dissatisfied with her native religion. Reason—*not* education or guidance from the Holy Spirit—convinces her that the pantheon is a fraud and that there must be only one true God.[40] Indeed, Bokenham devotes hundreds of lines to her "musings," "reasonings," and "syllogizings." Her father, like Katherine of Alexandria's, provides her with a first-rate education in the Liberal Arts, but that education does nothing to answer her questions about the one true God. Eager for knowledge, she turns to a Christian scholar, Origen, who is said to have "provid" the existence of only one God "by resons certeyn" (fol. 6).

Christianity, in Bokenham's "Barbara," is an open-minded faith that *encourages* intellectual curiosity and study, even among women. When he receives Barbara's letter, Origen is busy instructing the Empress and her household about "Cristis gospel" and the "principles of christen religion" (fol. 7). The Church Father is delighted that "withoute ony techyng" Barbara has "so busily . . . sought such meanys to knowe god by." To complete her education, he

---

39. See Baudouin de Gaiffier, "La légende Latine de Sainte Barbe par Jean de Wackerzeele," *Analecta Bollandiana* 77 (1959): 5–41. On the continental Barbara tradition that Bokenham is drawing upon, see Mathilde van Dijk, *Een rij van spiegels: De Heilige Barbara van Nicomedia als voorbeeld voor vrouwelijke religieuzen* (Hilversum: Hilversum Verloren, 2000) (for a summary of this study in English, see 236–47). An edition of the Middle English prose version can be found in *Supplementary Lives in Some Manuscripts of the Gilte Legende*, ed. Hamer and Russell, 381–470. For a discussion of that life, see Mathilde van Dijk, "Being Saint Barbara in England: Shifting Patterns of Holiness in the Later Middle Ages," in *Transforming Holiness: Representations of Holiness in English and American Literary Texts*, ed. Irene Visser and Helen Wilcox (Leuven: Peeters, 2006), 1–19.

40. Bokenham's emphasis on reason differentiates it from the Middle English prose life, which emphasizes the role played by God's grace in Barbara's conversion.

sends her books and a priest to instruct her in "gode livyng," "doctrine," and "lawe divine" (fol. 7v). His own cover letter includes a long and carefully reasoned discussion of the Trinity. After reading the letter, Barbara plies the priest with many questions about the Incarnation and other matters, "To which he made such declaracion / And in al thyngis hir aunswerid so reasonably" (fol. 8) that she is eager for Baptism. Bokenham sharply contrasts the responsiveness of Origen and his emissary with the rebuffs Barbara has received from the pagans she consulted earlier. With a dismissive condescension, they reproach the "studious ladie" for being "over busy and curious" (fol. 4v).

Barbara's knowledge of Christian doctrine and Scripture brings about and intensifies her persecution. Eager to share her new-found religious knowledge with her father, she launches into a long lecture on the Trinity, but while she "to dilaten was busy" (fol. 10), he swoons from anger and disbelief. When he comes to, he threatens her and sends her off to the prefect to be tried as a Christian. Barbara's ruminations on Scripture send the prefect into a frenzy: "Whan Marcian perceived thoccupacion / Of Barbara thus in ruminacion / Of hooly scripture he wex nere wode" (fol. 11v). Bokenham shows, however, that Barbara has the stamina to withstand the tortures he devises precisely because she "in holy scripture hir did exercyse."

Barbara is a woman with whom ordinary readers might readily identify, a self-styled "symple citezeyn" (fol. 6v). She is torn between her faith and her genuine love for her father. She's not too holy to experience doubt, perplexity, or even temptation.[41] Filial piety doesn't prevent her from fibbing to her father, scheming behind his back, and flat-out disobeying him. Though she's a great intellectual, Bokenham makes her dilations and syllogizings accessible to anybody. There could be no more eloquent argument for using one's native intelligence and common sense.

Bokenham is keenly aware of the destabilizing potential of education. Not only does it alienate Christian children from their pagan parents, as we see in the lives of Apollonia and Barbara, it also has the potential to stir up trouble even within Christian families. Bokenham makes that point clear in his verse life of Winifred. Eager that their daughter be "educat," Winifred's Christian parents encourage her to study with the monk Beuno:

> ... they dede here besynesse
> Whan Beunoon prechyd that she shuld be
> Present & syttyn euene undyr his kne
> Hyre chargyng ententysly for to lere
> What he seyde & yt awey to bere. (fol. 215)

---

41. Horobin notes Barbara's temptation in "Politics," 936–37.

Part 2, Chapter 3

In a move that, to my knowledge, has no precedent in any Latin or Middle English rendering of Winifred's legend, Bokenham contrasts what Winifred's parents expect her to learn from her religious instruction with what she actually learns. Her father counts on her, his only child, to ensure through her marriage "[t]he lyneal descens of hys kynrede" (fol. 214v). He and his spouse are confident that Beuno will teach her "wummanly honeste" and other virtues befitting a good Christian wife:

> That she shuld kun lyuyn verteuously
> Whan she to maryage aftyr were sent
> And aduouterye fleen & al leccherye
> As goddys lawe byddyth certeynly
> And in trewe weedlok hyre so to reule & gye
> That fruht in honeste she myht multyplye. (fol. 215)

But "contrarye to that hyre fadyr ment," she is "styryd by grace inward / And by blyssyd Beunons doctrine owtward" to desire a life of celibacy. The potential family conflict is never realized, of course; when Winifred is beheaded by a would-be rapist and restored to life through Beuno's prayers, it is obvious to everyone that she should dedicate herself to God by taking the veil. As a nun, being "excercysyd . . . in relygious lore" (fol. 218v) is a clear asset, for it makes Winifred ideally suited to be abbess.

REASSESSING BOKENHAM

The Abbotsford *Legenda aurea* reveals a bolder Bokenham, more creative in his selection and use of sources, more willing to portray his heroines in potentially controversial roles. Bokenham had always shown respect for women's abilities. There is no doubting Mary Magdalene's eloquence or Katherine's learning; Bokenham's doubts lie with the capacity of the *recipients* of his heroines' instruction to benefit therefrom—wouldn't they do better to stick to reciting the creed and proclaiming the power of God through miracles? Though miracles abound in the Abbotsford collection, they are no longer the principal means of effecting conversion. Bokenham seems more optimistic about the aptitude of ordinary people to listen and learn, and hence more optimistic about the efficacy of preaching and teaching. He seems more cognizant, also, of the spiritual rewards attending a more than basic understanding of one's faith.

Our ability to trace the evolution of Bokenham's thought is limited by our ignorance of exact dates for most of the lives comprising the Abbotsford collection. The collection was certainly compiled after 1449, because Bokenham revised a reference to Lydgate in his "Margaret" to mention Lydgate's death.[42] If, as seems probable, most or all of the prose lives were written specifically for the projected legendary, the 1450s seem a likely date for them. Most uncertain in date are the verse lives; as mentioned earlier, these appear to have originated as independent compositions. "Winifred" was written after 1448, because Bokenham mentions visiting the saint's shrine in that year, but about "Apollonia" and "Barbara" we have only the inference that they were written after 1445, drawn from Bokenham's not citing them, in his "Magdalene," among his "dyuers legendys." I strongly believe that they, like Winifred, are later compositions, because they are so much more complex than anything we find in Arundel 327. If so, the strain of intellectual liberalism I've identified in the Abbotsford *Legenda aurea* seems to represent a *change* in Bokenham's thinking—as opposed to Arundel 327 being Burgh's unrepresentative selection of the most conservative among available Bokenham compositions.

It would hardly be surprising if Bokenham were revisiting his views on Christian education during the 1450s. Christian education had become a hot topic, thanks in no small measure to the controversies swirling around Reginald Pecock. In 1447, Pecock, then bishop of St. Asaph, Wales, incensed pastorally oriented clergy with a sermon delivered at St. Paul's Cross defending bishops who did not preach and promoting writing as a more potent vehicle of Christian education.[43] Although he deprecated preaching, Pecock was a passionate advocate of lay religious instruction, opposing those who claimed that ordinary people were incapable of understanding matters like the Trinity.[44] In Middle English treatises written during the 1440s–50s and published during the 1450s, he championed a Christianity based both on natural reason and on the educated, clerically supervised reading of Scripture.[45] The allegation that Pecock valued reason over Scripture contributed to the condemnation of his writings as heretical. In 1457, Pecock returned to St. Paul's Cross to abjure his errors, confessing,

---

42. The reference originally read, "I dwellyd / neuere wyth the fresh rethoryens, / Gower, Chauncers, ner wyth lytgate, / Wych lyuyth yet, lest he deyed late" (*Legendys of Hooly Wummen*, 416–18). The emended lines read: "For I nevir duellid with the fressh reethorience / Gower, Chauncers ner with Lydgate / Which al be runnen to her fate" (fol. 130v).

43. For more on Pecock's writings and career, see, for example, R. M. Ball, "The opponents of Bishop Pecok." *The Journal of Ecclesiastical History* 48 (1997): 230–63; Roy Martin Haines, "Reginald Pecock: A Tolerant Man in an Age of Intolerance," *Studies in Church History* 21 (1984): 125–37; James H. Landman, "'The Doom of Resoun': Accommodating Lay Interpretation in Late Medieval England," in *Medieval Crime and Social Control*, ed. Barbara A. Hanawalt and David Wallace (Minneapolis: University of Minnesota Press, 1999), 90–123; and Wendy Scase, *Reginald Pecock* (Brookfield, VT: Ashgate, 1996).

44. See, for example, his discussion in *The Reule of Crysten Religioun*, ed. William Cabell Greet, EETS o.s. 171 (1927; reprint, Millwood, NY: Kraus, 1987), 85–99.

45. Ball writes, "Pecok published nothing until 1454," in "Opponents of Bishop Pecok," 230.

among other things, to "preferring the natural iugement of raison before th'Olde Testament and the Newe and th'auctorite and determinacion of oure modre Holy Chirche."[46] Pecock's books were banned and burned, and he was dispatched to Thorney Abbey, Cambridgeshire, where he lived confined to a single room, deprived of books and paper, until his death circa 1460.

Bokenham could not have been ignorant of Pecock's controversial ideas. In fact, he was rather close to the conflict: Archbishop Bourchier (Isobel's brother-in-law) launched the investigation into Pecock's alleged heresies in 1457, and in the same year Bokenham's Clare confrere John Bury wrote, at Archbishop Bourchier's request, a Latin treatise attacking the "nefandus" Pecock for privileging natural reason over Scripture.[47] Pecock's views were probably much discussed within Bokenham's circle of acquaintance, and it would be natural for those discussions to influence Bokenham's treatment of his materials, or indeed for Bokenham to use saints' lives, as Lydgate and Capgrave had, as a way of safely joining an incendiary debate. The numerous preaching bishops whose lives Bokenham tells—some for the first and only time—in the Abbotsford collection show preaching as an essential component of a bishop's duties. In fact, Bokenham's Saint John of Beverley resigns the bishopric of York when he can no longer preach: "whan he mygth no lenger labouren forto goon aboute and prechyn he by al the peplis assent committed his bisshopriche to his preste Wilfrid and went hym self to Bevyrlee" (fol. 102v).

But if Bokenham disagreed with Pecock on the importance of preaching, he was—or more probably *became*—more sympathetic to Pecock's views on lay education. His Barbara, as I noted earlier, was not propelled towards Christianity by any special grace but by musings that exemplify Pecock's natural reason—a faculty God gave *everyone* when he made mankind in his image.[48] Bokenham repeatedly refers to Barbara's "syllogizing," a mode of reasoning favored by Pecock.[49] In fact, one might read "Barbara" as a "test" of Pecock's ideas about lay religious instruction: How far *can* one rely on reason alone to reveal the truth about God? To what extent should lay Christians be trusted to study Scripture and/or theology on their own? How important is clerical guidance? With Barbara, Bokenham affirms the potency of reason but also insists that the reading of

---

46. Scase, *Reginald Pecock*, 59.

47. For extracts from Bury's "Gladius Salmonis," see Reginald Pecock, *The Repressor of Over Much Blaming of the Clergy*, ed. Churchill Babington (London: Longman, Green, Longman, and Roberts, 1860), 567–613, at 571. Bury was responding specifically to the *Repressor*.

48. In his *Repressor*, for example, which we know was available to Bury at Bokenham's Clare Priory, Pecock discusses at length the "doom of natural resoun, which is moral lawe of kinde and moral lawe of God, writun in the book of lawe of kinde in mennis soulis, prentid into the ymage of God" (18).

49. On the importance of syllogism in Pecock's thought, see James Simpson, "Reginald Pecock and John Fortescue," in *A Companion to Middle English Prose*, ed. A. S. G. Edwards (Cambridge, UK: D. S. Brewer, 2004), 271–87; especially 276–77.

Scripture and clerical instruction are essential to a true understanding of Christianity. Neither Pecock nor his enemies would have disagreed, but, at least by 1457 and most probably earlier, the public discourse had been reduced to caricatures, his pro-reason stance *versus* the Church's pro-Scripture stance.

Bokenham's work attests to the complexity of orthodoxy in mid-fifteenth-century England. If the specter of heresy provoked repression and censorship, especially during the early 1400s, it also provoked thoughtful clergy, such as Bokenham, to reflect upon the foundations of their faith and to think and rethink what it means to be an orthodox Christian. What better outlet for such reflections than imagining the lives and deaths of Christianity's earliest witnesses? Bokenham's female preachers and students of Scripture rebut the pernicious stereotype of the disorderly woman—inevitably a heretic—who quotes Scripture and prates about dogma, fancying herself a scholar. More broadly, they represent an intelligent laity, male and female, whose eagerness to learn can be harnessed for good—and a Church whose confidence in the truth makes it eager to teach and unafraid to confront error or dissent.

4

"Ete this book"

Literary Consumption and Poetic Invention in John Capgrave's *Life of St. Katherine*[1]

SHANNON GAYK

When we think of fifteenth-century considerations of poetic form, the Augustinian friar John Capgrave is likely not the first author to come to mind. Capgrave, after all, worked largely in a devotional context and his best-known writings are a series of hagiographical *vitae*. Instead, we may invoke the aureate rhetoric of John Lydgate or Stephen Hawes, the experimentation of John Skelton, or perhaps even the self-reflection of Thomas Hoccleve. The last decade has seen a renewed interest in the poetics and political posturing of fifteenth-century secular verse and an enthusiastic recuperation of such authors, many of whom, as Seth Lerer has demonstrated, sought in aureate diction "an idiom free from the possibility of temporal decay and patronly caprice."[2] One might argue that the "high style," embellished verse of aureation represents the governing literary aesthetic of the period. It is not, of course, restricted to secular poetry; much of the period's religious verse also employs aureate diction (as Meyer-Lee's contribution to this collection shows). Yet aureation represents only one mode by which fifteenth-century writers sought to elevate the status of English to make it an appropriate language for poetry. While aureation offers "an idiom

---

1. I am grateful for the helpful feedback that Paul Patterson, Elizabeth Schirmer, and Kathleen Tonry provided on earlier versions of this essay.
2. Seth Lerer, *Chaucer and His Readers: Imagining the Author in Late-Medieval England* (Princeton: Princeton University Press, 1993), 24. See also Robert J. Meyer-Lee, *Poets and Power from Chaucer to Wyatt* (Cambridge: Cambridge University Press, 2007), 15–27; and Lois Ebin, *Illuminator, Makar, Vates: Visions of Poetry in the Fifteenth Century* (Lincoln, NE: University of Nebraska Press, 1988).

free from the possibility of temporal decay," Capgrave locates in temporal decay the materials of vernacular invention. As this essay will argue, the prologues to his *Life of Saint Katherine* reveal Capgrave's commitment to a vernacular literary aesthetic that aims for "sweetness" rather than "gold," that prefers English vocabulary and forms over Latinate ones, that insists on both rhetorical play and formal plainness, and that meditates on the transformative powers of writing.

Although Capgrave's writing has been a relatively recent addition to the recuperation of fifteenth-century literature, he was one of the most prolific authors of his day; he composed dozens of Latin biblical commentaries, a number of vernacular saints' lives in both prose and verse, a pilgrim's guide to Rome, and a universal history.[3] Capgrave is now best known for his *Life of Saint Katherine*, a long vernacular version of the virgin martyr's *vita* and *passio* in five books, comprising over 8,000 lines and written around 1445. As Karen Winstead and others have recently shown, the *vita* explores contemporary questions and debates surrounding the role of lay learning, religious images, female piety, the nature of good governance, and orthodox reform.[4] For these reasons, Capgrave has played an increasingly important role in recent reassessments of the relationship between heresy and orthodoxy, and radicalism and reformism in fifteenth-century religious writing.

Despite the attention to Capgrave's reformism, there has been less interest in either the forms that his writing takes or his interest in form.[5] Admittedly, Capgrave has never been highly regarded for his poetic prowess (except perhaps by Osbern Bokenham, who noted admiringly that Capgrave composed Katherine's *vita* "in balaadys rymyd ful craftyly"[6]). Modern scholars have routinely contemned Capgrave's writing as formally uninteresting and generically inferior.

---

3. For a survey of Capgrave's life and writing, see M. C. Seymour, *John Capgrave*, Authors of the Middle Ages 11 (Aldershot: Variorum, 1996), 201–35.

4. See, for example: Karen Winstead, *Virgin Martyrs: Legends of Sainthood in Late Medieval England* (Ithaca: Cornell University Press, 1997) and *John Capgrave's Fifteenth Century* (Philadelphia: University of Pennsylvania Press, 2007); Sarah Stanbury, "The Vivacity of Images: St. Katherine, Knighton's Lollards, and the Breaking of Idols," in *Images, Idolatry, and Iconoclasm in Late Medieval England*, ed. Jeremy Dimmick, James Simpson, and Nicolette Zeeman (Oxford: Oxford University Press, 2002), 131–50; James Simpson, *Reform and Cultural Revolution*, Oxford English Literary History, ed. Jonathan Bate, vol. 2 (Oxford: Oxford University Press, 2002), 420–29; and Sarah James, "'Doctryne and studie': Female Learning and Religious Debate in Capgrave's *Life of Saint Katherine*," *Leeds Studies in English* n.s. 36 (2005): 275–302. See also my "John Capgrave's Material Memorials," in *Image, Text, and Religious Reform in Fifteenth-Century England* (Cambridge: Cambridge University Press, 2010).

5. The notable exception here is Jane Fredeman's helpful consideration of Capgrave's style in "Style and Characterization in John Capgrave's *Life of Saint Katherine*," *The Bulletin of the John Rylands University Library* 62 (1980): 347–87. But also see Derek Pearsall, "John Capgrave's *Life of St. Katharine* and Popular Romance Style," *Medievalia et humanistica* 6 (1975): 121–37; and Karen Winstead, "John Capgrave and the Chaucer Tradition," *The Chaucer Review* 30 (1996): 389–400.

6. Osbern Bokenham, *Legendys of Hooly Wummen*, ed. Mary S. Serjeantson, EETS o.s. 206 (London: Humphrey Milford, Oxford University Press, 1938; Kraus Reprint, 1988), 173, ln. 6359.

For instance, M. C. Seymour's biography of Capgrave emphasizes that his saints' lives neither have "anything to recommend [them] to another audience [nor rise] above the mediocrity of the genre."[7] Thomas Heffernan locates Capgrave as the last gasp of a dying tradition, suggesting that his works "have been somewhat eclipsed through comparison with the works of contemporaries who were more forward looking, more a product of their age, and who did not exhibit Capgrave's ready nostalgia for a past long gone."[8] And even though she has recently argued that Capgrave's works represent "a window into the mind of an innovative thinker," Winstead also comments that his style is "casual" and "makes no pretensions to high art."[9] This may be an accurate assessment, but as this essay will show, it is equally clear that Capgrave is a thoughtful rhetorical and poetic craftsman.

Capgrave takes up the relationship between rhetoric and reform in the prologues to the five books of his *Life of Saint Katherine*, which playfully appropriate a series of themes derived from *artes poetria* and *artes rhetorica* in order to reflect upon readerly reception, vernacular translation, and poetic invention.[10] In a number of these prologues, Capgrave uses images of textual consumption—both the literal and figural eating of books—to show how literary invention, form, and authority emerge from the processes of reflective reading. Whereas alimentary metaphors in fifteenth-century religious writing are sometimes associated with the orthodox infantilization of the laity (as in Nicholas Love's desire to restrict scriptural "mete" to the clergy), Capgrave uses images of eating texts and tasting their "sweetness" to model both meditative reading and vernacular composition.[11] Capgrave is, of course, writing nearly fifty years after Love and is better identified with the reformist vernacular theologies produced under Thomas Chichele's archbishopric. As Vincent Gillespie has recently argued, mid-fifteenth-century religious writers did not limit vernacular religious material to "milk," but rather "created for [vernacular theology] a whole new high-style register, seeking to reclaim the vernacular for orthodoxy and to make it fit for precise and nuanced thought."[12] In his *Life of Saint Katherine,* Capgrave contributes to the production of religious reform by reflecting on the type of poetic forms appropriate for

---

7. Seymour, *John Capgrave,* 218, 221.

8. Thomas J. Heffernan, *Sacred Biography: Saints and their Biographers in the Middle Ages* (Oxford: Oxford University Press, 1988), 171.

9. Winstead, *John Capgrave's Fifteenth Century,* ix; and Winstead, "Introduction," *Life of Saint Katherine,* 6.

10. On the articulation of Middle English literary theory in vernacular prologues, see Jocelyn Wogan-Browne, Nicholas Watson, Andrew Taylor, and Ruth Evans, eds., *The Idea of the Vernacular: An Anthology of Middle English Literary Theory, 1280-1520* (University Park, PA: The Pennsylvania State University Press, 1999), xv.

11. Michael Sargent, ed., *Mirror of the Blessed Life of Jesus Christ* (New York: Garland Press, 1992), 10. This distinction derives from Hebrews 5:12–14 and will be discussed further below.

12. Vincent Gillespie, "Vernacular Theology," in *Oxford Twenty-First Century Approaches to Literature: Middle English,* ed. Paul Strohm (Oxford: Oxford University Press, 2007), 417.

devotional topics, by supplying vernacular "meat" to the laity in theologically complex, vernacular writings, and by modeling for them how to read such writings.

Capgrave's prologues to *Life of Saint Katherine* thus render legible the relationship between literary form and reformist hermeneutics. As this essay will show, they do so by translating the alimentary metaphors common in rhetorical texts into a new setting—vernacular narrative poetry—and for a new audience—devout lay readers. This translation is not only linguistic and formal but also reformist insofar as it both enacts and represents the production and reception of vernacular religious writing. Capgrave's *Life of Saint Katherine* instructs its lay readers, in other words, in the rhetorical and hermeneutic methods of monks and scholars. My consideration of these issues begins with the literalized metaphor of textual consumption in the work's general prologue, which provides an authorizing narrative for Capgrave's translation and introduces the poem's recurring alimentary images. I next consider how textual incorporation generates vernacular invention. In the third section, I demonstrate how the metaphors for textual consumption, nourishment, and production in the prologue to the fourth book emphasize the aesthetic and spiritual product of consumption: sweetness. The essay concludes with a reflection on the place of Capgrave's aesthetic of sweetness in our literary histories of the fifteenth century. In sum, through his appropriation of rhetorical commonplaces in the prologues, Capgrave develops a critical vocabulary for describing both the nourishing power of religious writing and the ways such writing should be received. In so doing he models a fifteenth-century English poetics that is marked by rhetorical sophistication but not aureation, that is based on Latinate learning but rooted in English forms.

"THIS BOOK MUSTE THU ETE": TRANSLATION AND CONSUMPTION

As the work's lengthy opening prologue explains, Capgrave's versified English *Life* is the product of a series of linguistic, geographical, and material translations, but also translations of textual authorities and literary modes—both Latinate and vernacular.[13] In the poem's opening lines, Capgrave offers a rather convoluted chronology of this series of translations, but the essence of the story is as follows: Katherine's *vita* was originally written in Greek in the fourth century by an eyewitness, Athanasius, and translated into Latin in the fifth century

---

13. For a reading of the prologue that emphasizes its translations (and translation theory), see Nicholas Watson, "Theories of Translation," in *The Oxford History of Literary Translation in English*, ed. Roger Ellis (Oxford: Oxford University Press, 2006), 71–92.

by a priest named Arrek. This account was lost until an unnamed English priest traveled to Cyprus in the late fourteenth century in search of the *vita*, had a vision, and discovered it buried in a field. This priest, who died in Lynn but seems to have come from "the west cuntré . . . Be his maner spech and be his style" (Prologue 225–26), translated the Latin *vita* into a dialect of English that Capgrave suggests will be incomprehensible to his fifteenth-century readers: "whan it cam it was noght undyrstonde / Because, as I seyd, ryght for the derk langage" (Prologue 208–9).[14] It is for this reason, Capgrave explains, that he wishes "[t]o translate this story and set it more pleyne" (Prologue 232). He thus situates his poem as a translation, clarification, and modernization of this early English source.[15]

In insisting repeatedly that the text should be "open" and "plain," and modeling how the reader might open himself or herself to receiving the text, the prologue also offers a sustained meditation on receptivity more generally.[16] For instance, Capgrave tells the titular saint that he will "make thi lyffe, that more openly it schalle / Be know abowte of woman and of man" (Prologue 45–46). Several lines later he repeats this promise, noting that he is working from the earlier English source but pledges to "more openly make thi lyffe / Oute of his werk," with Katherine's help, so that "[i]t schall be know of man, mayde, and of wyffe" (Prologue 64–66).[17] In both cases, Capgrave links "openness" with readerly reception. He imagines a diverse audience for his book and seeks to render the story accessible to a full range of pious lay readers.

Central to opening the *vita* to a larger audience is finding an appropriate poetic register in the vernacular for his theological material, for as Capgrave notes later in the *Life,* "It is ful hard swech thingis forto ryme, / To uttir pleynly in langage of oure nacion" (IV. 2194–95). In the prologue to the third book, Capgrave similarly emphasizes his plain-style verse, "This have I pleynly now befor yow layde / In swech ryme as I coude best devyse" (III.12–13). Capgrave's emphasis on plainness throughout may derive from the Augustinian tradition of *sermo humilis*, in which the humility of the incarnation, the "lowliness of the sublime" finds its formal counterpart in the humble eloquence of the plain style.[18]

---

14. John Capgrave, *The Life of Saint Katherine,* ed. Karen Winstead (Kalamazoo, MI: Medieval Institute, 1999). Henceforth all citations will be to this edition and given parenthetically in the text.

15. Although some scholars have argued that this source text is an authorizing invention by Capgrave, his own highly alliterative style suggests an alliterative source. For this argument, see note 17 below.

16. Capgrave's emphasis on openness and plainness has some similarities with Lollard discourses. See Anne Hudson, "A Lollard Sect Vocabulary?" in *Lollards and Their Books* (London: Hambledon, 1985), 164–80.

17. This source has yet to be identified and may be a fiction. For a discussion of a close Latin parallel, see Auvo Kurvinen, "The Source of Capgrave's *Life of Saint Katherine of Alexandria,*" *Neuphilologische Mitteilungen* 61 (1960): 268–324.

18. On *sermo humilis,* see Erich Auerbach, "*Sermo Humilis,*" in *Literary Language and its Public in Late Latin Antiquity and in the Middle Ages,* trans. Ralph Manheim (Princeton: Princeton University Press, 1993), 27–66.

As Benvenuto da Imola notes in his fourteenth-century commentary on Dante's *Divine Comedy,* the "divine style is sweet and plain, not lofty and proud as that of Virgil and the poets."[19] For Capgrave, the linguistic humility of English need not be raised by mimicking Latinate forms or diction. Although he might find it a difficult medium for articulating theological material, he clearly views the vernacular as an entirely appropriate medium for communicating spiritual matters and producing sweetness. He chooses the native high-style, Chaucerian rhyme royal stanza to structure his verse.[20] Yet his lines also often retain the alliterative structures and syntactical doublings of English alliterative verse, such as in his explanation of the miraculous escape of the *vita* from heretics who "had brent the bokys, both the leffe and the brede" (Prologue 192).[21] Capgrave's use of high-style rhyme royal stanzas and alliterative structures is not at cross purposes with his articulated aim of plainness. Indeed, these formal choices emphasize the vernacular roots of his poem. Moreover, as Nicholas Watson has shown, while plainness often implies concision, in fifteenth-century literature it is also sometimes used as a mode of *amplificatio*: "under the influence of the French *plein,* the word takes on a second, quite different meaning, that of fullness or completeness."[22] In Capgrave's *Life,* plainness seems to imply verbal expansion, use of English forms, *and* rhetorical humility. In other words, for Capgrave, to insist on plainness is not necessarily to eschew rhetorical play.

While Capgrave expresses the value of openness and plainness throughout the *Life,* the opening prologue dramatizes how literary invention depends on embracing the value of plain, even unappealing, forms by narrating a humorous account of the earlier English translator's misreading of a rhetorical and hermeneutic commonplace: the command to eat a book. As Capgrave explains, after looking for the text of the *vita* for eighteen years, the priest has a vision in which he sees a richly dressed person, who commands him first to behold an old, rotten book and then to consume it:

For in his hand he held a boke ful elde,
With bredys rotyn, levys dusty and rent;
And evyr he cryed upon the preest, "Behelde!
Here is thi labour, here is all thin entente.

---

19. "sermo divines est sauvis et planus, non altus et superbus sicut sermo Virgilii et poetarum." Quoted in Auerbach, *"Sermo Humilis,"* 66.

20. Winstead has persuasively argued that Capgrave is likely following Lydgate's rhyme royal hagiographies rather than Chaucer's here. See *John Capgrave's Fifteenth Century,* 10–11 and "John Capgrave and the Chaucer Tradition," *The Chaucer Review* 30.4 (1996): 389–400.

21. For a discussion of these stylistic features with numerous examples, see Fredeman, "Style and Characterization," 349–57. Based on stylistic analysis, Fredeman has suggested that the lost source would have been alliterative prose, see 349–50.

22. Watson, "Theories of Translation," 85.

> I wote ful welle what thu hast sowte and ment;
> Ope thi mouth, this book muste thu ete;
> But if thu doo, thi wyll schall thu not gete." (Prologue 85–91)

Ostensibly, the priest now has in front of him that which he has most desired: the long-lost *vita* of Saint Katherine. But there is a catch: the priest will not find the text of the *vita*, the goal of both his labor and his desire, unless he physically consumes the book. The command to eat the book troubles the priest, who hesitates and protests because of the text's material form—its covers are rotten, pages dark, and it is far too large to fit comfortably inside a human mouth:

> Spare me now! Who schulde I this book ete?
> The roten bredys, these levys derk and dyme,
> I may in noo wyse into my mouth hem gete:
> My mouth is small and eke thei be so grete,
> Thei wyll brek my chaules and my throte—
> This mete to me is lykly to do noo note. (Prologue 93–98)

Here again, Capgrave emphasizes the material form of the codex as the reluctant priest juxtaposes the smallness of his mouth with the greatness of the book and insists that its ingestion would be both physically difficult and inconceivably painful. In short, the priest cannot see beyond the problematic physicality of the angel's command. Even as this passage gently pokes fun at the bewildered priest, it inaugurates some of the central themes of the poem: that external form may not accurately indicate internal value, and that forms have histories that must be understood to be read accurately.[23]

What is most significant about this encounter is what the priest fails to recognize: the scriptural precedents and figural resonances of the angel's command. Metaphors of taste, sweetness, and knowledge are everywhere in the Hebrew and Christian scriptures. The story of the fall equates eating with desire for knowledge (Genesis 3:6).[24] The psalmist frequently characterizes God as "sweet" and

---

23. I explore Capgrave's interest in historicizing form in greater detail in my chapter, "John Capgrave's Material Memorials," in *Image, Text, and Religious Reform*, 123–54.

24. On this point, see Nicolette Zeeman, *Piers Plowman and the Medieval Discourse of Desire* (Cambridge: Cambridge University Press, 2006), 2–6. In his commentary on this passage, Augustine associated eating from the Tree of Life (as opposed to the tree of knowledge) with spiritual, even sacramental knowledge. See Augustine, *The Literal Meaning of Genesis*, translated by John Hammond Taylor, Ancient Christian Writers 41–42 (New York: Newman, 1982), 8.4. Augustine, *De Genesi ad litteram, PL* 34, col. 375: "Nec sine mysteriis rerum spiritualium corporaliter praesentatis voluit hominem Deus in paradiso vivere. Erat ei ergo in lignis caeteris alimentum, in illo autem sacramentum." On this connection, see Ann Astell, *Eating Beauty: The Eucharist and the Spiritual Arts of the Middle Ages* (Ithaca: Cornell University Press, 2006), 32–35.

his words as sweeter "than honey" (Psalm 118:103).[25] The Christian scriptures similarly utilize alimentary metaphors to characterize spiritual knowledge, often drawing a distinction between the food/knowledge appropriate for the spiritually mature and immature.[26] The book of Hebrews, for instance, distinguishes between difficult theological matters and more elementary ones using the image of solid food and milk.[27]

These metaphorical representations of words as spiritual food are reinforced by several literal acts of consuming books in the scriptures, most notably those by the prophets Ezekiel and John. The prophet Jeremiah had exclaimed: "Thy words were found, and I did eat them, and thy word was to me a joy and gladness of my heart" (Jeremiah 15:16), but the metaphor is first radically literalized in the prophecy to Ezekiel.[28] In this passage an angel appears to Ezekiel bearing a scroll written on both sides with lamentations:

> And he said to me: "Son of man, eat all that thou shalt find: eat this book, and go speak to the children of Israel." And I opened my mouth, and he caused me to eat that book. And he said to me: "Son of man, thy belly shall eat, and thy bowels shall be filled with this book, which I give thee." And I did eat it: and it was sweet as honey in my mouth.[29]

After consuming the book, Ezekiel is called to take the words to the people of Israel, to translate the divine words into the native language of his own people. Here, eating comes before speaking; it is the prerequisite for prophecy. The Apocalypse appropriates this imagery with only subtle variations. In this account, an angel appears to John, the apostle: "And he said to me: Take the book, and

---

25. All English quotations from the Bible are taken from the Douay-Rheims version. Characterization of God as "sweet" in the Psalms alone is found in the following verses: 24:8; 33:9; 85:5, 99:5; 108:21; 134:3; 144:9.

26. The first epistle of Peter, for example, urges the letter's recipients: "As newborn babes, desire the rational milk without guile, that thereby you may grow unto salvation: If so be you have tasted that the Lord is sweet" (1 Peter 2:2-3). ["sicut modo geniti infantes rationale sine dolo lac concupiscite ut in eo crescatis in salutem si gustastis quoniam dulcis Dominus."] Also compare 1 Cor. 3:2.

27. Hebrews 5:12-14. In one of the most well-known lines from his prologue, Nicholas Love applies this passage to clerical and lay learning, explaining that the laity are like "symple creatures þe whiche as childryn hauen nede to be fedde with mylke of lyȝte doctryne & not with sadde mete of grete clargye & of hye contemplacion." Sargent, ed., *Mirror*, 10. On this infantilization in fifteenth-century religious writing, see Nicholas Watson, "Censorship and Cultural Change in Late-Medieval England: Vernacular Theology, the Oxford Translation Debate, and Arundel's Constitutions of 1409," *Speculum* 70 (1995): 822–64.

28. "inventi sunt sermones tui et comedi eos et factum est mihi verbum tuum in gaudium et in laetitiam cordis mei."

29. "et dixi ad me fili hominis quodcumque inveneris comede, comede volumen istud et vadens loquere ad filios Israhel. Et aperui os meum et cibavit me volumine illo. Et dixit ad me fili hominis venter tuus comedet et viscera tua conplebuntur volumine isto quod ego do tibi et comedi illud et factum est in ore meo sicut mel dulce." (Ezekiel 3:1–3).

eat it up: and it shall make thy belly bitter, but in thy mouth it shall be sweet as honey."[30] Here as before, the consumption of the word enables the prophetic voice. Neither Ezekiel nor John resist the divine commands and both find the text sweet (to the tongue if not to the stomach). Although the biblical act of textual consumption has been read as "an unusually vivid instance of the deconstruction of textuality," here it is ultimately generative: to eat the book is not to deconstruct it, but rather to incorporate and incarnate it.[31]

Eating words also becomes a commonplace for describing reflective reading in the Middle Ages. In his commentary on Ezekiel's consumption of the scroll, Jerome describes book-eating as "the starting point of reading," the beginning of memory, and the satiation of spiritual hunger.[32] By Capgrave's time, chewing (*ruminatio*) had long served as a metaphor for contemplative reading.[33] As Jean Leclerq and others since have noted, monastic *meditatio* and *ruminatio* were often represented as eating the word: tasting it, chewing it, savoring its sweetness.[34] Anselm, for instance, commands the careful reader: "chew the honeycomb of his words, suck their flavour which is sweeter than honey, swallow their wholesome sweetness. Chew by thinking, suck by understanding, swallow by loving and rejoicing."[35] While alimentary metaphors are quite common in Latin theological discourses, they also made their way into lay piety and vernacular religious writing, where eating and tasting are synonymous with experience, perception, and examination.[36] Caroline Walker Bynum has shown how continental mystics employ "images of food and eating to talk about the soul's desire for God."[37] Examples of spiritually hungry lay people are equally easy to

---

30. "et dicit mihi accipe et devora illum et faciet amaricare ventrem tuum sed in ore tuo erit dulce tamquam mel, et accepi librum de manu angeli et devoravi eum et erat in ore meo tamquam mel dulce et cum devorassem eum amaricatus est venter meus" (Apocalypse 10:9–10).

31. Jesse M. Gellrich, *The Idea of the Book in the Middle Ages* (Ithaca, NY: Cornell University Press, 1985), 21.

32. "Principia lectionis, et simplicis historiae, esus voluminis est. Quando vero assidue meditatione in memoriae thesauro librum Domini consideritus, impletur spiritualiter venter noster, et saturantur viscera." Jerome, *Commentarium in Ezekiel*, 3:5 (*PL* 25, 35D). Translated in Mary Carruthers, *Book of Memory: A Study of Memory in Medieval Culture* (Cambridge: Cambridge University Press, 1990), 45.

33. The source of this association is Leviticus 11:3: "omne quod habet divisam ungulam et ruminat in pecoribus comedetis." For a brief overview of the allegorization of this verse by early church fathers, see Philip J. West, "Rumination in Bede's Account of Caedmon," *Monastic Studies* 12 (1976): 217–26, at 218–19. This verse is sometimes associated with Song of Songs 7:9 and read figuratively. "Thy throat like the best wine, worthy for my beloved to drink, and for his lips and his teeth to ruminate" (Canticles 7:9). On rumination more generally, see Jean Leclerq, *The Love of Learning and the Desire for God: A Study of Monastic Culture*, trans. Catharine Misrahi (New York: Fordham University Press, 1961, rpt. 2007), 73.

34. Michael Camille, "Sounds of the Flesh—Images of the Word," *Public Access* iv.5 (1990): 161–69, at 165.

35. *Opera Omnia*, ed. F. S. Schmitt (1938–61), III. p. 84. Quoted and translated in Michael Clanchy, *From Memory to Written Record: England 1066–1307* (Oxford: Blackwell, 1993), 269.

36. MED, s.v. "tasten."

37. Bynum, *Holy Feast, Holy Fast: The Religious Significance of Food to Medieval Women*

find in late-medieval England.[38] Margery Kempe expresses her desire to hear the word preached in terms of appetite: "me thynkyth þat my sowle is euer a-lych hungry."[39] The prologue to the *Orchard of Syon* advises its reader to search the textual orchard, eschewing fruit that she finds "hard or bitter" and choosing the fruit she likes best, and instructs her to "chewe it wel and ete thereof for heelthe of youre soule."[40] Both Latin and Middle English devotional texts use alimentary metaphors to evoke the experiential acquisition of knowledge, memory, and literary production. In short, as Michael Clanchy emphasizes, medieval writers represent religious reading and writing as acts of "physical exertion."[41]

Remarkably, Capgrave's priest misses all of these associations; he is unable to see beyond the unappealing form (its "roten bredys") to its meaning. Seeing that the priest is reading the material form literally, the angel humors him, reassures him, and reminds him of the biblical precedents:

"Yys," seyd he, "thu mote nede ete this book—
Thu schalt ellys repente. Ope thi mowth wyde,
Receyve it boldly—it hath no clospe ne hook.
Let it goo down and in thi wombe it hyde;
It schal not greve thee neyther in bak ne syde;
In thi mowth bytter, in thi wombe it wyll be swete,
So was it sumetyme to Ezechyell the prophete." (Prologue 99–105)

Although Capgrave substitutes a medieval codex for the scroll, the situation closely parallels that of Ezekiel and John. Notably, the angel does not interpret the scene for the priest but only implies that the priest should imitate his prophetic forbearer, who received the book willingly. The angel also issues a series of commands—"Ope," "Receyve," "Let," and "hyde"—which redefine the priest as physical receptacle of the word. Indeed, the passage renders the priest as the sum of his bodily parts: "mowth," "wombe," "bak," and "syde." This emphasis on the priest's body is matched by the angel's emphasis on the physicality of the manuscript and reassurance that it will not hurt that much as it lacks a clasp and hook. Thus the literalization of the metaphor introduces the poem's interests in

---

(Berkeley: University of California Press, 1987), 150. For alimentary metaphors more generally, see E. R. Curtius, *European Literature and the Latin Middle Ages*, trans. Willard R. Trask (London, 1953; Princeton: Princeton University Press, rpt. 1991), 134–36.

38. Perhaps most famous is the dreamer's feasting on books with Clergy and Study in *Piers Plowman* B.13. See, for example, Jill Mann's article, "Eating and Drinking in *Piers Plowman*," *Essays and Studies* 32 (1979): 26–42. Also see, Britton Harwood, "Dame Study and the Place of Orality in *Piers Plowman*," *ELH* 57 (1990): 1-17, esp. 10–12.

39. Margery Kempe, *The Book of Margery Kempe*, ed. Stanford Brown Meech and Emily Hope Allen, EETS o.s. 212 (London: Oxford University Press, 1940), I. 58.

40. Excerpt from *The Orchard of Syon* in *The Idea of the Vernacular*, 236.

41. Clanchy, *From Memory to Written Record*, 269.

reading practices, in both the means and ends of reading well.

Yet alimentary images are not limited to the hermeneutic interests of the poem; they also indicate Capgrave's interest in the difference between form and substance and concern with distinguishing between the *sensus literalis* and *spiritualis* (what can be known by the senses and what must be discovered spiritually). These images resurface later in the poem when Katherine draws on Augustinian sign theory to reprimand Maxentius (the occupying ruler) for not reading material signs spiritually:

> Ye take the barke, whech is open to the yye,
> Then ye fede you ryght in youre dotage.
> The swete frute whech withinne doth lye,
> Ye desyre it nought. (IV. 687–90)

This is, to be sure, a hermeneutic commonplace. Like the priest of the prologue, Maxentius is a superficial reader; he overvalues external form, mistaking form for substance when he desires the bark and neglects the fruit. At this later moment, however, the semiotic lesson of the image is articulated more explicitly. Katherine first describes the image and then interprets it for the pagan ruler:

> The rotyn barke of thingis visible here,
> Whech ye se outwarde, this byte ye and knawe;
> The swete frute, the solace eke so dere,
> Whech schuld be the parfytnes of youre lawe,
> Fro that swetnes ye yourselve withdrawe. (IV. 708–12)

Echoing the description of the codex in the poem's prologue, this passage draws out the tension between "rotyn barke" and the "swetnes" within, between external form and internal meaning. But Katherine intensifies the image, representing Maxentius as gnawing on the rind. Maxentius, Katherine argues, is prone to worship created forms (a point Katherine makes in her larger argument against idolatry), but such a superficial reading prevents him from experiencing the sweetness of the fruit within.

Although the prologue's priest, who should know better, is also unable to see past the physical form of the rotten codex, when he finally eats the book, "[i]t semed swete, ryth as it hony were" (Prologue 107). Immediately after consuming the book, "New joye, new thowte, had he than there. / He awoke and was ful glad and blythe" (Prologue 110–11). The consumption of this book in the dream is generative insofar as it leads to the discovery of the physical book, which is full of sweetness and "solace." Capgrave thus seems to be suggesting in the opening prologue, as in Katherine's later debate with Maxentius, that sweetness often requires first overcoming formal prejudices, learning to see past formal plainness, or even "rotyn barke," to the nourishing fruit within, and second a special sort of hermeneutic diligence and labor. Capgrave thus encourages his readers to embrace rather than eschew difficult religious "food," emphasizing that although accessing the sweetness does not come easily to the priest, once digested, it is not only pleasant but also transformative.

"AMONG OLD TRESOURE": INVENTION

While in the biblical accounts the consumption of the book enables the prophetic voice, in Capgrave's poem the incorporation of the word enables literary discovery (*inventio*), bringing about the unearthing of the source text upon which, Capgrave claims, his poem is based. Upon tasting the sweetness of the book, skepticism and doubt become faith, and the priest's vision gives way to the discovery of the book itself: "Aftyr this not long, depe in a felde, / I-clad wyth flowres and herbys grete and smale / He dalf and fond this boke" (Prologue 113–15). "Finding" one's material is, of course, the first step of the *artes poetica* and *rhetorica,* but it is also the product of reading.[42] As Rita Copeland notes, in Augustinian hermeneutics "rhetorical invention is constituted through the *modus interpretandi.*"[43] Capgrave's general prologue makes this point by literalizing these rhetorical metaphors: the priest's consumption of the *vita* in his dream vision comes before and brings about its discovery in the flower-filled field. Rhetorically speaking, *lectio* brings about *inventio* and ultimately leads to *translatio*. However, this process is not simply linear. As later prologues make clear, the literary product of this compositional process (here Capgrave's English *vita*) is to be read reflectively and have the same generative effect on its readers. Reading and writing are reciprocal processes for Capgrave. By layering these tropes, he implies that although literary consumption leads to invention, invention and discovery always point back to the need for meditative reading.

Further, Capgrave explores the associations between hiddenness, discovery, and translation throughout the poem. When Capgrave's priest digs in a flower-filled field after his alimentary vision, he finds the *vita* "among old tresoure" (Prologue 120). The image of the treasure hidden in the field has biblical sources but here suggests another rhetorical trope: the wisdom stored in the well-trained

---

42. On rhetorical invention and its relationship to medieval exegesis, see Rita Copeland, *Rhetoric, Hermeneutics, and Translation in the Middle Ages* (Cambridge: Cambridge University Press, 1991), 158–59.

43. Capgrave would have been well aware of this tradition. See Copeland, *Rhetoric, Hermeneutics, and Translation,* 166. On Capgrave as an Augustinian thinker, see Winstead, *John Capgrave's Fifteenth Century,* 18-50.

memory.[44] One early rhetorical text, for instance, describes memory as "the treasurehouse of found-things."[45] Capgrave represents the long-lost book as both the treasure and the container of treasure insofar as it holds the memory of Katherine's life, which has, as he notes throughout his poem, been "kept all in cage" (Prologue 210).[46] The hiddenness and linguistic obscurity of the *vita* demand its translation into a more accessible form. In a later prologue, Capgrave notes that "[m]ech thing eke hyd in many dyverse lande. / Evene so was this lyffe, as I seyd in the prologe before, / Kept all in cage aboute, it was not bore" (III. 26–28). But where the *vita* was "hyd" by its earlier form, by Capgrave's pen, "[n]ow schall it walk wydere than evyr it dede" (III. 26, 29). The *vita*'s obscurity thus serves as the occasion for a new translation characterized by plainness. Yet Capgrave's emphasis on the hiddenness of the *vita* also serves as an authorizing move, enabling the poet to situate his poem as part of a recovery of a hagiographic tradition that was buried and forgotten by history and to locate himself in a genealogy of clerical poets that have sought to preserve the *vita*.[47] Capgrave's intent is to remember it, to resurrect memory of Katherine's *vita* through translation and make it more palatable to fifteenth-century literary tastes.[48]

The opening prologue thus draws out the complex relations among literary authority, hermeneutics, and form. The bookish meal in the opening prologue inaugurates a series of translations: the book is translated from the dream vision to the field of flowers; once found it is translated from Latin to English; and the reader is encountering a translation from one English dialect and form to another. Capgrave represents his translation as a new incarnation of the work, which is here embodied by his alliterative, rhyme royal verse, and which is plain but aims to produce sweetness in its readers—or at least in those readers that can see through the plainness of its form to the sweet fruit within.[49] Indeed, as we will see in the next section, discovering sweetness in a flower-filled field is not only the work of clerical translators, it is also the labor of the *Life*'s reader.

---

44. See, for example, Matthew 13:44. See also Romans 2:5 and Matthew 6:19–20.
45. Carruthers, *Book of Memory*, 34.
46. Capgrave's use of "cage" here and throughout has clear affiliations with mnemonic theory. See MED, s.v. "cage."
47. Given the popularity of the legend of Saint Katherine in Capgrave's time, one can only assume that he understands this recovery as a recuperation of her *vita*, which was far less common than her *passio*. For discussion of the book and saint as objects of recuperation via translation, see Watson, "Theories of Translation," 76–78.
48. In this association, as Watson has pointed out, Capgrave seeks to "make Capgrave's text as close a substitute for Katharine herself as possible" (Watson, "Theories of Translation," 77).
49. This sort of move suggests what Nicholas Watson has characterized as the connection between "the politics of vernacularization and the doctrine of the incarnation." See his "Conceptions of the Word: The Mother Tongue and the Incarnation of God," *New Medieval Literatures* 1 (1997): 85–124, at 91.

"LERNE AND TECHE, BOTH SOKE AND DRAWE": COLLECTION AND COMPOSITION

While Capgrave initially appropriates rhetorical tropes, including the images of textual consumption and buried treasure, to reflect upon the forms of reading and the reading of form in the opening prologue, he further develops these images later in the poem to suggest the ways in which literary consumption leads to composition. The prologue of the fourth book provides an imitative model for meditative reading and rhetorical invention: the flower-filled field gleaned by bees. This image recalls the opening prologue, rendering the field in more explicitly metaphorical terms and transforming its principal explorers into bees: "Thus semeth it to me that Holy Scripture is / In manere of a felde with flowres fayre arayde, / And Holy Kyrk is benethe iwys" (IV. 29–31). Although the opening books of the poem establish Katherine as a voracious reader who has mastered the Seven Liberal Arts and successfully defended her ability to remain unmarried and rule her country, it is only after her conversion that Capgrave characterizes her reading in terms of oral consumption.[50] After her mystical marriage to Christ in the third book, Katherine repudiates her pre-Christian learning, is catechized by the hermit Adrian, and is tutored in a sort of reading, Capgrave implies, that feeds the soul as well as the mind.

Capgrave takes up the exemplary function of Katherine's holy appetite in the fourth prologue by combining the Virgilian metaphor of society as a beehive with Christian images of scripture as a field:

> These erdely dwellers whech lyve now here
> Are lykened to bees whech dwell in hyve,
> Or ellys to dranes, if that ye lyst to lere.
> It faryth with men ryght thus in her lyve:
> Summe wyll labour and summe wyll nevyr thryve.
> Dyverse conceytes there be, and diverse eke degrees.
> The goode laboureres are likened to the bees. (IV. 1–7)

If Capgrave's appropriation of rhetorical models was subtle in earlier prologues, here he explains the analogies more directly. Like the other tropes appropriated by Capgrave, this one has academic roots but is also well attested in vernacular literature, where the honey-gathering of bees serves as an allegory for human labor, social order, and good governance.[51] For instance, *Mum and Sothsegger*

---

50. On Katherine's reading, see Karen Winstead, *Virgin Martyrs: Legends of Sainthood in Late Medieval England* (Ithaca: Cornell University Press, 1997), 167–80.

51. Karen Winstead glosses this passage by emphasizing that the Virgilian metaphor was a political one. Winstead, ed. *Life of Saint Katherine*, 304.

explores the ways in which "The bee of alle bestz beste is y-gouuerned / Yn lowlynes and labour and in lawe eek."[52] Other contemporary texts use the image to critique the laziness of the friars.[53] While Capgrave was certainly interested in social issues and would have known these associations (and indeed gestures toward them in the prologue's opening lines), he uses the metaphor to a different end: to explore again the relationship between reading and composition.

In addition to representing labor and social order, the gleaning and gathering of bees is a rhetorical commonplace for study, "books, book-collecting, memory, and scholarship."[54] The trope comes to the medieval tradition through Seneca, who writes: "We ought to imitate bees, as they say, which fly about and gather [from] flowers suitable for making honey, and then arrange and sort into their cells whatever nectars they have collected."[55] The image also is sometimes generalized to include other animals, as in Peter of Celle's description of reading as "a rich pasture where animals large and small . . . by interior rumination on the flowers of the Divine Word retain nothing else in their hearts and mouths."[56] In Capgrave's account, labor is working the field of Holy Scripture like bees that:

> Lerne and teche, bothe soke and drawe,
> Of goode exaumples of holy predecessoures
> Swete conceytes, wel famed savoures.
> Alle these be bees whech to the housolde bryng
> All her stuffe and alle her gaderyng. (IV. 9–14)

In a set of verbal pairings, Capgrave suggests that the labor of the bees involves both consumption (learning) and production (teaching) and in so doing again

---

52. Helen Barr, ed., *Mum and Sothsegger*, in *The Piers Plowman Tradition: A Critical Edition of Pierce the Ploughman's Crede, Richard the Redeless, Mum and the Sothsegger, and The Crowned King* (London: J. M. Dent, 1993), 173, lns. 997–98. The "Mum" author is relying on Bartholomaeus Anglicus (See Trevisa's Middle English translation, I. 609–14). This tradition follows Aquinas (*De Regimine Principum*, ch. 12) and continues to be appropriated into the Renaissance, for example, see Shakespeare, *Henry V*, I.ii.187–204.

53. *Pierce the Plowman's Crede*, for example, makes the following comparison: "ryght as dranes doth nought but drynketh up the huny, / Whan been with her bysynesse han brought it to the hepe, / Right so fareth freres with folke opon erthe." *Pierce the Plowman's Crede*, in Helen Barr, ed., *The Piers Plowman Tradition*, 92, lines 727ff. Also see Chaucer's prologue to the "Summoner's Tale" for a cruder version of this anti-fraternal analogy. Larry Benson, ed., *The Riverside Chaucer*, 3rd ed. (Boston: Houghton Mifflin, 1987).

54. Carruthers, *Book of Memory*, 38. I am indebted to Carruthers's overview of the trope for my brief summary here.

55. Quoted in Carruthers, *Book of Memory*, 192.

56. Peter of Celle, *Selected Works*, translated by H. Feiss (Kalamazoo, MI: Medieval Institute Publications, 1987), 103. Quoted by Michael Camille, "Mouths and Meanings: Towards an Anti-Iconography of Medieval Art," in *Iconography at the Crossroads*, ed. Brendan Cassidy (Princeton: Princeton University Press, 1993), 43–54, at 49. For a Middle English example, see Richard Rolle, *Meditations on the Passion*, 35: 274–75; and 36: 298–301.

emphasizes the reciprocity of the mnemonic and compositional process. Central to developing this relation is the rhetorical notion of "gathering" (*collatio*).[57] Capgrave's bees glean sweetness from "goode exaumples of holy predecessoures," thus mirroring the current labor of Capgrave's own readers, who are consuming his *Life of Saint Katherine*. Whereas earlier passages represented textual consumption at a distance, this prologue calls its readers to reflect on their own reading practices and imitate the virtuous bees.

Katherine is not mentioned until the seventh stanza of the prologue and only after Capgrave has described the labor of bees in a field more generally. She is, to be sure, a model bee, but her labor is not necessarily exceptional:

> On of these bees was this same qweene,
> The mayd Kateryne, whech with besynesse
> Of every floure whech was fayre to seene
> Sokyd oute hony of gret holynesse,
> Bare it to hyve, and there sche gan it dresse—
> For it wyll do servys bothe to God and man. (IV. 43–48)

Her labor is reading, and that reading is productive: she gathers honey, stores it, and prepares it, so that it might serve "bothe to God and man." Katherine's mode of reading the Bible, as expressed here, is characterized by consumption and composition. But Katherine's sacred reading also represents a model of replacement. As she will later tell the pagan philosophers, although she has been educated in the Seven Liberal Arts: "I hafe left all my auctoures olde, / I fonde noo frute in hem but eloquens" (IV. 1324–25). She leaves the "sotill bokes" of Aristotle, and Homer's "fayre terms in verse and eke in prose," claiming that she found nothing in these books other than "vanyte or thing that schall not lest" (IV. 1329, 1332, 1350). Although she will draw upon this learning and eloquence in her debates with the philosophers, she sees it as having only limited value. In contrast, she gathers the "sweet mete" she gleans from the natural law, written law, and law of grace and brings them into the hive of Holy Church where "ly thei yet as tresoure" (IV. 68).

This hidden treasure recalls the buried book of the opening prologue and links Katherine's reading and production with Capgrave's translation. In the next line, Capgrave again insists that this treasure is available to *all*: "Who that wyll laboure may fro that swetnes wryng / Mech bettyr than ony galey can bryng" (IV. 69–70). In other words, anyone who labors by reading can glean the sweetness of scripture as it has been mediated through the holy life of Katherine and her written *vita*. In the final lines of the prologue, Capgrave urges his readers to continue

---

57. Carruthers, *Book of Memory*, 35–36.

ruminating on the *vita*: "And forthe in this swetnesse wyll we now procede, / Whech that sche gadered, this lady, here lyvande" (IV. 71–72). Again, Capgrave promises sweetness and solace to all those who labor in the metaphorical field:

> I sey the grete labour
> That goode men have to rede exaumples olde,
> It is to hem of solace newe socour
> Her vertuous levyng stabyly to beholde
> And eke to fyght with corage fresch and bolde
> Ageyns this wordly deceyvable affluence,
> Ageyne the fleschly slulkyd neclygens. (IV. 36–42)

Thus the prologue serves as a mirror: Katherine's spiritual consumption and gathering is being replicated by those who are reading the literary treasure of the *vita*.[58] Just as Katherine sucks and gathers knowledge from old books, and just as the other bees gathered sweetness from old examples, so too Capgrave encourages his readers to "rede exaumples olde" and behold Katherine's "virtuous levyng." In a text so concerned with reading, it is natural that Capgrave is not only interested in the issue of *who* can read and *what* can be read, but in *how* to read, and in the effects of reading more generally. The reading modeled here is both intellectual and affective. The effect of careful reading should be "sweetness"—the experiential, affective property of knowing—just as it was for the hesitant priest in the opening prologue.

As this passage makes clear, one should not stop at reading and the sweetness that it produces; the gathering of bees is also a metaphor for writing. In the model proposed by Seneca, reading and writing should be alternated with each other, "so that what one reads is given body (*corpus*) by the writing."[59] Gathering thus leads to composition, an embodying of words so that something new is produced. As Mary Carruthers puts it, "merely to store memory by reading is an incomplete process without composition, for composition is the ruminative, 'digesting' process, the means by which reading is domesticated to ourselves."[60] Capgrave's prologues work out a model of the writing process in which rumination and invention blend, in which composition is a gathering of materials and a reassembling of them in new combinations. Thus, for Capgrave, composition is a process of rumination and digestion that ultimately produces sweetness.

---

58. As Winstead has shown, in the Books of Hours, "[r]eading provided an immediate way of identifying with the virgin martyrs . . . [because] the saint's behavior coincides exactly with that of her beholder" (*Virgin Martyrs*, 154).

59. On this topic, see John Scattergood, "Riddle 47 and Memory," in *Manuscripts and Ghosts: Essays on the Transmission of Medieval and Early Renaissance Literature* (Dublin: Four Courts Press, 2006), 85–86.

60. Carruthers, *Book of Memory*, 192.

"FORTHE IN THIS SWETNESSE": LITERARY FORMATION AND SPIRITUAL TRANSFORMATION

But what do Capgrave's uses of alimentary metaphors and reflection on transformative reading tell us about his understanding of poetic form and religious reform? On the one hand, Capgrave roots literary authority in rhetorical and theological tradition. On the other, he emphasizes the agency of the reader and insists that a text properly read is generative, producing both aesthetic and moral sweetness. Equally important as the form of the work, then, is its reception. The goals of sacred composition and devout reading are the same: sweetness. In the prologue to the fifth and final book of his *Life,* Capgrave reminds his readers that their hermeneutic labor is approaching its end and calls them to taste the sweetness of his book:

> Now is come oure leyser and oure space
> In whech we may—aftir oure grete labour
> Of other materis, now we have grace—
> Turne ageyn and tast the swete savour
> Of this clene virgine, of this wele savoured flour. (V. 1–5)

Capgrave here calls the readers of his book to remember that their reading represents a mode of laboring and of gleaning sweetness from the flower that is both Katherine herself and, as he soon suggests, his English *Life.* As we have seen, the metaphors of sweetness and "savour" that Capgrave employs in this passage are common ones in his lengthy verse *Life.* They provide a somatic aesthetic that runs through the work and is highlighted by its prologues, which provide a model of reading. Capgrave insists throughout that the reader's task is to taste the sweetness of Katherine's *Life*, a task that is simultaneously affective, aesthetic, and hermeneutic. And even as she is the aesthetic object upon which the reader's hungry gaze is fixed, Katherine herself serves as the model of how such aesthetic judgment functions.

In her recent work on the medieval concept of "sweetness," Carruthers has suggested that it is the aesthetic signifier par excellence: "no word is used more often in the Middle Ages to make a positive judgment about the effects of works of art."[61] Fifteenth-century poets such as John Lydgate frequently use the rhetoric of sweetness, sugar, and honey to characterize linguistic beauty and eloquence, describing the "sugred dites" and "the sugrid langage" of rhetoricians and poets

---

61. Carruthers develops this theme in two closely related essays: "Sweetness," *Speculum* 81 (2006): 999-1013, and "Sweet Jesus," in *Mindful Spirit in Late-Medieval Literature: Essays in Honor of Elizabeth D. Kirk,* ed. Bonnie Wheeler (New York: Palgrave, 2006), 9–19.

from Ovid to Chaucer.[62] For these poets, sweetness is a formal characteristic. Sweet words are beautiful words. In religious texts, however, the descriptive valences of the concept have as much to do with morality as with form. For instance, a version of Psalm 33 issues the command: "Gustate et videte quoniam sauvis est Dominus" [Taste and see that the Lord is sweet] (Psalm 33:9).[63] Here, sweetness is a spiritual quality. It is the moral beauty and delightfulness of God. More than simply an aesthetic signifier, spiritual sweetness is also the affective experience of beauty.

Sweetness serves as the bridge between the moral and the aesthetic for Capgrave. By consuming the nectar of flowers, Katherine becomes increasingly sweet and flower-like. Capgrave characterizes her as a "swete flowre" in the general prologue (171), but the references to her sweetness become more frequent as the poem proceeds. Her pre-baptism bath is "For to mak hir swete, for to make hir clene" (III. 1072), and after her conversion, baptism, and mystical marriage, she is often described as "this swete" (III. 1352)—as sweetness itself.[64] Indeed, by the prologue to the fifth book, Capgrave describes both Katherine herself and Capgrave's five-part *Life* as sweet-smelling, allegorical flowers: five-branched rose bushes (V. 1–42). Katherine herself is the rose bush, with green branches (signifying her life) and red flowers (signifying her martyrdom). Yet, as Capgrave explains, "These fyve leves, as I seyd wolate, / Betokenes these bokes whech we haven in hand" (V. 36–37). In other words, Capgrave's verse *Life of Saint Katherine* is also the flower from which the reader should gather honey. In this allegorical collapsing of Katherine's life and Capgrave's *Life* into one image, the written *Life* comes to mark Katherine's presence, a presence that readers are called to taste and consume. It reflects, one might even venture, a sort of transubstantiation.

This seemingly sacramental logic is especially striking given that the Eucharist is conspicuously absent from Capgrave's poem. His silence on this point has been read as a mark of his wariness about taking sides on contentious issues.[65]

---

62. Henry Bergen, ed., *Lydgate's Troy Book*, ed. by Henry Bergen, 4 vols., EETS e.s. 97, 103, 106, 126 (London: Kegan Paul, Trench, Trübner & Co., Limited, 1906–35; rpt. 1996), 2.2499, and Lydgate, *Fall of Princes*, ed. by Henry Bergen, 4 vols., EETS e.s., 121, 122, 123, 124 (London: Oxford University Press, 1924–27), 6.3467. Strikingly, most of the examples of "sugar" as an aesthetic term in the MED come from Lydgate's corpus; MED, s.v. "sugred."

63. This quotation is from the Gallic Psalter. Jerome changed the translation to "bonus" (rather than "sauvis"). For comment on these translations, see Carruthers, "Sweet Jesus," 12–13, and Rosemary Hale, "'Taste and See, For God Is Sweet': Sensory Perception and Memory in Medieval Christian Mystical Experience," in *Vox Mystica: Essays on Medieval Mysticism*, ed. Anne Clark Bartlett (Cambridge: D. S. Brewer, 1995), 3–14.

64. For other references to Katherine's sweetness, see, for example: III. 948, 1314, 1382; V. 352, 1392, 1958.

65. See, for example, Winstead, *John Capgrave's Fifteenth Century*, 84; and Simpson, *Reform and Cultural Revolution*, 462.

Yet the poem's frequent use of alimentary images and sustained interest in the transformative and nourishing power of consumption suggests, for Capgrave, the sacramental nature of spiritual writing and reading. Throughout the poem, books function as sanctifying signs. Capgrave's sacramental poetic is suggested first by textual resonances: as we noted, the opening prologue adapts two biblical scenes of book consumption, but the angel's command to eat the book also suggestively echoes the scriptural source of the Eucharistic ritual: "'Take and eat. This is my body.'"[66] In this association, Capgrave again suggests the transformative power of words well-written and well-received. Capgrave, in other words, elevates religious writing—and his book in particular—by associating it with the Eucharist.

Like the Eucharist, the objects of consumption throughout the poem reveal that, for Capgrave, physical forms do not necessarily signify internal reality or value. Although Capgrave's poem never denies the transformation of bread and wine into body and blood, it offers the parallel transformation of words into exemplary, sweet lives. Throughout his poem, Capgrave reiterates that one can "taste and see that the Lord is good" through reading. Capgrave's writing insists on the possibility of a sacramental poetics when it equates the transformative consumption of the word with spiritual food and when it suggests that material form is not a marker of internal sweetness.

However, as I have already noted, Capgrave expresses reservations several times throughout the *Life* about his ability to render theological ideas in plain, vernacular prose, articulating his desire for openness in the opening lines of the prologue and lamenting in a later aside that "It is ful hard swech thingis forto ryme, / To uttir pleynly in langage of oure nacion" the theological matters of his Latin source (IV. 2194–95). Despite the difficulty of translation, Capgrave seeks to craft a vernacular poetics appropriate for theological reflection. The prophetic, the visionary, the reformist, and even the *literary* for Capgrave do not emerge *ex nihilo*; they are the product of eating books. A text properly read is generative. Literary production is contingent upon literary consumption. Thus, for Capgrave, as for Jerome, "eating the book is the starting point of reading" but also of reformist religious instruction and literary production.

For Capgrave this reformism is also marked by a reformation of fifteenth-century poetic values. Capgrave's use of alimentary metaphors does not simply evince an interest in literary reception; it also serves as a reflection on the aesthetics of vernacular religious writing. Although Capgrave's *Life of Saint Katherine* may, at first glance, seem to follow the form of the embellished, rhyme royal saints' lives popularized by Chaucer and Lydgate, it diverges in some important

---

66. "Cenantibus autem eis, accepit Iesus panem, et benedixit ac fregit, deditque discipulis suis, et ait: Accipite et commendite: hoc est corpus meum" (Matthew 26:26).

ways from the works of these predecessors.[67] For instance, absent from Capgrave's intermittent articulations of authorial anxiety is the dullness *topos*.[68] This absence, alongside his repeated emphasis on openness and plainness, marks the difference of his poetic style from that of many of his contemporaries. And, as I have noted, the poem is almost entirely free of the aureate formulations found in the writings of many of his literary peers.[69] Like the work's protagonist, Capgrave uses, but seems to note the limited value of, rhetorical and poetic forms. Indeed, while the *Life of Saint Katherine* draws heavily on academic tropes, it models a non-Latinate fifteenth-century style; it represents a poetic that insists on its "Englishness" and weds multiple genres, forms, and styles: hagiography, romance, and poetic and rhetorical manuals; alliterative verse and rhyme royal; structural pairings and parallels. As Karen Winstead suggests, "[t]hough Capgrave acknowledges only one English source for his narrative . . . his *Life of St. Katherine* reads as if it were written by someone who had read Chaucer, was conversant with the works of Lydgate and Bokenham and with biblical drama, and knew of Margery Kempe's *Book*."[70] Capgrave's poetic method, like his use of rhetorical and poetic theory, works by means of association; like his protagonist, he gathers widely. As we have seen, his prologues are storehouses of exegetical, rhetorical, and poetic devices.[71] Thus, in his *Life of Saint Katherine,* Capgrave gives us a sense of the capaciousness of literary experimentation in the period.

Yet, as I have already noted, Capgrave's poetic style has not appealed to the aesthetic palates of modern literary critics. However, critical distaste for the period's formal values may say more about contemporary biases than literary worth. Our limited attention to fifteenth-century stylistics has been focused predominately on aureate, secular poets. To read fifteenth-century poetics through this partial lens, however, distorts the multiple and sometimes competing experiments in literary taste and form that characterize the period. Capgrave's *Life of Saint Katherine*, as this essay has sought to demonstrate, calls attention to the idea that "sweetness" may lie beneath a surface rather than *be* that surface (as the "sugrid eloquence" admired by Lydgate and others might suggest). Instead, Capgrave strives to write both plainly and eloquently so that his book, like its

---

67. Pearsall reads Capgrave's *Life* as a "continuation of the Chaucer-Lydgate tradition" but also suggests that the poem is influenced by romance style, see Pearsall, "Popular Romance Style," 123–24.

68. In Capgrave's poem, "dullness" and "rudeness" are only attributed to those that cannot understand Katherine's arguments (see, for example, IV. 615-16). On dullness as a characteristic pose of political or courtly poets in the long fifteenth century, see David Lawton, "Dullness and the Fifteenth Century," *English Literary History* 54 (1987): 761–99.

69. On Capgrave's "native," non-aureate, style, see Fredeman, "Style and Characterization," 357–58.

70. Winstead, "Introduction," *The Life of Saint Katherine,* 6.

71. Although this essay focuses primarily on images of consumption and incarnation, Capgrave's other two prologues employ equally common tropes: sparks rising from a fire (Book II) and a multi-branched rose bush (Book V).

subject, might be sweet to the reader's taste and nourishing to the reader's spirit.[72] And while Capgrave's poem aims to produce sweetness, it does not shy away from articulating the hermeneutic labor that gleaning will require. In fact, it is the reader's labor as much as the aesthetic object itself that generates sweetness. Sweetness is realized only through participation in the literary process, through the consumption, rumination, and reconstitution of form. Capgrave's poem thus challenges us to consider the ways in which fifteenth-century aesthetics may take up, after all, the matter of taste.

---

72. This, of course, is a relatively common understanding of the purpose of literature in the period. As D. Vance Smith has recently reminded us "Form in medieval texts is neither merely aesthetic nor aesthetically disinterested, it is always tuned to purpose" ("Medieval *Forma*," in *Reading for Form*, ed. Susan J. Wolfson and Marshall Brown [Seattle, WA: University of Washington Press, 2006], 66–79, at 71).

5

Jesus' Voice

Dialogue and Late-Medieval Readers

REBECCA KRUG

This essay considers three late-medieval English texts in which Jesus speaks: the well-known series of prayers called *The Fifteen Oes;* the vernacular translation of the fourth book of *The Imitation of Christ* composed by Margaret Beaufort; and Margery Kempe's *Book.* Although the three works differ greatly in their representations of Jesus' voice, they share a common interest, new to the long fifteenth century, in imagining *readers* of written texts as participating in direct conversation with Jesus through their reading. Although dialogue was popular throughout the Middle Ages, earlier dialogues rarely represented Jesus in conversation with humans who were not part of the gospel narratives.[1] In *The Fifteen Oes, The Imitation of Christ,* and Margery Kempe's *Book,* Jesus and a first-person narrator/speaker are represented as persons who engage in dialogue with one another. By using first-person perspective for the human characters represented, all three works identify their readers as participants in "conversation" with Jesus.

---

1. Misha von Perger provides a catalogue of dialogues in "Vorläufiges Repertorium philosophischer und theologischer Prosa-Dialoge des lateinischen Mittelalters" that sheds some light on the changes in the form over time. Aside from Anselm of Canterbury's late-eleventh-century "Monastic Dialogue" between a Benedictine monk and his Lord "Christus," no other dialogue in the register lists Jesus as a speaker until He appears in numerous works from the fifteenth century including items 126, 128, 138.2, 150.6, 150.9, 150.10, 162.2, 162.3. The register is not exhaustive. Nonetheless, it highlights general trends and indicates the growing presence of Jesus as a speaker in dialogues that appeared in the fifteenth century. Von Perger's catalogue is in *Gespräche Lesen: Philosophische Dialoge im Mittelalter,* ed. Klaus Jacobi (Tübingen: Gunter Narr Verlag, 1999), 435–94.

I argue that the growing popularity of written dialogues, in general, and of those in which Jesus speaks, specifically, resulted from late-medieval readers' desire to "talk back" to the written works that were "speaking" to them. Although orality is often discussed in relation to *writers* who composed written works as if they came from "a living heart through a living mouth," the present essay looks at the ways in which *readers* were attracted to dialogue form.[2] Readers in the period increasingly saw their books as vehicles for self-transformation.[3] Fifteenth-century readers "read" themselves into books; dialogues in which the reader might "speak" with Jesus were attractive because they offered audiences the opportunity to enter into direct conversation with the divine.[4]

Two of the three texts I consider, *The Fifteen Oes* and *The Imitation of Christ*, are often thought of as medieval "best-sellers." Their popularity, as Helen C. White demonstrated many years ago, continued well into the sixteenth century.[5] Margery Kempe's *Book*, in contrast, disappeared from view, with the exception of Wynkyn de Worde's printed excerpts, until the manuscript was rediscovered in the twentieth century. Although the analysis that follows is largely text-based, that is, it offers readings that attend to the manner in which interactions between Jesus and the first-person speaker/narrator are represented, this discussion is underwritten by a broader interest in reading practices and the ways that such practices changed in the sixteenth century. I return to this subject in my conclusion.

---

2. This is from the German mystic Suso's discussion of dialogue. See Heinrich Seuse, *Büchlein der Ewigen Weisheit* in *Deutsche Schriften,* ed. Karl Bihlmeyer (Stuttgart: Minerva, 1907; repr. 1961), 199. Suso's Middle High German reads: "als ungelich sint dú wort, dú in der lutren gnade werdent enpfangen und usser einem lebenden herzen dur einen lebenden munt us fliezent gegen den selben worten, so sú an daz tovt bermit koment." On orality and late medieval English literature see Jesse Gellrich, *Discourse and Dominion in the Fourteenth Century: Oral Contexts of Writing in Philosophy, Politics, and Poetry* (Princeton, NJ: Princeton University Press, 1995), 3–36.

3. See Rebecca Krug, *Reading Families: Women's Literate Practice in Late Medieval England* (Ithaca, New York: Cornell University Press, 2002), 153–212.

4. The best survey of dialogue in the period remains Francis Lee Utley's catalogue, "Dialogues, Debates, and Catechisms," in *A Manual of Writing in Middle English, 1050–1400,* vol. 3, ed. Albert E. Hartung (New Haven: Connecticut Academy of Arts and Sciences, 1972), 669–745. Scholars who mention dialogue usually discuss it in relation to debate poetry; see for example Thomas Reed, *Middle English Debate Poetry* (New York: Columbia University Press, 1990) and John W. Conlee, *Middle English Debate Poetry: A Critical Anthology* (East Lansing, MI: Colleagues Press, 1991). Dialogue form was used in medieval England to discuss an array of topics. Subjects ranged, for example, from the functioning of the Exchequer to instruction in the art of alchemy (delivered by the Queen of the Elves to Albertus Magnus!): for these examples see Richard Fitzneale, *Dialogus de Scaccario: The Dialogue of the Exchequer,* ed. Emilie Amt and S. D. Church (Oxford: Oxford University Press, 2007); Peter Grund, ed. "Albertus Magnus and the Queen of the Elves: A Fifteenth-Century English Verse Dialogue on Alchemy," *Anglia: Zeitschrift für Englische Philologie* 122 (2004): 640–62. There is a good deal more scholarship on sixteenth- and seventeenth-century dialogue than on dialogues from the Middle Ages. See, for example, *Printed Voices: The Renaissance Culture of Dialogue,* eds. Dorothea Heitsch and Jean-François Vallée (Toronto: University of Toronto Press, 2004).

5. Helen C. White, *The Tudor Books of Private Devotion* (Madison: University of Wisconsin Press, 1951), 28; 216–29.

THE FIFTEEN OES

Prayer, like all communicative activities necessitated by a lack of immediacy (letter-writing, for example) requires that the supplicant/writer/reader imagine she is addressing another person.[6] But it looks, at first glance, like a monologue, a solitary, imaginative exercise in which the person praying enacts a communal, or at least multi-personed, relationship that seems, in reality, largely imagined: in unscripted, personal prayer, God's voice is hard to find. The late-medieval answer to this problem was to assign God a voice. Often, that voice spoke through the authority of what I will call "inscription," by which I mean the insertion of authoritative written texts into a written work.[7] Although scholars of contemporary literature tend to associate this kind of stylized quotation with modernism, it was a common feature in medieval literature, and the very popular, late-fourteenth-century *Fifteen Oes* offer a good example of this.[8]

The *Fifteen Oes* is a series of prayers on the Passion that scholars now believe originated in England. They were traditionally attributed to Saint Bridget of Sweden, but this attribution is no longer accepted. The prayers were originally composed in Latin and subsequently translated into various vernaculars. Several Middle English versions of the *Oes* circulated in manuscript and print throughout

---

6. This essay emerged from a talk Kathleen Tonry and Shannon Gayk kindly invited me to give at the International Medieval Congress in Kalamazoo, Michigan in May 2007. It was called "The Comfort of Form: Lay Women's Prayers in the Fifteenth Century." Although the present piece differs a great deal from that talk, I continue to use "she" to refer to the reader throughout the essay. Readers of the *Fifteen Oes* were often women; Margaret Beaufort was a female reader who read and then translated the last book of the *Imitation of Christ* into Middle English; and Margery Kempe was a writer and aural reader—in the sense that others read to her—who seems to have written at least in part out of her sense of the difficulties of gender for women believers and with an interest in female readers. In the present essay, I draw no conclusions about the relationship between gender and dialogue as a form. For a discussion of dialogue and gender see Janet Levarie Smarr, "A Female Tradition? Women's Dialogue Writing in Sixteenth-Century France," in *Strong Voices, Weak History: Early Women Writers and Canons in England, France, and Italy,* eds. Pamela Joseph Benson and Victoria Kirkham (Ann Arbor: University of Michigan Press, 2005), 32–57.

7. My thinking about inscription grew out of work done with my teacher Ingeborg Hoesterey on intertextuality, pastiche, and bricolage; see Hoesterey, *Pastiche: Cultural Memory in Art, Film, Literature* (Bloomington: Indiana University Press, 2001) and Hoesterey, ed., *Zeitgeist in Babel: The Postmodernist Controversy* (Bloomington: Indiana University Press, 1991). For the affective possibilities of pastiche, see Richard Dyer, *Pastiche: Knowing Imitation* (London: Routledge, 2006). Seeta Chaganti's discussion of inscription has also influenced my discussion: see *The Medieval Poetics of the Reliquary: Enshrinement, Inscription, Performance* (New York: Palgrave, 2008).

8. For an introduction to, modernized version of, and transcription that follows the first printed edition of the *Oes* see Krug, "The Fifteen Oes," in *Cultures of Piety: Medieval English Devotional Literature in Translation,* eds. Anne Clark Bartlett and Thomas H. Bestul (Ithaca, New York: Cornell University Press, 1999), 107–117 and 212–16. The present essay cites the modernized version from this anthology. Middle English versions of the prayers began circulating in the late fourteenth century, and the *Oes* were well known to late-medieval English readers including Elizabeth of York and Margaret Beaufort, who commissioned Caxton's printing. See also John C. Hirsh, "A Middle English Metrical Version of *The Fifteen Oes* from Bodleian Add MS B 66," *Neuphilologische Mitteilungen* 75 (1974): 98–114, and White, *The Tudor Books of Private Devotion,* 216–29.

the fifteenth century, including several anonymous metrical versions, a verse translation by John Lydgate, and at least two prose versions. William Caxton produced a print version of the *Oes* as a single book (STC 20195), which he stated was commissioned by the queen mother Margaret Beaufort and her daughter-in-law Elizabeth of York, in 1491. Wynkyn de Worde reprinted that version as a supplement to a Sarum book of hours in 1494 (STC 15875).[9]

The prayers' title comes from the fact that each of the fifteen prayers begins with the exclamation "O." This is the most obvious formal aspect, but the structure of the sequence is actually based on the "Seven Words," Jesus' last utterances before the crucifixion. These seven phrases were culled from various biblical sources and appeared frequently in prayers and poems. In the *Fifteen Oes* they appear in the following order: "Father, forgive them, for thy know not what they do" (third O); "This day you shall be with me in paradise" (fifth O); "Lo, woman, your son" (sixth O); "I thirst" (seventh O); "O my God, why have you forsaken me?" (ninth O); "Now is it done" (thirteenth O); and "Father, into your hands I commend my spirit" (fourteenth O). This last of the Seven Words is the only one that is not quoted directly in the *Fifteen Oes*.[10] The incorporation of the Seven Words into the *Fifteen Oes* is an obvious example of the authoritative inscription of Jesus' "traditional" voice into the prayers.

But the *Fifteen Oes* does more than simply offer the reader an authorized version of the divine voice.[11] Rather, by redeploying Jesus' words from the cross, the *Fifteen Oes* allows its reader the experience of articulating her own voice, as supplicant, and, at the same time, of *speaking* through God's voice. So, for example, in the fifth O, the supplicant requests that Jesus "show me mercy in the hour of my death" (the voice of the supplicant) and then associates this prayer with Jesus' words to the thief on the cross. The supplicant asks that Jesus show her mercy as he has done to others in the past. Her request is framed in this way: "Mindful of the depth of the great mercy you had for us, lost and desperate sinners, and espe-

---

9. This material is drawn from my introduction in *Cultures of Piety*, 107–112.

10. *Cultures of Piety*, 109. In the fourteenth O it appears as a "reminder" by the speaker to Jesus: "remember how you meekly commended your spirit into the hands of your Father," *Cultures of Piety*, 116.

11. The best-known modern commentator on dialogue and literature is Mikhail Bakhtin: for his analysis of the role of dialogue in the novel see *The Dialogic Imagination*, ed. Michael Holquist, trans. Caryl Emerson and Michael Holquist (Austin: University of Texas Press, 1981). Following Bakhtin, critics often assume that medieval dialogue is "univocal" and does not offer the same possibilities of polyphony found in literature of modernity. Nonetheless, medievalists sometimes apply Bakhtin's terms to medieval literature. For such an account see Nicole Rice, *Lay Piety and Religious Discipline in Middle English Literature* (Cambridge: Cambridge University Press, 2009). Rice makes an interesting case, using Bakhtin's term "dialogic," for the influence of medieval readers on devotional writers. On dialogism and early period literature see also Peter Burke, "The Renaissance Dialogue," *Renaissance Studies* 3 (1989): 1–12; Francois Rigolot, "Problematizing Renaissance Exemplarity: The Inward Turn of Dialogue From Petrarch to Montaigne," in *Printed Voices*, esp. p.17; and Nicola McLelland, "Dialogue and German Language Learning in the Renaissance," in *Printed Voices*, 206–26.

cially for the great mercy you showed to the thief who hung on your right side, to whom you said, 'This day you shall be with me in paradise'" (fifth O). The reader, in the *Fifteen Oes,* speaks to Jesus directly and calls him "you." The Jesus who speaks back, via quotation from the Seven Words, addresses His audience as "you." However, by relying on the Seven Words, the prayer must represent Jesus as speaking across time: His original words are directed at the characters from the gospel narratives. How, then, does the reader claim this voice as her own?

The supplicant's appropriation of that voice, a voice of inscripted authority, comes through the emotional symmetry that the *Fifteen Oes* establishes between the supplicant's affective condition and the Savior's. This is made, first, through representations of physical penetrability. In the eleventh O, for example, the supplicant asks Jesus to "draw me out of sin and hide me in the holes of your wounds from the face of your wrath, until the time, Lord, in which your dreadful judgment has passed." Although she asks for mercy, the grounds for this request are identified in terms of physicality rather than spiritual considerations: the speaker asks Jesus for such merciful protection on account of "the depth of your wounds, which went through your tender flesh, through your bowels, and through the marrow of your bones." In the supplicant's request, Jesus' body is imagined as present and penetrable. That body is a physical refuge for the reader. It is not just the object of distant, historical implements of torture, nor is it simply the authoritative subject of gospel narrative. And, although the image of Jesus' body as a protective enclosure is conventional, the presentation in the *Oes* is striking. The prayers fuse together the physical aspects of the crucifixion with the physical aspects of human, spiritual vulnerability in an intricate and highly elaborate manner: the depth of mercy needed by the speaker can be measured in relation to the depth of the wounds.

The *Oes* insist on Jesus' dual nature as man and God. The biological connection means that the Savior, like the supplicant, experiences pain physically and, like a great deal of late-medieval art and literature, the *Fifteen Oes* attends to the physical aspects of the Passion and uses bodily pain to heighten the identification between reader and Jesus.[12] But even as they draw attention to such physical identification, the prayers' greatest power lies in their ability to return, insistently, to the supplicant's need to feel that God is present *as a person who speaks.* It is not enough to represent Jesus as a suffering body. Rather, the *Oes* ask repeatedly that God assume personal responsibility for enunciating His promises to the reader.[13]

---

12. A great deal has been written about affective piety in recent years. Giles Constable's "The Ideal of the Imitation of Christ," in *Three Studies in Medieval Religious and Social Thought* (Cambridge: Cambridge University Press, 1995), 143–248 is a particularly lucid account that takes into consideration historical change. Laurelle Levert's "'Crucifye hem, Crucifye hem': The Subject and Affective Response in Middle English Passion Narratives," *Essays in Medieval Studies* 14 (1997): 73–90 is a useful exploration of reader response and affective devotion.

13. The *Oes* often appeared with an introductory legend promising spiritual benefits from the prayers'

As the supplicant repeats Jesus' words to the characters of the gospel narratives including His Father, His Mother, and the thief, she makes the *voice* behind those words her own and reads herself into the promises. Those promises, expressly verbalized, grant the supplicant access to divine presence.

The reader of the *Fifteen Oes* is not asked to simply bow to the authority of the Seven Words but, instead, fuses the Words' original meanings from the gospel contexts with her own needs and interpretations. In the seventh O, for example, the reader is taught to claim the phrase "I thirst" as her own speech. The *Oes* do not lose sight of the gospel narrative: Jesus' desire to drink is thwarted in the eighth O by the soldiers who offer him "vinegar and gall." But the prayers do not stop at this literalization. So, in the seventh O, thirst is spiritualized. Jesus thirsts for "the salvation of man's soul." This allegorical reading is then taken up by the supplicant. The Savior's substitution of another kind of desire for bodily thirst parallels the supplicant's prayer for herself: "Mindful of this blessed desire . . . quench my thirst for all worldly love and desire." Reinterpretation of water imagery is one of the *Fifteen Oes*'s central themes, and, following the same pattern in which the supplicant assumes a spiritualized meaning in imitation of Jesus' allegorized reading, in the tenth O "I thirst" is coupled first with the reader's memorialization of Jesus' blood as "water" in which he "drowned." The blood/water is then linked with her own sense that she herself has "drowned in foul sin."

In this way, the speaker hears Jesus' words and then speaks them as her own. Yet, despite this fusion of the supplicant's prayer with Jesus' words, in the *Fifteen Oes* the reader's voice and Jesus' are distinct. When they are joined together it is through an echo-like effect: the supplicant reads Jesus' words in her voice—an enactment of Jesus' voice—and the Words, or at least words and phrases from them, then return but are vocalized in her own voice and are accompanied by her own interpretations. For example, in the ninth O, "'O my God, why have you *forsaken* [ital. added] me?'" is transformed into "On account of this painful anguish, our blessed God, do not *forsake* [ital. added] us in the anguish of our own death." In the third O, "'Father, *forgive* [ital. added] them, for they know not what they do'" becomes "mindful of this bitter Passion, grant me absolute remission and *forgiveness* [ital. added] of my sins." Sometimes, the vocabulary of the Words is exchanged: "'Now it is done'" in the thirteenth O becomes a synonym for death—here life's "end"—as the supplicant asks "have mercy on me at the *end* [ital. added] of my life when my soul shall be anguished and my spirit troubled."

The *Oes* conclude with a return to the supplicant's voice. In doing so, the prayers exchange the roles that the speaker and Jesus have assumed throughout

---

repetition. See, for example, Cameron Louis, *The Commonplace Book of Robert Reynes of Acle: An Edition of Tanner MS 407* (New York: Garland, 1980), 264–68; 463–64.

the verses. In the fifteenth O, the supplicant asks that Jesus "wound my heart so that my soul may be fed sweetly with the water of penance and with tears of love," but it also offers that heart as a home for the Savior. The speaker says, "And good Jesus, turn me wholly to you that my heart may always be a dwelling place for you." This opening up of her body to Jesus as a refuge shows the supplicant returning to her reflections on Jesus' wounds as a safe haven (found in the eleventh O) but shifts the relational dynamic found in this final verse. By the end of the *Oes,* the *speaker* is ready to offer her body and her voice as sanctuaries in which *Jesus* will be able to find what He needs. The fusion of voices, in which Jesus' Seven Words seem to stand authoritatively, is used to offer the supplicant an active role in protecting God. The prayers' final verse fixes that role firmly in the supplicant's body and "manner of living."

In the experience of reexpressing Jesus' actual words, the speaker of the *Fifteen Oes* follows the divine exemplar's verbal and linguistic model. By "speaking" in Jesus' voice as she prays, the supplicant performs a type of *imitatio Christi.* Claiming Jesus' words as her own, she enacts her desire to follow the example modeled by the Savior by reexperiencing and reexpressing inscripted, authoritative language. In doing so, the supplicant finds new ways to speak. The next text under consideration, the fourth book of the fifteenth-century *Imitation of Christ,* also invites the reader to respond to Jesus' voice. However, in this case, the text's author does not limit himself to using authoritative, traditional words to animate Jesus but instead constructs a Jesus who speaks and responds directly to the supplicant in the present time.

IMITATION OF CHRIST

In the fourth book of the *Imitation of Christ,* Jesus' dialogue fluctuates between three registers: the authoritative/inscriptive (a voice like that found in the *Fifteen Oes*); an intimate voice that speaks to the supplicant personally; and an expert voice that sounds like that of an authoritative clergyman. Practically, we might think of them as three separate Jesuses. The first appears in the prologue, which begins: "Come to me, seythe our mercyfull lorde / all that laboreth and be charged / and I shal gyue vnto you refeccyon." The lines are represented as spoken by Jesus—not just included as voiceless epigrams—in the *Imitation*'s prologue, and much like the Seven Words in the *Fifteen Oes,* they are authoritative and traditional.[14] The passage cited above is a late Middle English rendering of Matthew

---

14. *The Imitation of Christ,* ed. John K. Ingram, EETS, e.s., 63 (London: Kegan Paul, Trench, Trübner, 1893), 259. The last two books of the *Imitation* are both written in dialogue form. My original interest in the fourth book stemmed from the fact that it was translated into English by Margaret Beaufort, Henry VII's mother, in 1504. Subsequent references to the *Imitation* are cited in parentheses

11:28; the entire, extremely brief prologue is, in fact, a string of lines spoken by Jesus in the New Testament. Following the quotation from Matthew are a series of phrases that are associated with celebration of the Eucharist, for example, "And the bredde that I shall gyue vnto you, shalbe my flesshe for the lyfe of the worlde. Take and ete it, for it is my body that for you shalbe gyuen in sacryfice."[15]

The compilation of verses comes, as the supplicant notes at the opening of the book, from "my lorde Iesu cryst." Despite the fact that the words "haue not ben sayd in one self tyme, nor wrytten in one selfe place," she explains they are "yet for that . . . thy wordes" and argues that she "ought feythfully / & agreably to vnderstande them / [that] they be thy wordes / and thou hast proferred them" (259). After identifying Jesus' voice as the source of the biblical quotations, she then goes on to claim Jesus' words for herself, much as the supplicant does in the *Fifteen Oes*. In the *Imitation* the speaker makes that appropriation explicit: she explains that those words "be now myn, for thou hast sayd them for my helthe. I will gladlye receyue them of thy mouthe, to thende they may be the better sowen & planted in my herte" (259).

Although the speaker says the words come from Jesus' mouth, suggesting presence, the passage forms part of an episode in which the speaker is thinking aloud and appears unable to "hear" Jesus. This aspect is emphasized by the isolated nature of the speaker's voice: the desire for direct access to the Savior is expressed by the supplicant in a long, opening sequence in which she agonizes, without interruption by other speakers, over her feelings of unworthiness as she contemplates receiving the sacrament of holy communion. The book's first chapter is filled with first-person questioning and exclamations, for example, "Howe dare I than, cursed / & right poore amonge other creatures, receyue the into my house, which vnneth can knowe that I haue well passyd and enployed one hour of tyme?"[16] The speaker in the *Imitation*'s fourth book is loquacious, intimate, and anxious as she expresses her need for divine intervention. She worries over her inner spiritual life, observing, for instance:

---

within the text. On the work's textual history, see Roger Lovatt, "The *Imitation of Christ* in Late Medieval England," *Transactions of the Royal Historical Society* 18 (1968): 97–121. On Margaret Beaufort's translation see Krug, *Reading Families*, 106–11. Scholars seem to now agree that Thomas à Kempis was the author of the Latin text: see Constable, "The Ideal of the Imitation of Christ," 239–40. The work was first written in Latin and appeared anonymously in the 1420s.

15. *Imitation*, 259. The first sentence is John 6:51; the second is 1 Corinthians 11:24.

16. *Imitation*, 260. Up until the fifth chapter, the supplicant's is the only voice found in the book with the exception of the gospel citations in the prologue. The fifth chapter introduces an "expert" voice that is confusingly lacking identification. This is considered below. For a survey of various kinds of "inwardness" in late medieval devotional writing see Jennifer Bryan, *Looking Inward: Devotional Reading and the Private Self in Late Medieval England* (Philadelphia: University of Pennsylvania Press, 2007), 35–74. Bryan mentions the *Imitation* in passing. For an investigation of selfhood in the Middle Ages that complements Bryan's study see Katherine C. Little, *Confession and Resistance: Defining the Self in Late Medieval England* (Notre Dame, IN: University of Notre Dame Press, 2006).

> Lorde, whan I thynke of thy worthynesse and of my great fylthynes / I tremble strongly and am confounded in my selfe. For if I receyue the nat, I fle the eternall lyfe / & yf I vnworthyly receyue the, I renne in to thy wrath. what shall I thanne do, my good lorde . . . in all myne infyrmytes / and necessities? (268)[17]

The passage expresses the supplicant's dilemma and, after a staccato of first-person questioning that seems not to bring any relief, she reaches out to Jesus for an answer by imagining his mercy as she speaks to herself. Despite the fact that she "may nat be heuenly enflamed as the cherubyns and ceraphyns," she tells herself that "enforc[ing]" her own "deuocion" will grant her a "lytel flame of that goodly loue" (267). The chapter concludes with a prayer for mercy from Jesus that she claims as her due by repeating Jesus' words from the opening scriptural passage from the prologue: "come ye all vnto me that labour and be charged, and I shal refresshe you."[18] Despite her own unworthiness, the promise of Jesus' voice, she hopes and prays, will lead her to "the lyfe eternal."

This last book of the *Imitation* opens with a series of imaginary conversations between the reader and the divine. In its first four chapters, the book presents the supplicant as the voice of the reader. The supplicant/reader is encouraged to take solace in these "conversations" with Jesus, and the anxiety of spiritual loneliness is answered by personal reflection: talking to oneself and imagining the absent Jesus are held up as vehicles for finding encouragement and consolation. This kind of "conversation" is traditional—the psalms are well-known examples—and the supplicant explicitly acknowledges her place in this spiritual lineage.[19] She compares herself with "right deuout kynge dauyd" and her preparation for the sacrament with his composition and singing of songs of praise to the "inuysyble" God (261).

Like the *Fifteen Oes*, the *Imitation* takes Jesus' words from the gospels and identifies them as divine speech that has the ability to draw the supplicant closer to God. As the first-person speaker asks how she dares, given her unworthiness, to receive "holy communyon of thy precyous bodye" (260), she emphasizes the vitality of Jesus' voice. Scripture, in the *Imitation,* is spoken rather than written, and the supplicant invests speech with the highest authority. She exclaims, "Lorde, who shulde beleue thys thynge to be true / if thy selfe dyd not *say it?* [ital. added]" (260). Yet, in contrast with the *Fifteen Oes,* the *Imitation* moves beyond the idea that Jesus speaks to the believer through the words of the gospels alone, and models direct conversation as an additional method by which the supplicant

---

17. This is a paraphrase of I Corinthians 11:27.
18. This is a slightly different rendering of Matthew 11:28 from the one with which the fourth book of the *Imitation* opens. Compare *Imitation,* 259, and the present instance, *Imitation,* 267.
19. On the psalms see Shannon Gayk, "'Among psalms to fynde a cleer sentence': John Lydgate, Eleanor Hull, and the Art of Vernacular Exegesis," *New Medieval Literatures* 10 (2008): 161–89.

can hear the divine. In this way, the personal anxiety of the first-person speaker is relieved by imagined answers to her imagined questions.

The book's author goes even further in his exploration of Jesus' voice: the supplicant's longing for *Jesus* to speak to her anxieties is answered halfway through the book. A new voice—one clearly set apart from the speaker's—is introduced at the end of the seventh chapter. This is a Jesus who speaks directly to the supplicant and responds to her pressing, individual questions about her unworthiness. At the conclusion of the seventh chapter, Jesus addresses the supplicant, assuring her that if His advice is followed: "than wyl I nomore remembre his synnes & trespaces, but all shalbe forgyuen & pardoned vnto hym" (270). In the book's eighth chapter, this new Jesus continues to speak pointedly to the supplicant/reader: "O Man, as I dyd offre my selfe / and my free wyll vnto god my fader ... in lyke wyse thou oughtest to offre vnto me wyllyngly thy selfe" (270). Incorporating personal desire into His responses, the intimate Jesus insists, "What aske I of the more, but that thou study to resygne thy selfe vnto me enterely? what thynge so euer elles thou gyuest vnto me I haue no cure. For I demaunde nat thy gyftes, but only thy selfe" (270). This is, clearly, a Jesus who speaks in His own voice and not through the imaginings of the supplicant.

The introduction of a Jesus who speaks in an intimate and assertive voice reverberates fascinatingly with the first-person questioning of the supplicant. Before Jesus' insistence that the supplicant offer herself to Him wholly and exclusively, the supplicant had said, "My soule desyreth thy body, my herte desyreth to be vnyght, & onely with the. gyue thy selfe vnto me, good lorde / & than I suffysed, for withoute the no consolacyon nor comforte is good / without the I may not be" (264). Although this passage is framed by the chapter heading as an exploration of the "great profyte" of "receyu[ing] the body of our lorde Iesu cryst," its meaning extends beyond observation of the sacrament to meditation on spiritual existence. The supplicant longs for Jesus' presence as the means of self-fulfillment. Jesus' response is, however, to demand self-renunciation: He insists on the "fre oblacyon of thy selfe" (270), that is, sacrifice of self.[20] Throughout the fourth book, Jesus repeats his insistence that the supplicant's solution lies in self-renunciation. In the twelfth chapter, he advises the reader to "shet" herself "in thy chaumbre, as doeth a solytary byrde vnder the euesynges of an house" (276). He then reminds her, chillingly, "thou hast moche nede of me" but "I haue none of the" (276). If this were a relationship between humans, we might consider Jesus' responses emotional abuse.

The supplicant is complicit in this arrangement. Loss of self is represented as her greatest desire in the *Imitation*. She longs for annihilation of the self and

---

20. Oblation is a term used in the Eucharistic service. The "lesser oblation" involves presentation of the unconsecrated bread and wine; the "greater oblation" is presentation of the consecrated elements. The *Imitation* employs the language of the service to reflect on self-sacrifice as well as ritual.

Jesus, her lover, not only promises that this is possible but demands it. He tells her, "I am he to whome thou oughtest to gyue the by such maner that from hensforth thou liue nomore in thy selfe, but in me only" (277). In the next chapter, she responds by asking when they can be alone together and she can "vterly forgete my selfe" (277). Reflecting on Jesus' "familiar spekynge," the supplicant imagines a conversation in which Jesus says, "If thou wilt be with me, I will be with the," and she replies, "blessed lorde, I beseche the, dwell with me, for all the desyre of my herte ys to be with the inseparable without departynge" (278). These intimate conversations between the supplicant and Jesus are focused on negating the supplicant's essential being. Rather than desiring to imitate Christ, she longs to lose herself entirely and become part of Him. This dramatic loss of identity, the text suggests, is an answer to the supplicant's anxious prayers at the opening of the book.

Yet, although the *Imitation* represents direct access to Jesus and His voice as the supplicant's greatest desire, it fractures and mediates the interpersonal and private relationship it represents by returning insistently to discourse that associates Jesus with the voice of the clergy. The intimate Jesus responds directly to the supplicant's anxious queries in the eighth and twelfth chapters of the book, but these responses are framed by chapters of dialogue (chapters five, seven, ten, fifteen, and eighteen) spoken by an expert cleric who is, belatedly, identified as Jesus Himself.[21]

The dialogue spoken by the clerical Jesus supplements the conversation between the supplicant and intimate Jesus by framing seemingly individual anxieties as definitions of the human condition. The supplicant's desire for direct experience of God, her first-person longing for divine presence in place of her human loneliness and corruption is initially answered by the expert, clerical figure in the fifth chapter; it is only after this that her concerns are taken up by the intimate Jesus a few chapters later. Rather than reassuring the supplicant that she is worthy, the speaker in chapter five underscores the supplicant's lack of worth: "If thou haddest the puryte of aungels, and the holynes of saynt John Baptyst, thou shuldest nat be worthy to receyue / or trete of that holye sacrament" (267). He generalizes the unworthiness that the supplicant presented as individualized and personal and in doing so replaces conversation with doctrine. Following this impulse, the expert, clerical speaker then proceeds to identify the wonder of God's mercy with the "dygnyte of prestes" (267).

The clerical speaker answers the supplicant's worried queries, but he does so

---

21. The only way we know that the expert clerical figure is Jesus is because, forty or so lines into the seventh chapter, He refers to himself as "me" in a context in which His divine status is unmistakeable: the reader, He says, should amend herself by "offre[ing] thy selfe with plaine resignacion and entier wyll to the honoure of *my name* [ital. added]," *Imitation,* 269. This expert, clerical speaker had been introduced in chapter five.

by employing the voice of a preacher to the clergy: his responses are framed as institutional advice to institutional representatives. In the *Imitation,* Jesus can be *imagined* as speaking directly to the anxious supplicant, but that imagining seems to require mediation and explication that can best be understood in the language of a priest. The intimate Jesus is drowned out by the expert voice of the priest. This occurs even in the set speeches in which Jesus is primarily intimate. In the passage about "oblation of self," for example, Jesus concludes his comments by returning to scripture: "none may be my disciple without he renounceth all that he hath."[22] Biblical authority is reinforced by clerical expertise, and the language of personal obligation that Jesus uses when He speaks in His intimate voice is supplemented by universal doctrine. The last chapters of the book, thirteen through eighteen, continue to incorporate the supplicant's intimate longings but replace the personal Jesus with the clerical figure. The voice of the expert who relies on admonition—the chapters are littered with "behooves" and "oughts"—dominates the dialogue.

The effect of this reliance on the clerical speaker is to return the supplicant to the loneliness of her own voice. The clerical voice may offer comfort through its explicit didacticism and promises of success if proper techniques are applied, but it does this by seemingly distancing the supplicant from the private relationship that she desires. The final chapter's heading sums this up neatly: the supplicant is urged not to be too "curious" about the sacrament and instead to be a "meke follower of crist iesu" by submitting her "reason & felynge to the holy feyth" (282). Although the reader of the *Imitation of Christ* is, of course, free to identify with any, all, or none of the speakers in the dialogue, the text's increasing emphasis on institutional voices of authority works to direct the reader in a specific manner.[23] Discipline replaces emotional investment, ultimately, in the *Imitation,* and it is trust in the voice of the clergy that the treatise insists will see the supplicant through her longings for Jesus' presence.[24]

---

22. *Imitation,* 270. Jesus' words come from Luke 14:33.

23. This is only true, of course, if the work is read as a whole and in the order of its presentation. The reader may find herself aligned with the clerical Jesus and the newly minted priest, or she may not. She may understand herself most completely in relation to the voice of the lonely, desperate supplicant, or she may align herself with the "abusive" Jesus. She might find herself unsatisfied with a representation of faith as a negation of self and choose to concentrate on the advocacy of active, institutionally sanctioned practice found in the final chapters of the book and spoken by the clerical Jesus. There need not be any consistent identification with a single voice, and the treatise can be read in different ways at different times. This holds true of any written work, but it is particularly significant when multiple voices are represented since such representation invites readers to imagine themselves inhabiting the speakers' voices.

24. The text understands the direct experience of Jesus' presence as impossible in this lifetime: the supplicant says, "For all thynges that I here / or see in this worlde, I compte as no thynge so longe as I se nat my lorde god in his glorye. Lorde God, thou arte my wytnes that nothynge can gyue vnto me comforte, nor no creature may gyue vnto me rest, but thou, my lorde god, whom I desyre eternally to beholde. But that is a thynge to me not possible / whyle that I am in this mortall lyfe," *Imitation,* 274.

Yet, even as the book reinforces the speaker's isolation, it offers the reader a new language of community that implicitly replaces the imagined intimacy of the divine voice. This comes in part via identification of the supplicant herself as a priest. Taking the reader quite by surprise, Jesus-the-cleric in chapter five says to the supplicant, "Beholde nowe thou arte made a preste / and sacreyd to doo this holye mysterye" (267). This identification might seem to exclude readers who are in fact *not* priests. However, the looseness of the identification—the fact that it is only clearly made in two passages and might easily be missed—and the subsequent popularity of the book with lay readers suggests that this identification was not conceived of as exclusionary.[25] Rather, it seems to have functioned in a broad, inclusive manner, much as the phrase "priesthood of believers" is understood to encompass the laity and the clergy.[26]

More importantly, the *Imitation* encourages readers of book four to experience the loss of self demanded by Jesus in chapters eight and twelve as an invitation to exchange personal anxiety for the surety of membership in the institutional Church. One way to think about the *Imitation* is to see the author as inventing a Jesus who speaks like a priest to priests, but another is to see him as a writer who teaches readers a new way of talking with God through institutional practices. The intimate dialogue between Jesus and the supplicant is represented as understandable, human, and for overly excited *beginners* whom, as Jesus puts it in the last chapter, may be "dysceyued" if they rely on their own feelings too much (283).

Rather, the *Imitation* suggests, the supplicant needs to stop worrying about her individual experience and feelings of isolation and follow the Church's teachings: the book's reader/newly-minted-priest is introduced to a different way of understanding her isolation when the clerical Jesus offers religious practice as the solution to her problems. Jesus tells her that she needs to "do after the councell of the wyse" and "take away this anxyete & stryple" by following the traditions of the Church. She should receive the sacrament, confess her sins, and keep "the comon maner" with those people that she "lyuest amonge"; she should do this rather than having "to great solycytude for deuocyon" (272–73). Instead of thinking of her "owne deuocyon or pryuate pleasure" (273) she is encouraged to

---

25. The supplicant refers to herself as "we which haue taken the offyce of presthode" in chapter eleven.
26. 1 Peter 2:9. The idea was popular with dissident groups: see, for example, Hawisia Moon's testimony in *Heresy Trials in the Diocese of Norwich, 1428–1431*, ed. Norman P. Tanner, Camden Society, ser. 4, vol. 20 (London: Office of the Royal Historical Society, 1977) and my discussion of that testimony in which she declares that every believer is a "very pope" in *Reading Families*, esp. 135–36. Claire Water's discussion of the idea of "shared speech" in which preachers are both "a group with special access to instructive speech" and "participants in a conversation that requires them to understand that speech in a cooperative rather than a hierarchical mode" is useful in this regard: see *Angels and Earthly Creatures: Preaching, Performance, and Gender in the Later Middle Ages* (Philadelphia: University of Pennsylvania Press, 2004), 71.

follow the example of saints, to read "holy bokes," and to observe the sacrament of holy communion (274–75).

The fourth book of the *Imitation* offers the reader multiple positions from which to reimagine her spiritual state. The supplicant/reader is engaged in an imaginative performance of Jesus' words: as she speaks, she recites Jesus' words from scripture, enacts Jesus' imagined words to her as spoken by the clerical and intimate incarnations, and mimics His clerical authority. For all the seriousness of the *Imitation,* there is a playful quality to the dialogues. The various subject positions are provided as heuristic devices or experiments that the reader can engage with imaginatively as she considers her emotional condition and its relationship to her spiritual life. Aside from Jesus' words from scripture, the book never suggests that these words are actually those of Jesus in any historical sense. This play-acting in the *Imitation* contrasts sharply with the presentation of dialogue in Margery Kempe's early-fifteenth-century *Book,* the final text under consideration, in which the author insists on the veracity of recorded conversations with Jesus.

THE BOOK OF MARGERY KEMPE

Despite the fact that they are not framed in relation to oralization, current arguments about authorship and Margery Kempe's *Book* are largely about the voice of the author, the person who we hear as we read the *Book.*[27] Modern critics tend to want to hear Margery's voice. Some are anxious to make sure we recognize this voice as fragmented by social conditions, to be certain that we understand her position as sole author as fictional.[28] Others want to argue for the serious, intellectual work that this woman writer did and to find how her voice differs from the voice of others.[29]

---

27. On oralization, that is, "recourse to speech, actual or imagined" as "an essential part of our ability to read texts" (89) see anthropologist Johannes Fabian, "Keep Listening: Ethnography and Reading" in *The Ethnography of Reading,* ed. Jonathan Boyarin (Berkeley: University of California Press, 1993), 80–97.

28. Contemporary critics have shown a great deal of interest in this subject. See, for example, Leonard Lawlor "The Beginnings of Thought: The Fundamental Experience in Derrida and Deleuze," in *Between Deleuze and Derrida,* eds. Paul Patton and John Protevi (London: Continuum, 2003), 67–83. Lawlor discusses "univocality" versus "equivocality": "Inside myself when I speak to myself, I make no actual vocalisation. . . . In this experience, according to Derrida, I must hear myself speak at the very moment I speak. It is the same me speaking as hearing. Univocal. Yet, given that I am not the one speaking when I am the one hearing and vice versa, it is not the same me speaking as hearing; equivocal. Because there is always a retention inseparable from the now, from the very moment in which I am hearing, there is always an other in me, in the same, speaking to me," 79.

29. Nicholas Watson and Felicity Riddy play out this argument in their essays about Margery Kempe in *Voices in Dialogue: Reading Women in the Middle Ages* (Notre Dame, IN: University of Notre Dame Press, 2005), 395–458. Riddy's response to Watson outlines their disagreement, at least in part: "I

Modern scholars want to hear Margery's voice because that is what we are missing. We do not have access to her, we cannot hear her in the ways, for instance, her scribes could. For them, Margery's voice was not mysterious, not lost. It was the voice the scribes heard (as they read the *Book*, as they wrote the *Book*), at least when they did not hear their own voices. In contrast, the voice that medieval readers (the scribes and the later, anonymous readers) of the *Book* were missing, the one that they were unable to hear, was God's. God is "hid," as the *Book* explains in several instances.[30] The attentive reader is encouraged to pay attention to "signs" of God's presence. Reading (of this *Book*, of other books) is offered as one means of experiencing God intimately, directly, aurally.

Dismay over God's hiddenness is a condition shared by Margery, her scribes, and the medieval readers of her *Book*. It is the starting point of her book's compilation and, narratively, of Margery's redemption. In the *Book*, she is represented as believing that God has deserted her. She, in turn, "forsakes" Him and experiences a psychological breakdown. When Jesus appears and speaks to her in the *Book*'s first chapter He assures her that He has not left her, despite her feelings about the matter. Jesus asks: "'Dowtyr, why hast thow forsakyn me, and I forsoke nevyr the?'" (23). His question makes Him present for Margery, and the direct speech allows readers to see Him as "re-presented" each time the passage is read.

Margery's anxious feelings are mirrored by those that the prologue describes as motivating the *Book*'s readers. Here, the scribe represents the *Book*'s audience as miserable: it is composed of "synful wrecchys" who are in desperate need of "solas and comfort" (17). They have, like Margery, deserted God and forgotten that Jesus actively intervenes in their lives "now in ower days" (17). This inclusive "our" makes it clear that the scribe counts himself among the "unworthy" in whose lives Jesus, despite that unworthiness, "deyneth to exercysen hys nobeley and hys goodnesse" (17). The aim of the *Book* is to provide its readers with examples of God's "wonderful werkys" (17) as evidence of His active and immediate participation in the readers' lives.

It is, according to the prologue, through the "forme of her levyngs" that God's "goodnesse myth be knowyn to alle the world" (19). The *Book*, then, takes the form of Margery's experience, which it identifies as both the pattern of repeated

---

cannot accept the simple dictation model—she speaks, he writes—because the syntax is obviously not that of speech, and so it must have gone through a process of modification. We cannot know what role the priest played in composition or whose language we are reading: with Foucault, I believe that 'Who is the author?' is not the important question," 457. On the *Book*'s embrace of phonocentrism, Derrida's term for the privileging of voice over writing, see Diana R. Uhlman, "The Comfort of Voice, the Solace of Script: Orality and Literacy in the *Book of Margery Kempe*," *Studies in Philology* 91 (1994): 50–69.

30. *The Book of Margery Kempe*, ed. Lynn Staley, TEAMS Middle English Texts (Kalamazoo, MI: Medieval Institute Publications, 1996), 194. Subsequent references are noted parenthetically. God Himself reminds Margery in this passage that He is a "hyd God" and that she should, therefore, be "the mor besy" to search for Him.

upheavals and restorations, and the articulation of that pattern as the basis for understanding what the life can teach its readers about God's mercy. It is explicitly in the *shape* of experience that, according to the prologue, readers can find God; here we see one of the *Book*'s central concerns. Margery, of course, has a privileged position; she can see and hear God, as she does in the passage in the first chapter. Although the reader does not have this gift, she can, nonetheless, experience God's presence through the *Book*'s words.

The voices of Margery Kempe's *Book* (hers, the scribes', God's, Jesus', those of the saints, those of her neighbors, even those of her enemies) become expressions of God's voice. For the believer desperate to find the hidden God, the *Book* offers the promise of consolation via reading, and it does so by promising to exchange temporal, human voices (the reader's own, the scribes', Margery's) for the sound of eternal significance. Margery Kempe's earthly voice, for the medieval reader eager to find God, becomes one among many important ways to hear the divine.

This might explain why her voice nearly disappears from the text when the printer Wynkyn de Worde takes hold of the *Book* and prints his abstract, the "shorte treatyse of contemplacyon taught by our Lorde Jhesu Cryste, or taken out of the boke of Margerie Kempe of Lynn" (STC 14924) seventy-five or so years later. De Worde's treatise leans heavily on the proverbial and emphasizes the catechism-like sound of some of Jesus and Margery's conversations. It replaces the sound of singular voices with what look, to modern audiences, like platitudes ("Pacyence is more worthe than myracles-doyng," for example). One way to understand this is to see it as squeezing the life out of Margery; another, though, is to read it as part of the same cultural movement that made proverbial wisdom so appealing to late-medieval readers.[31]

The medieval readers of Margery Kempe's *Book,* like Margery herself, were offered the experience of *hearing* as the best way to escape from their own isolation. Margery's descent into madness, the consequence of not having a chance to speak as the priest hurried her through confession ("And, whan sche cam to the poynt for to seyn that thing whech sche had so long conselyd, hir confessowr was a lytyl to hastye . . . so sche wold no more seyn" [22]), is, ultimately, not about a failure to speak but a failure to hear. Singular human voices block out the hidden voice. The sound of her own voice, the sound of voices that drowned out God's (like the man who says he will seduce her and leaves Margery incapable of hearing divine service: she was "so labowrd wyth the mannys wordys that sche mygth not heryn hir evynsong, ne sey hir Pater Noster, er thynkyn ony other good thowt"

---

31. On de Worde's treatise see Elizabeth Schirmer, "Orthodoxy, Textuality, and the 'Tretys' of Margery Kempe," *Journal X: A Journal of Criticism and Culture* 1 (1996): 31–55 and Rebecca Schoff, "Editing the Books of Margery Kempe," in *Reformations: Three Medieval Authors in Manuscript and Movable Type* (Turnhout, Belgium: Brepols, 2007), 91–140. De Worde printed the treatise in 1501.

[29]) are shown to be the source of her desolation. It is when Margery learns to listen that she is redeemed.

First, Margery has to learn to hear God's promises as they apply to particular situations in her life. Many of Jesus' words in the *Book* are guarantees made to Margery exclusively or prompts in which Jesus tells Margery to offer a third person particular information. The level of specificity in these instances make the encounters seem lifelike, much as Henry Suso maintained in his discussion of the use of multiple characters. For example, as Margery makes her way to Venice after her pilgrimage to the Holy Land, the *Book* mentions that many of her fellow travelers had fallen sick. Jesus reassures Margery by promising that everyone in her ship would survive the journey: "Drede the not, dowtyr, ther schal no man deyin in the schip that thu art in" (82). This guarantee is for Margery who, the *Book* notes, "fond hir felyngys ryth trewe" (82). A few lines further in this chapter, Jesus speaks to her again, telling Margery, "Drede the not, dowtyr, for I schal ordeyn for the ryth well and bryng the in safté to Rome and hom ageyn into Inglond" (82) as long as she follows his command to put on white clothing.[32]

Similarly, passages in which Jesus prompts Margery by providing answers to the questions of a third party are explicitly situational and intended for Margery's ears alone.[33] Yet even in their specificity, these conversations between Margery and Jesus are used to teach the reader how to listen. Margery's worries about the weather and sickness, as mundane as they might seem, are important because they illustrate a habit of attention that is offered as a model for readers. If Margery listens, Jesus answers.

These conversations in which Jesus offers Margery specific assurance about specific issues, as important as they are to Margery, differ from those in which Jesus and Margery talk over ideas about assurance that stretch beyond the immediate moment and help Margery imagine her future. These dialogues offer Margery and her *Book*'s readers methodological advice about conducting their spiritual lives. Striking examples of this occur in two episodes in which Jesus helps Margery overcome the sense of worthlessness that she feels arises from her physical condition. In the first, she has just discovered she is pregnant again and she feels because of her sexual activity with her husband that she does

---

32. Instances of this sort are too frequent to catalogue here; Book I, chapter twenty-three, for example, includes four such promises in fifty or so lines.

33. For example, when a monk asks her whether he will be saved or not and what kinds of sins he has committed, Jesus tells Margery, "My derworthy dowtyr, sey in the name of Jhesu that he hath synned in letthery, in dyspeyr, and in worldly goodys kepyng" (39–40). The reader in this instance and the others like it is asked to admire an exchange that resembles a magic trick in which the "invisible" Jesus provides Margery with answers that would not be available to her under normal circumstances. Further examples of Jesus' verbal prompting of Margery include the instances when Margery sues Bishop of Lincoln Philip Repingdon for permission to take the vow and assume the habit of married chastity (I, chapter fifteen); when she is involved in a tangled encounter with a widow (I, chapter eighteen); and when a vicar comes to her looking for answers about his career (I, chapter twenty-three).

not deserve "to heryn" Jesus "spekyn" (59). Jesus explains to her that his love extends to "wyfes" as well as holy maidens and that he "take[s] non hede what a man hath ben" but, rather, "take[s] hede what he wyl ben" (59).

In the second, Jesus explains to Margery that believers need different things at different times in their lives. Those who are early in their spiritual journey are well advised to mortify their bodies by fasting or wearing hair shirts, but Margery, He explains, has advanced to the point in which her love for God allows her to please Him best through "thynkyng, wepyng, and hy contemplacyon."[34] She should feel confident in this, Jesus assures her, because He "take[s] non hed what thu has be but what thu woldist be" (94). In both passages, the emphasis on the future—to the point of using the same phrasing—gives Margery and the *Book*'s readers a sense of dynamic hopefulness. Rather than feeling trapped in the bodily present, readers of the passages are taught to imagine themselves as perfected in the future and told by Jesus Himself that this is how He sees them.[35]

Readers of the *Book*, despite their obvious differences from Margery, are encouraged, nonetheless, to identify with Margery's ability to hear and converse with Jesus. This is done by making Margery's experience of Jesus' voice more like that of her readers. Both passages above take the form of give-and-take dialogue between Jesus and Margery and yet both, unexpectedly, insist that this dialogue is not conducted aloud but is, rather, a silent affair in which "owyr Lord spak onto hir sowle" (59). In chapter twenty-one, the internal nature of the conversation is revealed only at the close of the passage. Chapter thirty-six, in contrast, carefully frames the dialogue as part of God's practice of speaking silently to Margery: the previous chapter asserts that external signs of grace such as sounds, melodies, and repeated episodes in which she saw white objects flying through the air are all "tokens" that prove that "God . . . spekyth in the" (93). According to these chapters of the *Book*, outer signs point to the importance of soul over body. The soul's eternal nature is a guarantee that feelings of desperation tied to bodiliness are transitory and ultimately insignificant. Jesus tells Margery that she should feel secure in His love because "God schal nevyr partyn fro thi sowle" since God and her soul are "onyd togedyr wythowtyn ende" (93).

The *Book*'s emphasis on the interior nature of many of Margery's conversations with Jesus effectively reinforces the sense that readers can, like Margery, listen to God's voice. After an episode in which Margery first doubts that she hears God internally and God, to teach her a lesson, "drow fro hir alle good thowtys and alle good mendys of holy spechys and dalyawns and the hy contemplacyon" (142), Margery learns in short space to trust that God speaks to her. She

---

34. *Book*, 94. The passage uses literal vocabulary of the "marriage bed" to describe the relationship.

35. I discuss this idea in relation to the generic nature of the *Book* as a "treatise": see "Margery Kempe," in *The Cambridge Companion to Medieval English Literature*, ed. Larry Scanlon (Cambridge: Cambridge University Press, 2009).

concludes "I schal belevyn that every good thowt is the speche of God" (143).[36] The *Book*'s embrace of thinking as listening encourages the reader to imagine the possibility of conversation with Jesus. If thinking is listening, and responding in one's mind to thoughts is talking, then even readers who do not receive the unusual gifts that Margery is granted—such as hearing Jesus speak aloud—are able to engage in dialogue with Jesus.

Although the *Fifteen Oes,* the *Imitation,* and Margery Kempe's *Book* differ in their representations of Jesus' voice, all three are fascinated by the ways that treating written language as speech helps believers find divine presence. The liveliness of dialogue is not just a description of the animated presences in the text but, instead, an effect of the reading experience: the reader herself is enlivened by the experience of reading dialogue. What is perhaps most interesting about this sense of the power of spoken language is the way that all three works imagine speaking as interior and aural—silent—and not simply sound-based. This helps to solve one of the main problems with the entirely orthodox idea that Jesus, who is both dead and alive, speaks to believers. Although the promise that Jesus speaks can be understood as metaphorical, late-medieval audiences appear to have preferred a Jesus who actually spoke, even when that speaker was silent.

All three texts empower readers to speak with Jesus. Why, then, if this kind of dialogue was especially appealing to fifteenth-century readers and continued to attract sixteenth-century readers, does Margery Kempe's *Book* disappear, only to be replaced by the proverbial and impersonal statements in de Worde's printed extract, while *The Fifteen Oes* and *The Imitation of Christ* continue to be read widely?[37] It is of course possible to ascribe the *Book*'s fate to accidental causes: perhaps it was simply set aside and unnoticed for hundreds of years. But it seems equally likely, given a consideration of the differences between the *Book* and the other two works, that it vanished because it was no longer the kind of book readers wanted despite its representation of a speaking Jesus. Although there are many differences between the *Book* and the other works, the main one, at least in relation to my argument about dialogue, is its insistence on the veracity of the conversations recorded. As I point out in my discussion of silent reading, the *Book* encourages its audience to understand all "good thowtys" as words spoken by Jesus, thus diffusing the sense that readers are attending to and responding to specific strings of language produced by the divine. Nonetheless, it also insists

---

36. In one of the strangest passages in the *Book,* Margery must experience twelve days of of "horybyl syghtys" including the "beheldyng of mennys membrys" because she has doubted that it was God who told her that all people will not be saved. Margery finds these visions of men's penises "delectabyl" in spite of her desire not to feel this way and nearly falls into despair. Before this happens, an angel comes and explains the situation to her (I, chapter fifty-four).

37. For a discussion of the very few late-fifteenth- and early-sixteenth-century readers of the *Book* with whom we are familiar (from marginal commentary) see Karma Lochrie, *Margery Kempe and the Translations of the Flesh* (Philadelphia: University of Pennsylvania Press, 1991), 206–28.

on the historical, factual accuracy of Jesus' words to Margery. In contrast, *The Fifteen Oes* makes Jesus' words transhistorical but personally meaningful and *The Imitation of Christ* labels them, ultimately, as personally and institutionally significant but fictional.

The difference, then, is in veracity versus literariness. The pressing, personal, and literal dialogue of the *Book*, even when it makes allowances for readers who cannot hear Jesus' voice directly, seems to have lost its appeal for sixteenth-century readers. This may have been because the personal identification with one's own books that I described at the opening of this essay as a characteristic of the late fifteenth century had, in fact, become so entrenched by the sixteenth century that readers did not want to imagine their own responses through Margery's. Rather, the conservative and disciplinarily driven speech of Jesus in *The Fifteen Oes* and *The Imitation of Christ* appealed to later readers not because it was less "affective" or less "superstitious" than Jesus' speech in the *Book*, but because it allowed sixteenth-century readers to do away with the necessity of seeing the world through another person's eyes. Like lyric poetry in which first-person speakers claim universality, the speakers in *The Fifteen Oes* and *The Imitation of Christ,* unlike Margery Kempe, allow readers to hear themselves in direct conversation with Jesus.

part 3

REFORMING SKELTON

6

Conception Is a Blessing

Marian Devotion, Heresy, and the Literary in Skelton's *A Replycacion*

ROBERT J. MEYER-LEE[1]

What discursive quality, if any, categorically distinguishes literary from other uses of language? This question has been, somewhat ironically, a perennial one of literary theory from Plato to the present. Faced with the sheer number and variety of possible answers, one may be tempted simply to declare the question irrelevant and insist, along with Terry Eagleton, "There is no 'essence' of literature whatsoever. . . . Anything can be literature, and anything which is regarded as unalterably and unquestionably literature . . . can cease to be literature."[2] Yet such critical agnosticism, historically perspicacious as it may be, leaves in place the long history of authors claiming some special quality for their writing. Such claims, in part, are intrinsic to the phenomenon of a literary tradition—reflecting, for example, authors' attempts to co-opt their precursors' authority—but they also arise out of specific historical circumstances and thus have particular cultural and political implications, among others. A disbelief in the literary as something "eternally given and immutable" should therefore not discourage us from paying close attention to what Stephen Greenblatt has described as "the status of the literary, its position in shifting and contested

---

1. In addition to those individuals mentioned below who offered assistance on particular points, I thank Steven Justice for his encouraging response to the initial version of this paper, presented at Kalamazoo in 2007, and to the editors of this volume for including me in that session and for all their subsequent help.
2. Terry Eagleton, *Literary Theory: An Introduction,* 2nd ed. (Minneapolis: University of Minnesota Press, 1996), 8–9.

133

cultural systems"—attention to how, that is, distinct versions of the literary arise and the uses to which these are put within specific historical contexts.³ Greenblatt writes further that "literary history is always the history of the possibility of literature," and here I take this to imply that authors' articulations of this possibility, especially when these articulations are self-exemplifying, form a special sort of historical evidence, along with the contingencies that enable them and the effects they incur.⁴

How and why an articulation of the "possibility of literature" emerges among "shifting and contested cultural systems" in John Skelton's *A Replycacion against Certayne Yong Scolers Abjured of Late* is the principal topic of this chapter. Skelton's remarkably grandiose claims for the literary in this poem, I argue, take their peculiar shape in response to a synchronic political history and a diachronic literary one: respectively, the poem's immediate polemical purposes recorded in its title, and a specific tradition of English poetry in which the literary was deployed for analogous purposes in a similar fashion. This latter literary and diachronic history recognizes that one of the innovations of fifteenth-century English poets—as their critical recuperation over the last two decades has emphasized—is their explicit celebrations of a vernacular literary per se, an idea that appears more inchoately and with less confidence in the productions of Ricardian poets, but which in the fifteenth century emerges as a signal feature of proto-high-culture English verse.⁵

For a consideration of Skelton's *A Replycacion*—which almost certainly appeared in 1528, shortly before the poet's death in 1529—the most pertinent precursor text is John Lydgate's *Life of Our Lady*, which cannot be dated with confidence but was most likely composed sometime between 1409 and 1422.⁶ Elsewhere, in the companion piece to this present chapter, I have argued at some length that Lydgate's poem articulates a vernacular literary as a potential sacral power wielded by an authoritative English poet in respect to Mariology and the threat of heresy; it is a power marshaled in defense of both Lydgate's own and his religious order's relation to the crown and alternative orthodox vernacular theologies.⁷ To substantiate the diachronic element of my claims here, in the following

---

3. Eagleton, *Literary Theory*, 9; Stephen Greenblatt, "What is the History of Literature," *Critical Inquiry* 23 (1997): 460–81, at 475.

4. Greenblatt, "What is the History," 470.

5. This point was well established by Lois A. Ebin, *Illuminator, Makar, Vates: Visions of Poetry in the Fifteenth Century* (Lincoln: University of Nebraska Press, 1988), and has since become a critical commonplace within the resurgence of interest in fifteenth-century English poetry.

6. The date has been the topic of some dispute. See Derek Pearsall, *John Lydgate (1371–1449): A Bio-bibliography* (Victoria: University of Victoria, 1997), 19–20, for discussion.

7. See Robert J. Meyer-Lee, "The Emergence of the Literary in John Lydgate's *Life of Our Lady*," *JEGP* 109.3 (2010): 322–48, which also contains, as its conclusion, a brief preview of this present chapter on Skelton. I thank the University of Illinois Press for permission to incorporate portions of this article.

first section I reproduce the most germane details of this argument. In the second and principal section, I argue that Skelton's *A Replycacion*, despite its many differences from the *Life of Our Lady,* offers a very similar (if grandly inflated) articulation of the literary; and yet, at the same time, the manifest instrumentality of *A Replycacion* siphons off the sacral aura upon which its claims for the literary depend. Skelton's final poem, I suggest in my conclusion, marks the boundary of a characteristically fifteenth-century articulation of the literary, signifying one of the ways that we might say that the "long fifteenth century," as a distinct literary culture, ends.

To set the bearings of this trajectory, let us first consider a passage from the third part of *A Replycacion:*

> Ye saye that poetry
> May nat flye so hye
> In theology,
> Nor analogy,
> Nor philology,
> Nor philosophy,
> To answere or reply,
> Agaynst suche heresy. (306–13)[8]

These exuberant Skeltonics immediately suggest three things about the notion of the literary that this poem articulates. First (as conventional New Historical wisdom would hold) the literary is not entirely distinct from other learned discourses, since Skelton depicts "poetry" here as a discursive weapon that flies in, or depends upon, these other discourses to achieve an instrumental (that is, not solely aesthetic) aim—"To answere or reply, / Agaynst suche heresy."[9] Second, the literary is nonetheless enough distinct from these other discourses that the image of it flying in them makes sense. Third, in this passage's ventriloquism of its opponents, Skelton is plainly asserting the opposite view—namely, that poetry is somehow specially equipped to reach the intellectual and epistemological heights of a variety of discourses, and that this unique quality makes it the most effective weapon to combat heresy. The basis for Skelton's assertion, what conditions its appearance in this poem, and what it represents for fifteenth-century

---

8. All quotations of *A Replycacion* and translations of its Latin, except where otherwise indicated, are from *John Skelton: The Complete English Poems,* ed. John Scattergood (Harmondsworth: Penguin Books, 1983), and cited in the text by line number. (The edition henceforth cited as *English Poems.*)

9. See, for example, Louis Montrose, "Renaissance Literary Studies and the Subject of History," *English Literary Renaissance* 16 (1986): 5–12, who claims that "during the sixteenth and seventeenth centuries, the separation of 'Literature' and 'Art' from explicitly didactic and political discourses or from such disciplines as history or moral and natural philosophy was as yet incipient" (12).

articulations of the literary are the topics on which I will focus, after reviewing what may be the first appearance in English verse of a similar assertion, in Lydgate's *Life of Our Lady.*

1. GOLD DEW: LYDGATE'S *LIFE OF OUR LADY*

The best-known lines in Lydgate's ambitious, six-book, 5,932-line mixture of Marian adoration, instruction, and narrative are doubtless the ones he directs not at the Virgin but at his recently deceased poetic forebear:

> And eke my maister Chauser is ygrave,
> The noble Rethor, poete of Brytayne,
> That worthy was the laurer to haue
> Of poetrye, and the palme atteyne;
> That made firste to distille and rayne
> The golde dewe dropes of speche and eloquence
> Into our tunge thurgh his excellence,
>
> And fonde the floures firste of Retoryke,
> Our Rude speche only to enlumyne;
> That in our tunge, was neuere noon hym like. (2.1628–37)[10]

It has often been observed that these and similar lines in Lydgate's corpus are singularly focused on Chaucer's rhetorical accomplishments, to the exclusion of all other qualities.[11] Many reasons have been offered for the narrowness of Lydgate's praise, one of the most persuasive being that he celebrates his predecessor for precisely the stylistic tendencies that most characterize his own writing—the excessive rhetorical ornamentation and Latinate diction that he collectively terms *aureate.*[12] And, in so doing, he calls attention to those tendencies as they are exemplified in this very passage. Hence with this paean to Chaucer Lydgate claims—like Skelton more directly does in *A Replycacion*—that his own

---

10. All quotations are from *A Critical Edition of John Lydgate's Life of Our Lady,* ed. Joseph A. Lauritis, Ralph A. Klinefelter, and Vernon F. Gallagher (Pittsburgh: Duquesne University, 1961) and cited in the text by book and line number. (The edition henceforth cited as *Critical Edition.*) I have added and modified punctuation, which is inconsistently given in the edition.

11. For example, Derek Pearsall, *John Lydgate* (London: Routledge & Kegan Paul, 1970), 65.

12. See, for example, Richard Firth Green, *Poets and Princepleasers: Literature and the English Court in the Late Middle Ages* (Toronto: University of Toronto Press, 1980), 178, and, in more depth, Ebin, *Illuminator,* 19–48. For a rich discussion of Lydgate's use of the term aureate (which he coined), see chapter 1 in Seth Lerer, *Chaucer and His Readers: Imagining the Author in Late-Medieval England* (Princeton: Princeton University Press, 1993), 22–56.

"poetrye," as reflexively exemplified by this passage's aureation, possesses a special discursive value. The very narrowness of his praise represents his attempt to delineate something like what we now call the literary and to provide for this discursive quality both a description and an illustration.

Why such a paean to Chaucer appears in this particular poem, however, and in the position it occupies, has been less explored.[13] Importantly, this digression appears at the emergence of the project of the poem's third book—which is to "make mencion / Of the feste and solempnyte / That called is the Incarnacion" (2.1615–17). Facing this prospect, Lydgate suddenly becomes aware of the passing of literary power out of the world, in the form of the "Retorykes swete / Of petrak Fraunces," "Tullyus," and, most crucially, Chaucer: those former masters of this power who are "dede alas and passed into faate" (2.1623–27). As Christopher Cannon and others have observed, this eulogistic lament for the dead, here and elsewhere in Lydgate's corpus, is a tacit but relatively obvious claim to poetic inheritance.[14] It is an assertion that some portion of a former age's "Retorykes swete" is reborn in the present and is in Lydgate's possession, as evidenced by the rhetorical polish of the very lines that follow, which as we have seen mournfully ascribe Lydgatean poetics to Chaucer, and conclude with the revealingly self-referential wish that Chaucer could "amende eke and corecte / the wronge traceȝ of [Lydgate's] rude penne" (2.1648–49). As the link to the matter of the third book, therefore, this articulation of the literary appears both in conjunction and in parallel with the key event not just in Mary's life but also in Christian history: the implied rebirth of the literary, in the figure of Lydgate, emerges alongside the birth of Christ.

Yet, notably, Lydgate does not position this paean to Chaucer in book three itself but at the end of book two, which is concerned, above all, with Mary's conception of Christ and the scrutiny and doubt leveled at that conception's virginal status and divine origin. In this regard, Lydgate's petition for divine assistance earlier in book two takes a revealing form:

So late thy grace to me discende a downe

My rude tonge to exployte and spede
Som what to saye, in commendacion
Of hir that is well of womanhede. (2.435–38)

---

13. Indeed, while the *Life of Our Lady* has received some penetrating analyses, studies of the poem are relatively few. Among recent work, my interests most resemble those of Nancy Bradley Warren, *Spiritual Economies: Female Monasticism in Later Medieval England* (Philadelphia: University of Pennsylvania Press, 2001), 137–47, and Katherine K. O'Sullivan, "John Lydgate's *Lyf of Our Lady*: Translation and Authority in Fifteenth-Century England," *Mediaevalia* 226 (2005): 169–201.

14. Christopher Cannon, *The Making of Chaucer's English: A Study of Words* (Cambridge: Cambridge University Press, 1998), 185.

In the figurative positioning of himself that this petition realizes, Lydgate clearly implies that, inasmuch as God's grace has descended into Mary's womb, Lydgate's petition has been answered, and grace has likewise descended "a downe" into him, bestowing upon him the ability to celebrate and defend precisely this divine conception. The book's ensuing long narration of the doubts regarding Mary's pregnancy and the heaven-sent confirmations of its divinity are thus, at the same time, arguments for the divine origin and authority of Lydgate's poem.

Furthermore, the "daring parallel between the poet and Mary herself" that Philippa Hardman has observed in regard to this passage, and that in fact pervades the entire work, helps determine the later singular focus on style in the celebration of Chaucer.[15] In the equivalence between the impregnating and inspiring powers of the Holy Spirit, and between the respective receivers of these powers, Mary and Lydgate, what corresponds to the product of Mary's conception must be the *Life of Our Lady* itself. This equivalence is evident as early as the opening invocation of book one:

> So late the golde dewe of thy grace fall
> Into my breste, like skales fayre and white,
> Me to enspyre of that I wolde endyte,
> With thylke bame, sent downe by miracle,
> Whan the hooly goost the made his habitacle;
>
> And the licour of thy grace shede
> Into my penne, t'enlumyne this dite[.] (1.52–58)

Here, Lydgate requests from the heavenly Mary that same "bame" that impregnated her on earth in order to "enlumyne" the "dite" that is the poem at hand (in the process transforming this seminal trope into the more gender-appropriate figure of the illuminating ink of his "penne"). And this term *enlumyne,* along with the metaphoric description of Mary's "grace" as "golde dewe," brings us back to Lydgate's later focus on style in the Chaucer eulogy.[16] As we have seen, Lydgate reuses both of these terms in that encomium of style, and this further elaborates the analogy between the *Life of Our Lady* and the outcome of Mary's conception. Like Christ, Lydgate's poem possesses a compound nature: like Mary's contribution of the flesh of Christ's body,[17] Lydgate contributes the matter of the poem,

---

15. Phillipa Hardman, "Lydgate's *Life of Our Lady:* A Text in Transition," *Medium Aevum* 65 (1996): 248–68, at 250. See also Warren, *Spiritual Economies,* 143.
16. For the importance of the term *enlumyne* for Lydgate, see Ebin, *Illuminator,* 20–24.
17. For this theological point, see, e.g., Thomas Aquinas, *Summa Theologiae,* vol. 52, trans. Roland Potter (Manchester: Blackfriars, 1972), 3a. 31, 4 (p. 21).

but, like Christ's possession of eternal divinity, the poem possesses a quality divinely bestowed upon its mortal author, the "grace" that was "shede" into his "penne," which is evident in—that is, signified by—the illumined, "golde dew dropes of speche and eloquence" that are the manifestations of discursive grace.

In this light, we can understand Lydgate's positioning of the Chaucer eulogy at the narrative juncture between conception and incarnation as the metonymic hinge that firmly establishes the analogy between Holy Spirit/Mary/Christ and poetic inspiration/Lydgate/poem, at the very moment in the unfolding of that analogy when its third and greatest claim, the equation of Christ with the poem, is about to occur. Lydgate's strategy with this eulogy, as the above quotation of the first ten of its twenty-eight lines indicates, is to dwell obsessively on the fact of Chaucer's death and simultaneously to proclaim his perfection. In effect, Lydgate figures his precursor as a saint, in which role Chaucer approaches (and therefore stands metonymically alongside) the divine agency of Mary, the mediator par excellence between human and divine.[18] In the logic of the culminating passage of the first two books of the *Life of Our Lady*, Lydgate thus associates with himself both Mary's divine procreativity and her mediating agency: he becomes Mary inasmuch as he proves himself to be Chaucer's heir, and both the evidence for and outcome of this double (and hermaphroditic) self-elevation is the sacral and specifically literary quality to which the poem lays claim.

If this description is accurate, it raises the question of what might have motivated Lydgate, at this juncture in history, to produce such a long Marian devotion that is, at the same time, a defense of poetry—and, specifically, of poetry in the English vernacular. In respect to the first half of this question, one frequently cited clue for the rationale behind the poem qua devotional work is the introductory rubric that occurs, along with a list of chapter headings, in eleven of the forty-three more or less complete manuscripts:

> This booke was compilede by Iohn Lidgate Monke of Bury, at the excitacion and styyryng of our worshipfull prince, kyng Harry the fifthe, in the honour, glory, and worship of the byrthe of the moste glorious maide, wife, and modir of our lord Ihesus criste.[19]

The particular "excitacion and styyryng" of Henry V mentioned here, as Derek

---

18. As Carolyn P. Collette, *Performing Polity: Women and Agency in the Anglo-French Tradition, 1385–1620* (Turnhout: Brepols, 2006), puts it, the Virgin in late medieval Marian devotion is "a vates. . . . Because of who and what she is, her words have enough power to open the gates of salvation. . . . To invoke the Virgin is to mantel oneself with this power, to align oneself, insofar as humanly possible, with it" (91).

19. For this rubric, see *Critical Edition*, 240, and n. 1 on the same page for the list of manuscripts containing it.

Pearsall has speculated, may be his "desire to encourage quasi-liturgical English composition in the high style, and . . . his understanding that such writing struck at the claims of the Lollards to own the religious vernacular.[20] In the light of this possibility, it seems not merely coincidental that Lydgate drew heavily on the pseudo-Bonaventuran *Meditationes Vitae Christi* for the *Life of Our Lady* in the same period in which the Carthusian monk Nicholas Love's bluntly anti-Lollard English adaptation of the *Meditationes* was making its appearance.[21]

Unlike Love's *Mirror of the Blessed Life of Jesus Christ,* however, the *Life of Our Lady* does not explicitly position itself as an anti-Lollard text, never mentioning Lollards or Wyclif specifically. Nonetheless, its acknowledgment of some sort of royal interest, its thoroughgoing orthodoxy, and the fact that it, like the *Mirror,* offers its snapshots of scripture within an elaborate, exegetical framework that emphasizes officially sanctioned devotional practice, lend it, in the era of Arundel's Constitutions, a distinct ideological valence.[22] A comparison with Lydgate's *A Defence of Holy Church* suggests his modus operandi in this regard. This poem, which appears to be addressed to Henry V, is to most readers unambiguously anti-Lollard, even though Lydgate includes only a few lines about "sectys newe" (93) specifically; he hence appears to prefer indirect communication of his position on the topic rather than blunt engagement.[23] In this light, we thus have some justification for understanding the 289-line diatribe in the middle of book two of the *Life of Our Lady* (2.652–940)—which is addressed to a representative "blynde man" (2.652) who doubts the divinity of Mary's conception of Christ—as being more than a mere rhetorical device to usher in a list of learned analogies for the miracle. The culmination of this diatribe conveys enough genuine ferocity that the designation of these doubters as "heretykeȝ" (2.938) would seem to have an indirect, historically specific reference as well as a rhetorically general one.

To be sure, several recent studies have persuasively argued against seeing a Lollard hiding in every corner of early fifteenth-century orthodox religious writing, and some have emphasized instead, as Mishtooni Bose puts it in this present volume, more complex "interactions between Wycliffism and orthodox reform."[24] In addition, what would seem to make the association of "heretykeȝ"

---

20. Pearsall, *Bio-bibliography,* 19.
21. See *Nicholas Love's Mirror of the Blessed Life of Jesus Christ,* ed. Michael G. Sargent (New York: Garland Publishing, 1992). For the sources of the *Life of Our Lady,* see *Critical Edition,* 57–182.
22. O'Sullivan, "John Lydgate's *Lyf,*" closely compares Lydgate's effort to Love's and concludes that they shared aims in this regard.
23. For *A Defence,* see *John Lydgate: Poems,* ed. John Norton-Smith (Oxford: Clarendon Press, 1966), 30–34.
24. See p. 160. For reassessments of the influence of the official anti-Lollard program on late medieval English writing, see, e.g., Kathryn Kerby-Fulton, *Books under Suspicion: Censorship and Tolerance of Revelatory Writing in late Medieval England* (Notre Dame: University of Notre Dame Press, 2006), esp. 397–401, and Vincent Gillespie's forthcoming "Chichele's Church: Vernacular Theology after Thomas

with Lollards doubtful in this instance is that skepticism toward the virgin birth hardly characterizes their brand of heresy. But perhaps more at issue in this case is Wyclif's denigration of the mediating agency of saints, which also extended to Mary, as did later Lollard rejections of prayers to saints.[25] This denigration, if hardly responsible for the *Life of Our Lady* as a whole, may nonetheless have been a key catalyst for its particular expression of orthodoxy. Since Lydgate metonymically translates Mary's mediating agency into a sacral literary quality wielded by a sanctified Chaucer, inherited by himself, and manifest in aureate style, the heretical denial of this agency may well have helped prompt the project and also, through a key strategic displacement, this peculiar attack on the unnamed "heretyke3" that doubt the virgin birth.[26]

If we can thus claim with some confidence that the *Life of Our Lady* is a gospel meditation that, at some level of indirection, is ideologically freighted with anti-Lollard sentiment, we can also understand the second half of the question of its motivation, that pertaining to its defense of poetry, in this light. The introductory rubric's notably vague terms "excitacion and styyryng" suggest not so much direct patronage as some sort of less assured response to Henry, and, with this in mind, an assemblage of circumstantial evidence further suggests that an important part of Lydgate's aim in this work was to advertise the political usefulness of his Benedictine order in general and of himself as monastic poet in particular. Here, in lieu of presenting this evidence, I offer only the summary that, in the period spanning Henry's 1412 commissioning of Lydgate's *Troy Book* and the 5 May 1421 meeting on Benedictine reform that Henry personally initiated, Lydgate experienced a unique set of intersecting historical pressures: a climate of anxiety about heresy and rebellion, royal concern in regard to the Benedictines' value to the kingdom, royal favor shown to the more austere Carthusian order, the popularity and official sanction of Love's *Mirror* (reemphasized by a new French translation of the *Meditationes*), and Lydgate's need to consolidate his own role—figured so strikingly in the *Troy Book*—as Henry's unofficial poet laureate. If, as one of the editors of the critical edition of the *Life of Our Lady* argues, Lydgate completed this work at around the time of Henry's return to England in 1421, then we must understand the work's articulation of the literary in light of the complex combination of these pressures.[27]

Arundel." I thank Professor Gillespie for providing me a draft of his article.

25. See Anne Hudson, *The Premature Reformation: Wycliffite Texts and Lollard History* (Oxford: Clarendon Press, 1988), 311–13.

26. That this attack does indeed represent such a displacement finds support in the Latin poem *Carmen super multiplici viciorum pestilencia* written by John Gower in 1396, an explicitly anti-Lollard text which provides a revealing parallel to the visceral animus that Lydgate seemingly misdirects at a doubter of the virgin birth. See *John Gower: The Minor Latin Works*, ed. R. F. Yeager and Michael Livingston (Kalamazoo: Medieval Institute Publications, 2005), 16–32.

27. See *Critical Edition*, 7, and, for the entire discussion of dating, pp. 4–10.

Even if, however, Lydgate was engaged with the work several years earlier or following the death of Henry, enough of the historical pressures still apply in some fashion to support the conclusion that, with the *Life of Our Lady*, Lydgate seeks to defend the value of poetry as a means of defending not only doctrinal orthodoxy but also his own and his order's value to the kingdom. Ultimately, then, in this instance the literary is most simply a form of potential power; it is not a mask for power—not, that is, sacerdotal or royal power in disguise—but a potential for power that arises in response to the pressures of these powers, aligned with but independent of them, and possessing similar qualities of mystery and aura.

2. ORATOR REGIUS: SKELTON'S A REPLYCACION

The great claim of Lydgate's poetic enterprise—that the "golde dewe" of his aureate style possesses a sacral, even sacramental, power—helped inaugurate an English poetic tradition in which vernacular aureation signifies a protean authority potentially active across multiple dimensions: spiritual, moral, political, and social, as well as literary. One hundred years later, Skelton's contemporaries Stephen Hawes and Alexander Barclay would still be writing in this tradition, as would Skelton himself, as most evident in such aureate, rhyme royal efforts as *Upon the Dolorus Dethe*.[28] In comparison with the latter poem, the idiosyncratic, multiform, macaronic, and only slightly aureate *A Replycacion* would at first glance appear a stark departure from this tradition. Yet, juxtaposed with the above account of the *Life of Our Lady*, Skelton's poem unfolds, in many ways, as a strikingly similar project, only one at once more witty and blunt, and, in a manner of speaking, turned inside out: if the *Life of Our Lady* is an orthodox Marian devotion that modulates at times into a defense of poetry and, more subtly, a response to early fifteenth-century Lollardy, *A Replycacion* is a direct satiric attack on early sixteenth-century Lollard-like heretics that marshals both Marian orthodoxy and a defense of poetry to its cause.[29]

---

28. The development of this Lydgatean tradition is one of the principal topics of my *Poets and Power from Chaucer to Wyatt* (Cambridge: Cambridge University Press, 2007); for the relation of Hawes, Barclay, and Skelton to this tradition, see chapter 5, pp. 174–219. For a differently inflected but congruent account of these early Tudor writers, see Antony J. Hasler, "Cultural Intersections: Skelton, Barclay, Hawes, André," in *John Skelton and Early Modern Culture: Papers Honoring Robert S. Kinsman*, ed. David R. Carlson (Tempe: Arizona Center for Medieval and Renaissance Studies, 2008), 63–84.

29. Theodore L. Steinberg, in "Poetry and Prophecy: A Skelton Key," in *Prophet Margins: The Medieval Vatic Impulse and Social Stability*, ed. E. L. Risden, Karen Moranski, and Stephen Yandell (New York: Peter Lang, 2004), 149–65, makes a strong argument that many of Skelton's works, including *A Replycacion*, are more aptly termed prophetic rather than satiric. As is evident from the argument that follows, I am in agreement on this point, although I retain the term satiric as it more straightforwardly

This poem survives in its first print edition, which, as Jane Griffiths observes, "is unique among Skelton's works in being published by the King's Printer, at this time Richard Pynson." Griffiths persuasively suggests, moreover, that Skelton was at least in part responsible for the complex layout and extensive paratext of this edition, which makes shrewd use of typeface and *mise-en-page* to emphasize the significance of the organization of the work and to call attention to various aspects of its content.[30] Pynson's edition presents the poem in three parts that foreground the poem's instrumental function as a satiric attack on heresy and a defense of orthodoxy. The edition, twenty pages in all, devotes its first part—the initial three pages—to a belligerent, amusingly amplified statement of the *raison d'être* of the poem: the "remordying" of "dyvers recrayed and moche unresonable errours of certayne sophystycate scolers and rechelesse yong heretykes lately abjured"; or, in other words, the berating and belittling of two Cambridge scholars, Thomas Bilney and Thomas Arthur, who had recently renounced and been punished for heresy. Skelton excoriates these two with relish, as "fervently reboyled with the infatuate flames of their rechelesse youthe and wytlesse wontonnese."[31] As figures 6.1 and 6.2 show, the first quotation appears in Pynson's edition in a prose passage occupying the top half of the second page and is set off with a highly ornamental initial letter, while the wonderfully alliterative abuse of the second quotation appears in a prose passage that introduces the second part of the poem and occupies the entire fourth page.[32]

Embedded within this instrumental framework, the Virgin appears at the top of Pynson's fifth page, which marks the opening of the verse portion of the work's second part and, in a sense, of the poem proper, after the extensive context-setting of its first part. In this passage, although Skelton begins writing "In the honour of our blessed lady," his point is not so much to venerate the Virgin as it is to depict Bilney and Arthur's "horrible heresy" as specifically anti-Marian. Here is the entire initial verse paragraph:

---

conveys the surface distinction in genre between *A Replycacion* and the *Life of Our Lady*.

30. Jane Griffiths, *John Skelton and Poetic Authority: Defining the Liberty to Speak* (Oxford: Oxford University Press, 2006), 28, 108–10. See also her earlier study, "What's in a Name? The Transmission of 'John Skelton, Laureate' in Manuscript and Print," *Huntington Library Quarterly* 67 (2004): 215–35. Skelton's likely hand in this edition gives the critic interpretive advantages that are lacking for many of the poet's other texts. For discussion of some of the latter, see A. S. G. Edwards, "Deconstructing Skelton: The Texts of the English Poems," *Leeds Studies in English,* New Series 36 (2005): 335–53. For Pynson's edition, see *A Replycacion agaynst Certayne Yong Scolers,* STC 22609 (London: Richard Pynson, [1528]), held in the Huntington Library but viewable on Early English Books Online. I thank Dr. Griffiths for bringing to my attention the revealing features of this edition.

31. For a recent discussion of Skelton's involvement in what was apparently, in the aftermath of Bilney and Arthur's trial, a concerted propaganda effort orchestrated by Cardinal Wolsey and also involving Thomas More, see chapter 7 in Greg Walker, *Persuasive Fictions: Faction, Faith and Political Culture in the Reign of Henry VIII* (Aldershot: Scolar Press, 1996), 166–77.

32. For the edited text, see *English Poems,* 373–74.

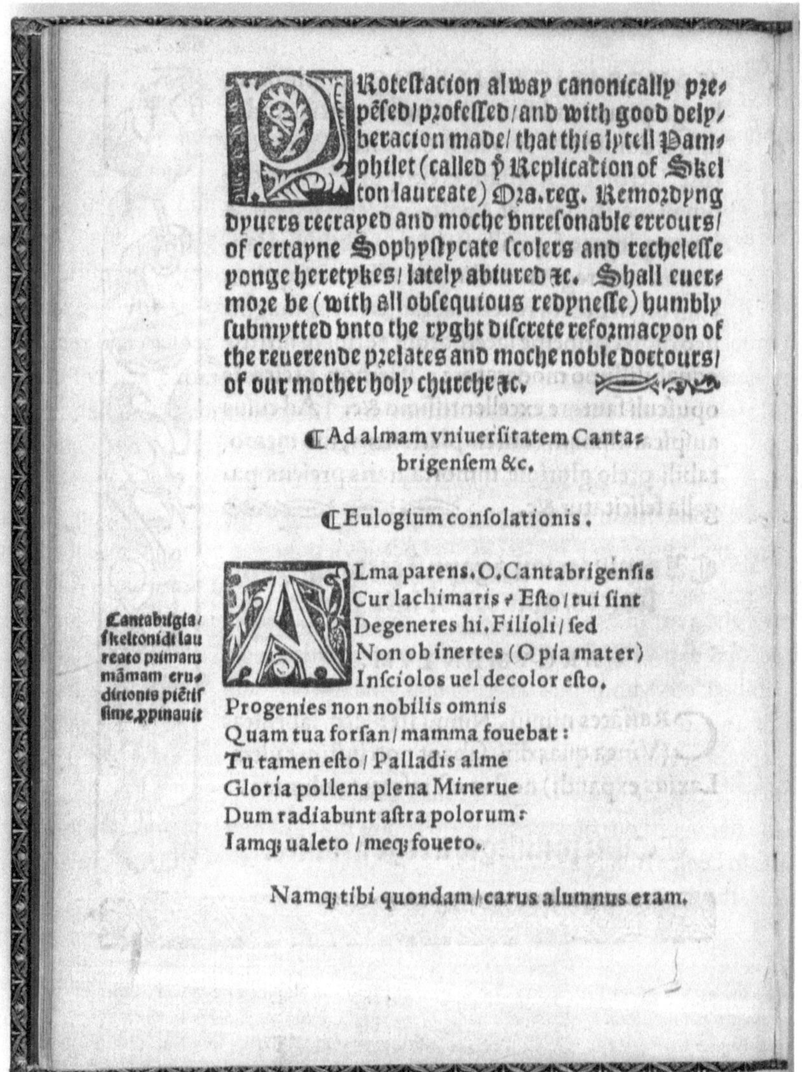

Rotestacion alway canonically pre⁎
pesed / professed / and with good delp⁎
beracion made / that this lytell Pam⁎
phlet (called ẏ Replicacion of Skel
ton laureate) Ora. reg. Remordyng
dyuers recrayed and moche vnresonable errours /
of certayne Sophysticate scolers and recheleſſe
yonge heretykes / lately abiured etc. Shall euer⁎
more be (with all obsequious redynesse) humbly
submytted vnto the ryght discrete reformacyon of
the reuerende prelates and moche noble doctours /
of our mother holy churche etc.

     ¶ Ad almam vniuersitatem Canta⁎
            brigensem &c.

     ¶ Eulogium consolationis.

Cantabrigia /
skeltonidi lau
reato primariu
māmam eru⁎
ditionis pictiſ
sime, ppinauit

Lma parens, O, Cantabrigensis
Cur lachimaris ? Esto / tui sint
Degeneres hi, Filioli / sed
Non ob inertes (O pia mater)
Insciolos uel decolor esto,
Progenies non nobilis omnis
Quam tua forsan / mamma fouebat :
Tu tamen esto / Palladis alme
Gloria pollens plena Minerue
Dum radiabunt astra polorum ?
Iamq; ualeto / meq; foueto.

     Namq; tibi quondam / carus alumnus eram.

FIGURE 6.1. San Marino, Calif., Huntington Library: Skelton's *A Replycacion* (printed by Richard Pynson, 1528), STC 22609, A1v. Reproduced by permission of The Huntington Library, San Marino, California.

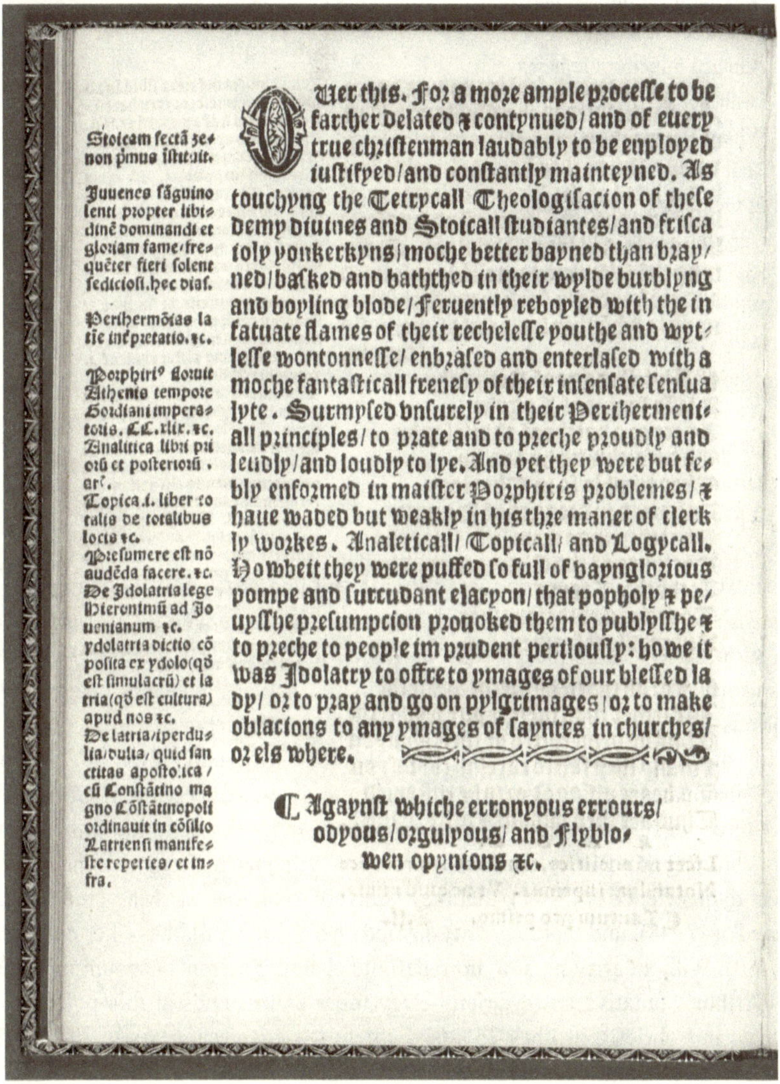

Stoicam sectã ʒe-
non p̄mus īstituit.

Iuuenes sãguino
lenti propter libi-
dinē dominandi et
gloriam fame, fre-
quēter fieri solent
sediciosi. hec Diaf.

Perihermēias la-
tie īnp̄retatio. ꞇc.

Porphiri⁹ scrut
Athenis tempore
Sordiani imperas
toris. CC.xlix. ꞇc.
Analitica libri pri
orū et posteriorū,
ar̄.
Topica.i. liber to
talis de totalibus
locis ꞇc.
Presumere est nō
audēda facere. ꞇc.
De Idolatria lege
Hieronimū ad Io-
uenianum ꞇc.
ydolatria dictio cō
posita ex ydolo(qd̄
est simulacrū) et la
tria(qd̄ est cultura)
apud nos ꞇc.
De latria, iperdu-
lia, Dulia, quid san
ctitas aposto.ica /
cū Constātino ma
gno Cōstātinopoli
ordinauit in cōsilio
Latriensi manife-
ste reperies, et in-
fra.

Uer this. For a more ample processe to be
farther delated & contynued, and of euery
true christenman laudably to be enployed
iustifyed, and constantly mainteyned. As
touchyng the Tetrycall Theologisacion of these
demy diuines and Stoicall studiantes, and frisca-
ioly yonkerkyns, moche better bayned than bray-
ned, basked and baththed in their wylde burblyng
and boylyng blode, feruently reboyled with the infatuate flames of their rechelesse youthe and wytlesse wontonnesse, enbraced and enterlaced with a
moche fantasticall frenesy of their insensate sensua-
lyte. Surmysed vnsurely in their Periherment-
all principles, to prate and to preche proudly and
leudly, and loudly to lye. And yet they were but fe-
bly enformed in maister Porphiris problemes, &
haue waded but weakly in his thre maner of clerk-
ly workes. Analeticall, Topicall, and Logycall.
Howbeit they were puffed so full of vayngloryous
pompe and succudant elacyon, that popholy & pe-
uysshe presumpcion prouoked them to publysshe &
to preche to people im prudent perilously: howe it
was Idolatry to offre to ymages of our blessed lady, or to pray and go on pylgrimages, or to make
oblacions to any ymages of sayntes in churches,
or els where.

⁋ Agaynst whiche erronyous errours,
odyous, orgulpous, and flyblo-
wen opynions ꞇc.

FIGURE 6.2. San Marino, Calif., Huntington Library: Skelton's *A Replycacion* (printed by Richard Pynson, 1528), STC 22609, A2v. Reproduced by permission of The Huntington Library, San Marino, California.

> In the honour of our blessed lady,
> And her most blessed baby,
> I purpose for to reply
> Agaynst this horrible heresy
> Of these yong heretikes, that stynke unbrent,
> Whom I nowe sommon and convent,
> That leudly have their tyme spent,
> In their study abhomynable,
> Our glorious lady to disable,
> And heinously on her to bable
> With langage detestable,
> With your lyppes polluted,
> Agaynst her grace disputed,
> Whiche is the most clere christall
> Of all pure clennesse virgynall,
> That our Savyour bare,
> Which us redeemed from care. (18–34)[33]

Mariolatry is plainly secondary to satire in these lines; the point is not so much to express adoration for the Virgin as it is to condemn those who do not. Moreover, the virtuoso vitriol of the passage leaves curiously unclear precisely what the "yong heretikes" in their "study abhomynable" actually declared against "Our glorious lady"—though the vivid concluding contrast between the "lyppes polluted" of the "heretikes" and the "pure clennesse virgynall / That our Savyour bare" insinuates a charge of their doubting the divine conception of Christ. The next three verse paragraphs offer no more specificity but continue this insinuation, claiming that Bilney and Arthur preached "Agaynst her magnificence, / That never dyde offence" (43–44), that they "brayed" "baudrie" at "Mary, mother and mayed" (47–48), and that they "mysnamed" her "And would have her defamed" (59–60). Without arriving at a more definite charge, Skelton's account of Bilney and Arthur's putative anti-Marian heresy more or less ends at this point, reappearing only briefly in lines 254–62—where the charge appears to be that the Cambridge scholars claimed it "idolatry" to "reverence" the "ymage" of "That glorious mayde and mother"—and more obliquely in line 287, where Skelton distinguishes *hyperdulia* (the veneration due Mary) from *latria* (the worship reserved only for God) and *dulia* (the reverence appropriate to saints). Altogether, Mariology of some vague variety occupies at most 62 of the poem's 409 lines of English verse as printed in John Scattergood's modern edition, or—taking into account

---

33. Scattergood prints this passage as two verse paragraphs, placing a division after "That leudly have their tyme spent," but in Pynson the seventeen lines form one unbroken sentence. I have also modified Scattergood's punctuation after lines 28 and 29 to emphasize this continuity.

the elaborate paratext—only about two of the work's nineteen text-bearing pages, as printed by Pynson. Nonetheless—and remarkably for a work supposedly written in confutation of heretics—these lines on Mary constitute the most devoted to any particular point of doctrine, however ambiguous that point is.[34]

As a whole, the poem may thus be more accurately characterized as intellectually ingenious, sustained name-calling rather than doctrinal polemic, which has led some its best readers to conclude that Skelton was not very well informed about the incident.[35] In fact, as evident in the account of the trial in John Foxe's *Acts and Monuments,* while Bilney perhaps believed that Mary did not remain a virgin *after* the birth of Christ, specifically Marian dogma played a very small role in the charges brought against him and made no appearance in those brought against Arthur.[36] Among Bilney's thirty-four "interrogatories" was just the one question, "Whether that a man may beleue without spot of heresie, that our Lady remayned not always a virgin"; Bilney's somewhat equivocal response was apparently allowed to stand: "To the seuenth Article he said, that it is not to be thought contrary."[37] Moreover, as I have noted, neither Wyclif nor his Lollard followers ever questioned the virgin birth, nor did Luther (all of whom Skelton associates with Bilney and Arthur—see lines 166, 167, 204, and 266); nor is it likely, regardless of whatever Skelton had heard about the trial, that a suspicion of this particular heresy would have been circulating in England among enforcers of orthodoxy in the 1520s. As Beth Kreitzer discusses, Lutherans in the early sixteenth century generally maintained Marian orthodoxy and even devotion, but they did deny her intercessory agency, as they did for all saints.[38] (Later in the century, in a Counter-Reformation climate of emphasis on Marian piety, Lutheran views of Mary became more commonly disparaging, although the virgin birth was never rejected.) In England in the 1520s, the principal suspected heresies involving Mary were among those that pertained to all saints: to quote Foxe's

---

34. Second to this point is Skelton's concern over the "worshyppe [of] ymages of sayntes" (291), the somewhat diffuse topic of lines 254–299, including the aforementioned lines on the worship of images of the Virgin.

35. For example, Vincent Gillespie, "Justification by Faith: Skelton's *Replycacion,*" in *The Long Fifteenth Century: Essays for Douglas Gray,* ed. Helen Cooper and Sally Mapstone (Oxford: Clarendon Press, 1997), 273–311, at 278.

36. For the lists of charges against Bilney and Arthur and their responses, see John Foxe, *Acts and Monuments* [. . .] (1583 edition), Foxe's Book of Martyrs Variorum Edition Online v. 1.1 (Sheffield: hriOnline, 2006), http://www.hrionline.shef.ac.uk/foxe/ (accessed 26 May 2008), 8.998–1000. For a thorough account of the trial, see John F. Davis, "The Trials of Thomas Bylney and the English Reformation," *The Historical Journal* 24 (1981): 775–90, which reappears in part in John F. Davis, *Heresy and Reformation in the South-East of England, 1520–1559* (London: Royal Historical Society, 1983), 46–53.

37. Foxe, *Acts and Monuments,* 8.999–1000.

38. Beth Kreitzer, *Reforming Mary: Changing Images of the Virgin Mary in Lutheran Sermons of the Sixteenth Century* (Oxford: Oxford University Press, 2004). See also Miri Rubin, *Mother of God: A History of the Virgin Mary* (New Haven: Yale University Press, 2009), 367–76.

account of the charges against Arthur, "That men should praye to no Saintes in heauen, but onely to God, and they should vse no other Mediatour for them, but Christ Iesu our redeemer only"; and "that they shoulde worship no Images of Saintes, whiche were nothing but stockes and stones."[39]

It is thus not surprising that Skelton only suggests Bilney and Arthur's doubts about Mary's divine conception of Christ without accusing them of this outright. As becomes clear in the poem's third and concluding part, Skelton's Mariology, like Lydgate's, is not so much directly related to the details of the heresy at hand as it is to his role as vatic poetic defender of orthodoxy. In this regard, the heretical rejection of the mediating agency of saints in general and Mary in particular may have been, as perhaps it was for Lydgate, the more basic prompt for the Marian passage and its conjunction with the work's defense of poetry. This heresy, with its Lollard pedigree, would have been familiar to Skelton regardless of his knowledge of the trial (in fact, as indicated, it did figure relatively prominently in the charges against Bilney and Arthur), and it becomes an explicit concern in the poem, as evident in Skelton's aforementioned remarks on the distinction between *dulia* and *hyperdulia* (line 287). The early-sixteenth-century rejection of Mary's mediating agency, in both its Lollard and Lutheran varieties, effectively reduced the Virgin from "the powerful, merciful, mother Queen of Heaven" to merely a "humble, chaste, obedient girl," if not, as in more radical formulations, simply "a receptacle for the celestial body of Christ"; as John Morris, a Rochester weaver, put it in 1505, "as for ouer blessid lady[,] She is but a sakk."[40] As the third part of *A Replycacion* goes on to suggest, the figure of Mary as "powerful . . . Queen of Heaven" is for Skelton, as it was for Lydgate, a metonym for the vatic poet, and therefore the supposed diminishment of the former serves well as the provocation for a defense of the latter. Consequently, because Mary's conception of Christ provides for Skelton, as for Lydgate, both the more specific metonym for vatic inspiration and, in its supposed denial, a synecdoche for heresy—and thus as well the link between the two—we should also not be surprised that Skelton *does* insinuate that Bilney and Arthur held doubts about the conception, notwithstanding whatever incomplete knowledge about, intentional misconstrual of, or irrelevance in regard to their trial this insinuation involves.

One incidental fact from the trial, however, that plainly did supply Skelton an excuse for this insinuation—and, more generally, for invoking Mariology at all—was the particular date of Bilney and Arthur's public punishment: as he records at the end of the four verse paragraphs discussed above, "At the feest of

---

39. Foxe, *Acts and Monuments*, 8.999. As Davis notes, Bilney and Arthur held views more Lollard than Lutheran, and "bishops used the smear of Lutheranism on suspects who plainly held Wycliffite views" ("The Trials of Thomas Bylney," 778). See also Hudson, *The Premature Reformation*, 496–500.

40. For the former two quotations, see Kreitzer, *Reforming Mary*, 141; for the latter two, Davis, *Heresy and Reformation*, 37.

her concepcion / Ye suffred suche correction" (67–68). Seizing on this one detail, in the second and third parts of the poem Skelton constructs an intricate thematic and figurative architecture, in which Mariology, prosecution of heresy, and a defense of poetry are all interlinked by means of what Victor Scherb has well demonstrated to be Skelton's "triple pun on conception." As Scherb summarizes:

> The poem connects Mary's conception, Bilney and Arthur's flyblown heretical conceptions, and finally Skelton's own divinely inspired poetic conceptions. Generational processes metaphorically link these three meanings, as Skelton appropriates liturgical themes, mediaeval scientific lore concerning flies, and exegetical commentary in order to refute and attack Bilney and Arthur while exalting his own role as poet. The three types of conception are brought together by the occasion of Mary's feast, which provides true doctrine, confounds heresy, and inspires the *vates* to true poetry.[41]

Likely prompted by the heretical rejection of Mary's mediating agency and provided a convenient rationale by the date of Arthur and Bilney's punishment, Skelton was irresistibly drawn to the figural and rhetorical flexibility of Mary's conception. Like Lydgate, with this flexibility Skelton is able to fuse the catachresis between supposed doctrinal error and an articulation of the literary as a power possessed by his person and exemplified in the present poem. And, like Lydgate, Skelton accomplishes this fusion by identifying himself with Mary in the moment of her conception.

The passage in which this identification is most evident is Skelton's famously grand claim for the divine origin of poetry. These lines are worth quoting at length:

> With me ye must consent
> And infallibly agre
> Of necessyte,
> Howe there is a spyrituall,
> And a mysteriall,
> And a mysticall
> Effecte energiall,
> As Grekes do it call,
> Of suche an industry
> And suche a pregnacy,
> Of heavenly inspyracion

---

41. Victor I. Scherb, "Conception, Flies, and Heresy in Skelton's 'Replycacion,'" *Medium Aevum* 62 (1993): 51–60, at 51.

> In laureate creacyon,
> Of poetes commendacion,
> That of divyne myseracion
> God maketh his habytacion
> In poetes whiche excelles,
> And sojourns with them and dwelles.
>
> By whose inflammacion
> Of spyrituall instygacion
> And divyne inspyracion
> We are kyndled in suche facyon
> With hete of the Holy Gost,
> Which is God of myghtes most,
> That he our penne dothe lede,
> And maketh in us suche spede
> That forwith we must nede
> With penne and ynke procede[.] (362–88)

In separate studies, Griffiths and Vincent Gillespie have shown how in this passage Skelton draws on and marvelously condenses various theological, humanist, and philosophical sources to culminate his "most passionate and emphatic defence of his poetic calling[.]"[42] For present purposes, it suffices to point out the sheer density of the passage's imagery of holy conception and divine indwelling. In almost graphic specificity, Skelton figures the "heavenly inspyracion" of "laureate creacyon" as a "pregnacy";[43] he claims that "God maketh his habytacion / In poetes whiche excelles, / And sojourns with them and dwelles";[44]

---

42. Gillespie, "Justification by Faith," 276. See also Griffiths, *John Skelton*, 129–35, and her earlier "A Contradiction in Terms: Skelton's 'effecte energiall' in *A Replycacion*," *Renaissance Studies* 17 (2003): 55–68. For Scherb's comments on the passage, see "Conception," 57. For a more skeptical view of the ingenuousness of Skelton's claims here, see Bose's essay in this volume (chapter 7). Perhaps the political and ecclesial instrumentality that underwrites the poem as a whole does indeed result in the sort of multiform self-cancellation that Bose perceives here and elsewhere in the piece, although, as will become evident, my sense of the precise reasons for this differ from hers.

43. Though Scattergood glosses this noun as "productiveness, inventiveness," it also held its corporeal meaning—see O.E.D. *pregnancy* n. (1), as well as the adjectival form, *pregnant* adj. (1) and n.

44. A Latin sidenote to these lines, combining Ovid's *Fasti* 6.5 and *Ars amatoria* 3.550, emphasizes their meaning, as well as that of lines 382–83: "Est deus in nobis; agitante calecimus illo. / Sedibus aetheriis spiritus iste venit." ["There is a god within us. It is when he stirs us that our bosom warms. / From celestial places comes our inspiration."] Interestingly, the preceding line in *Ars amatoria* and the following one in *Fasti* much resemble the quoted lines from the respective other poems, which perhaps accounts for their conflation (or perhaps Skelton could not resist such a coincidence of the sacred and profane). Here is the "alternative" conflation: "Est deus in nobis, et sunt commercia caeli. / Impetus hic sacrae semina mentis habet." ["There's a god in us; we are in touch with heaven. / It is his impulse that sows the seeds of inspiration."] The sidenote appears at the top of Pynson's p. 18; for the edited Latin, see *The Poetical Works of John Skelton*, ed. Alexander Dyce, 2 vols. (London: Thomas Rodd, 1843), rpt.

and, most revealingly, describes poets, in their "divyne inspyracion," as having been "kyndled" with the "hete of the Holy Gost." Indeed, this last example, in its depiction of the kindling of the Holy Spirit as the agency behind the movement of the poet's phallic "penne"—and hence poetry as the product of divine conception—recalls the similar figuration in the *Life of Our Lady*. Although a side note references Psalm 44:2 (Vulgate) for the trope ("Lingua mea calamus scribae velociter scribentis" ["My tongue is the pen of a scrivener that writeth swiftly"]),[45] Skelton's imagery is much closer to Lydgate's, as when the latter beseeches the Virgin for "thylke bame, sent downe by miracle, / Whan the hooly goost the made his habitacle" (cf. Skelton's "habytacion") and for her to "shede" "the licour" of her "grace" into his "penne" (1.55–58).

With this comparison, I do not mean to claim the *Life of Our Lady* as a direct source for *A Replycacion* (although this is certainly possible: Skelton shows ample knowledge of Lydgate elsewhere, and, along with one of the many manuscript copies of this particular poem, he may have seen Caxton's 1484 edition). But I do mean to claim that Skelton was consciously writing in a tradition that Lydgate inaugurates, a consciousness that he signals by what is, in this poem, a striking stylistic anomaly: the sudden intrusion of two aureate rhyme royal stanzas positioned, significantly, between his initial claims for poetry as able to fly high in such discourses as theology and philosophy and his subsequent figuration of poetry as the result of divine impregnation. Rhyme royal is of course the stanza form that Chaucer made famous as the armature for lofty works such as *Troilus and Criseyde* and religious ones such as the "Prioress's Tale." Over the course of Lydgate's long career, the form became closely associated with the aureate high style of such works as the *Life of Our Lady*. Although Skelton uses rhyme royal for a variety of purposes, one of them is quite evidently to signify his participation in this tradition of aureate verse, as illustrated in his *tour de force* self-encomium, the *Garlande or Chapelet of Laurell,* in which he depicts Lydgate as ushering him on to the court of Fame.

In *A Replycacion* these two stanzas of aureate rhyme royal translate a passage from the letter of Jerome to Paulinus that often prefaced the Vulgate Bible and the *Glossa ordinaria*. As Gillespie shows, this passage, which Skelton supplies verbatim just before his translation, underwrites Skelton's claim of *poeta theologus* in multiple ways, especially given the bearing of other aspects of Jerome's letter

---

The Poetical Works of John Skelton, ed. Alexander Dyce, 3 vols. (Boston: James R. Osgood, 1871), vol. 1, 248. For the translation (and the Latin of the "alternative" conflation), see Ovid, *Fasti,* trans. James George Frazer and rev. G. P. Goold (Cambridge: Harvard University Press, 1989), and Ovid, *The Art of Love, and Other Poems,* trans. J. H. Mozley and rev. G. P. Goold (Cambridge: Harvard University Press, 1979). For brief discussion, see John Scattergood, *Reading the Past: Essays on Medieval and Renaissance Literature* (Dublin: Four Courts Press, 1996), 296.

45. See Pynson, 18, and *Poetical Works,* ed. Dyce, 249; Douay-Rheims translation. *English Poems* inadvertently gives the psalm as 54, but Scattergood corrects this in *Reading the Past,* 296.

on the events that prompted *A Replycacion*. For present purposes, two aspects of the translation are notable. First is the translation's expansiveness—as figure 6.3 shows, in Pynson's edition it occupies fourteen lines of English for four lines of Latin and neatly ends the sixteenth page. And second is how it draws particular attention to Jerome's concern with poetic tradition, in which King David shines supreme over Greek and Latin poets:

> Kyng David the prophete, of prophetes principall,
> Of poetes chefe poete, saint Jerome doth wright,
> . . .
> Flaccus nor Catullus with hym may nat compare,
> Nor solempne Serenus . . .
> . . .
> For Davyd our poete, harped so meloudiously
> Of Our savyour Christ in his decacorde psautry,
> That at his resurrection he harped out of hell
> Olde patriarkes and prophetes in heven with him to dwell. (329–42)

Taken all together, this concern with poetic tradition in general, these stanzas' singular and expansive intrusion of aureate rhyme royal, and Skelton's ensuing vernacular defense of "poetes laureate" (359) form a clear nod to the Lydgatean English laureate tradition, and perhaps specifically to the aureate defenses of vernacular poetry inaugurated by Lydgate in the *Life of Our Lady* and elsewhere.

In addition, by foregrounding Skelton's formal choices through their stark stanzaic and stylistic contrast, these stanzas call attention to Skelton's return, for the grand claims for poetry that follow, to the idiosyncratic verse form that we now term Skeltonics—with Skelton signaling this transition, as figure 6.3 shows, with the remark, "Returne we to our former process." Stanley Fish long ago alerted us to the meaningfulness of Skelton's stylistic choices and, in particular, of the contrast between the aureate and the plain:[46] following these two stanzas, Skelton turns from the aureate to the plain to mark the transition from a declaration of David's divinely underwritten poetic superiority over the classical, pagan tradition to a declaration of his own divinely underwritten poetic superiority—thereby at once implicitly asserting his membership in, and surpassing of, the Lydgatean tradition. The position Skelton takes up vis-à-vis Lydgate is, in other words, precisely parallel to how Jerome positions David vis-à-vis classical poets—as at once, as Gillespie says, "the equal of and successor to the poets of classical antiquity."[47] Hence, in the third part of *A Replycacion*, Lydgatean aureate claims to poetic authority culminate in, are reinvigorated by, and are superseded by, the

---

46. Stanley E. Fish, *John Skelton's Poetry* (New Haven: Yale University Press, 1965), 250 and passim.

47. Gillespie, "Justification by Faith," 291. See also Griffiths, *John Skelton*, 32.

Vos igit omnes irrisores/ contēptoresq; poetarū erudicie cū ignominosa verecundia eriticosaq; cōfusio operiat facies vestras. hec ñ.

Poete of poetes all
And Prophete pryncypall
Thus may nat be remorded
For it is wele recorded
In his pystell ad Paulinum
Presbyterum diuinum
Where worde for worde ye may
Rede/ what Jerome there dothe say.

Dauid (inquit) Siphonides nf̄ / Pindar⁹ et Alcheus/ Flaccus quoq;/ Catullus/ atq; Serenus/ Christū lira personat/ et in decachordo psalterio ab inferis ercitat resurgētem. Hec Hier.

⁊The Englysshe.

Kyng Dauid the pphete / of pphetes pricipall
Of poetes chefe poete/ saith Jerome dothe wright
Resembled to Symphonides/that poete lyricall
Among the Grekes/ most relucent of lyght
In that faculte: whiche shyned as Phebus bright
Lyke to Pyndarus/ in glorious poetry
Lyke vnto Alcheus/he dothe hym magnify.

⁊Flaccus nor Catullus/ wᵗ hym may nat cōpare
Nor solempne Serenus/for all his armony
In metricall muses/ his harpyng we may spare
For Dauyd our poete/ harped so melodiously
Of our sauyour Christ/in his decacorde psautry
That at his resurrection/he harped out of hell
Olde patriarks & prophets/ i heuen w̄ him to dwell

⁊Returne we to our former processe.

"ragged" rhyme of Skelton's clipped, irregular plain style.[48] So highly characteristic of his poetry, this style, in the concluding movement of this poem, becomes the sign of the poetic grace bestowed upon the poet as *Skeltonis laureatus*—the sign which at once justifies and is the form of his service to king and cardinal and his repression of heresy.

In comparison with the *Life of Our Lady*, however, notably missing from *A Replycacion* is the mediating role of the dead precursor as poetic saint, the role played by Chaucer in Lydgate's poem as the metonymical hinge in the analogy between poet and Mary. In that work, Chaucer, a mortal become immortal, forms the bridge between the poem before us and its transcendental claims. For Skelton, this bridge is the one he so thoroughly fabricates in the *Garlande or Chapelet of Laurell,* since for Skelton what bridges the realms of time-bound and timeless is, instead of a sanctified precursor, the office signified by the title *laureatus,* which appears eight times in *A Replycacion.*[49] As Gillespie has shown, Skelton, drawing on continental humanistic defenses of poetry, would have understood this office as, in principle, at once a thing of this world and a thing of heaven, the divine sanction of mortal poets doing God's work; in *A Replycacion,* "perhaps for the first time explicitly in all his writings, Skelton is able to conflate his laureate status with his perception of his role as the priest-prophet-poet."[50]

Because a laureateship (however different from the modern institution) was, unlike in Lydgate's day, something Skelton could officially possess and, in addition, associate with the office of *orator regius* (which also did not exist for Lydgate), it would seem to underwrite more forcefully his claim to wield the sacral power of the literary than would the merely notional laureate status of a precursor who, as Lydgate says in the *Life of Our Lady* about Chaucer, "worthy was the laurer to haue" (2.1630). Yet the institutionalization of the formally notional status of laureate in fact demystified that status, and hence severely undermined its transcendental claims.[51] The poet laureate, in Henry VIII's court, was quite visibly a household servant, and hence the laureate's poems, despite what else they may claim to be, were manifestly objects of socioeconomic *quid pro quo.*

---

48. I glance here at Skelton's famous description of his style in *Collyn Clout*: "For though my ryme be ragged, / Tattered and jagged, / . . . / Yf ye take well therwith / It hath in it some pyth" (lines 53–58 in *English Poems*).

49. In the opening Latin dedication to Wolsey, in the prose following the Latin *argumentum,* in the sidenote to the Latin verse "Eulogium consolationis," in the prose introduction to the third part of the poem, in the English verse lines 301 and 358, in the Latin epilogue, and in the colophon.

50. Gillespie, "Justification by Faith," 293, and, for discussion, 293–311.

51. For this point, see my *Poets and Power,* esp. 174–78, and, for some of the ideas in the following two paragraphs, 217–18. See also chapter 1 in Griffiths, *John Skelton,* 18–37, who similarly analyzes the lurking deflation of Skelton's laureate status in the early Tudor court, focusing in particular on the conflict between the ideas of laureate and *orator regius.*

Such a status is readily evident in the contrast between *A Replycacion* and the *Life of Our Lady* in respect to how the relationship between the poem and ecclesial and royal authority is signaled. That relationship in Lydgate's poem is ambiguous and indirect, whereas in *A Replycacion* it is prominently foregrounded, inescapably thrust forward at the reader with the lengthy, hyperbolically obsequious, Latin dedication to Cardinal Wolsey, which occupies the entire top half (and more) of the work's title page in Pynson's edition (see figure 6.4).[52] In this dedication, what jumps out at the reader are the two words in all capitals: the initial one, "Honorificatissimo" ["To the most honorable"], and, after more superlatives, the dedicatee's given name, "Thome." Buried in the middle of the passage, Skelton identifies himself as "Skeltonis laureatus, ora*tor* reg*ius*," but encases these titles within the groveling of a humility topos: "humillimum, dicit obsequium cum omni debita revere*n*tia" ["the laureate Skelton, royal orator, makes known his most humble obeisance with all the reverence due"]. Prominently positioned at the bottom of the page in the same large, bold print as the work's title ("A replycacion agaynst certayne yong scolers abjured of late, etc," which follows the dedication as the only English on the page) is then the phrase "Cum privilegio a rege in dulto" ["with the privilege granted by the king"]. Although this is not Skelton's statement but rather Pynson's advertisement of his authority, as royal printer, to publish the work, it nonetheless fittingly punctuates the overall import of the page.[53]

Even more revealing in this regard is the poem's Latin verse epilogue, where, after insisting, "reor ergo poetas / Ante alios omnes divine flamine flatos" ["Therefore, I think that poets, / before all others, are filled with divine inspiration"], Skelton adds, "sic Caesar, maximus heros / Romanus, celebres semper coluere poetas" ["thus Caesar, the greatest / of Roman heroes, always honored famous poets"] (6–10). With these lines, we see that the subtle advertisement of the poet's royal usefulness in the *Life of Our Lady* becomes at the end of *A Replycacion* a kind of billboard addressed to England's Caesar, reminding him of the necessity of honoring famous poets, such as the one named repeatedly in this very poem. Indeed, the very strangeness of some of the second-person plural accusations in the third part of the poem—which sound as if the most egregious of Bilney and Arthur's heresies was their rejection of Skelton's laureate authority (e.g., "Ye do moche great outrage / For to disparage / And to discorage /

---

52. The apparent relationship between the *Life of Our Lady* and royal authority is less ambiguously signified in the version Skelton may have seen, Caxton's 1484 edition (STC 17023), which begins with the rubric about Henry V's "excitation"—a feature which perhaps makes the influence of Lydgate's poem on Skelton in this respect more likely. For brief discussion of Caxton's print, see Alexandra Gillespie, *Print Culture and the Medieval Author: Chaucer, Lydgate, and Their Books 1473–1557* (Oxford: Oxford University Press, 2006), 72–73.

53. For this statement as Pynson's, see Griffiths, "What's in a Name," 224–26.

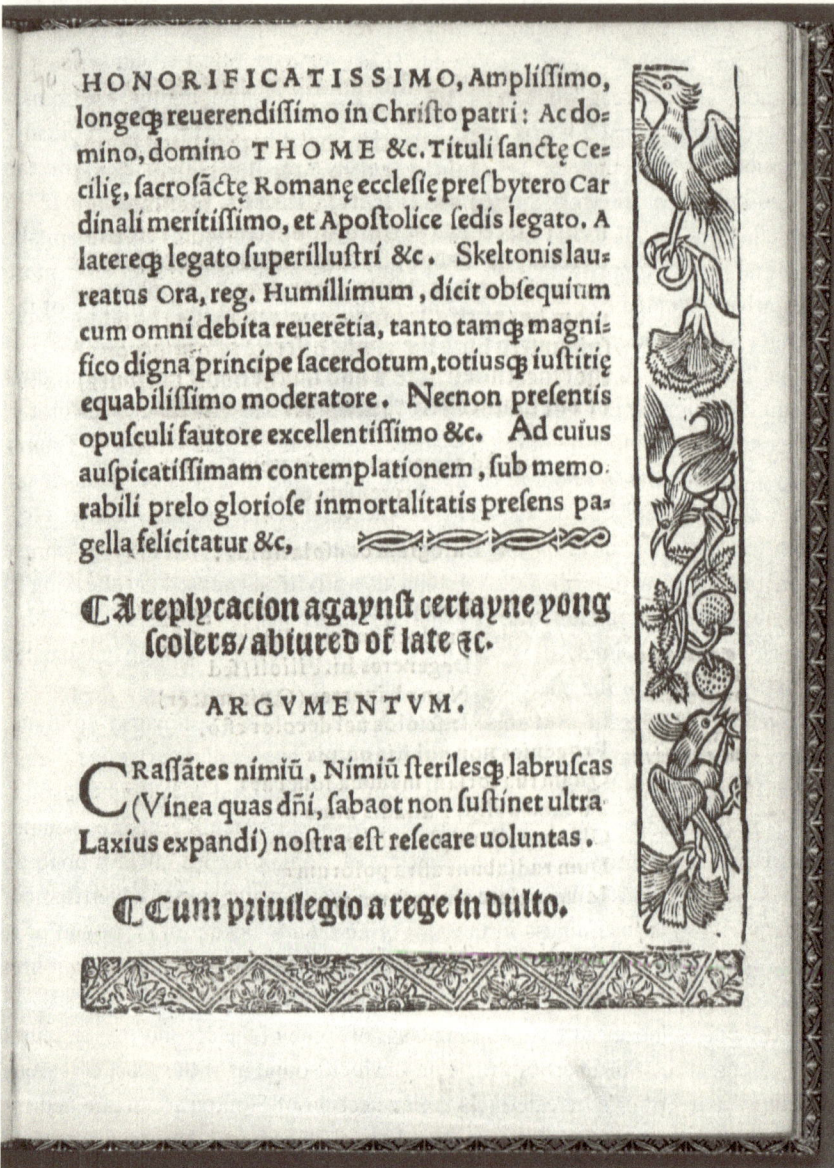

FIGURE 6.4. San Marino, Calif., Huntington Library: Skelton's *A Replycacion* (printed by Richard Pynson, 1528), STC 22609, A1r. Reproduced by permission of The Huntington Library, San Marino, California.

The fame matryculate / Of poetes laureate" [354–58])—suggests that Skelton's more vital addressees in this defense of poetry are, in fact, his dedicatee Wolsey and his boss, Henry VIII. Given that just a few years before writing this poem, Skelton, banished from court, was living in sanctuary after somehow earning the ire of Wolsey and spending his time writing masterful, vitriolic satires against the cardinal, we may find that the status of the laureate here has devolved to the point of abjection.[54]

To be sure, at one point in *A Replycacion* Skelton does appear once again to flex his satiric muscles in regard to Wolsey, when he remarks, "Some of you had ten pounde, / Therewith for to be founde / At the unyversyte" (146–48). Griffiths suggests, following William Nelson, that this remark—as signaled by the side note "Obscurus sarcasmos" ["an obscure sarcasm"]—takes Wolsey to task for earlier supporting Bilney financially: "It thus ironically undermines the authority of one of the poem's own potential authorizers, and implies that the reconciliation between Skelton and the cardinal was not all it seemed."[55] Although this reading is persuasive, Skelton's undermining of Wolsey is, as his own gloss says, *obscurus,* and is as well quite brief and framed by his polite remark, "I saye it for no sedicion" (140). It may mark a moment of resistance, but one that eventually dissipates into the obsequiousness of the epilogue.

Admittedly, too—as with Lydgate and Henry V—the precise nature of Wolsey's prompting of *A Replycacion* remains somewhat of a mystery and did not, in any event, necessarily represent the will of the king. As Greg Walker remarks, the poem "is probably best considered a work for the church rather than state"—but he quickly adds, "in this period the distinction is, of course, at best a problematic one."[56] It is clear, however, that in this poem and elsewhere, regardless of how far Skelton actually stood from the crown, royal power occupies the center of his imagination. Notwithstanding what I have argued about the similarities between the *Life of Our Lady* and *A Replycacion,* then, the two poems are in an important way the inverse of one other. In Lydgate's poem, political instrumentality arises *out of* its articulation of the literary, which is a form of potential power independent of those with which it may align itself. In contrast, in Skelton's poem, political instrumentality *gives rise to* an articulation of the literary, and hence the literary cannot ultimately be distinguished from the power Wolsey represents. The arc from Lydgate to Skelton thus maps both the triumph of one kind of

---

54. For two somewhat different views of Skelton's relations with Wolsey and, more generally, his status at court, see part 3 in Alistair Fox, *Politics and Literature in the Reigns of Henry VII and Henry VIII* (Oxford: Basil Blackwell, 1989), 131–205, and Greg Walker, *John Skelton and the Politics of the 1520s* (Cambridge: Cambridge University Press, 1988), esp. 188–217.

55. Griffiths, *John Skelton,* 112. See also William Nelson, *John Skelton, Laureate* (New York: Columbia University Press, 1939), 217–19.

56. Greg Walker, "John Skelton and the Royal Court," in *John Skelton and Early Modern Culture,* ed. Carlson, 3–18, at 13.

articulation of the literary and its waning. While the indirect and figural defense of poetry in the *Life of Our Lady* becomes an explicit, learned, impassioned defense in *A Replycacion*, the literary itself devolves from an independent form of potential power to something finally not so different from Pynson's authority to print the work: a "privilege granted by the king."

Already so devolved, the articulation of the literary that Skelton inherits from Lydgate would not have long to suffer. In Reformation England—whose proximity to the 1528 *A Replycacion* lends the poem a historical irony that its vatic author did not seem to prophesy—the profound shifts in the relations between royal and ecclesial power, orthodox and heretical devotion, and clerical and lay poetic production would quickly send into extinction the remaining vestiges of this articulation. In 1531—the very year in which the convocations of Canterbury and York acquiesced, under threat of the charge of *praemunire*, to Henry VIII's demand to be recognized as "Supreme Head of the English Church and Clergy" (but only, they added at this point, "so far as the law of Christ allows")—Redman reprinted Caxton's text of the *Life of Our Lady;* it would not be published again in its entirety until the 1961 modern edition.[57] In 1538, one of Bilney's famous Cambridge converts, Hugh Latimer, wrote to Thomas Cromwell about how the image of the Virgin at Worcester "hath been the devil's instrument," gleefully suggesting that "she herself," along with other images of the Virgin, "would make a jolly muster in Smithfield," where heretics—and, in Latimer's day, recusants—were burned; he adds, "They would not be all day in burning."[58] In this world, a literary that rests on a triangulation of Marian devotion, counterheresy, and political utility was simply no longer feasible, and thus, with *A Replycacion*, one sort of articulation of the literary in the English vernacular came to an end.

---

57. For the events of 1531, see A. G. Dickens, *The English Reformation*, 2nd ed. (University Park: The Pennsylvania State University Press, 1989), 124–25. For the publication history of the *Life of Our Lady*, see Alain Renoir and C. David Benson, "John Lydgate," in *A Manual of the Writings in Middle English*, ed. Albert E. Hartung (Hamden: The Connecticut Academy of Arts and Sciences, 1980), 1809–1920, 2071–2175 at 2129–30. Pearsall also notes that Simon Quinlan edited the work in his 1957 University of London dissertation (*John Lydgate*, 292). For Redman's edition (STC 17025), see Gillespie, *Print Culture*, 176–78; interestingly, this edition, as Gillespie's reproduction of f. A1r shows, foregrounds the Henry V rubric even more than Caxton's does.

58. Qtd. in James Simpson, *Reform and Cultural Revolution* (Oxford: Oxford University Press, 2002), 414. Simpson also notes the chronological proximity of Redman's edition of the *Life of Our Lady* to the "strippings of the Virgin in 1538, the suppression of female monastic houses mostly in 1536, and the derisive gendering of the Roman Church" (416). For further accounts of the suppression of Marian devotion, see Rubin, *Mother of God*, 376–78.

7

Useless Mouths

Reformist Poetics in Audelay and Skelton

MISHTOONI BOSE

The "useless mouths" in the title of Simone de Beauvoir's play, *Les bouches inutiles* (1945), are those of the women, children, the old and the infirm of Vaucelles, a fourteenth-century Flemish city.[1] When the city is under siege, they threaten to cause a dangerous drain on energy and provisions, and the resulting emergency gives rise to a debate as to whether or not they should be sacrificed by exposure in order to ensure the city's survival. Hardship brings with it a perspective from which the human being, synecdochically shrunk to a "useless mouth," is surplus to requirements. In the present essay, I use the image of the useless mouth to bring into focus an important theme in English poetry written during the long fifteenth century: the clerical poet as *bouche inutile,* his paradoxical situation and singular self-image arising from the tension between his empowering vocation and his prophetic compulsions. Such compulsions generate their own paradoxes, requiring the poet-priest to situate himself in the margins of discourses and institutions, analyzing, lamenting, yet, above all, compulsively re-creating their problems. And consequently, the would-be prophetic voice is itself subject to necessary contamination by self-consciousness and irony.

The suspicion that poetry, whatever its ostensible commitment to modeling and instigating ethical and religious reform, may be nothing more than the ambivalent mutterings of a useless mouth, had been memorably articulated by Ymaginatif in *Piers Plowman:*

---

1. Ed. Catherine Léglu (London: Bristol Classical Press, 2001).

> And thow medlest thee with makynges—and myghtest go seye thi Sauter,
> And bidde for hem that yyveth thee breed: for ther are bokes ynowe
> To tell men what Dowel is, Dobet and Dobest bothe,
> And prechours to preve what it is, of many a peire freres. (B.XII.16–19)[2]

The two poet-priests considered in this essay, John Audelay and John Skelton, must have shared with the author of *Piers Plowman* the common knowledge that there were "bokes ynowe" to guide people in the moral life. More pertinently still for a priest, there were the sacraments themselves to ensure salvation. Thus in these and other writers we find a dialectic between priestly awareness of Ymaginatif's argument and the urge to speak prophetically, resulting in poems that compulsively retrace the fault-lines between authority and vulnerability not only in the personae of the speakers themselves, but in the clerical or curial institutions to which, and within which, they speak. But *Piers Plowman* had also set up a parallel world beyond the control of any one institution in which such fault-lines are not merely represented, but framed and relativized, and in which even Ymaginatif is the outcome of a poetic vocation whose other fruits he impugns. And it is in their comparable compulsion to create imaginative worlds in which the clashing energies of institutional reform and collapse are given full play that Audelay and Skelton test the eloquence of the useless mouth to the limit. Both exhibit a distinctive clerical subjectivity produced by, and active within, established literary traditions of ecclesiastical satire. But exploration of the fortuitous affinities between their poetic worlds must go further, focusing not merely on the literary traditions that they inherited, but, more substantially, on their shared concerns with reformist poetics.

James Simpson's characterization of late-medieval English literature as broadly reformist in the sense that it is "[a] cultural field characterized by a diverse and highly segmented set of jurisdictions" is suggestive and enabling, but my use of the term "reformist" in the present essay is more purely driven by reflections on the interplay between ecclesiastical mentalities and literary developments in the fifteenth century.[3] The essay is thus part of a wider current phenomenon: the emergence of new literary histories—and, in particular, new fifteenth centuries—generated by the recent shift in critical attention to the interactions between Wycliffism and orthodox reform, and the cumulative impact of these interactions on intellectual, religious, and literary life in late-medieval England. Fiona Somerset puts it well: "[n]ow that Lollardy is on the map, everything else seems to have moved."[4] As the study of heresy has melded with investiga-

---

2. The citation is from *The Vision of Piers Plowman*, ed. A. V. C. Schmidt, 2nd ed. (London, 1995).

3. *Reform and Cultural Revolution, 1350–1547, Oxford English Literary History*, ed. Jonathan Bate, vol. 2 (Oxford: Oxford University Press, 2002), 2.

4. *Lollards and Their Influence in Late Medieval England*, ed. Fiona Somerset, Jill C. Havens, and

tions into the literary consequences of concern with church reform—a far more prominent feature of late-medieval English intellectual life than heresy ever was—what is gradually coming into focus is a picture of persistence, resilience, and audacity across a number of discursive fields, as writers in both English and Latin sought to preserve the topic of intraclerical and lay–clerical relationships as a subject for dispute, conjecture and often invective.[5] It is natural to consider how Audelay and Skelton might benefit from the resulting critical plate tectonics, and I essay that process here. Audelay has just been granted a place in this new literary landscape.[6] By contrast, the ecclesiastical, as distinct from the curial, Skelton is hardly a new figure in literary criticism, as the discussion below will make clear.[7] Nevertheless, listening to his poetry with an ear attuned to the various attitudes and textual strategies generated during and after the Wycliffite controversies suggests new ways of historicizing the pleasurable discomfort that his work forces upon its readers. To approach Skelton via Audelay enables us to appreciate two phases in the evolution of English reformist poetics: first, an audacious and strong-minded modification of Langlandian idioms, designed to emphasize the ambiguities and problems of perception that afflicted clerical identities and vocations in the immediate aftermath of the Wycliffite controversies; and second, the reinvention of goliardic poetry to forge a new poetic idiom that nearly broke with the literary and institutional past altogether, only permitting it to be replayed in fragmented and diminished form.[8] Thus, in what follows, I propose that Audelay's and Skelton's writings be considered as separate but comparable poetic evocations of an essentially turbulent and discursively capacious religious orthodoxy.[9] And one hopes that a poet who complained, in *Agenst*

Derrick G. Pitard (Woodbridge: Boydell, 2003), 16.

5. I consider intraclerical and lay–clerical debates at greater length in "Writing, Heresy and the Anticlerical Muse," in *The Oxford Handbook of Medieval English Literature,* ed. Greg Walker and Elaine Treharne (Oxford: Oxford University Press, 2010), 276–96.

6. See most recently *My Wyl and My Wrytyng: Essays on John the Blind Audelay,* ed. Susanna Fein (Kalamazoo, MI: Medieval Institute Publications, 2009). The present essay was substantially completed when this collection appeared, but there are obvious points of contact between it and several essays in the Fein collection, notably that of Robert J. Meyer-Lee ("The Vatic Penitent: John Audelay's Self-Representation," 54–85) and that of Derek Pearsall ("Audelay's *Marcolf and Solomon* and the Langlandian Tradition,"138–52).

7. For one version of the ecclesiastical Skelton, see Arthur Kinney, *John Skelton, Priest as Poet: Seasons of Discovery* (Chapel Hill and London: University of North Carolina Press, 1987). I share one reviewer's view, however, that in this book "the interrelationship is pushed too hard" in ways that flatten much of the poetry (Christine M. Rose, *Speculum* 65 [1990]: 442–45 [442]).

8. In the most comprehensive recent study of Skelton, Jane Griffiths briefly suggests a possible origin for the Skeltonic in the medieval lyric: *John Skelton and Poetic Authority: Defining the Liberty to Speak* (Oxford: Clarendon Press, 2006), 18, n. 8.

9. James Simpson briefly but suggestively adumbrates such a comparison: "Resources of the kind deployed by Audelay re-surfaced in the new theological environment of the 1520s to 1550s. . . . Like Audelay, Skelton positions himself outside the Church and addresses it in what is perhaps the last orthodox example of traditional anti-ecclesiastical satire" (*Reform and Cultural Revolution,* 380–81).

Garnesche, that "I was made poete lawreate. / To cal me lorell ye are to lewde" (84–85) would not actively disapprove of the reading that follows, which presents his poetic world as a place where Tutivillus, the genius of linguistic discord, vies with Tully, avatar of eloquence, for the role of presiding genius.[10]

I

It is essential to the reading of Skelton to be pursued here that we keep constantly before us the uncertain, and unregulated, *bouche inutile* through which much of his language pours, for this will determine much about the way in which we assess the tone of what he writes. James Simpson has observed that in the *Bowge of Courte*, "Drede is drawn by the desire of the 'bouche,' or 'pouch' of court, but this desire diminishes the authority of his own *bouche* or mouth."[11] Simpson further suggests that Skelton's growing bid for agency may be discerned in the changing role of conversational fragments in his poetry: according to such a reading, "scraps of conversation" hurled at the narrator in *Bowge* later mutate into purposefully wrought linguistic and cultural *bricolage* endowed by increasingly active narrators with a heavily satiric charge.[12] It is fruitful to consider the point at which Skelton began to regroup his poetic energies in this way; that is, the point at which "form and reform" first coalesced meaningfully in his writing. This decisive shift came after his ordination, during his years as rector of Diss, in Norfolk, a period during which he pioneered the Skeltonic and thus invented an entirely new way through which poetic and institutional worlds might speak to one another. It is in the first major poem from the Diss years, *Ware the Hauke*, that we see the testing and exploring of both his professional and poetic self-reinventions.

The incident that this poem records, or simply imagines, is well known. While at Diss, Skelton claims to have discovered a priest hawking in his church. The poem does not merely describe the desecration and its discovery, but grotesquely inflates the roles of both the vandal priest and his righteously indignant witness, so that a familiar clerical transgression that had long given cause for concern is

---

10. On Tutivillus, see Margaret Jennings, "*Tutivillus. The Literary Career of the Recording Demon*," *Studies in Philology* 74.5 (1977): 1–93; Kathy Cawsey, "Tutivillus and the 'Kyrkchaterars': Strategies of Control in the Middle Ages," *Studies in Philology* 102 (2005): 434–51; Sandy Bardsley, *Venomous Tongues. Speech and Gender in Late Medieval England* (Philadelphia: University of Pennsylvania Press, 2006), 52–57; Susan E. Phillips, *Transforming Talk: The Problem with Gossip in Late Medieval England* (University Park, PA: Penn State University Press, 2007), 21–31.

11. *Reform and Cultural Revolution*, 248.

12. "The Death of the Author?: Skelton's *Bowge of Courte*," in *The Timeless and the Temporal: Writings in honour of John Chalker by friends and colleagues*, ed. Elizabeth Maslen (London: QMW Department of English, 1993), 58–79, esp. 69–70. This essay is developed further in chapter 8 of the present volume.

interpreted as an assault not merely on the fabric of a particular building, but on the fundamental authority of the Church.[13] Skelton swiftly recasts the hawking priest as a full-blown heretic, and his witness as both a defender of orthodoxy and an instigator of reform:

> That preest that hawkys so,
> All grace is far hym fro.
> He semeth a sysmatyke
> Or else an heretike,
> For faith in hym is faynte.
> Therefore to make complaynt
> Or such mysadvysed
> Parsons and dysgysed,
> Thys boke we have devised,
> Compendyously comprysed,
> No good preest to offend,
> But suche dawes to amend . . . (15–26).[14]

But things are not this simple. As Stanley Fish long ago pointed out, "For the reader, *Ware the Hauke* is an uncomfortable experience. . . . What of pastoral care, judicial corruption, heresy, considerations too large, perhaps, for the incident in question, but nonetheless there? In short, there is in *Ware the Hauke* no clear moral focus [. . .]."[15] These seem to me among the most honest comments that the poem has ever provoked. For this poem does not merely burlesque the tensions between heresy and reform: it exacerbates them. There is much more than the blame function of *epideixis* at work here. Instead Skelton deliberately builds a poem in which nothing may be seen in its proper perspective, as in the subliminally Chaucerian maneuver whereby the fall of Constantinople is belittled by comparison with the hawking at Diss (216–19).[16] Skelton goes far beyond merely denouncing the abuse: he presides over, re-stages and even elaborates it. He expresses his horror at the transgression, but cannot suppress the reporting of the wayward priest's imagined wish that "the dowves donge downe might fall / Into my chalys at mas" (183–84). Although that particular act of vandalism does

---

13. John Scattergood, "Skelton and Traditional Satire: *Ware the Hauke*," *Medium Aevum* 55 (1986): 203–216; Janet Wilson "Skelton's *Ware the Hauke* and the 'Circumstances' of Sin," *Medium Aevum* 58 (1989): 243–57.

14. All quotations from Skelton's poetry are taken from *John Skelton: The Complete English Poems*, ed. John Scattergood (Harmondsworth: Penguin, 1983).

15. *John Skelton's Poetry* (New Haven and London: Yale University Press, 1965), 97.

16. Skelton's tactics here recall the famous claim in the *Nun's Priest's Tale* that "Certes, he Jakke Straw and his meynee / Ne made nevere shoutes half so shrille / When that they wolden any Flemyng kille, / As thilke day was maad upon the fox" (3394–97).

not actually take place—only the *corporas* is defiled in this way, in a parody of the descent of the Holy Spirit in the form of a dove—a confused reader might be forgiven for thinking that it had. Skelton has exploited the unregulated arena of the poem to amplify the priest's transgression further, sadistically inviting his readers to enact a further phase of desecration in their imagination, and thus to come close to the satirical speculations disseminated among earlier generations of Wycliffite writers concerning the ontological status of fragments of the consecrated host that had been eaten by mice.[17] And Skelton invites his readers to think that the poem's most immediate cause is a failure of ecclesiastical discipline: bribery ("mayden Meed," 149) has ensured that his allegations about the matter have not been given a fair hearing in the courts.

Above all, however, the newly minted Skeltonic was a most unlikely delivery system for the clear moral dichotomies between heresy and orthodoxy that the poem's narrator proposes. For in this verse form, Skelton has deliberately crafted an undiscriminating engine of goliardic compression that reduces the muniments of ecclesiastical legislation, so necessary for a full understanding of, and participation in, religious controversy, to vulnerable fragments. Thus the pejorative suffix "-ista" in lines 250–58 razes the *sophista, silogista* and "dogmatista" to the level of doggerel-fodder. In particular, feminine rhymes littered throughout the poem drain concepts of their semantic fullness—and thus their institutional and cultural dignities—by prioritizing their sounds, as in lines 103–105, in which the authority of the Sarum rite is undermined via contamination from its rhyme-words:

Sed non secundum Sarum
But lyke a March harum
His braynes were so *parum.*

Rhyme similarly induces insidious parataxis in lines 13–14, where the doctrinal edification provided by the Church "[t]hat of our fayth the grownd is" is trivialized by its collocation with "the holy church bowndis" within which the petty outrage of the hawking took place.

Most importantly, the simple act of pluralizing "decretals . . . sinodals . . . [and] provincials"—the institutions, processes and documentary genres through which religious orthodoxy is brokered, authorized, defended and disseminated—threatens to reduce them to nothing more than a pile of dusty, impotent books and irrecoverable procedures:

---

17. Anne Hudson, "The Mouse in the Pyx: Popular Heresy and the Eucharist," *Trivium* 26 (1991): 40–53.

> Or els is thys Goddis law,
> Decrees or decretals,
> Or holy sinodals,
> Or els provincyals,
> Thus within the wals
> Of holy church to deale,
> Thus to ryng a peale
> Wyth his hawkys bels?
> Dowtles such losels
> Make the churche to be
> In smale auctoryte;
> A curate in specyall
> To snappar and to fall
> Into this opyn cryme;
> To loke on this were tyme. (130–44)[18]

The instruments of ecclesiastical discipline—the "correctyon" whose lack is lamented in line 162—are here exposed by Skelton's poetic idiom in a manner that makes clear, and thus frays even further, the fragile consensual threads by which their authority is legitimated. It is not only the hawking priest here who has made the Church "in smale auctoryte": the cumulative impact of the Skeltonic in this poem is that of mimetic degradation. There is a consistency here with the effect achieved by a remark that had been attributed to Reginald Pecock at his interrogation for heresy, namely, that his interlocutors were doctors, like Jerome and Augustine, so they might as well cite themselves. Whilst ostensibly flattering his contemporaries, the remark casually dethrones the Fathers, thereby anticipating the Skeltonic both in its compression of a vast swath of time and in the consequent dismantling of *auctoritas* that typically depended on the preservation of a decorous temporal distance between writers and readers.[19] How had things got to this point?

---

18. "Muniments" is a particularly pertinent term here because both its current sense ("A document . . . preserved as evidence of rights or privileges") and its obsolete sense ("Something serving as a defense or protection") could aptly describe the documents and processes passing through the Skeltonic shredder in these lines. See *OED, muniment* (n).

19. "Quare vos non allegatis vosmet, cum estis doctores, ut Jeronimus et Augustinus?" ["Why don't you cite yourselves in support of your arguments, since you are doctors, as Jerome and Augustine were?"], quoted by Thomas Gascoigne in his *Liber Veritatum* and printed in *Loci e Libro Veritatum*, ed. James E. Thorold Rogers (Oxford: Oxford University Press, 1881), 217.

II

One way of answering that question is to turn to Audelay's poetry, extant in a single manuscript (Oxford, Bodleian Library MS Douce 302).[20] Audelay's body of work not only exemplifies, on its own terms, the literary resourcefulness of English reformism, but also shows that Skelton's provocative maneuverings in *Ware the Hauke* are not without precedent, however fortuitously. The second poem in this collection, *De concordia inter rectores fratres et rectores ecclesie*, which takes the form of a dialogue between the characters of Marcol and Solomon, shows what happened to Langlandianism in the early decades of the fifteenth century.[21] Marcol, "the more fole mon," in his "mad wyse," gives "broder Salamon" an evangelical commission: "to say, as I here": that is, to be his mouthpiece (66–67). Marcol, who has a long lineage in multilingual literary histories, appears here in his familiar guise as the subversive so-called fool who, like a prophet, is "touchid upon the tong, the soth for to say" (236).[22] And the risks that this poem takes are broached, not without some seriousness, when the poem's speaker declares that "Fore to stond at a stake, bren ther Y wolde / ȝif Y say falslé at my wyttyng" (501–502). The poem proposes an accord between friars and secular priests (thus 390: "I make a loue day" and 393: "Spare not to say the soth, and make a loue day"). Given the existence of long-established tensions between the two, there are several literary analogues for Audelay's poetic loveday, not least in the lengthy dialogue in the Carmelite Thomas Netter's near-contemporary *Doctrinale* (1420s) in which a regular and secular priest praise each other's status and regard each other as brothers rather than as rivals.[23] Early in the poem, Marcol authorizes Solomon to "Do thi message mekely to preste and to frere; / Thai are the lanternys of lyf, the leud men to lyght" (70–71). The phrase "lantern of light" that is fragmented by the line anchors the poem in the rhetoric of reform, connecting as it does the biblical phrase *lucerna pedibus meis* (Psalm 118, *v.* 105: "Thy word is a lamp to my feet, and a light to my paths") with

---

20. All references are taken from John the Blind Audelay, *Poems and Carols (Oxford, Bodleian Library MS Douce 302)*, ed. Susanna Fein (Kalamazoo, Michigan: Medieval Institute Publications, 2009), accessed via the TEAMS website: http://www.lib.rochester.edu/camelot/teams/fsjacmsf.htm (accessed 21st February 2010).

21. On the Langlandian context of Audelay's poetry, see Pearsall, "Audelay's *Marcolf and Solomon*," an important response (and in certain respects a corrective) to James Simpson, "Saving Satire after Arundel's *Constitutions*: John Audelay's 'Marcol and Solomon,'" in *Text and Controversy from Wyclif to Bale: Essays in Honour of Anne Hudson*, eds. Helen Barr and Ann M. Hutchison (Turnhout: Brepols, 2005), 387–404. I prefer the Latin title *De concordia*, derived from Scribe B's incipit to this poem, to the unauthorized *Marcolf and Solomon*.

22. I have discussed other incarnations of Marcol and his interlocutor Solomon in "From Exegesis to Appropriation: the Medieval Solomon," *Medium Aevum* 65 (1996): 187–210.

23. I compare and contrast Audelay and Netter more fully in "Writing, Heresy and the Anticlerical Muse."

the title of a vernacular treatise deemed to be Wycliffite. Its continued validity in reformist polemic would later be marked by Skelton in *Collyn Clout*, in which the "bysshopes of estates" are urged to "com forthe at large / Lyke lanternes of light, / In the peoples syght" (690, 693–95).

Marcol often addresses Solomon, whom he authorizes to broadcast and act on his criticisms; but his is a notoriously mobile voice, and the addressees of successive stanzas change abruptly, with Marcol swerving between secular priests and friars without warning in an attempt to balance his criticisms of the different clerical strata, homing in now on the necessity of friars preaching, now on the sin of simony amongst secular priests, and latterly turning to "al Cristun men" to command them to participate in the sacrament of the altar, and of confession. The result is, as James Simpson has aptly put it, "a voice under pressure," a feature that becomes particularly clear in passages such as the following:[24]

> Yif ther be a pore prest, and spirituale in spiryt,
>   And be deuoute with deuocion, his seruyse syng and say,
> Thay lekon hym to a Lollere and to an epocryte;
>   Yif he be besé in his bedus þe Prince of heuen to pay,
> And holde hym in Holé Cherche, dulé uche day
>   Oute of þe curse of cumpané, and kepe his concyans clene,
> He ys a nyþyng, a noght, a negard, thai say. (131–37)

The meaning of the first few lines quoted here is clear enough: moral panic over an ill-defined "Lollardy" has reached such a pitch that even sacerdotal zeal might be regarded by some as a form of dissent. The phrase "thai say" (137) and its variants recur throughout the poem and are essential in creating its prevailing atmosphere of ill-founded rumor and premature accusation. But a reader lulled into confidence by this stanza might easily be thrown by lines 664–688, with their rapid shifts in focus. In the first stanza of this extract, shifts of perspective enact the armed truce that apparently exists between laypeople and curates over the matter of tithes, with each side withdrawing into either avarice (on the part of the curates) or righteous indignation corroborated by anticlerical prophecy (on the part of the laypeople):

> The prophecy of the prophetus, ale nowe hit doþ apere,
> That sumtyme was sayd be þe clergé:
> That leud men þe laue of God that schuld loue and lere,
> Fore curatis fore here couetyse, wold count noght þer-by,
> Bot to talke of here teythys, Y tel you treuly.

---

24. "Saving Satire," 389.

> And yif þe secular say a soth, anon thai bene eschent,
> And lyen apon the leud men and sayn, "Hit is Lollere!"
> Thus the pepul and the prestis beth of one asent;
> > Thai dare no noder do,
> > Fore dred of þe clergé
> > Wold dampnen hem vnlaufully
> > To preche apon þe pelere,
> > And bren hem after too.
> *Ve vobis qui dicitis malum bonum et bonum malum.* (664–77)[25]

The interpretative challenge posed by this stanza is partly caused by Audelay's use of a carefully coded lexis that insists on separating out the "curatis" from the "secular," "prestis" from "clergé," "leud men" from "pepul." It may be a difficulty partly created by the requirements of alliteration, but it infects the reader with the interpretative paranoia, arising from perpetually unstable points of reference, that is not merely depicted but enacted throughout the poem. Its suggestion that secular priests might, under pressure, elide what is "soth" with what is "Lollere" certainly casts a heavily ironic light on the curse from Isaiah, with its insistence that good and bad are easily distinguished. The following stanza is less syntactically challenging, but is nevertheless remarkable for its change in perspective:

> Lef thou me, a Loller his dedis thai wyl hym deme.
> Yif he withdraue his deutes fro Holé Cherche away,
> And wyl not worchip the cros, on hym take good eme,
> And here his matyns and his masse apon the haleday,
> And belevys not in þe sacrement, that hit is God veray,
> And wyl not schryue him to a prest on what deþ he dye,
> And settis noght be þe sacrementus, sothly to say,
> Take him fore a Loller, Y tel you treuly,
> > And false in his fay!
> . . .
> Deme hym after his saw;
> Bot he wyl hym withdraw,
> > Neuer fore hym pray. (677–88)

Having declared that a layperson's deeds will expose him as a "Loller" if he withholds his tithes, the voice switches aggressively to the imperative in line 684 and takes refuge in condemnation: "Take him fore a Loller." But despite the disorientating changes of focus in Audelay's poem, one issue remains prominent: what

---

25. Isaiah 5:20.

unites the disparate perspectives tried out by the poem's speaker is a recurrent concern that the transgressions—real or misconceived—of all the clerical orders will alienate the "leud" men: "I am heuy in my hert and chaunget al my chere, / To wyt leud men, unleryd, lagh hem to scorne" (395–96). Thus when the friars cash in on the vogue for trentals, "Hit is no ferly thagh the folke in hom thai han no fay!" (472). The poem's chief concern is not merely that the clergy should act as viable intermediaries between God and the laity: they must be seen and thought to do so. Even though the speaker stops well short of Donatism, maintaining that the sacrament of the altar may not be "enpayrd" if the priest sings Mass "unworthelé" (833–34), an explicit assumption runs throughout the poem that the laity have a role in validating this; and equally, there is an ever-present fear that the various kinds of corruption to which both friars and secular priests may fall prey will result in either apathy or scorn amongst the laity.

This aspect of the poem has attracted little attention, but is quite possibly its most nuanced contribution to the discourse of reform. It brings to the fore a vexed emphasis throughout this period on the ways in which perception could create reality.[26] In one sense, the poem endorses the application of critical scrutiny on all sides, not least in its repeated insistence that "deeds" could "deme" (judge—and, in this case, condemn) a person, whether lay or clerical. But in the slippery mobility of the voice in the passages I have quoted, there is both a collusion with, and a recoiling from, the way in which sympathy for the zeal of a "pore prest" misunderstood and condemned as a Lollard could suddenly mutate into condemnation (from a priest's perspective) of a layperson who will not pay his tithes—and who is equally vulnerable to being called a Lollard.[27] The term "Loller" in this poem emerges as what Jeremy Catto has suggested it may have become: "effectively meaningless," an imprecisely used, generalized term of abuse, thrown about as carelessly, or at least as highly subjectively, by the voices in this poem as it is by the monks at Canterbury in their chiding of Margery Kempe.[28] At such moments as the ones that I have quoted here, the poem rests content to transmit a medley of voices that see a sequence of episodes in lay/clerical relations from incompatible perspectives. Occasionally this cacophony is wrapped up in the voice of the prophet—in this case, Isaiah. But the perspective transmitted by the Latin, in which conduct is divided up between the good and the bad, sits uneasily in a vernacular arena so assiduously mimetic of an ecclesiastical world in which vested

---

26. The necessity for discrimination between "rumor and hearsay" and "reliably reported suspicion" is invoked as a context for this poem in Ian Forrest, *The Detection of Heresy in Late Medieval England* (Oxford: Clarendon Press, 2005), 167–68.

27. For another appraisal of the poem's "mobility of voice," see Simpson, "Saving Satire," 401.

28. Catto offers a nuanced appraisal of what the term "Lollard" might or might not mean in "Fellows and Helpers: the religious identify of the followers of Wyclif," in *The Medieval Church: Universities, Heresy and the Religious Life. Essays in Honour of Gordon Leff*, eds. Peter Biller and Barrie Dobson (Woodbridge: Boydell and Brewer, 1999), 141–61, esp. 160.

interests or apathy on all sides make it difficult to discern good conduct from bad, or zeal from dissent.

Audelay had thus modeled one distinctive way in which fifteenth-century poets could have the courage of their Langlandianism. There are several routes from this poem to Skelton's poetic world. Firstly, the outpourings from Marcol's *bouche inutile* (the paradoxical phrase working particularly well here as a description of a fool's mouth) are undoubtedly among the most compelling features of this poem and sustain the case for its formal and ideological affinities, however accidental, with Skelton's later reformist polyvocality. In a poetic idiom that combines lexis and alliteration derived, however indirectly, from *Piers Plowman,* Audelay has interjected the tensions and suspicions circulating around him and vocalizes them deftly, frankly and with an allusiveness that results in a plethora of ambiguities.[29] It is this quality that explains why it has been argued that Audelay's voicing of Marcol the fool could be regarded as "a kind of funnel, through which scraps of reported speech, including prophecy and official legislation, flow."[30] Secondly, Audelay peddles anticlerical satire by lampooning an unlearned priest, comparing him to a caged bird whose ignorance leaves him at the mercy of his own utterances:

> Moné men of Holé Cherche thei ben ale to lewd;
> I lekyn ham to a bred is pynud in a cage.
> When he hath shertly hymselfe ale bescherewd,
> Then he begynys to daunse, to harpe, and to rage,
> For he is leud and understond not his oune langwage;
> Therfore he settes therby bot a lytyl prise,
> For he lerde hit in his youthe and in his yenge age,
> And castis hym neuer to lerne more al att here oun devyse.
>   I say you forewhy—
> Thus leud men þai can say,
> He is an honest prest in good faye,
> Yif his goune be pynchit gay,
>   He getis a salary. (547–59)

It is difficult not to see in this passage an uncanny preview (however accidental) of Skelton's avian satires, and *Speke Parott* in particular; and such a fortuitous poetic precedent suggests that Skelton risked creating merely an object of contempt: the shrieking, caged priest. No less than that of Marcol, Parott's voice in

---

29. On the poem's Langlandian affiliations, see Pearsall, "Audelay's *Marcolf and Solomon,*" and Simpson, "Saving Satire," 389, 402–403.

30. Simpson, *Reform and Cultural Revolution,* 380.

the early stanzas of *Speke Parott* runs the risk of being yet another potentially "useless mouth." In this poem, Skelton has created a syntactically and epistemologically paratactic, parallel world in which ephemeral and authoritative utterances often disconcertingly occupy the same plane. The resulting linguistic chaos, mimetic of a "decentered" world in which both political and academic spheres are bereft of "central unifying concepts" has led Greg Walker, for example, to argue that in this poem discourse rebounds against both bird and poet: "language in turn betrays Parott, and finally the text itself . . . betrays its author."[31] He finds no less "chaos, irrationality and caprice" in the anaphoric idioms of the poem's envoy (449–518) than of the bird-chatter that precedes it. Although Walker's reading of *Parott* here corroborates the characterization of Skelton as reformist self-saboteur that I have pursued in relation to *Ware the Hauke,* and will continue below, I would argue that in this case Parott's prophetic monologue drives the poem's linguistic and conceptual energies in another direction, suggesting how the compulsion to speak might be transformed into a purposeful vocation: castigation that names Chaos without capitulating to it, and does so in a reconstituted poetic idiom. As Theodore Steinberg observes concerning the Old Testament prophets that are one model for Parott, and Skelton, here: "Not only are they unafraid to speak the truth, however painful that truth may be, but they are unable to stop themselves from speaking it."[32]

In the hands of both Audelay and Skelton, the reformist poem became a place in which anger and anxiety might coalesce into prophecy or satire at any moment, and in which the two modes were forced to find a place alongside one another.[33] There are further fortuitous but specific connections between the preoccupations of these two poets: the apparent failure of a consistory court beguiled by Lady Meed (bribery) and thus unable to deliver justice, a situation of which *De concordia* keenly takes note (717–18), would become the ostensible pretext for *Ware the Hauke.* And in *De concordia* we have another precedent for *Ware the Hauke* in the form of a poem whose fragmented idiom reenacts the very institutional breakdown that has called the poem into existence. Finally, if we look beyond *De concordia* to a fragment from the Audelay manuscript, there is another suggestive link between these two poetic worlds in the form of the recording demon, Tutivillus, the presiding genius of the next phase in our argument.

---

31. Greg Walker, "'Ordered Confusion'?: The Crisis of Authority in Skelton's *Speke Parott,*" *Spenser Studies* 10 (1992): 213–28. The phrases quoted here appear on 225, 218, and 227 respectively.

32. "Poetry and Prophecy: A Skelton Key," in *Prophet Margins. The Medieval Vatic Impulse and Social Stability,* ed. E. L. Risden, Karen Moranski, and Stephen Yandell (New York: Peter Lang, 2004), 149–65, esp. p. 151.

33. The vatic motives of Audelay's poetry are more fully explored in Meyer-Lee, "The Vatic Penitent."

III

> My name is Collyn Cloute.
> I purpose to shake oute
> All my connynge bagge,
> Lyke a clerkely hagge.
> For though my ryme be ragged,
> Tattered and jagged,
> Rudely rayne-beaten,
> Rusty and mothe-eaten,
> Yf ye take well therwith,
> It hath in it some pyth.
> For, as farre as I can se,
> It is wronge with eche degree;
> For the tempralte
> Accuseth the spirytualte;
> The spirytualte agayne
> Dothe grudge and complayne
> Upon the temporall men. (*Collyn Clout*, 49–65)

The opening of Collyn's "connynge bagge," at once both receptacle and orifice, and therefore yet another paradigm of the useless mouth, has its own lineage in English literary history. In the decades that intervened between Lydgate and Skelton, aureate diction and the epistemological and institutional hierarchies that it served and represented had been constantly assailed, most notably in vernacular drama. Tutivillus, who thrives on linguistic fragmentation, was one of the means by which this subversion of institutional discourses was represented.[34] There is a "snatch of verse" at the end of the Audelay manuscript in which Tutivillus and another devil, Rofyn, act as *agents provocateurs,* "acting in collusion to tempt and then claim the sinners of mouth, who neglect their prayers and the holy service." They divide the task between them, Tutivillus provoking them to chatter during services, and Rofyn recording their words so that these may be used against them on Doomsday. Chief among the sinners are "Ouer-hippers and skippers, moterers and mumlers"—that is, those who vandalize language through laziness, pride, or simple inattention.[35] As a fifteenth-century verse has it: "Fragmina verborum TUTIVILLUS colligit horum" ["Tutivillus collects the fragments

---

34. "Sermons mention the sack in which he collects the syllables and syncopated words and verses which clerics steal from God by lazily omitting them from their prayers, and also the roll of parchment on which he writes down idle chatter spoken in church": G. A. Lester, "Introduction" to *Three Late Medieval Morality Plays. Mankind, Everyman, Mundus et Infans* (New York: Norton, 1981), xxii.

35. Susanna Fein, "A Thirteen-Line Alliterative Stanza on the Abuse of Prayer from the Audelay MS," *Medium Aevum* 63 (1994): 61–74, esp. pp. 63–64.

of these words"].³⁶ In one of his most famous appearances in English literature, the demon carries a "gret sacchell full of thing" in which he carries "sylablys and woordys, ouerskyppyd and synkopyd, and verse and psalmys the whiche these clerkys han stolyn in the qweere, and haue fayled in here seruyse."³⁷ *Mankind*, a play that resonates with noise emanating from morally useless mouths, provides some of the best-known examples of the all too easy degradation of Latin, whether via translation from English, or exploitation of the random connections in sound and disruptions of register that occur when the two languages come too close together. This aspect of a play in which the character "Nought" becomes "our Tully" (691) has often been discussed, most comprehensively by Janette Dillon, whose lucid account of dramatic language throughout this period underpins this phase of my argument.³⁸ Tutivillus presides over this inflicting of linguistic chaos, and even when he is not on stage, his function is recalled by other characters, as when Nowadays urges Mischief to translate obscenities into Latin: "Now, open your satchel with Latin words, / And say me this in clerical manner!" (133–34). Collyn Clout would inherit from Mischief, Tutivillus and Rofyn the moment at which the satchel is opened and the discursive decorums that prevent coherence and chaos from colliding with one another temporarily collapse.³⁹ Nor is this proposed alignment between clerical scourge and demon of indecorum so unlikely. Far from being simply an agent of Bakhtinian misrule, Tutivillus might equally be seen as the mouthpiece—far from useless this time—of religious rigour and authoritarianism, an *outré* embodiment of the Church's compulsive auto-critique. He could thus be viewed, like Skelton's Collyn and like satirists in general, as a self-administered poison that provokes the body's immune system into responding. But a larger question remains of whether or not the dethroning of Latin, or the fragmentation of prayers, or the proliferation of gossip—acts of discursive anarchy that occur under the sign of Tutivillus and comprise a notional hinterland for Skelton's poetic world—are processes that, once imagined and unleashed, can be controlled and directed, even by clerics. In Skelton's poetry we hear the syncopation not simply of individual words but of an entire Latinate culture. A. R. Heiserman claims that the "shredis of sentence" that Parott gathers in his crop (*Speke Parott*, 92, 95) are "fragments shored against the world's madness to create a buffer of hedonism."⁴⁰ But there is another sense in which, rather like

---

36. Ibid., 65.
37. *Jacob's Well*, ed. Arthur Brandeis, EETS o.s., 115 (London: Kegan Paul, Trench, Trübner, 1900), 115.
38. *Language and Stage in Medieval and Renaissance England* (Cambridge: Cambridge University Press, 1998), particularly pp. 31–69.
39. Cf. Simpson: "Scraps of different voices are ventriloquized by Colin, including prophecies and official threats against the very kind of discourse practiced by the poem itself" (*Reform and Cultural Revolution*, 381).
40. *Skelton and Satire* (Chicago: University of Chicago Press, 1961), 145.

Tutivillus in his role as *agent provocateur,* Skelton has to engineer such fragmentation, to splinter rather than to shore up, in order to make his poetry happen at all: "Fragmina verborum SKELTON colligit horum," perhaps. In *A Replycacion,* at the end of his career, he retained the same Skeltonic idioms that he had pioneered at Diss, and thus allowed the same destabilizing energies to remain in circulation. It remains for us to weigh the consequences of this decision.

IV

Janet Wilson has argued that Skelton rarely used parody after his return to Westminster.[41] Nevertheless, stylistic affiliations stubbornly subsist between *Ware the Hauke* and *A Replycacion* (1527/8), which Skelton appears to have written at the behest of Cardinal Wolsey and in tandem with Thomas More's *Dialogue Concerning Heresies,* to commemorate and to condemn the relapse into heresy of Thomas Bilney, a Cambridge student.[42] It would be unwise to claim that the *Dialogue* was nothing more than the "straight man" of this distinctive literary double act, for More's text conducted its own complex experiments with bodies of knowledge, resourcefully vernacularizing knowledge and juxtaposing scholastic disputation with folk wisdom. To bring these very different texts into focus on the same critical plane, it is only necessary to take into account Erasmus's notably eirenic view of the permissibility of widely contrasting discursive resources in the collective endeavor of vanquishing heresy:

> There is diversity of gifts and tastes; men are drawn to godliness by a thousand means. . . . Hilary thunders against heretics, Augustine disputes, Jerome contends in dialogues, Prudentius wars in various forms of verse, Thomas and Scotus fight with the help of dialectic and philosophy. All have the same purpose but each uses a different method. Variety is not condemned so long as the same goal is sought.[43]

But this leaves unresolved the fundamental question whether poetry and dialogue can serve only as the instruments of power or as the delivery systems for doctrine or penitential scourging, or whether they slip the noose of ideological determinism

---

41. "Skelton's *Ware the Hauke,*" 251.
42. On this episode, and the respective contributions of Skelton and More, see Greg Walker, "John Skelton, Thomas More, and the 'lost' history of the early Reformation in England," *Parergon* 9 (1991): 75–85; John Scattergood, "Skelton and Heresy," in *Early Tudor England: Proceedings of the 1987 Harlaxton Symposium,* ed. Daniel Williams (Woodbridge: Boydell, 1989), 157–70. The liturgically informed literariness of Skelton's *Replycacion* is assessed in Victor Scherb, "Conception, Flies, and Heresy in Skelton's 'Replycacion,'" *Medium Aevum* 62 (1993): 51–60.
43. "On the Usefulness of Colloquies," in *The Colloquies of Erasmus,* trans. and annot. Craig R. Thompson (Toronto, Buffalo and London: University of Toronto Press, 1997), 633.

too easily. More had anticipated the failure of persuasion in the *Letter to Dorp*, with his merciless and unanswerable claim that "one little bundle of faggots" was far more effective in deterring heretics than "many large bundles of syllogisms."[44] If syllogisms could not be relied upon to work—and it was a major humanist contention that they had failed—what could be achieved, not simply by poetry, but by *Skeltonic* poetry? It is possible to argue, as Vincent Gillespie has done, that in this late poem Skelton makes a robust case for the dignity of his poetic vocation, and for the ability of poetry to convey and defend theological truths.[45] According to this reading, the poet's voice in *A Replycacion* is anything but a useless mouth, even if one takes into account the peculiar discursive privileges enjoyed by fools, parrots, and prophets. But what, precisely, makes the famous protestation about the "effecte energiall," the image of "hevenly inspyracion," with which the poem closes, a statement of fact rather than wishful thinking? This is, after all, a poem in which Skelton is still haunted by the specter of his redundancy, and he is compelled to continue giving voice to such a specter, to resonate quasi-passively as these poetic winds blow through him:

Why fall ye at debate
With Skelton laureate,
Reputyng hym unable
To gainsay replycable
Opinyons detestable
Of heresy execrable?
Ye saye that poetry
Maye nat flye so hye
In theology,
Nor analogy,
Nor philology,
Nor philosophy,
To answere or reply
Agaynst suche heresy. (300–313)

It is curious that Skelton answers his anonymous detractors with nothing more argumentatively robust than hopeful assertions. Gillespie has re-created the creatively and broadly Hieronymian context in which Skelton takes refuge at this point in the poem ("Rede what Jerome there dothe say,"l. 328), as "Kyng David the prophet, of prophetes principal" is asserted to be "chefe poete," and the roles

---

44. *Letter to Dorp* (1515) in *In Defense of Humanism*, ed. Daniel Kinney. *The Yale Edition of the Complete Works of St. Thomas More*, 15 vols. (New Haven and London, 1986), 15:71.

45. "Justification by Faith: Skelton's *Replycacion*," in *The Long Fifteenth Century. Essays for Douglas Gray*, eds. Helen Cooper and Sally Mapstone (Oxford: Clarendon Press, 1997), 273–311.

of prophet, priest and poet are aligned.[46] But as with *Ware the Hauke*—and in contrast to the envoy of *Speke Parott*—there is something *tonally* wrong with this tableau. If Skelton is prophetic here, he is so in a particularly distinctive way, for even if one subscribes to the view that poetry can do theological work, *A Replycacion* is a problematic example of such poetry because it is composed from the impurities of satire and parody (including self-parody), refusing to organize them into a hierarchy, or simply to tidy them away. Like Gillespie, Heiserman is sympathetic to Skelton's aspirations here: if the "effecte energiall" whereby God "maketh his habytacion / In poetes" (376–77) really is infused, "even the ragged Skeltonic . . . has a source which makes it worthy," for "not only does this divine source make distinctions of style petty . . . [but] species of poems might be distinguished, not by their styles, but by their differing ends."[47] This would also accord with Erasmus's generous assessment of the legitimacy of employing different discursive styles in the fight against heresy. But *A Replycacion*'s lofty assertions and its inconsistent modes are insuperably at odds. When he translates Jerome's arguments for the superiority of David over all other poets, Skelton uses rhyme royal. When he returns to "our former processe," it is to the Skeltonics through which he had first fused the roles of priest and poet and, moreover, to a notably shaky argument:

> Than, if this noble kyng,
> Thus can harpe and syng
> With his harpe of prophecy
> And spirituall poetry,
> And saynt Jerome saythe,
> To whom we must gyve faythe,
> Warblynge with his strynges
> Of suche theologicall thynges,
> Why have ye then disdayne
> At poetes, and complayne
> How poetes do but fayne? (343–53)

Since David sang of "theologicall thynges," Skelton argues, poetry should be immune from the criticism that it is nothing but "feigning." Such an argument makes no allowance for any distinction between genres of poetry, let alone between modes or, less comfortably still, quality. And this assertion is not an argument: David is an exceptional case by any standards. In the passage that follows, Skelton makes another famous claim that poets are, like Mary, "kyndled in

---

46. Ibid., 287–93.
47. *Skelton and Satire*, 290.

suche facyon" by the Holy Ghost that "forthwith we must need / With penne and ynke procede." Pen and ink have replaced the image of the funnel-like mouth. And perhaps it *is* possible to see this image as exerting the Pentecostal authority necessary to do away, once and for all, with the undiscriminating babble of the *bouche inutile*. But can it entirely expel the image, gratuitously evoked in *Ware the Hauke,* of another dove's chaotic descent? There is another echo of *Hauke* in the Latin that follows, in which Skelton claims that there are an infinite number of sophists, logicians, philosophers and theologians, teachers and masters, "but poets are few and rare" (*sed sunt pauci rarique poete*). The effect that he risks producing here is similar to the one deliberately procured in *Hauke* whereby the pluralizing of entities had the effect of trivializing them: a tricky maneuver indeed in a poem ostensibly dedicated to the defense of orthodoxy for which, as he must surely have known, logicians, theologians, and teachers are at least as necessary as poets. And thus, once again, a Skelton poem playfully guys the annihilation of institutions and hierarchies in order that it might come into being.

V

The critical renaissance that Skelton is currently enjoying recently attracted the following warning from Helen Cooper: "We are beginning to feel comfortable with Skelton; and that may be the worst possible reaction to him."[48] I have attempted to respond to the implicit challenge in Cooper's observation by suggesting how a discomfiting Skelton might be rediscovered. And in this enterprise, it has been particularly valuable to have the opportunity of writing for a volume containing essays on the poet by Robert Meyer-Lee and James Simpson, both of whom have influenced our understanding of Skelton's work in important ways. In this essay I have sought to respond to some lines of inquiry suggested in their work. As I have acknowledged, I have found Simpson's brief collocations of Audelay and Skelton particularly suggestive. And like Meyer-Lee in the present volume, I propose an arc of development in English poetry that has one possible point of origin in the early decades of the fifteenth century and perhaps concludes with Skelton; but I propose an alternative lineage for Skelton from the Lydgatean one that Meyer-Lee delineates here. I do not discuss this trajectory in terms of laureateship and its discontents, since I do not see "Skelton's court career" as "the single most essential element of his poetic identity."[49] Some concluding words are therefore necessary on the question as to how Skelton might be resituated

---

48. "Skeltonics," *London Review of Books,* 14th December 2006, 32–34, esp. p. 34.
49. Robert Meyer-Lee, *Poets and Power from Chaucer to Wyatt* (Cambridge: Cambridge University Press, 2007), 205.

within the distinctly ecclesiastically inflected version of literary history that I have privileged here.

In her recent survey of Skelton criticism, Kathleen Tonry has identified a dialectical movement over time between formalist and historicist approaches to the poet.[50] Two essays, by John Scattergood and Bernard Sharratt respectively, which appeared fortuitously in the same year (1986), might seem at first simply to confirm the view that these distinct tendencies in Skelton criticism are not merely dialectical but dichotomous.[51] Scattergood locates *Ware the Hauke* in literary history, resourcefully uncovering the thick context of long-established legal and satirical traditions on which it draws, and hence finding "nothing unorthodox" in it.[52] Sharratt explores parallels between Skelton and Bakhtin, proceeding from the statement in *The Dialogical Imagination* that "language is heteroglot from top to bottom."[53] He issues a powerful warning against the temptation simply to revel in Skelton's verbal polyphonies for their own sake, and thus to depoliticize his poetry.[54] Instead, he suggests parallels between Bakhtin's engagements with the centralizing tendencies of the "Great Russian hegemony" and Skelton's opposition to "the centralising tendencies of arrogant power and blind wilfulness."[55] If we fuse the two approaches represented here by Scattergood and Sharratt, a hybrid critical position emerges whereby the poetry of orthodox reform has a duty to draw on all the polyphonic resources at its disposal, including a range of satirical tropes, in the face of the monologic readings of the world imposed either by heresy, or secular ambition, or both. This might be considered a persuasive reading of what happens in Skelton's poems, but in my view it still does not accommodate the cumulative impact of the stylistic ruptures and gratuitous fragmentation of bodies of knowledge from which Skelton's readers also derive their singular pleasures. If more emphasis is placed on these elements, what results is a polyvocality whose triumphs are far less assured: a style that does not merely reflect, but is constitutive of, a restless, dissonant orthodoxy constantly testing its latitudes and even risking its own collapse, since "frensy nor jelousy / Nor heresy wyll never dye" (*A Replycacion,* 407–408). As Sharratt intimates, Skelton's displays of linguistic and cultural fecundity might be interpreted as a series of attempts to forge the stylistic correlative of a broad-minded and resilient orthodoxy threatened with closure by a preemptive, impudent, and intellectually impoverished heresy. But the poetic idioms that he pioneered keep a stubbornly

---

50. "John Skelton and the New Fifteenth Century," *Literature Compass* 5 (2008): 721–39.

51. Scattergood, "Skelton and Traditional Satire"; Bernard Sharratt, "John Skelton: Finding a Voice—Notes after Bakhtin," in *Medieval Literature: Criticism, Ideology and History,* ed. David Aers (Brighton: The Harvester Press, 1986), 192–222.

52. "*Ware the Hauke,*" 206.

53. "John Skelton: Finding a Voice," 195.

54. Ibid., 218.

55. Ibid., 217, 219.

ambiguous, dissonant reality before his readers. The Skeltonic compresses and elides, thriving on plurals and diminutives. The resulting verbal music evokes an orthodoxy that was every bit as turbulent for Skelton as it had been for Audelay: a state in which, in my view, the inspiration that authorized the *bouche inutile* could be hoped for, but not taken for granted. Whenever Skelton gives in to his compulsion to revisit the edge of the precipice, the moment at which human systems of knowledge are annihilated orally, whether by cacophony or bird-talk, he comes nearer to committing the acts of epistemological terrorism imagined by Chaucer in *House of Fame* and *Parliament of Fowls*. Although the *Garlande or Chapelet of Laurel* is Skelton's most explicit reworking of *House of Fame,* in the poems discussed here, he showed, with much greater subtlety, the more profound level at which he had registered what is really at stake in Chaucer's dream poems: a cultural and epistemological free-fall from which there might be scant possibility of recovery, unless the world of the poem is granted validity—however fragile, however contingent—independent of the institutions that it reduces to rubble. Chaucer never recovered the nerve that it must have taken to write the last lines of *Fame,* choosing instead to replay the tidings of useless mouths more diffusely and often less courageously in the *Canterbury Tales*. And for all that the Skeltonic reprises the audacity of *Fame* by enshrining in poetic form the epistemological impasse invited by the Eagle's claim that "soune ys aire ybroke" (770), Skelton never quite brought himself to resolve the paradox of the poet's useless mouth by acknowledging outright that poetry is not obliged to do any moral or theological work at all, but can legitimately be a place in which mimesis prevails over moralizing. But the ultimate inheritor of the poetic lineage that he helped to create was an English poet who would pursue the uncomfortable implications of that possibility, in a text that confronts its readers with the indelible image of the poet's tongue impaled: Edmund Spenser.

Killing Authors

Skelton's Dreadful *Bowge of Courte*

JAMES SIMPSON[1]

Wynkyn de Worde's "publication of Skelton's *Bowge of Courte*, c. 1499, marks the first appearance in print of any substantial poem by a living English poet."[2] How ironic, then, that the first living poet to be published in England should represent himself, in this very poem, as committing suicide. The text is also published anonymously. No sooner does the living author achieve the immortality of print than he is stripped of his name and attempts to kill himself.

Of course authors have fictionally "died" long before Roland Barthes' essay, "The Death of the Author,"[3] but few so strikingly as Skelton's Drede in *The Bowge of Courte*, written between 1480 and 1498, in Skelton's first period of court association, before his removal to Diss.[4] At the end of the dream sequence,

---

1. An earlier form of this essay appeared as "The Death of the Author?: Skelton's *Bowge of Court*," in *The Timeless and the Temporal, Writings in Honour of John Chalker*, ed. Elizabeth Maslen (London: Queen Mary and Westfield College, 1993), 58–79. I thank the publishers for permission to reprint this revised version.
2. STC 22597. A. S. G. Edwards, "From Manuscript to Print: Wynkyn de Worde and the Printing of Contemporary Poetry," *Gutenberg Jahrbuch* 66 (1991): 143–48, at 143–44.
3. Roland Barthres, "La mort de l'auteur," *Manteia* 5 (1968): 12–17. The original text can be found in Roland Barthes, *Essais critiques IV, Le bruissement de la langue* (Paris: Seuil, 1984), 61–67, from which all citations in this essay are drawn. Further page numbers will be cited in the body of the text. The translation into English of this essay by Stephen Heath (*Image-Music-Text* (London: Fontana, 1977), 42–148) is reproduced in *Modern Criticism and Theory, a Reader*, ed. David Lodge (Harlow, UK: Longman, 1988), 167–72. The citations are from Heath, *Image, Music, Text*. Further page numbers will be cited in the body of the text.
4. For a convenient summary of the argument surrounding dating, see *John Skelton, The Complete English Poems*, ed. John Scattergood (Harmondsworth: Penguin, 1983), 395. See also Jane Griffiths,

and almost at the very end of the poem, the ship-borne Drede (unequivocally a poet), sees his enemies approach in a nightmarish rush, grabs the ship's handrail, and attempts to hurl himself overboard. Not only this, but there is no formal divide between the voice of Drede (speaking from within the dream) and that of the narrator-poet (hereafter "the poet") who frames the dream with a Prologue and Epilogue: both poet and Drede are indifferently the "I" of the poem—it is the poet's nightmare as much as Drede's. We can see how these two figures, really one, are merged syntactically in the penultimate stanza, as dream merges seamlessly into Epilogue:

> And as they came, the shypborde faste I hente,
> And thoughte to lepe; and even with that woke,
> Caughte penne and ynke, and wroth this lytell boke. (530–32)[5]

The poem thus ends with a spectacular death, the represented death of its own author. But, my reader might object, the poet, as distinct from Drede, *is* writing: the act of the epilogue is to assert the presence and coherence of the authorial act outside the nightmarish dream. If this is true, then the author here hasn't really "died" at all; his "death" through dread is only the terrible shadow-play of nightmare, whereas in waking life he is confidently writing.

But is he confidently writing? What he is recounting is, after all, the experience of Drede: the movement away from the dream to the solidities of waking rational life turns out to be recursive, right back into the very nightmare experience of dread, silence and suicide. Dreams and poems (as Freud and many late-medieval poets understood) are closely related experiences, which make similar hermeneutic demands on their "audiences"; isn't this the point that Skelton is making in his last stanza?

> I wolde therwith no man were myscontente;
> Besechynge you that shall it see or rede,
> In every poynte to be indyfferente,
> Syth all in substaunce of slumbrynge doth procede.
> I wyll not saye it is mater in dede,
> But yet oftyme suche dremes be founde trewe.
> Now construewe ye what is the resydewe. (533–39)

If it is the case that dream and poem are merged, and that Drede and poet are

---

John Skelton and Poetic Authority: Defining the Liberty to Speak (Oxford: Clarendon Press, 2006), 56 and further references. Griffiths dates the *Bowge* c. 1488.

5. All citations from the works of Skelton are taken from *John Skelton, The Complete English Poems*, ed. Scattergood.

merged, then are we not left with the same possibility I have already raised: that the poem is no more, or less, than the nightmare of the dream, just as evanescent, just as frightening, and just as ruthlessly efficient in doing away with authors?

What is the "resydewe" of this poem: court satire, or simply the inability to produce court satire? Is this a text in which the author's position is wholly subsumed in the fear from which he is trying to escape, by suicide? Is there any difference between the discursive conditions represented from *within* the poem (i.e., the impossibility of speaking), and those *of* the poem itself? If the poet's voice is as much subject to the powerful undertow of fear as Drede's, then what can be said by either Drede or the poet to recenter the poet's voice? If Drede holds true to his name, then the very possibility of political satire is neutralized, since personification allegory is iterative; personified concepts can, after all, only repeat their name's semantic range, and so Drede can only be frightened. There is only so much he can say (which will wholly consist of saying what he can't say). Drede (and therefore the poet) is effectively a "dead," or at best a dying poet.[6] Satire is by definition devoted to reform, but a dreadful satirist can reform nothing, since a dreadful satirist is no satirist at all.

So the question I put, and attempt to answer, in this essay arises from the response required of us by the poem's last line: "Now construewe ye what is the resydewe." What is the "resydewe" of *The Bowge of Courte,* the irreducible truth behind the poem's coding? In my first section I argue as strong a case as I can to persuade you that the author is effectively dead here, or, as I say, at least making his last gasps. This is a serious idea—*The Bowge of Courte* underlines just how serious it is. But it is also an extremely frightening idea—the audience represented from within the poem practices a Barthian reading, whereby its members happily enjoy (at least when it suits them) the free play of meanings, without reference to authorial intention. *The Bowge of Courte* reveals the authorial experience of such a readerly world from the inside. And so in the second, and final, section I argue that an ethical response to the poem is inseparable from the attempt at understanding the living authorial "residue." A reformist impulse does survive in this poem, but it does so only through the interpretive choices made by its readers. The very layout of the poem in de Worde's editions of both (?)1499 and (?)1510 thrusts this decision upon us,[7] since the poem's apparently

---

6. For an exceptionally penetrating argument about the dead end of allegory in the context of literalist philology, and how it feels (bad), see Helen Cooney, "Skelton's *Bowge of Court* and the Crisis of Allegory in Late-Medieval England," in *Nation, Court and Culture: New Essays on Fifteenth-Century English Poetry,* ed. Helen Cooney (Dublin: Four Courts Press, 2001), 153–67. I am very grateful to Helen Cooney for sending this article to me.

7. Respectively, STC 22597 and 22597.5. Jane Griffiths argues the same point, with reference to the narrative shock of Drede's attempted suicide: "By concluding on such a destabilizing note, *The Bowge of Court* fiercely startles the reader into engagement with his work." See Griffiths, *John Skelton and Poetic Authority,* 64.

authorial explicit "Thus endeth the Bowge of Court" is set together with, indeed seamlessly elided with in the later edition, the printer's colophon: "Enprinted at Westmynster By me Wynkyn the worde" (*sic*).[8]

I am acutely conscious that this essay does not explicitly situate Skelton's poem within traditions of authorship contemporary with the poem. It calls instead for an ethical response to the work of authors, as if that response, and the concept of the author, were ahistorical. I do not believe for a moment that the concept of the author is ahistorical, but I do believe that late-medieval court poetry is a locus in which one tradition of authorship easily recognizable to us, that of potentially pathological author under censorship (and pathological *because* under censorship), comes into view.[9] The authorial precariousness of Tudor court poetry is partly a matter of organizational shifts within court; partly of political centralizations; and partly a matter of correlative shifts in discursive practice.[10]

I

A very brief theoretical frame sets the ethical and hermeneutic issues into larger perspective. Every hermeneutic tradition reveals a particular set of power relations between the different loci from which textual and interpretative authority derive. The history of textual interpretation (in biblical, legal, and literary traditions, for example) is made up of a wide spectrum of different answers to the question as to where authority is to be located. But even within this wide spectrum of possible answers, the main currents of Anglo-American and French

---

8. This point is made by Anthony J. Hasler, "Cultural Intersections: Skelton, Barclay, Hawes, André," in *John Skelton and Early Modern Culture: Papers Honoring Robert S. Kinsman*, edited by David R. Carlson (Temple, AZ: Arizona Center for Medieval and Renaissance Studies, 2008), 63–84, at 72–73. I am grateful to Kathleen Tonry for pointing me to this locus. The misprint "Wynkyn the Worde" appears only in the earlier edition.

9. For medieval theories of authorship, see A. J. Minnis, *Medieval Theory of Authorship: Scholastic Literary Attitudes in the Later Middle Ages*, 2nd ed. (Aldershot, UK: Scolar Press, 1988). For the precarious position of early Tudor poets, see Colin Burrow, "The Experience of Exclusion: Literature and Politics in the Reigns of Henry VII and Henry VIII," in *The Cambridge History of Medieval English Literature*, ed. David Wallace (Cambridge: Cambridge University Press, 1999), 793–820.

10. For organizational shifts within the early Tudor court, see David Starkey, "The Age of the Household: Politics, Society and the Arts c.1350–c.1550," in *The Later Middle Ages*, ed. Stephen Medcalf (London: Methuen, 1981), 225–90, and, with specific reference to the *Bowge of Courte*, Greg Walker, "John Skelton and the Royal Court," in *John Skelton and Early Modern Culture*, ed. Carlson, 3–18, at 7–10. For the cultural centralizations and their attendant cultural disciplines, see James Simpson, *Reform and Cultural Revolution, 1350–1547*, volume 2 of *The Oxford English Literary History* (Oxford: Oxford University Press, 2002), especially chapter 5. For the shifts in discursive practice (especially the rising status of the literal sense and its attendant paranoia), see Cooney, "Skelton's *Bowge of Court* and the Crisis of Allegory in Late-Medieval England," and James Simpson, *Burning to Read: English Fundamentalism and its Reformation Opponents* (Cambridge, MA: Harvard University Press, 2007), Chapter 5 especially.

literary criticism in the latter half of the twentieth century were all agreed, curiously, on the banishment of one source of authority, the author. Despite their divergences, significant critical traditions each proscribed authors from the realm of critical discussion, and different centers of authority in the literary commonwealth have instead assumed the function of authors: the formal unity of texts (New Criticism), conventional codes (Structuralism), the textual community of readers (Reader-response Criticism), discursive formations (Foucauldian analysis), the unconscious (psychoanalytic criticism), and the differential instability of signifying systems themselves (Deconstruction) all conspired to keep discussion of authors well out of critical parlance.

The fact of literary authority was certainly preserved by these movements (even in the case of Deconstruction), but in each case displaced from its etymological source, the author, who was told to leave.[11] Sometimes he or she was sent packing merely by the cold shoulder of labelling author-talk as "naive," but when we review this series of movements at a glance, we notice that antipathy to discussion of authors was in fact a passionately held point of principle in each case; the Barthian metaphor of death signals the deadly seriousness (in an otherwise playful writer) with which the question of authorship is held.[12] Barthes' word "death" in fact doesn't seem willing to register the real extremity of his position, since it is more the case that Barthes is executing the author, rather than simply observing him or her pass away. A genteel snub won't do here—what's required is nothing short of revolutionary violence.

In his celebrated essay Barthes in fact describes the author's death in a variety of ways, with quite different implications for how it actually happens. He begins with a philosophical point, which suggests that writing is a kind of voluntary suicide, since the moment an event "est raconté, à des fins intransitives, et non plus pour agir directement sur le réel, c'est-à-dire finalement hors de toute fonction autre que l'exercise même du symbole, la voix perd son origine, l'auteur entre dans sa propre mort, l'écriture commence" (61) [" . . . is narrated no longer with a view to acting directly on reality but intransitively, that is to say, finally outside of any function other than that of the very practice of the symbol itself . . . the voice loses its origin, the author enters into his own death, writing begins" (142)]. This scenario, in which the author conveniently does the work of dying, soon gives way to another, in which the author clearly requires a certain help in putting himself to death: in his discussion of linguistics, Barthes says that this science "vient de fournir à la destruction de l'Auteur un instrument analytique précieux,

---

11. I argue this more fully in James Simpson, "Faith and Hermeneutics: Pragmatism versus Pragmatism," *Journal of Medieval and Early Modern Studies,* 33 (2003): 215–39.

12. For an intelligent account of this critical phenomenon, see Seán Burke, *The Death and Return of the Author: Criticism and Subjectivity in Barthes, Foucault, and Derrida,* 2nd ed. (Edinburgh: Edinburgh University Press, 1998).

en montrant que l'énonciation dans son entier est un processus vide . . . le langage connait un 'sujet,' non une 'personne'" (63) [" . . . has recently provided the destruction of the Author with a valuable analytical tool by showing that the whole of the enunciation is an empty process . . . language knows a 'subject,' not a 'person'" (145)]. This sentence leaves it unclear as to who is to wield the precious "*instrument*" for "destroying" the author, but the fact that a tool is required suggests that the author's death is to be something more than passive, painless suicide.

After a few accounts of the funeral festivities ("Having buried the author . . . " (146); "Once the author is removed . . . " (147)), discussion of the author's death is underwritten not by the language of suicide, but rather by that of revolutionary execution: Barthes says that "literature," by refusing to assign a secret, ultimate meaning, "libère une activité que l'on pourrait appeler contre théologique, proprement révolutionnaire, car réfuser d'arrêter le sens, c'est finalement refuser Dieu et ses hypostases, la raison, la science, la loi" (66) ["liberates an anti-theological activity, an activity that is truly revolutionary, since to refuse to fix meaning is, in the end, to refuse God and his hypostases—reason, science, law" (147)]. The final sentence is a rallying call to the guillotine: " . . . nous savons que, pour rendre à l'écriture son avenir, il faut en renverser le mythe: la naissance du lecteur doit se payer de la mort de l'Auteur" (67) [" . . . we know that to give writing its future, it is necessary to overthrow the myth: the birth of the reader must be at the cost of the death of the Author" (148)]. Barthes published this essay in 1968; the Ayatollah Khomeini, who himself later also developed an interest in the death of authors, was briefly in exile in France in 1978. That the Ayatollah was reading Barthes at the time is of course unlikely, despite the common interest.

I'd like this theoretical introduction, however brief, to direct the turn of this essay: Skelton's text is valuable in this context precisely because it represents exactly the championing of the free play of readerly meanings at the expense of the author's life. The poem is acutely aware of the ways in which authors can indeed be killed, certainly metaphorically, and possibly literally. The procedures of this "murder" will, as I say, be the subject of the first part of this essay. Whereas for Barthes (championing the reader's newfound power) the death of the author is the occasion for celebration, Skelton, however, represents the same experience from the point of view of the victim, the author. The pressure of this authorial perspective directs discussion in the last section.

Many readers will not know *The Bowge of Courte,* and might require the one further preliminary of a plot summary: in autumn the poet thinks of writing poetry in the tradition of the ancients, but is unable to begin (1–28); he sleeps and dreams that he sees a ship, which is discovered to be full of royal merchandise; the owner is Dame "Saunce-Pere" and the royal merchandise consists of this lady's favor. Saunce-Pere's lady-in-waiting, Danger, accuses the narrator of arrogance, and is told, on request, that the narrator's name is Drede. Drede tells Danger that he wants some of the ship's wares, at which point Danger leaves him disdainfully. Another, more kindly lady (Desire) approaches, who encourages Drede to speak up for what he wants, and gives him the jewel of "Bone aventure." He is to seek the favor of Fortune, which he promptly does, along with the other "merchants" who have come on board (29–126). The rest of the dream sequence is recounted as a series of encounters between Drede and his "companions," respectively Flattery (Favell), Suspicion, Hervy Hafter, Disdain, Riot, Dissimulation, and Deceit. Each of these encounters is prefaced with a monologue by Drede, and the sequence concludes with Drede's attempted suicide and the poet's writing of the poem when awake (127–532); there follows a short conclusion, in which the poet addresses his readers (533–39).

II

In the traditions of classical and medieval satire within which Skelton is writing, dread is often presented as the experience of the satirist. This is true, for example, of *Piers Plowman,* where Conscience (a supposedly courageous voice) is represented as unwilling, through fear, to push his case to its end ("*culorum*" means "conclusion"):

> The *culorum* of this cas kepe I noght to shewe;
> On aventure it noyed me, noon ende wol I make,
> For so is this world went with hem that han power
> That whoso seith hem sothest is sonnest yblamed. (B.3.280–83)[13]

We also find the same kind of thing being said in the intelligent early-fifteenth-century satirical poem, *Mum and the Sothsegger* (*Keeping Mum and the Truth-teller*). As soon as the truth-teller opens his mouth, he is hushed by Mum, who advises political expediency through silence. The truth-teller insists that he should speak out, despite the fact that many others don't through fear; there are many potential truth-tellers, he says,

> But the king ne his cunseil cunne not mete with thaym,
> But cleerly the cause I knowe not for sothe
> But dreede of the deeth dryveth thaym thens,
> Or elles looste of thaire likerous life uppon erthe. (125–28)[14]

---

13. William Langland, *The Vision of Piers Plowman,* ed. A. V. C. Schmidt, 2nd ed. (London, 1995).
14. *Mum and the Sothsegger,* in *The Piers Plowman Tradition,* ed. Helen Barr (London: Dent, 1993).

In Skelton's own poetry we find the same constraint on speaking, dread, defined as the inevitable experience of the satirist.[15] At the end of his *Colin Clout,* for example, he imagines the voices of his powerful enemies:

> Howe darest thou, daucocke, mell?
> How darest thou, losell,
> Allygate the gospell
> Agaynst us of the counsell?
> Avaunt to the devyll of hell!
>
> Take him, wardeyn of the Flete,
> Set hym fast by the fete!
> I say, lieutenaunt of the Toure,
> Make this lurdeyne for to loure. (1160–68)

All these poems that represent dread as the characteristic experience of the satirist nevertheless manage to overcome fear and to speak out. Their voice is represented as being situated outside, and as bravely addressing the court.[16] In *The Bowge of Courte,* however, Skelton makes a critical shift from the conventions of court satire, by placing the voice of the satirist as within the court, subject to the same desires as those he might be satirizing.[17] Instead of being the uplandish, "boistous" (or uncouth) satiric figure, Skelton's narrator is subject to the desire for courtly advancement, the "Bowge," or pouch of court—that's why he's on

---

Letter forms have been modernized. For other late-medieval examples of fear of speaking, see James Simpson, "The Constraints of Satire in *Piers Plowman* and *Mum and the Sothsegger,*" in *Langland the Mystics and the Medieval English Religious Tradition,* ed. Helen Phillips (Cambridge: Brewer, 1990), 11–30. See also Kathryn Kerby-Fulton, *Books under Suspicion: Censorship and Tolerance of Revelatory Writing in Late Medieval England* (Notre Dame, IN: University of Notre Dame Press, 2006).

15. For an extremely useful survey of Skelton studies, see Kathleen Tonry, "John Skelton and the New Fifteenth Century," *Literature Compass* 5 (2008): 721–39. I am grateful to Kathleen Tonry for allowing me to see this essay before publication.

16. For an expert survey of curial satire, with astute arguments about the *Bowge of Court,* see Ad Putter, "Animating Court Satire," in *The Court and Cultural Diversity,* ed. Evelyn Mullally and John Thompson (Woodbridge, Suffolk: Brewer, 1997), 67–76. See also Helen Barr and Kate Ward-Perkins, "'Spekyng for one's sustenance': the Rhetoric of Counsel in *Mum and the Sothsegger,* Skelton's *Bowge of Court,* and Elyot's *Pasquil the Playne,*" in *The Long Fifteenth Century: Essays in Honour of Douglas Gray,* ed. Helen Cooper and Sally Mapstone (Oxford: Oxford University Press, 1997), 249–72.

17. This point has been best made by Stanley Fish, *John Skelton's Poetry* (New Haven and London: Yale University Press, 1965), 77; Fish is arguing against the earlier argument of A. R. Heiserman, *Skelton and Satire* (Chicago: University of Chicago Press, 1961), who has it that Skelton merely rearranged the stylistic possibilities of satire to attack satire's conventional objects (chapter 2, *passim*). Fish, instead, argues that the focus is not on the court vices, but rather on Drede himself: "we watch him rather than them; his situation (mental and physical), not their exposure, is our point of focus" (77). I agree with Fish entirely here; I register my disagreement with him below.

board.[18] The discursive conditions of court life are represented from within.

If this is so, can the poem gain any purchase on the conditions of court life to attack or satirize it? Or does the poem, in the way of personification allegory, simply reiterate the dreadfulness of Drede's condition? I first consider the case that the poem remains wholly marginal in its discursive timidity.

The Prologue begins with a chronographia of autumn, a low point of the year. The lowness of the season spills over, or at least characterizes, the narrator's own position as a writer, unable as he is to begin. He recalls the skill, the freshness, and the courage of a presumably classical and late-medieval tradition of broadly satirical poetry:

> I, callynge to mynde the great auctoryte
> Of poetes olde, whyche, full craftely,
> Under as coverte termes as coude be,
> Can touche a troughte and cloke it subtylly
> Wyth fresshe utteraunce full sentencyously;
> Dyverse in style, some spared not vyce to wrythe,
> Some of moralyte nobly dyde endyte. (8–14)

Like Henryson's *Moral Fables,* then, *The Bowge of Courte* begins with praise of a moralizing, allegorical tradition of authoritative poetry. Unlike Henryson, however, Skelton declines to place his own poem in this tradition. No sooner is the tradition defined than the narrator declares his incapacity to contribute to it. Ignorance, he says, advised silence, "my penne aweye to pulle" (21), and not to attempt what is beyond his capacity. To do so would be to incur a threat:

> But of reproche surely he maye not mys
> That clymmeth hyer than he may fotynge have;
> What and he slyde downe, who shall hym save? (26–28)

As it is posed here, this threat seems rather limited, simply a matter of having committed a poetic indiscretion by attempting more than one is capable of. Failure would incur embarrassment, and the threat of embarrassment provokes silence.[19] But is the silence simply the product of poetic discretion? The terms Skelton uses to define the threat of embarrassment suggest not only a poetic, but also a political threat that hangs over the writing of poetry. The reference to climbing higher than one has footing might, for example, recall Wyatt's slightly

---

18. For the low stylistic register of satire, see Simpson, "The Constraints of Satire," esp. n. 32.

19. For the theme of poetic discretion, see James Simpson, "Dante's 'Astripetam Aquilam' and the Theme of Poetic Discretion in the *House of Fame,*" *Essays and Studies* n.s. 39 (1986): 1–18.

later poem of the 1530s about shaky footing (i.e. his Senecan "Stand whoso list, upon the slipper toppe / Of courtes estates . . . "), which describes that kind of courtier who

> death grip'th right hard by the crop
> That is much known of other, and of himself, alas,
> Doth die unknown, dazed, with dreadful face.[20]

The threat registered by Skelton is, it seems to me, both poetic and political: by failing to write courageous, morally forthright satire, Skelton equally fails to join an ancient poetic tradition in which poets, or at least some of them, "spared not vyce to wrythe."

When we look to the action of the dream, we can see that the poet's fear certainly is political. The narrator is not only a poet in the Prologue, but in the dream, too, he is presented as a skilful, learned, cultivated poet. But in each case where he is so characterized, the characterization is made by figures who wish to undermine, rather than bolster, the narrator's confidence as a poet. Praise of a poet's skill in the dream appears simply as a strategy to undermine the powers of poetry. The first address to the narrator is by Favell, or Flattery. It opens in this way:

> Noo thynge erthely that I wonder so sore
> As of your connynge, that is so excellent;
> Deynte to have with us suche one in store,
> So vertuously that hath his dayes spente;
> Fortune to you gyftes of grace hath lente:
> Loo, what it is a man to have connynge!
> All erthely tresoure it is surmountynge. (148–54)

In this encounter, as in all others, Drede himself does not speak; Flattery's praise of "connynge" serves, in fact, to silence and neutralize knowledge. The "great auctoryte / Of poetes olde" is here evacuated of any force or power to resist corruption, largely because the very strategies of "olde poets" are more skilfully commanded by Flattery himself than by Drede.[21] For it is Flattery who promises to be "playne," and who assures Drede that he can "cracke" a "bolde worde"; but of course these professions of satirical courage only cloak a truth (that Flattery

---

20. Cited from *Sir Thomas Wyatt, The Complete Poems,* ed. R. A. Rebholz (Harmondsworth, UK: Penguin, 1978), 94.

21. Jane Griffiths accurately goes further in arguing that the *Bowge* "disconcertingly calls into question the validity of the distinction between poetic and courtly feigning." See Griffiths, *John Skelton and Poetic Authority,* 60.

won't be plain) subtly. Flattery insinuates himself with Drede first by praising him as a scholar, and then by planting fear in Drede's mind, by saying that he, Favell, is on Drede's side against those who wish to overthrow him.

Hervy Hafter, too, approaches Drede by reference to Drede's activity as a poet: "me thynke ye make a verse, / I coude it skan and ye wolde it reherse" (244–45). Poetry is, interestingly, felt to be covert activity, but so covert that Drede doesn't, of course, "reherse" what he writes—he's too afraid. Poetry is in no way reformist, since it never sees publication. And finally Dissimulation also approaches Drede by praising the power of book learning and the skill of poets. From the envious, he says, the literate poet need fear nothing:

> I knowe your vertu and your lytterkture
> By that lytel connynge that I have.
> Ye be malygned sore, I you ensure,
> But ye have crafte your selfe alwaye to save.
> It is grete scorne to se a mysproude knave
> With a clerke that connynge is to prate.
> Lete theym go lowse theym, in the devylles date. (449–55)

Once again, the power of poetry to preserve a space for identity and integrity is here championed in such a way as to dissolve that power altogether. What Dissimulation really celebrates is the remarkable power of the ignorant, or at least of those who care nothing for learning. The virtues of the "poetes olde"—their "craft" (meaning both skill and power), and their ability to disguise the truth with "coverte termes"—are here in the possession of the enemies of poetry.[22] And Drede's enemies deny Drede's own possession of the power ("vertu") and skill of poetry even as they praise him so lavishly for it. As the word "literature" (449) is first used in something like its modern, literary critical sense, it is revealingly mangled and neutralized.[23] As with printed authors, so too with literature: they are under threat even as they come into focus.

So poetry, then, is represented from within the poem as having no autonomous power to resist or denounce corruption; the discursive conditions of court life, as they are represented, would seem entirely to disallow the space of integrity preserved by "the grete auctoryte / Of poetes olde," who could "touch" a truth "full craftely." Here "craft" is not deployed by the poet, but rather by his enemies.

This invasion of the space of poetry and of the poet is manifest in the very form of the poem. As I mentioned earlier, the narrative is constructed out of a

---

22. This point has been made by Anna Torti, *The Glass of Form, Mirroring Structures From Chaucer to Skelton* (Cambridge: Brewer, 1991), 112.

23. For the formation and function of the "literary" in the century leading up to Skelton, see the cogent essay of Robert J. Meyer-Lee in this volume.

series of encounters, in which different court types address Drede. Characteristically, Drede himself does not reply in these addresses; they are not dialogues, since the voices of the corrupt court types wholly invade and eclipse Drede's own voice, entirely silencing him. But, you might object, Drede does speak in the poem: he speaks to us, in the interim periods between the encounters. That is true, but his narration of what happens turns out to report *other* voices, to report what his perceived enemies are saying about him. This is a world in which private identity is largely, or wholly, a matter of public reputation. This is implicit in the formal presentation of Drede's voice: whenever we are alone with him, we are not privileged with the private, intimate voice the monologue promises; instead the voices of others invade the private voice of Drede, and fatally erode any sense of coherence and integrity in that private voice. After Favell passes from Drede, for example, we are left alone with Drede as our private narrator: "than thanked I hym for his grete gentylnes" (176); we expect to be in the presence of Drede alone, but, on the contrary, Drede relates how he sees Favell meet Suspicion, and, he says, "I drewe nere to herke what they two sayde." Then follows the reported conversation, of which I cite a part here:

"In fayth," quod Suspecte, "spake Drede no worde of me?"
"Why? What than? Wylte thou lete men to speke?
He sayth he can not well accorde with the."
"Twyst," quod Suspecte, "goo playe; hym I ne reke!"
"By Cryste," quod Favell, "Drede is soleyne freke!" (183–87)

Drede's persona is, as I say, invaded by other voices, and constituted by his public reputation. Paradoxically, it is the very fact that Drede's being is wholly public property that renders Drede so lonely, a "soleyne freke" [solitary fellow].

In *The Bowge of Courte,* then, dialogue occurs only between Drede's enemies, not between Drede and his interlocutors. Solidarity, such as it is in the shifting world of the court, is the preserve of others. The very bases of dialogue are denied Drede, since he is cut off from any real understanding of what he is told. Understanding, like solidarity, is located outside the narrator himself. As a result, direct speech at times degenerates into scraps of conversation, hints of gossip, where the vital connections of sense are deliberately, and threateningly, truncated. Thus Deceit, for example, falls into a code language, whose inner sense is unavailable to Drede:

But by that Lorde that is one, two and thre,
I have an errande to rounde in your ere.
He tolde me so, by God, ye maye truste me.
Parde, remembre when ye were there,

> There I wynked on you—wote ye not where?
> In A *loco,* I mene *juxta* B:
> Woo is hym that is blynde and maye not see! (512–18)

The gesture of intimacy here serves to underline the alienating quality of the non-communication.

Skelton as a poet more generally, it might be observed, is himself a master of the "scrap," the truncated (non-) message. In his other satirical poems, *Speke Parrott* or *Colin Clout,* for example, he deliberately speaks through scraps of information—what the bird parrots uncomprehendingly, or what "clouts," or bits of satirical information are drawn out of the satirist's bag. The very rhyme is "ragged, / Tattered and jagged, / Rudely rayne-beaten, / Rusty and mothe-eaten" (*Colin Clout,* 53–56). But in those poems Skelton is deploying the truncated scrap as a satirical strategy, presumably protecting himself from attack and/or instilling fear in the objects of his attack precisely through alienating them. In *The Bowge of Courte,* however, the narrator is the *object* of these scraps, and is not in a position to deploy them himself.[24]

III

> *[Danger:] "What is thy name?" and I sayde it was Drede.* (77)

Drede comes into being through his interlocutors: in response to the question of Danger (i.e., haughtiness, domination, danger), then of course Drede names himself as "Fear"; and even in my description of the poem in the previous section, I have been effectively elucidating tautologies: "Drede does not speak"; "Drede doesn't rehearse what he writes"; "the very bases of dialogue are denied Drede"; "the voices of others invade the private voice of Drede." All these statements are designed to elucidate the discursive conditions that pertain to Drede, but when we reflect on the matter, these statements are already implicit in the name "Drede" itself; they merely fill out the semantic content of the name, which itself is a product of the world Drede ostensibly describes. *The Bowge of Courte* seems to reverse the "normal" relationship that pertains between narrator and the world he or she describes: instead of the narrator being given at least theoretical priority to the world he describes, he is instead posterior to that world, a product of it, and wholly absorbed by it. The "author" disappears into the fabric of his world; for even if Drede comes into being through his interlocutors, that very

---

24. For the larger history and instability of the satirical scrap across the fifteenth century, see the penetrating essay by Mishtooni Bose in this volume.

moment of coming into being is equally his undoing as an author. The author is "dead." And, indeed, the author tries to commit suicide.

In this final section, however, we might ask ourselves whether or not there is a difference between the discursive situation represented *in* the poem, and the discursive position *of the poem itself.* It might theoretically be the case that a poem could *represent* the total evanescence of the author but itself make powerful demands on readers to make a commitment to understanding an authorial voice and strategy. Skelton's poem is, after all, published—we have it, which wouldn't be the case if Skelton really were Drede.

At the end of the poem the very act of writing the text we have read is represented; whereas the narrator had been unwilling to write at the beginning of the poem, by its end there is no hesitation: "and even with that woke, / Caughte penne and ynke, and wroth this lytell boke" (531–32). This decisive act of writing is coupled with the act of publishing, for in the last stanza (533–39, cited above) the poet addresses the audience directly, as audience, for the first time. And for the first time, at the end of the poem, we are invited to consider not so much the poem's represented action as the poem itself, "this lytell boke" that has just been written. The poet invites us to see in this book precisely the kind of thing that seems to have been so completely negated in the action of the dream—that is poetry, in the tradition of the ancients, as presenting a truth that requires interpretation to be understood, poetry that can "touche a troughte and cloke it subtylly" (11).

Of course, even in the very act of suggesting the poem's truth, Skelton allows for the possibility of its ephemerality and insubstantiality. It's a dream, which "in substaunce of slumbrynge doth procede" (536); as such, the poet disavows that it is "mater in dede." We are perfectly free to dismiss the whole poem as a dream, and therefore as insubstantial. But this self-deprecatory move (so frequent in satirical dream poetry—we find it in *Piers Plowman* and *Mum and the Sothsegger*)[25] itself implies, of course, the substantial quality of what we have before us, and the truth of the poem, the irreducible "resydewe" that we have been asked to construe.

We are now being asked to interpret the poem as a dream poem. This might suggest that the poet's nightmare has more substance than the shadowy fictions of Drede's interlocutors. Certainly the kind of relationship implied here between poet and audience—polite, serious, knowing as it is—is quite different from every other relationship depicted within the poem's world. All those other relationships are governed by nothing more than self-interest, the "Desire" who rules the ship of court. In such a world, pledges of fidelity consistently dissolve in their very formulation. The relationship between poet and audience, on the contrary,

---

25. See, for example, *Piers Plowman,* B.7.144–51; and *Mum and the Sothsegger,* line 1293.

implies the possibility that the poem, unlike the world it represents, will allow for a perspective that is at once trusting (we are gently asked to trust the poet that there is a "truth" behind the shadowy fiction of the poem), and disinterested (we are asked, indeed, "in every poynte to be indyfferente"). So the kinds of relationship that pertain in the realm of literature are presented as being altogether different from those in the malicious world of the court.

But the premise of the trusting yet disinterested attitude we are asked to bring to the text can only be our disinterested trust in Skelton, or at least the poet-narrator, himself. And what trust can we have in him? Is there any perspective we can gain on this poem that does not collapse back into the frightening, deceptive, shifting world of the court? Might our trust in "Skelton" be no more than a new move in an endless game of fundamentally self-interested self-promotion, in which we become the victims? Authenticity might be only one more counter in the courtly game (a counter that almost all Drede's interlocutors effortlessly deploy).

Or might our trust in "Skelton" turn out to have rather shaky foundations? We are asked to interpret the poem as a dream poem, reasonably enough. Reading late medieval/early modern dream poetry involves trying to identify the authority figure from within the dream. Of course sophisticated poets like Chaucer will frustrate this attempt, but the frustration wouldn't exist if the invitation hadn't been made in the first place. Where is the authority figure in Skelton's dream? There isn't one, or no obvious one, at any rate. For not only does Drede's authority approach zero-point, since being Drede he can't really be said to "speak about" his experience at all; in fact it is perfectly possible that his "authority" is below zero-point, since it is easy to read the whole poem as issuing from Drede's fearful, "dredful" imagination.[26] Fear is the source of paranoia, and it is possible to read the dream as a paranoid nightmare; the narrator's constant affirmations that he *seemed* to hear or see people talking about him serve to make us question whether or not he really *did* see such things ("me thoughte" is a constant qualifier to Drede's account). One sense of the word "drede," indeed (and one that Skelton activates) is "doubt, uncertainty."[27] If we were to read the poem as a paranoid nightmare, then one could argue that it becomes even more insubstantial than it at first appeared: it is not so much the case that corrupt court figures neutralize the power of poetry and poets, so this argument would run, but rather that the poet's fearful imagination actively precipitates this process of neutralization, by imagining threats where none exist. Just as Drede comes into being through

---

26. For Drede's failure of authority, see Griffiths, *John Skelton and Poetic Authority*, 63.
27. Besides sense 1 (a), "Fear, fright, terror," *Middle English Dictionary* also lists under "drede" sense 4 (a) "Doubt, uncertainty."

his interlocutors, so too, more worryingly, do the interlocutors come into being through Drede.

And if Drede's authority *might* be below zero-point, then it is: we invest a speaker with authority on the basis of confidence; once that confidence is questioned (and the doubt unable to be answered), then we remain unable to listen to a speaker or read a narrator's voice without questioning the status of their account of events.

This essay might seem to be running into trouble: I wanted to devote this section to "construing the residue" of Skelton's poem—to elucidating what is irreducible after we sift out the phantasma of fear from "mater in dede." The only possibility of making this elucidation seemed to lie in our relationship with the poet-narrator. As we are seeing now, however, that relationship can only be constructed on infirm territory. The argument that we should seek to establish our relationship not with Drede but with the narrator of Prologue and Epilogue is no escape, since, as I argued in my introduction, Skelton goes to considerable lengths to blur narrator and Drede (and the narrator is, furthermore, long on board before the Prologue ends at line 126).

The point to which I seem to be heading in my reading is the world of the poem itself. I seem to be heading, that is, to a world in which all relationships are open to distrust: just as Drede distrusts all his interlocutors, so too do we distrust Drede; just as there is almost certainly no substance to the threats dreamed up by Drede's enemies, so too there may be no substance to the narrator's own threats; just as the last stanza is, as I argued in my introduction, recursive into the nightmare experience of dreadful distrust, so too is our own reading heading in the same direction. Paranoia is an infectious disease.

It is impossible to get around an interpretation of this poem as the fearful projection of paranoia. Does that necessarily destroy its authority? I do not think so. I am reminded of the maxim that "just because you're paranoid doesn't mean they're not out to get you." It's impossible to deny the plausibility of paranoia in *The Bowge of Courte,* but so too is it impossible to deny the power of the poem as a whole in expressing the experience of paranoia. The poem's power derives from the extraordinary way in which it says "I cannot say anything." The poet's voice never escapes its marginality—it is forever perched on the ship's edge, ready to jump. And precisely as such, it traces the nature of that marginality with frightening force, brilliantly, even luridly, highlighting the pain and fear that exist at the edges of articulation, immediately before the silence of death, "dazed, with dreadful face."

But it isn't *actually* silent: even if narrator and Drede are fundamentally similar, the single act that differentiates the narrator from Drede is the unhesitating act of writing and publication. The very fact of articulating paranoia is the first move in an attempt to locate the sources of fear; even if the poem does nothing more than articulate the experience, it has its own authority.[28] Whether we choose to invest the speaker with the kind of authority I am describing depends on an ethical choice as to whether we remain in a hermeneutics of a free play of meanings, or whether we aim at the minimal authorial closure to which I'm pointing. It is our decisions as readers, not something ineradicably there "in" the text, which bring an author into being.[29] If we do accept this minimal closure of written paranoia's own authority, however, then we must equally recognize that the author does not, as Barthes would have it, "die" at the moment of writing, but rather that he "lives" through that very act:

>   . . . the shypborde faste I hente,
> And thoughte to lepe; and even with that woke,
> Caughte penne and ynke, and wroth this lytell boke. (530–32)

---

28. For another late medieval poem whose advice to princes is essentially that they have most to learn from the *emptiness* of advice poetry, see James Simpson, "'For al my body . . . weieth nat an unce': Empty Poets and Rhetorical Weight in Lydgate's *Churl and the Bird*," in *John Lydgate: Poetry, Culture, and Lancastrian England*, ed. Larry Scanlon and James Simpson (Notre Dame, IN: University of Notre Dame Press, 2006), 129–46.

29. While Stanley Fish rightly argues that the focus of *The Bowge of Courte* is interior, rather than on the traditional objects of court satire, I disagree with the ending of his chapter on the poem, where he says that, given Drede's attempted suicide, and given the inseparability of the narrator and Drede, the Skeltonic problem here is "insoluble—in later poems there will be an alternative solution—a 'leap of faith'" (81). I think Fish restricts his reading to the represented action of the poem, rather than extending it to include the poem itself, and its relationship with us as readers. My point is that a leap of faith is required here, too (from the reader, towards the author), but the faith is of a purely ethical kind. Presumably the later, "reader-response" Fish would agree with me in wanting to extend the problematic of the poem to its relationship with its readers; but if he did so, then he would also agree that this particular version of reader-response criticism requires that we posit the existence of authors. For a critique of the pragmatism of Fish and Richard Rorty for its failure to grant any place to trust in reading and interpretation, see Simpson, "Faith and Hermeneutics."

bibliography

MANUSCRIPTS
Cambridge, Newnham College, MS 4 [Yates-Thompson MS]
Cambridge, University Library, MS Dd.i.17
Cambridge, University Library, MS Ll.iv.14
Dublin, Trinity College Library, MS 432
London, British Library, MS Additional 35290 [York Register]
London, British Library, Arundel MS 327
New Haven, Beinecke Library, MS 365 [Book of Brome]
Oxford, Corpus Christi College, MS 201
Oxford, Bodleian Library, MS Tanner 407
Oxford, Bodleian Library, MS Douce 302
Oxford University Archives, NEP/supra/Reg F [Registrum F]
San Marino, Huntington Library, MS HM 1
Washington DC, Folger Shakespeare Library, MS V.a.354

EARLY PRINTED EDITIONS
Anon. *Fifteen Oes* (Westminster: William Caxton, 1491; STC 20195 and Westminster, Wynkyn de Worde, 1494; STC 15875)
Kempe, Margery. *A Short Treatise* (London: Wynkyn de Worde, 1501; STC 14924)
Skelton, John. *The Bowge of Courte* (Westminster: Wynkyn de Worde, 1499; STC 22597)
——. *A Replycacion against Certayne Yong Scolers* (London: Richard Pynson, 1528; STC 22609)

PRIMARY SOURCES
[A Kempis, Thomas]. *The Imitation of Christ.* Ed. John K. Ingram. EETS e.s. 63. London: Kegan Paul, Trench, Trübner, 1893.
Anstey, Henry, ed. *Epistolae Academicae Oxon. (Registrum F)*. 2 vols. Oxford: Oxford Historical Society, 1898.
Aquinas, Thomas. *Summa Theologiae.* Trans. Roland Potter. Manchester: Blackfriars, 1972.

Audelay, John. *Poems and Carols (Oxford, Bodleian Library MS Douce 302)*. Ed. Susanna Fein. Kalamazoo, Michigan: Medieval Institute Publications, 2009.
Augustine of Hippo, St. *The Literal Meaning of Genesis*. Trans. John Hammond Taylor. Ancient Christian Writers 41–42. New York: Newman, 1982.
———. *De Genesi ad litteram, Patrologia Latina* 34, col. 375.
Barr, Helen, ed. *The Piers Plowman Tradition: A Critical Edition of Pierce the Ploughman's Crede, Richard the Redeless, Mum and the Sothsegger, and The Crowned King*. London: J. M. Dent, 1993.
Blamires, Alcuin, ed. "The Trial of Walter Brut (1391)." In *Woman Defamed and Women Defended*, ed. Alcuin Blamires, Karen Pratt, and C.W. Marx, 250–55. Oxford: Oxford University Press, 1992.
Bokenham, Osbern. *Bokenham's Legendys of Hooly Wummen*. Ed. Mary S. Serjeantson. EETS o.s. 206, 1938; reprint, New York: Kraus, 1971.
———. "Mappula Angliae, von Osbern Bokenham." Ed. Carl Horstmann, *Englische Studien* 10 (1997): 1–34.
Brandeis, Arthur, ed. *Jacob's Well*. EETS o.s. 115. London: K. Paul, Trench, Trübner & Co, 1900; rpt. 1973.
Capgrave, John. *The Life of Saint Katherine*. Ed. Karen A. Winstead. Kalamazoo, MI: Medieval Institute, 1999.
Chaucer, Geoffrey. *The Riverside Chaucer*. Ed. Larry D. Benson. 3rd ed. Boston: Houghton Mifflin, 1987.
Coldewey, John C., ed. *Early English Drama: An Anthology*. New York and London: Garland, 1993.
D'Ardenne, S.R.T.O. and E. J. Dobson, eds. *Seinte Katerine*. EETS s.s. 7. Oxford: Oxford University Press, 1981.
Davis, Norman, ed. *Non-Cycle Plays and Fragments*. EETS s.s. 1. Oxford: Oxford University Press, 1970.
———, ed. *Non-Cycle Plays and the Winchester Dialogues*. Leeds Texts and Monographs, Medieval Drama Facsimiles 5. Leeds: School of English, 1979.
De Voragine, Jacobus. *The Golden Legend: Readings on the Saints*. Trans. William Granger Ryan. 2 vols. Princeton, New Jersey: Princeton University Press, 1993.
Enright-Clark Shoukri, Doris, ed. *Liber apologeticus de omni statu humanae naturae*. New York: Modern Humanities Research Council in conjunction with Renaissance Society of America, 1974.
Erasmus, Desiderius. "On the Usefulness of Colloquies." In *The Colloquies of Erasmus*, trans. and annot. Craig R. Thompson. Toronto, Buffalo and London: University of Toronto Press, 1997.
Eusebius. *History of the Church*. Trans. G. A. Williamson. New York: Penguin, 1965.
Foxe, John. *Acts and Monuments [. . .]* (1583 edition), Foxe's Book of Martyrs Variorum Edition Online v. 1.1 (Sheffield: hriOnline, 2006), http://www.hrionline.shef.ac.uk/foxe/.
Fitzneale, Richard. *Dialogus de Scaccario: The Dialogue of the Exchequer*. Ed. Emilie Amt and S. D. Church. Oxford: Oxford University Press, 2007.
Gascoigne, Thomas. *Liber Veritatum*. In *Loci e Libro Veritatum*. Ed. James E. Thorold Rogers. Oxford: Oxford University Press, 1881.
Gower, John. *John Gower: The Minor Latin Works*. Ed. R. F. Yeager and Michael Livingston. Kalamazoo: Medieval Institute Publications, 2005.
Hamer, Richard, and Vida Russell, eds. *Gilte Legende*, 2 vols., EETS o.s. 327–28. Oxford: Oxford University Press, 2006–2007.

———, eds. *Supplementary Lives in Some Manuscripts of the Gilte Legende*. EETS o.s. 315. Oxford: Oxford University Press, 2000.
Kempe, Margery. *The Book of Margery Kempe*. Ed. Emily Hope Allen and Sanford Brown Meech, EETS o.s. 212. Oxford: Oxford University Press, 1940.
———. *The Book of Margery Kempe*. Ed. Lynn Staley. TEAMS Middle English Texts. Kalamazoo, MI: Medieval Institute Publications, 1996.
Langland, William. *The Vision of Piers Plowman*. Ed. A. V. C. Schmidt. 2nd ed. London, 1995.
Love, Nicholas. *Nicholas Love's Mirror of the Blessed Life of Jesus Christ*. Ed. Michael G. Sargent. New York: Garland Publishing, 1992.
Lumiansky, R. M., and David Mills, eds. *The Chester Mystery Cycle*. EETS s.s. 3 and 9. London: Oxford University Press, 1974, 1986.
Lydgate, John. *A Critical Edition of John Lydgate's Life of Our Lady*. Ed. Joseph A. Lauritis, Ralph A. Klinefelter, and Vernon F. Gallagher. Pittsburgh: Duquesne University, 1961.
———. *Fall of Princes*. Ed. Henry Bergen, EETS e.s. 121, 122, 123, 124. Oxford: Oxford University Press, 1924–27; rpt. 1967.
———. *Lydgate's Troy Book*. Ed. Henry Bergen, EETS e.s. 97, 103, 106, 126. Kegan Paul, Trench, Trübner & Co., 1906–35; rpt. 1996.
———. *John Lydgate: Poems*. Ed. John Norton-Smith. Oxford: Clarendon Press, 1966.
Mills, David, ed. *The Chester Mystery Cycle: A New Edition with Modernised Spelling*. East Lansing, MI: Colleagues Press, 1992.
Mitchell, W. T., and Pantin, W.A., eds. *The Register of Congregation, 1448–1463*. Oxford: Clarendon Press, 1972.
More, Thomas. *The Yale Edition of the Complete Works of St. Thomas More*. Ed. Daniel Kinney, 15 vols. New Haven and London, 1986.
Ovid. *The Art of Love, and Other Poems*. Trans. J. H. Mozley and rev. G. P. Goold. Cambridge: Harvard University Press, 1979.
———. *Fasti*. Trans. James George Frazer and rev. G. P. Goold. Cambridge: Harvard University Press, 1989.
Pecock, Reginald. *The Repressor of Over Much Blaming of the Clergy*. Ed. Churchill Babington. London: Longman, Green, Longman, and Roberts, 1860.
———. *The Reule of Crysten Religioun*. Ed. William Cabell Greet, EETS o.s. 171. London: H. Milford, Oxford University Press, 1927; rpt, Millwood, NY: Kraus, 1987.
Peter of Celle. *Selected Works*. Trans. H. Feiss. Kalamazoo, MI: Medieval Institute Publications, 1987.
[Reynes, Robert]. *The Commonplace Book of Robert Reynes of Acle: An Edition of Tanner MS 407*. Ed. Cameron Louis. New York: Garland, 1980.
Skelton, John. *The Poetical Works of John Skelton*. Ed. Alexander Dyce, 2 vols. London: Thomas Rodd, 1843, rpt. Boston: James R. Osgood, 1871.
———. *John Skelton, The Complete English Poems*. Ed. John Scattergood. Harmondsworth: Penguin, 1983.
[Suso, Henry] Seuse, Heinrich. *Büchlein der Ewigen Weisheit* in *Deutsche Schriften*. Ed. Karl Bihlmeyer. Stuttgart: Minerva, 1907; repr. 1961.
Tanner, Norman P., ed. *Heresy Trials in the Diocese of Norwich, 1428–1431*. Camden Society, ser. 4, vol. 20. London: Office of the Royal Historical Society, 1977.
Toulmin-Smith, Lucy, ed. *A Commonplace Book of the Fifteenth Century: Containing a Religious Play and Poetry, Legal Forms, and Local Accounts*. London: Trübner and Co., 1886.

Uhlman, Diana R. "The Comfort of Voice, the Solace of Script: Orality and Literacy in the *Book of Margery Kempe.*" *Studies in Philology* 91 (1994): 50–69.
Wyatt, Thomas. *Sir Thomas Wyatt, The Complete Poems.* Ed. R. A. Rebholz. Harmondsworth: Penguin, 1978.

SECONDARY SOURCES

Astell, Ann. *Eating Beauty: The Eucharist and the Spiritual Arts of the Middle Ages.* Ithaca: Cornell University Press, 2006.
Aston, Margaret. *Lollards and Literacy in Late Medieval Religion.* London: Hambledon Press, 1984.
Auerbach, Erich. *Scenes from the Drama of European Literature.* Minneapolis: University of Minnesota Press, 1984.
———. *Literary Language and its Public in Late Latin Antiquity and in the Middle Ages.* Trans. Ralph Manheim. Princeton: Princeton University Press, 1993.
Bakhtin, Mikhail. *The Dialogic Imagination.* Ed. Michael Holquist and trans. Caryl Emerson and Michael Holquist. Austin: University of Texas Press, 1981.
Ball, R. M. "The opponents of Bishop Pecok." *The Journal of Ecclesiastical History* 48 (1997): 230–63.
Bardsley, Sandy. *Venomous Tongues. Speech and Gender in Late Medieval England.* Philadelphia: University of Pennsylvania Press, 2006.
Barr, Helen and Kate Ward-Perkins. "'Spekyng for one's sustenance': the Rhetoric of Counsel in *Mum and the Sothsegger,* Skelton's *Bowge of Court,* and Elyot's *Pasquil the Playne.*" In *The Long Fifteenth Century: Essays in Honour of Douglas Gray,* ed. Helen Cooper and Sally Mapstone, 249–72. Oxford: Oxford University Press, 1997.
Barthes, Roland. "La mort de l'auteur." *Manteia* 5 (1968): 12–17.
———. *Image-Music-Text.* Ed. Stephen Heath. London: Fontana, 1977.
———. *Essais critiques IV, Le bruissement de la langue.* Paris: Seuil, 1984.
Biddick, Kathleen. *The Typological Imaginary: Circumcision, Technology, History.* Philadelphia: University of Pennsylvania Press, 2003.
Benson, C. David, and Lynne S. Blanchfield. *The Manuscripts of* Piers Plowman: *The B-Version.* Cambridge: D. S. Brewer, 1997.
Bischoff, Bernhard. *Latin Paleography: Antiquity and the Middle Ages.* Trans. Dáibhí Ó Cróinín and David Ganz. Cambridge: Cambridge University Press, 1990.
Blamires, Alcuin. "Women and Preaching in Medieval Orthodoxy, Heresy, and Saints' Lives." *Viator* 26 (1995): 135–52.
Boffey, Julia, and John J. Thompson. "Anthologies and Miscellanies." In *Book Production and Publishing in Britain, 1375–1475,* ed. Jeremy Griffiths and Derek Pearsall, 279–315. Cambridge: Cambridge University Press, 1989.
Bose, Mishtooni. "From Exegesis to Appropriation: the Medieval Solomon." *Medium Aevum* 65 (1996): 187–210.
———. "Writing, Heresy and the Anticlerical Muse." In *The Oxford Handbook of Medieval English Literature,* ed. Greg Walker and Elaine Treharne, 276–96. Oxford: Oxford University Press, 2010.
Braekman, W. L. "Fortune-Telling by the Casting of Dice: A Middle English Poem and Its Background." *Studia Neophilologica* 52 (1980): 3–29.
Brantley, Jessica. *Reading in the Wilderness: Private Devotion and Public Performance in*

Late Medieval England. Chicago: University of Chicago Press, 2007.
Bruster, Douglas. "The Materiality of Shakespearean Form." In *Shakespeare and Historical Formalism,* ed. Stephen A. Cohen, 31–48. Aldershot: Ashgate, 2007.
Bryan, Jennifer. *Looking Inward: Devotional Reading and the Private Self in Late Medieval England.* Philadelphia: University of Pennsylvania Press, 2007.
Burgess, C. F. "Art and Artistry in the *Brome Miracle Play of Abraham and Isaac.*" *Cithara* 1 (1962): 37–42.
Burke, Peter. "The Renaissance Dialogue." *Renaissance Studies* 3 (1989): 1–12.
Burke, Seán. *The Death and Return of the Author: Criticism and Subjectivity in Barthes, Foucault, and Derrida.* 2nd ed. Edinburgh: Edinburgh University Press, 1998.
Burrow, Colin. "The Experience of Exclusion: Literature and Politics in the Reigns of Henry VII and Henry VIII." In *The Cambridge History of Medieval English Literature,* ed. David Wallace, 793–820. Cambridge: Cambridge University Press, 1999.
Bynum, Caroline Walker. *Holy Feast, Holy Fast: The Religious Significance of Food to Medieval Women.* Berkeley: University of California Press, 1987.
Camargo, Martin. *Ars Dictaminis, Ars Dictandi.* Turnhout: Brepols, 1991.
———. "If You Can't Join Them, Beat Them; or, When Grammar Met Business Writing (in Fifteenth-Century Oxford)." In *Letter-Writing Manuals and Instruction from Antiquity to the Present,* ed. Carol Poster and Linda C. Mitchell, 67–87. Columbia: University of South Carolina Press, 2007.
Camille, Michael. "Sounds of the Flesh—Images of the Word." *Public Access* iv.5 (1990): 161–69.
———. "Mouths and Meanings: Towards an Anti-Iconography of Medieval Art." In *Iconography at the Crossroads,* ed. Brendan Cassidy, 43–54. Princeton: Princeton University Press, 1993.
Cannon, Christopher. *The Making of Chaucer's English: A Study of Words.* Cambridge: Cambridge University Press, 1998.
———. *The Grounds of English Literature.* Oxford: Oxford University Press, 2004.
———. "Form." In *Oxford Twenty-First Century Approaches to Literature: Middle English,* ed. Paul Strohm, 177–90. Oxford: Oxford University Press, 2007.
Carlson, David R. *English Humanist Books: Writers and Patrons, Manuscripts and Print, 1475–1525.* Toronto: University of Toronto Press, 1993.
Carruthers, Mary. *The Book of Memory: A Study of Memory in Medieval Culture.* Cambridge: Cambridge University Press, 1990.
———. "Sweetness." *Speculum* 81 (2006): 999–1013.
———. "Sweet Jesus." In *Mindful Spirit in Late-Medieval Literature: Essays in Honor of Elizabeth D. Kirk,* ed. Bonnie Wheeler, 9–19. New York: Palgrave, 2006.
Catto, Jeremy. "Followers and Helpers: The Religious Identity of the Followers of Wyclif." In *The Medieval Church: Universities, Heresy and the Religious Life. Essays in Honour of Gordon Leff,* eds. Peter Biller and Barrie Dobson, 141–62. Studies in Church History, Subsidia 11. Woodbridge: Boydell and Brewer, 1999.
———. "Chaundler, Thomas." In *Oxford Dictionary of National Biography,* ed. H. C. G. Matthew and Brian Harrison, 11.268–69. 60 vols. Oxford: Oxford University Press, 2004.
———, and Ralph Evans, eds. *The History of the University of Oxford,* vol. 2. Oxford: Clarendon Press, 1992.
Cawsey, Kathy. "Tutivillus and the 'Kyrkchaterars': Strategies of Control in the Middle Ages." *Studies in Philology* 102 (2005): 434–51.
Chaganti, Seeta. *The Medieval Poetics of the Reliquary: Enshrinement, Inscription, Perfor-*

mance. New York: Palgrave, 2008.

Clanchy, Michael. *From Memory to Written Record: England 1066–1307.* Oxford: Blackwell, 1993.

Clark, James G. *A Monastic Renaissance at St. Albans: Thomas Walsingham and His Circle, c. 1350–1440.* Oxford: Clarendon Press, 2004.

Coens, Maurice. "Une 'passio S. Apolloniae' inédite suivie d'un miracle en Bourgogne." *Analecta Bollandiana* 70 (1952): 138–59.

Cohen, Stephen. "Between Form and Culture: New Historicism and the Promise of Historical Formalism." In *Renaissance Literature and Its Formal Engagements,* ed. Mark David Rasmussen, 17–41. New York: Palgrave, 2002.

——, ed. *Shakespeare and Historical Formalism.* Aldershot, UK: Ashgate, 2007.

Cole, Andrew. "Heresy and Humanism." In *Twenty-First Century Approaches to Literature: Middle English,* ed. Paul Strohm, 421–37. Oxford: Oxford University Press, 2007.

——. "Staging Advice in New College MS 288: On Thomas Chaundler and Thomas Bekynton." In *After Arundel: Religious Writing in Fifteenth-Century England,* ed. Vincent Gillespie and Kantik Ghosh. Turnhout: Brepols, 2011.

Collette, Carolyn P. *Performing Polity: Women and Agency in the Anglo-French Tradition, 1385–1620.* Turnhout: Brepols, 2006.

Coletti, Theresa. *Mary Magdalene and the Drama of Saints: Theater, Gender, and Religion in Late Medieval England.* Philadelphia: University of Pennsylvania Press, 2004.

Conlee, John W. *Middle English Debate Poetry: A Critical Anthology.* East Lansing, MI: Colleagues Press, 1991.

Constable, Giles. "The Ideal of the Imitation of Christ." In *Three Studies in Medieval Religious and Social Thought,* 143–248. Cambridge: Cambridge University Press, 1995.

Cooney, Helen. "Skelton's *Bowge of Court* and the Crisis of Allegory in Late-Medieval England." In *Nation, Court and Culture: New Essays on Fifteenth-Century English Poetry,* ed. Helen Cooney, 153–67. Dublin: Four Courts Press, 2001.

Cooper, Helen. "Skeltonics." *London Review of Books,* 14 December 2006. 32–34.

Cooper, Lisa H., and Andrea Denny-Brown, eds. *Lydgate Matters: Poetry and Material Culture in the Fifteenth Century.* New York: Palgrave, 2007.

Copeland, Rita. *Rhetoric, Hermeneutics, and Translation in the Middle Ages.* Cambridge: Cambridge University Press, 1991.

——. *Pedagogy, Intellectuals, and Dissent in the Later Middle Ages: Lollardy and Ideas of Learning.* Cambridge: Cambridge University Press, 2001.

Curtius, E. R. *European Literature and the Latin Middle Ages.* Trans. Willard R. Trask. London, 1954. Princeton: Princeton University Press, rpt., 1991.

Davis, John F. "The Trials of Thomas Bylney and the English Reformation." *The Historical Journal* 24 (1981): 775–90.

Davis, Norman. "The Brome Hall Commonplace Book." *Theatre Notebook* 24 (1969–70): 84–86.

de Gaiffier, Baudouin. "La légende Latine de Sainte Barbe par Jean de Wackerzeele." *Analecta Bollandiana* 77 (1959): 5–41.

de la Mare and Richard Hunt. *Duke Humfrey and English Humanism in the Fifteenth Century: Catalogue of an Exhibition held in the Bodleian Library, Oxford.* Oxford: Bodleian Library, 1970.

——. "Duke Humfrey's English Palladius (MS. Duke Humfrey d. 2)." *Bodleian Library Record* 12.1 (1985): 39–51.

Delany, Sheila. *Impolitic Bodies: Poetry, Saints, and Society in Fifteenth-Century England:*

The Work of Osbern Bokenham. Oxford: Oxford University Press, 1998.

Derolez, Albert. *Codicologie des manuscrits en écriture humanistique sur parchemin*, 2 vols. Turnhout: Brepols, 1984.

———. *The Palaeography of Gothic Manuscript Books: From the Twelfth to the Early Sixteenth Century*. Cambridge: Cambridge University Press, 2003.

Dickens, A. G. *The English Reformation*. 2nd ed. University Park: The Pennsylvania State University Press, 1989.

Dillon, Janet. *Language and Stage in Medieval and Renaissance England*. Cambridge: Cambridge University Press, 1998.

Dodd, Gwilym. *Justice and Grace: Private Petitioning and the English Parliament in the Late Middle Ages*. Oxford: Oxford University Press, 2007.

Doyle, A. L. and M. B. Parkes. "The Production of Copies of the *Canterbury Tales* and the *Confessio Amantis* in the Early Fifteenth Century." In *Medieval Scribes, Manuscripts and Libraries: Essays Presented to N. R. Ker*, ed. M. B. Parkes and Andrew G. Watson, 163–203. London: Scolar Press, 1978.

Duffy, Eamon. *The Stripping of the Altars*. New Haven: Yale University Press, 1992.

Dyer, Richard. *Pastiche: Knowing Imitation*. London: Routledge, 2006.

Eagleton, Terry. *Literary Theory: An Introduction*, 2nd ed. Minneapolis: University of Minnesota Press, 1996.

Ebin, Lois A. *Illuminator, Makar, Vates: Visions of Poetry in the Fifteenth Century*. Lincoln: University of Nebraska Press, 1988.

Edwards, A.S.G. "From Manuscript to Print: Wynkyn de Worde and the Printing of Contemporary Poetry." *Gutenberg Jahrbuch* 66 (1991): 143–48.

———. "The Transmission and Audience of Osbern Bokenham's *Legendys of Hooly Wumen*." In *Late Medieval Religious Texts and their Transmission*, ed. Alastair Minnis, 157–67. Cambridge, UK: Brewer, 1994.

———. "Deconstructing Skelton: The Texts of the English Poems." *Leeds Studies in English* New Series 36 (2005): 335–53.

Enenkel, Karl. "In Search of Fame: Self-Representation in Neo-Latin Humanism." In *Medieval and Renaissance Humanism*, ed. Stephen Gersh and Bert Roest, 93–113. Leiden: Brill, 2003.

Fabian, Johannes. "Keep Listening: Ethnography and Reading." In *The Ethnography of Reading*, ed. Jonathan Boyarin, 67–83. Berkeley: University of California Press, 1993.

Fein, Susanna, ed. *My Wyl and My Wrytyng: Essays on John the Blind Audelay*. Kalamazoo, MI: Medieval Institute Publications, 2009.

———. "A Thirteen-Line Alliterative Stanza on the Abuse of Prayer from the Audelay MS." *Medium Aevum* 63 (1994): 61–74.

Fish, Stanley E. *John Skelton's Poetry*. New Haven: Yale University Press, 1965.

Forrest, Ian. *The Detection of Heresy in Late Medieval England*. Oxford: Clarendon Press, 2005.

Fort, Margaret Dancy. "The Metres of the Brome and Chester Abraham and Isaac Plays." *PMLA* 41.1 (1926): 832–39.

Fox, Alistair. *Politics and Literature in the Reigns of Henry VII and Henry VIII*. Oxford: Basil Blackwell, 1989.

Frantzen, Allen J. "Tears for Abraham: The Chester Play of Abraham and Isaac and Anti-sacrifice in Works by Wilfred Owen, Benjamin Britten, and Derek Jarman." *Journal of Medieval and Early Modern Studies* 31.3 (2001): 445–76.

Fredeman, Jane. "Style and Characterization in John Capgrave's *Life of Saint Katherine*." *The*

Bulletin of the John Rylands University Library 62 (1980): 347–87.
Gayk, Shannon. "'Among psalms to fynde a cleer sentence': John Lydgate, Eleanor Hull, and the Art of Vernacular Exegesis." *New Medieval Literatures* 10 (2008): 161–89.
———. *Image, Text, and Religious Reform in Fifteenth-Century England.* Cambridge: Cambridge University Press, 2010.
Gellrich, Jesse. *The Idea of the Book in the Middle Ages.* Ithaca, NY: Cornell University Press, 1985.
———. *Discourse and Dominion in the Fourteenth Century: Oral Contexts of Writing in Philosophy, Politics, and Poetry.* Princeton: Princeton University Press, 1995.
Giancarlo, Matthew. *Parliament and Literature in Late Medieval England.* Cambridge: Cambridge University Press, 2007
Gibson, Gail McMurray. "Saint Anne and the Religion of Childbed: Some East Anglian Texts and Talismans." In *Interpreting Cultural Symbols: Saint Anne in Late Medieval Society,* ed. Kathleen Ashley and Pamela Sheingorn, 95–110. Athens: University of Georgia Press, 1990.
Gilchrist, Roberta and Marilyn Oliva. *Religious Women in Medieval East Anglia: History and Archaeology, c. 1100–1540.* Norwich: Centre of East Anglian Studies, University of East Anglia, 1993.
Gillespie, Alexandra. *Print Culture and the Medieval Author: Chaucer, Lydgate, and Their Books 1473–1557.* Oxford: Oxford University Press, 2006.
Gillespie, Vincent. "Justification by Faith: Skelton's *Replycacion.*" In *The Long Fifteenth Century: Essays for Douglas Gray,* ed. Helen Cooper and Sally Mapstone, 273–311. Oxford: Clarendon Press, 1997.
———. "Vernacular Theology." In *Oxford Twenty-First Century Approaches to Literature: Middle English,* ed. Paul Strohm, 401–20. Oxford: Oxford University Press, 2007.
———. "Chichele's Church: Vernacular Theology after Thomas Arundel." (forthcoming).
Green, Richard Firth. *Poets and Princepleasers: Literature and the English Court in the Late Middle Ages.* Toronto: University of Toronto Press, 1980.
Greenblatt, Stephen. "What is the History of Literature?" *Critical Inquiry* 23 (1997): 460–81.
Griffiths, Jane. "A Contradiction in Terms: Skelton's 'effecte energiall' in *A Replycacion.*" *Renaissance Studies* 17 (2003): 55–68.
———. "What's in a Name? The Transmission of 'John Skelton, Laureate' in Manuscript and Print." *Huntington Library Quarterly* 67 (2004): 215–35.
———. *John Skelton and Poetic Authority: Defining the Liberty to Speak.* Oxford: Clarendon Press, 2006.
Grund, Peter, ed. "Albertus Magnus and the Queen of the Elves: A Fifteenth-Century English Verse Dialogue on Alchemy." *Anglia: Zeitschrift für Englische Philologie* 122 (2004): 640–62.
Haines, Roy Martin. "Reginald Pecock: A Tolerant Man in an Age of Intolerance." *Studies in Church History* 21 (1984): 125–37.
Hale, Rosemary. "'Taste and See, For God Is Sweet': Sensory Perception and Memory in Medieval Christian Mystical Experience." In *Vox Mystica: Essays on Medieval Mysticism,* ed. Anne Clark Bartlett, 3–14. Cambridge: D. S. Brewer, 1995.
Hardman, Phillipa. "Lydgate's *Life of Our Lady:* A Text in Transition." *Medium Aevum* 65 (1996): 248–68.
———. "Lydgate's Uneasy Syntax." In *John Lydgate: Poetry, Culture, and Lancastrian England,* ed. Larry Scanlon and James Simpson, 12–35. Notre Dame, IN: University of Notre Dame Press, 2006.

Harper, Carrie A. "A Comparison between the Brome and Chester Plays of Abraham and Isaac." In *Studies in English and Comparative Literature by Former and Present Students at Radcliffe College, presented to Agnes Irwin, Dean of Radcliffe College, 1894–1909,* Radcliffe College Monographs 15. Boston and London: Ginn, 1910.

Harwood, Britton. "Dame Study and the Place of Orality in *Piers Plowman.*" *English Literary History* 57 (1990): 1–17.

Haskins, James. "Humanism and the Origins of Modern Political Thought." In *Cambridge Companion to Renaissance Humanism,* ed. Jill Kraye, 118–41. Cambridge: Cambridge University Press, 1996.

Hasler, Anthony J. "Cultural Intersections: Skelton, Barclay, Hawes, André." In *John Skelton and Early Modern Culture: Papers Honoring Robert S. Kinsman,* ed. David R. Carlson, 63–84. Tempe, Arizona: Arizona Center for Medieval and Renaissance Studies, 2008.

Heffernan, Thomas. *Sacred Biography: Saints and their Biographers in the Middle Ages.* Oxford: Oxford University Press, 1988.

Heiserman, A. R. *Skelton and Satire.* Chicago: University of Chicago Press, 1961.

Heitsch, Dorothea, and Jean-François Vallée, eds. *Printed Voices: The Renaissance Culture of Dialogue.* Toronto: University of Toronto Press, 2004.

Hirsh, John C. "A Middle English Metrical Version of *The Fifteen Oes* from Bodleian Add MS B 66." *Neuphilologische Mitteilungen* 75 (1974): 98–114.

Hoesterey, Ingeborg, ed. *Zeitgeist in Babel: The Postmodernist Controversy.* Bloomington: Indiana University Press, 1991.

——. *Pastiche: Cultural Memory in Art, Film, Literature.* Bloomington: Indiana University Press, 2001.

Hohlfeld, Alexander R. "Two Old English Mystery Plays on the Subject of Abraham's Sacrifice." *Modern Language Notes* 5.4 (1890): 111–19.

Horobin, Simon. "The Angle of Oblivioun: A Lost Medieval Manuscript Discovered in Walter Scott's Collection." *Times Literary Supplement,* 11 November 2005, 12–13.

——. "A Manuscript Found in Abbotsford House and the Lost Legendary of Osbern Bokenham." *English Manuscript Studies, 1100–1700* 14 (2007): 132–64.

——. "Politics, Patronage, and Piety in the Work of Osbern Bokenham." *Speculum* 82 (2007): 932–49.

Hudson, Anne. "A Lollard Sect Vocabulary?" In *Lollards and Their Books,* 164–80. London: Hambledon, 1985.

——. *The Premature Reformation: Wycliffite Texts and Lollard History.* Oxford: Clarendon Press, 1988.

——. "The Mouse in the Pyx: Popular Heresy and the Eucharist." *Trivium* 26 (1991): 40–53.

Jacob, E. F. "To and From the Court of Rome in the Early Fifteenth Century." In *Studies in French Language and Mediaeval Literature: Presented to Professor Mildred K. Pope, by pupils, colleagues, and friends,* 161–82. Freeport, NY: Books for Libraries Press, 1969.

James, M. R. *The Chaundler MSS.* London: J. B. Nichols and Sons, 1916.

James, Sarah. "'Doctryne and Studie': Female Learning and Religious Debate in Capgrave's *Life of St. Katharine.*" *Leeds Studies in English* 36 (2005): 275–302.

Jansen, Katherine Ludwig. *The Making of the Magdalen: Preaching and Popular Devotion in the Later Middle Ages.* Princeton, NJ: Princeton University Press, 2000.

Jayne, Sears Reynolds. *Plato in Renaissance England.* Dordrecht: Kluwer Academic Publishers, 1995.

Jennings, Margaret. "Tutivillus: The Literary Career of the Recording Demon." *Studies in Philology,* Texts and Studies 74.5 (1977): 1–93.

Johnson, Ian. "Xpmbn: The Gendered Ciphers of the Book of Brome and the Limits of Misogyny." *Women: A Cultural Review* 18.2 (2007): 145–61.
Kahrl, Stanley J. "The Brome Hall Commonplace Book." *Theatre Notebook* 22 (1968): 157–61.
Kerby-Fulton, Kathryn, ed. *Voices in Dialogue: Reading Women in the Middle Ages.* Notre Dame, IN: University of Notre Dame Press, 2005.
——. *Books under Suspicion: Censorship and Tolerance of Revelatory Writing in Late Medieval England.* Notre Dame, IN: University of Notre Dame Press, 2006.
Kinney, Arthur. *John Skelton, Priest as Poet: Seasons of Discovery.* Chapel Hill and London: University of North Carolina Press, 1987.
Knapp, Ethan. *The Bureaucratic Muse: Thomas Hoccleve and the Literature of Late Medieval England.* State Park, PA: Pennsylvania State University Press, 2001.
Kolve, V. A. *The Play Called Corpus Christi.* Stanford: Stanford University Press, 1966.
Kreitzer, Beth. *Reforming Mary: Changing Images of the Virgin Mary in Lutheran Sermons of the Sixteenth Century.* Oxford: Oxford University Press, 2004.
Krug, Rebecca. "The Fifteen Oes." In *Cultures of Piety: Medieval English Devotional Literature in Translation,* ed. Anne Clark Bartlett and Thomas H. Bestul, 107–117 and 212–16. Ithaca, NY: Cornell University Press, 1999.
——. *Reading Families: Women's Literate Practice in Late Medieval England.* Ithaca, NY: Cornell University Press, 2002.
——."Margery Kempe." In *The Cambridge Companion to Medieval English Literature,* ed. Larry Scanlon, 217–28. Cambridge: Cambridge University Press, 2009.
Kurvinen, Auvo. "The Source of Capgrave's *Life of Saint Katherine of Alexandria.*" *Neuphilologische Mitteilungen* 61 (1960): 268–324.
Landman, James H. "'The Doom of Resoun': Accommodating Lay Interpretation in Late Medieval England." In *Medieval Crime and Social Control,* ed. Barbara A. Hanawalt and David Wallace, 90–123. Minneapolis: University of Minnesota Press, 1999.
Lawlor, Leonard. "The Beginnings of Thought: The Fundamental Experience in Derrida and Deleuze." In *Between Deleuze and Derrida,* ed. Paul Patton and John Protevi, 67–83. London: Continuum, 2003.
Lawton, David. "Dullness and the Fifteenth Century." *English Literary History* 54 (1987): 761–99.
Leach, Arthur F. *The Schools of Medieval England.* London: Methuen, 1915.
Leclerq, Jean. *The Love of Learning and the Desire for God: A Study of Monastic Culture.* Trans. by Catharine Misrahi. New York: Fordham University Press, 1961, rpt. 2007.
Lerer, Seth. *Chaucer and His Readers: Imagining the Author in Late-Medieval England.* Princeton: Princeton University Press, 1993.
——. "The Endurance of Formalism in Middle English Studies." *Literature Compass* 1 (2003): 1–15.
Lester, G. A., ed. *Three Late Medieval Morality Plays. Mankind, Everyman, Mundus et Infans.* New York: W. W. Norton, 1981.
Levert, Laurelle. "'Crucifye hem, Crucifye hem': The Subject and Affective Response in Middle English Passion Narratives." *Essays in Medieval Studies* 14 (1997): 73–90.
Levinson, Carol. "What Is New Formalism?" *PMLA* 122.2 (2007): 558–69.
Lewis, C. S. *English Literature in the Sixteenth Century Excluding Drama.* Oxford: Clarendon Press, 1954.
Lewis, Katherine J. *The Cult of St Katherine of Alexandria in Late Medieval England.* Woodbridge, Suffolk: Boydell Press, 2000.
Little, Katherine C. *Confession and Resistance: Defining the Self in Late Medieval England.*

Notre Dame, IN: University of Notre Dame Press, 2006.

Lochrie, Karma. *Margery Kempe and the Translations of the Flesh*. Philadelphia: University of Pennsylvania Press, 1991.

Lovatt, Roger. "The *Imitation of Christ* in Late Medieval England." *Transactions of the Royal Historical Society* 18 (1968): 97–121.

MacDonald, Nicola. "Fragments of *(Have your) Desire:* Brome Women at Play." In *Medieval Domesticity: Home, Housing, and Household in Medieval England*, ed. Maryanne Kowaleski and P. J. P. Goldberg, 232–58. Cambridge: Cambridge University Press, 2008.

Mann, Jill. "Eating and Drinking in *Piers Plowman*." *Essays and Studies* 32 (1979): 26–42.

Marston, Thomas E. "The Book of Brome." *Yale University Library Gazette* 41.4 (1967): 141–45.

Matthews, David. "The Medieval Invasion of Early Modern England." *New Medieval Literatures* 10 (2008): 223–44.

Mauss, Marcel. *The Gift: The Form and Reason for Exchange in Archaic Societies*. Trans. W. D. Halls, with a foreword by Mary Douglas. New York: W. W. Norton, 1990.

McLelland, Nicola. "Dialogue and German Language Learning in the Renaissance." In *Printed Voices: The Renaissance Culture of Dialogue*, ed. Dorothea Heitsch, and Jean-François Vallée, 206–26. Toronto: University of Toronto Press, 2004.

McSheffrey, Shannon. *Gender and Heresy: Women and Men in Lollard Communities, 1420–1530*. Philadelphia: University of Pennsylvania Press, 1995.

Meyer-Lee, Robert J. *Poets and Power from Chaucer to Wyatt*. Cambridge: Cambridge University Press, 2007.

———. "The Vatic Penitent: John Audelay's Self-Representation." In *My Wyl and My Wrytyng: Essays on John the Blind Audelay*, ed. Susanna Fein. 54–85. Kalamazoo, MI: Medieval Institute Publication, 2009.

———. "The Emergence of the Literary in John Lydgate's *Life of Our Lady*." *Journal of English and Germanic Philology* 109.3 (2010): 322–48.

Mills, David. "The Doctor's Epilogue to the Brome Abraham and Isaac: A Possible Analogue." *Leeds Studies in English* 11 (1980): 105–10.

Minnis, A. J. *Medieval Theory of Authorship: Scholastic Literary Attitudes in the Later Middle Ages*, 2nd ed. Aldershot, UK: Scolar Press, 1988.

———. *Fallible Authors: Chaucer's Pardoner and Wife of Bath*. Philadelphia: University of Pennsylvania Press, 2008.

Montrose, Louis. "Renaissance Literary Studies and the Subject of History." *English Literary Renaissance* 16 (1986): 5–12.

Mooney, Linne. "Chaucer's Scribe." *Speculum* 81 (2006): 97–138.

———. "Some New Light on Thomas Hoccleve." *Studies in the Age of Chaucer* 29 (2007): 293–340.

Mortimer, Nigel. *John Lydgate's Fall of Princes: Narrative Tragedy in Its Literary and Political Contexts*. Oxford: Oxford University Press, 2005.

Nelson, William. *John Skelton, Laureate*. New York: Columbia University Press, 1939.

Nolan, Maura. *John Lydgate and the Making of Public Culture*. Cambridge: Cambridge University Press, 2004.

O'Sullivan, Katherine K. "John Lydgate's *Lyf of Our Lady:* Translation and Authority in Fifteenth-Century England." *Mediaevalia* 226 (2005): 169–201.

Pade, Marianne. *The Reception of Plutarch's Lives in Fifteenth-Century Italy*, 2 vols. Copenhagen: Museum Tusculanum Press, 2007

Parkes, M. B. *English Cursive Book Hands, 1250–1500*. London: Scolar Press, 1979.

Pearsall, Derek, *John Lydgate*. London: Routledge and Kegan Paul, 1970.
———. "John Capgrave's *Life of St. Katharine* and Popular Romance Style." *Medievalia et humanistica* 6 (1975): 121–37.
———. *John Lydgate (1371–1449): A Bio-bibliography*. Victoria: University of Victoria, 1997.
———. ed. *Chaucer to Spenser: An Anthology of Writings in English, 1375–1575*. Oxford: Blackwell, 1999.
———. "Audelay's *Marcolf and Solomon*." In *Text and Controversy from Wyclif to Bale. Essays in Honour of Anne Hudson,* ed. Helen Barr and Ann M. Hutchison, 387–404. Turnhout: Brepols, 2005.
———. "Audelay's *Marcolf and Solomon* and the Langlandian Tradition." In *My Wyl and My Wrytyng: Essays on John the Blind Audelay,* ed. Susanna Fein, 138–52. Kalamazoo, MI: Medieval Institute Publication, 2009.
Perkins, Nicholas. *Hoccleve's 'Regiment of Princes': Counsel and Constraint.* Cambridge: D. S. Brewer, 2001.
Petrina, Alessandra. *Cultural Politics in Fifteenth-Century England: The Case of Humphrey, Duke of Gloucester.* Leiden: Brill, 2004.
Petti, Anthony G. *English Literary Hands from Chaucer to Dryden.* London: Edward Arnold, 1977.
Phillips, Susan E. *Transforming Talk: The Problem with Gossip in Late Medieval England.* University Park, PA: Penn State University Press, 2007.
Polak, Emil J. *Medieval and Renaissance Letter Treatises and Form Letters: A Census of Manuscripts found in Eastern Europe and the former U.S.S.R.* Leiden: E. J. Brill, 1993.
———. *Medieval and Renaissance Letter Treatises and Form Letters: A Census of Manuscripts found in part of Western Europe, Japan, and the United States of America.* Brill, 1994.
Price, Paul. "Trumping Chaucer: Bokenham's *Katherine*." *Chaucer Review* 36 (2001): 158–83.
Putter, Ad. "Animating Court Satire." In *The Court and Cultural Diversity,* ed. Evelyn Mullally and John Thompson, 67–76. Woodbridge, Suffolk: Brewer, 1997.
Reed, Thomas. *Middle English Debate Poetry.* New York: Columbia University Press, 1990.
Rendall, Thomas. "Visual Typology in the Abraham and Isaac Plays." *Modern Philology* 81.3 (1984): 221–32.
Renoir, Alain, and C. David Benson. "John Lydgate." In *A Manual of the Writings in Middle English,* ed. Albert E. Hartung. Hamden: The Connecticut Academy of Arts and Sciences, 1980.
Rice, Nicole. *Lay Piety and Religious Discipline in Middle English Literature.* Cambridge: Cambridge University Press, 2009.
Riddy, Felicity. "Text and Self in *The Book of Margery Kempe*." In *Voices in Dialogue: Reading Women in the Middle Ages,* ed. Kathryn Kerby-Fulton, 435–53. Notre Dame, IN: University of Notre Dame Press, 2005.
———, and Nicholas Watson. "Afterwords." In *Voices in Dialogue: Reading Women in the Middle Ages,* ed. Kathryn Kerby-Fulton, 454–57. Notre Dame, IN: University of Notre Dame Press, 2005.
Rigg, A. G. *A History of Anglo-Latin Literature, 1066–1422.* Cambridge: Cambridge University Press, 1992.
Rigolot, François. "Problematizing Renaissance Exemplarity: The Inward Turn of Dialogue From Petrarch to Montaigne." In *Printed Voices: The Renaissance Culture of Dialogue,* ed. Dorothea Heitsch, and Jean-François Vallée, 3–24. Toronto: University of Toronto Press, 2004.

Roest, Bert. "Rhetoric of Innovation and Recourse to Tradition in Humanist Pedagogical Discourse." In *Medieval and Renaissance Humanism: Rhetoric, Representation and Reform*, ed. Stephen Gersh and Bert Roest, 115–48. Leiden: Brill, 2003.

Rooney, Ellen. "Form and Contentment." In *Reading for Form*, ed. Susan J. Wolfson and Marshall Brown, 25–48. Seattle: University of Washington, 2006.

Rosenthal, Joel T. "Local Girls Do It Better: Women and Religion in Late Medieval East Anglia." In *Traditions and Transformations in Late Medieval England*, ed. Douglas Biggs, Sharon D. Michalove, and A. Compton Reeves, 1–20. Leiden: Brill, 2002.

Rubin, Miri. *Mother of God: A History of the Virgin Mary*. New Haven: Yale University Press, 2009.

Rundle, David. "On the Difference between Virtue and Weiss: Humanist Texts in England during the Fifteenth Century." In *Courts, Counties, and the Capital in the Later Middle Ages*, ed. Diana E. S. Dunn, 181–203. The Fifteenth Century Series, 4. Stroud, Eng.: Sutton, 1996.

——. "Of Republics and Tyrants: aspects of quattrocento humanist writings and their reception in England, c. 1400–c. 1460." D.Phil. thesis, University of Oxford, 1997.

Sammut, Alfonso. *Unfredo duca di Gloucester e gli umanisti italiani*. Padova: Antenore, 1980.

Sanok, Catherine. *Her Life Historical: Exemplarity and Female Saints' Lives in Late Medieval England*. Philadelphia: University of Pennsylvania Press, 2007.

Saygin, Susanne. *Humphrey, Duke of Gloucester (1390–1447) and the Italian Humanists*. Leiden: Brill, 2002.

Scanlon, Larry. *Narrative, Authority and Power*. Cambridge: Cambridge University Press, 1994.

——. "Lydgate's Poetics: Laureation and Domesticity in the *Temple of Glass*." In *John Lydgate*, ed. Larry Scanlon and James Simpson, 61–97. Notre Dame, IN: University of Notre Dame Press, 2006.

——, and James Simpson, eds. *John Lydgate: Poetry, Culture and Lancastrian England*. Notre Dame, IN: University of Notre Dame Press, 2006.

Scase, Wendy. *Reginald Pecock*. Brookfield, VT: Ashgate, 1996.

——. *Literature and Complaint in England, 1272–1553*. Oxford: Oxford University Press, 2007.

Scattergood, John. "Skelton and Traditional Satire: *Ware the Hauke*." *Medium Aevum* 55 (1986): 203–216.

——. "Skelton and Heresy." In *Early Tudor England: Proceedings of the 1987 Harlaxton Symposium*, ed. Daniel Williams, 157–70. Woodbridge: Boydell, 1989.

——. *Reading the Past: Essays on Medieval and Renaissance Literature*. Dublin: Four Courts Press, 1996.

——. "Riddle 47 and Memory." In *Manuscripts and Ghosts: Essays on the Transmission of Medieval and Early Renaissance Literature*, 83–94. Dublin: Four Courts Press, 2006.

Schell, Edgar. "Fulfilling the Law in the Brome Abraham and Isaac." *Leeds Studies in English* 25 (1994): 149–58.

Scherb, Victor I. "Conception, Flies, and Heresy in Skelton's 'Replycacion.'" *Medium Aevum* 62 (1993): 51–60.

Schirmer, Elizabeth. "Orthodoxy, Textuality, and the 'Tretys' of Margery Kempe." *Journal X: A Journal of Criticism and Culture* 1 (1996): 31–55.

Schoff, Rebecca. *Reformations: Three Medieval Authors in Manuscript and Movable Type*. Turnhout, Belgium: Brepols, 2007.

Severs, J. Burke. "The Relationship between the Brome and Chester Plays of Abraham and Isaac." *Modern Philology* 42.3 (1945): 137–51.
Seymour, M. C. *John Capgrave*. Authors of the Middle Ages 11, 201–35. Aldershot: Variorum, 1996.
Sharratt, Bernard. "John Skelton: Finding a Voice—Notes after Bakhtin." In *Medieval Literature: Criticism, Ideology and History*, ed. David Aers, 192–222. Brighton: The Harvester Press, 1986.
Simpson, James. "Dante's '*Astripetam Aquilam*' and the Theme of Poetic Discretion in the *House of Fame*." *Essays and Studies* n.s. 39 (1986): 1–18.
———. "The Constraints of Satire in *Piers Plowman* and *Mum and the Sothsegger*." In *Langland, the Mystics, and the Medieval English Religious Tradition*, ed. Helen Phillips, 11–30. Cambridge: Brewer, 1990.
———. "The Death of the Author?: Skelton's *Bouge of Courte*." In *The Timeless and the Temporal. Writings in honour of John Chalker by friends and colleagues*, ed. Elizabeth Maslen, 57–79. London: QMW Department of English, 1993.
———. *The Oxford English Literary History, Volume 2: 1350–1547; Reform and Cultural Revolution*, general editor Jonathan Bate. Oxford: Oxford University Press, 2002.
———. "Faith and Hermeneutics: Pragmatism versus Pragmatism." *Journal of Medieval and Early Modern Studies* 33 (2003): 215–39.
———. "Reginald Pecock and John Fortescue." In *A Companion to Middle English Prose*, ed. A. S. G. Edwards, 271–87. Cambridge: D.S. Brewer, 2004.
———. "Saving Satire after Arundel's *Constitutions:* John Audeley's 'Marcol and Solomon.'" In *Text and Controversy from Wyclif to Bale: Essays in Honour of Anne Hudson*, ed. Helen Barr and Anne M. Hutchinson, 387–404. Turnhout: Brepols, 2005.
———. "'For al my body . . . weieth nat an unce': Empty Poets and Rhetorical Weight in Lydgate's *Churl and the Bird*." In *John Lydgate: Poetry, Culture, and Lancastrian England*, ed. Larry Scanlon and James Simpson, 129–46. Notre Dame, IN: University of Notre Dame Press, 2006.
———. *Burning to Read: English Fundamentalism and its Reformation Opponents*. Cambridge, MA: Harvard University Press, 2007.
Smarr, Janet Levarie. "A Female Tradition? Women's Dialogue Writing in Sixteenth-Century France." In *Strong Voices, Weak History: Early Women Writers and Canons in England, France, and Italy*, ed. Pamela Joseph Benson and Victoria Kirkham, 32–57. Ann Arbor: University of Michigan Press, 2005.
Smith, D. Vance. "Medieval *Forma:* The Logic of the Work." In *Reading for Form*, ed. Susan J. Wolfson and Marshall Brown, 66–79. Seattle: University of Washington Press, 2006.
Somerset, Fiona, Jill C. Havens, and Derrick G. Pitard, eds. *Lollards and Their Influence in Late Medieval England*. Woodbridge: Boydell, 2003.
Stanbury, Sarah. "The Vivacity of Images: St. Katherine, Knighton's Lollards, and the Breaking of Idols." In *Images, Idolatry, and Iconoclasm in Late Medieval England*, ed. Jeremy Dimmick, James Simpson, and Nicolette Zeeman, 131–50. Oxford: Oxford University Press, 2002.
———. *The Visual Object of Desire in Late Medieval England*. Philadelphia: University of Pennsylvania Press, 2008.
Starkey, David. "The Age of the Household: Politics, Society and the Arts c.1350–c.1550." In *The Later Middle Ages*, ed. Stephen Medcalf, 225–90. London: Methuen, 1981.
Steinberg, Theodore L. "Poetry and Prophecy: A Skelton Key." In *Prophet Margins: The Medieval Vatic Impulse and Social Stability*, ed. E. L. Risden, Karen Moranski, and Ste-

phen Yandell, 149–65. New York: Peter Lang, 2004.

Strier, Richard. "How Formalism Became a Dirty Word and Why We Can't Do without It." In *Renaissance Literature and its Formal Engagements,* ed. Mark Rasmussen, 207–15. New York: Palgrave Press, 2002.

Strohm, Paul. *England's Empty Throne.* New Haven: Yale University Press, 1998.

Symes, Carol. "The Appearance of Early Vernacular Plays: Forms, Functions, and the Future of Medieval Theater." *Speculum* 77 (2002): 778–831.

Tonry, Kathleen. "John Skelton and the New Fifteenth Century." *Literature Compass* 5 (2008): 721–39.

Torti, Anna. *The Glass of Form, Mirroring Structures from Chaucer to Skelton.* Cambridge: Brewer, 1991.

Utley, Francis Lee. "Dialogues, Debates, and Catechisms." In *A Manual of Writing in Middle English, 1050–1400,* vol. 3, ed. Albert E. Hartung, 669–745. New Haven: Connecticut Academy of Arts and Sciences, 1972.

van Dijk, Mathilde. *Een rij van spiegels: De Heilige Barbara van Nicomedia als voorbeeld voor vrouwelijke religieuzen.* Hilversum: Hilversum Verloren, 2000.

——. "Being Saint Barbara in England: Shifting Patterns of Holiness in the Later Middle Ages." In *Transforming Holiness: Representations of Holiness in English and American Literary Texts,* ed. Irene Visser and Helen Wilcox, 1–19. Leuven: Peeters, 2006.

von Perger, Misha. "Vorläufiges Repertorium philosophischer und theologischer Prosa-Dialoge des lateinischen Mittelalters." In *Gespräche Lesen: Philosophische Dialoge im Mittelalter,* ed. Klaus Jacobi, 435–94. Tübingen: Gunter Narr Verlag, 1999.

Wakelin, Daniel. *Humanism, Reading and English Literature, 1430–1530.* Oxford: Oxford University Press, 2007.

Walker, Greg. *John Skelton and the Politics of the 1520s.* Cambridge: Cambridge University Press, 1988.

——. "John Skelton, Thomas More, and the 'lost' history of the early Reformation in England." *Parergon* 9 (1991): 75–85.

——. "'Ordered Confusion'?: The Crisis of Authority in Skelton's *Speke, Parott.*" *Spenser Studies* 10 (1992): 213–28.

——. *Persuasive Fictions: Faction, Faith and Political Culture in the Reign of Henry VIII.* Aldershot: Scolar Press, 1996.

——. "John Skelton and the Royal Court." In *John Skelton and Early Modern Culture,* ed. David R. Carlson, 3–18. Tempe, AZ: Arizona Center for Medieval and Renaissance Studies, 2008.

Warren, Nancy Bradley. *Spiritual Economies: Female Monasticism in Later Medieval England.* Philadelphia: University of Pennsylvania Press, 2001.

Warton, Thomas. *The History of English Poetry from the Twelfth to the Close of the Sixteenth Century,* ed. W. Carew Hazlott. London: Reeves and Turner, 1871; orig. pub. 1774–1781.

Waters, Claire. *Angels and Earthly Creatures: Preaching, Performance, and Gender in the Later Middle Ages.* Philadelphia: University of Pennsylvania Press, 2004.

Watson, Nicholas. "Censorship and Cultural Change in Late-Medieval England: Vernacular Theology, the Oxford Translation Debate, and Arundel's Constitutions of 1409." *Speculum* 70 (1995): 822–64.

——. "Conceptions of the Word: The Mother Tongue and the Incarnation of God." *New Medieval Literatures* 1 (1997): 85–124.

——. "The Making of *The Book of Margery Kempe.*" In *Voices in Dialogue: Reading Women in the Middle Ages,* ed. Kathryn Kerby-Fulton, 395–434. Notre Dame: University of

Notre Dame Press, 2005.
———. "Theories of Translation." In *The Oxford History of Literary Translation in English*, ed. Roger Ellis, 71–92. Oxford: Oxford University Press, 2006.
Watts, John. "Introduction: History, the Fifteenth Century and the Renaissance." In *The End of the Middle Ages? England in the Fifteenth and Sixteenth Centuries*, ed. John Watts. Gloucestershire, UK: Sutton Publishing, 1998.
Weiss, Roberto. *Humanism in England during the Fifteenth Century*, 3rd ed. Oxford: Basil Blackwell, 1967.
West, Philip J. "Rumination in Bede's Account of Caedmon." *Monastic Studies* 12 (1976): 217–26.
White, Helen C. *The Tudor Books of Private Devotion*. Madison: University of Wisconsin Press, 1951.
Wilson, Janet. "Skelton's *Ware the Hauke* and the 'Circumstances' of Sin." *Medium Aevum* 58 (1989): 243–57.
Winstead, Karen. "John Capgrave and the Chaucer Tradition." *The Chaucer Review* 30 (1996): 389–400.
———. *Virgin Martyrs: Legends of Sainthood in Late Medieval England*. Ithaca, NY: Cornell University Press, 1997.
———. *John Capgrave's Fifteenth Century*. Philadelphia: University of Pennsylvania Press, 2007.
———. "Hagiography after Arundel: Expounding the Trinity." In *After Arundel: Religious Writing in Fifteenth-Century England*, ed. Kantik Ghosh and Vincent Gillespie. Turnhout, Belgium: Brepols, 2011.
Wogan-Browne, Jocelyn, Nicholas Watson, Andrew Taylor, and Ruth Evans, eds. *The Idea of the Vernacular: An Anthology of Middle English Literary Theory, 1280–1520*. University Park: The Pennsylvania State University Press, 1999.
Wolfson, Susan. "Introduction." In *Reading for Form*, ed. Susan Wolfson and Marshall Brown, 3–24. Seattle and London: University of Washington Press, 2006.
Woolf, Rosemary. "The Effect of Typology on the Mediaeval Plays of Abraham and Isaac." *Speculum* 32.4 (1957): 805–25.
———. *The English Mystery Plays*. Berkeley and Los Angeles: University of California Press, 1972.
Wright, Elizabeth Cox. "Continuity in XV Century English Humanism." *PMLA* 51 (1936): 370–76.
Zeeman, Nicolette. *Piers Plowman and the Medieval Discourse of Desire*. Cambridge: Cambridge University Press, 2006.

contributors

MISHTOONI BOSE is Christopher Tower Student and Tutor in English (Christ Church) and CUF Lecturer in the Faculty of English, University of Oxford. She has published several articles on the literature of orthodox reform in late-medieval England, focusing on prophecy, anticlericalism, and the work of Thomas Gascoigne, and has completed an analytical survey of recent work on intellectual life in fifteenth-century England (*New Medieval Literatures* 12). She is writing a study of reformist voices in late-medieval England and her future work will explore the possibilities offered by post-historicism and the cognitive turn for the study of literature from this period.

JESSICA BRANTLEY is associate professor of English at Yale University. She is the author of *Reading in the Wilderness: Private Devotion and Public Performance in Late Medieval England* (Chicago, 2007) as well as many shorter pieces on the relation of text and image in late medieval reading. She is the recipient of fellowships from the Fulbright Commission and the National Humanities Center. Other projects in process address the role of the artifact in visionary writing from the *Dream of the Rood* to Julian of Norwich, and the relation between vernacular literature and the book of hours.

ANDREW COLE is associate professor of English at Princeton University. He is author of *Literature and Heresy in the Age of Chaucer* (Cambridge, 2008), and is completing a book on medieval dialectic and modern theory. He has co-edited *The Legitimacy of the Middle Ages: On the Unwritten History of Theory* (Duke, 2010) and *The Cambridge Companion to Piers Plowman* (forthcoming). He has co-edited seven volumes of the *Yearbook of Langland Studies* and was a Visiting Fellow at All Souls College, Oxford.

SHANNON GAYK is associate professor of English at Indiana University, Bloomington. She is the author of *Image, Text, and Religious Reform in Fifteenth-Century*

England (Cambridge, 2010) and other essays on late medieval religious poetry and culture. She is currently working on projects on religious lyrics across the Long Reformation and on the *arma christi* in late-medieval and early-modern literary cultures.

REBECCA KRUG is associate professor of English at the University of Minnesota. She is the author of *Reading Families: Women's Literate Practice in Late Medieval England* (Cornell, 2002). She has recently written essays about Margery Kempe, medieval gardens, and *Piers Plowman*. Krug is currently working on two book projects, one about ideas of "self help" in the Middle Ages and the other about Margery Kempe.

ROBERT J. MEYER-LEE is associate professor of English at Indiana University, South Bend. He is the author of *Poets and Power from Chaucer to Wyatt* (Cambridge, 2007) and several essays on fourteenth- and fifteenth-century poets. He is currently working on a project on Chaucer and literary value.

JAMES SIMPSON is Donald P. and Katherine B. Loker Professor of English at Harvard University. He was formerly Professor of Medieval and Renaissance English at the University of Cambridge. His most recent books are *Reform and Cultural Revolution*, being volume 2 in the *Oxford English Literary History* (Oxford, 2002), *Burning to Read: English Fundamentalism and its Reformation Opponents* (Harvard, 2007), and *Under the Hammer: Iconoclasm in the Anglo-American Tradition* (Oxford, 2010). He is currently working on medieval and early modern representations of making recalcitrant speakers speak, including the exercise of torture.

KATHLEEN TONRY is assistant professor of English at the University of Connecticut, Storrs. Her work concentrates on late-medieval literary culture and textual production, and she is currently finishing a monograph entitled *The Common Profits of Early Print: English Printing, 1475—1535*, which will be appearing with Brepols as part of the Texts and Transitions series. Her published and forthcoming work includes articles on Skelton and Caxton's *Polychronicon*.

KAREN WINSTEAD is professor of English at The Ohio State University. She is the author of *Virgin Martyrs: Legends of Sainthood in Late Medieval England* (Cornell, 1997) and *John Capgrave's Fifteenth Century* (Pennsylvania, 2006). She has edited and translated Middle English saints' lives, including John Capgrave's *Life of Saint Katherine*. Her current research deals with late medieval and early modern saints' lives and biography.

index

Page references to illustrations are given in italics.

Abraham and Isaac (Book of Brome), 10–11, 19–25, 30–39
Adrian and Epotys, 22, *27*, 28; devotional emblem, 36
alliterative verse, 7, 100, 108; mistaken for prose, 33; in Skeltonics, 143
Ambrose (Church Father), 68, 71
Anselm of Canterbury
  Monastic Dialogue, 110
anticlerical satire, 160, 161n9, 170–71, 177. *See also* Audelay: "Marcol and Solomon"; Skelton: *Ware the Hauke*
Aquinas, Thomas
  De Regimine Principum, 102n52
  Summa Theologiae, 138n17
ars epistolandi. See letter-writing
Arthur, Thomas, 143, 146–49, 157, 174
Arundel's Constitutions, 55n52, 69, 140
Ashby, George, 7
Audelay, John, 13–14, 159–61, 166–72
  "Marcol and Solomon" (*De concordia inter recortes fraters et rectores ecclesie*), 166–71
Augustine, 165, 174; rhetoric, 54–55, 92
  Confessions, 54
  De Genesi ad litteram, 94n24
aureation, 13, 88, 108, 136, 141–42, 151–54, 172; absence of, 91, 108; challenged, 172; Lydgate, use of term, 136. *See also* Hawes, Stephen; Lydgate, John; Skelton, John

authority, 118, 142, 155, 160; authorial, 162, 184; of characters, 194; divine, 138, 177; ecclesiastical, 10, 12, 123, 163, 165; figures, 64, 71, 194; by inscription, 112–15, 118; institutional, 64, 121; 170–71; literary, 9–10, 90, 100, 105, 133, 154, 157, 183–84, 195–96; political, 61n77, 155; to print, 155, 158; of Sarum rite, 164; of scripture, 71, 121. *See also* Skelton, John; Langland, William; Tutivillus
author, theories of, 181–85

Bakhtin, Michel, 113n11, 178
Barclay, Alexander, 7, 142
Barthes, Roland, 180, 182, 184–85, 196
Beaufort, Margaret, 112n6, 112n8, 113, 116n14, 117n14
  Imitation of Christ, 12, 110–11, 112n6, 116–123, 128–29
Beauvais, Vincent de, 70
Bible: women lacking training in, 70; women scholars of, 12, 69, 75, 81–83, 87
  Apocalypse (Revelation) 10:9–10, 95–96
  Ezekiel 3:1–3, 95–96
  Genesis 3:6, 94
  Hebrews 5:12–14, 95n27
  Isaiah 5:20, 168

215

Index

Jeremiah 15:16, 95
Matthew 11:28, 116–17
Psalm 33:9, 106
Psalm 44:2, 151
Psalm 108:21, 95
Psalm 118:103, 95
Psalm 118:105, 166
Bilney, Thomas: heresy, 143, 146–48, 174; Latimer converted by, 158; Lollard views, 18n39; punishment date, 148–49; rejection of laureate authority, 157
Boccaccio, Giovanni, 1
Bokenham, Osbern, 7, 67–87, 89, 108; intellectual liberalism, 9, 12; reappraisal of, 11–12
  works of: *Mappula Angliae*, 68
  works in *Legenda aurea*: *Agatha*, 67–68; *Agnes*, 67–68; *Ambrose*, 68; *Anne*, 67–68, 71; *Apollonia*, 12, 68–69, 79–80, 83, 85; *Audrey*, 68; *Barbara*, 12, 68–69, 82–83, 85–86; *Cecilia*, 68, 73, 76–78; *Christine*, 67–68; *Claire of Assisi*, 78; *Dorothy*, 67–68, 77; *Elizabeth*, 67–68, 71; *Faith*, 67–68; *Katherine of Alexandria*, 67–68, 70, 73–77, 84; *Margaret*, 67–68, 85; *Martha*, 78–79; *Martina*, 78, 81; *Mary of Egypt*, 68; *Mary Magdalene*, 67–73, 76–78, 84–85; *Monica* (Augustine's mother), 78, 81–82; *Paul the Hermit*, 68; *Priscilla*, 78; *Ursula*, 67–68, 77; *Vincent*, 68; *Winifred*, 12, 68, 83–85
Book of Brome, 7, 10–11, 19–39; rubrication in, 29–39
books of hours, 104n58, 113
Bourchier, Isobel, 67, 78, 86
Bradshaw, Henry, 7
Bridget of Sweden
  Fifteen Oes (traditional attribution), 112
Brut (prose), 33
Bury, John
  Gladius Salmonis, 86

Cannon, Christopher, 3–4, 21, 137
Capgrave, John, 7, 9, 69, 86, 88–109; allit-erative source, 92n15, 93; consumption as metaphor for reading, 90–99, 103–9; critical denigration of, 89–90, 108; Englishness, 88–89, 91–93, 100, 108; Eucharist, 106–7; internal vs. external, 94, 97–99, 107; literary form, 88–91, 93, 100, 105–8; literary invention, 90–91, 93, 99, 101–4; memory, 96–97, 100, 104; readerly reception, 90–92, 100, 104–9; reading linked with writing, 97, 99, 101–2, 104, 107; religious reform, 89–91, 105, 107; rhetoric of, 89–91; sweetness as aesthetic, 12, 89–91, 93, 105–6; sweetness in religious texts, 94–96; translation and hiddenness linked, 99–100, 103; translation practices, 90–93, 100, 107; vernacular theology, 90–92, 107
  Life of Saint Katherine, 12, 73–74, 82, 88–109. *See also* dream visions: *Life of Saint Katherine*
Caxton, William, 7, 112n8, 113, 151, 155, 158
Chaucer, Geoffrey, 85n42, 106, 163, 194; as authority figure, 154; begging poems, 55; in contemporary collections, 22, 28; dream poem, 179; as exemplar, 9, 14, 93, 136, 141; hagiographer, 107–8; praise of, 136–39, 141, 154–55; rhyme royal use, 93, 107–8, 151
  Canterbury Tales, 33: "Prioress's Tale," 151; Prologue to the "Summoner's Tale," 102n53; "Nun's Priest's Tale," 163n16
  House of Fame, 179
  "Lak of Stedfastnesse," 22
  Parliament of Fowls, 179
  Troilus and Criseyde, 151
Chaundler, Thomas, 40–64; chancellor, 43, 51, 61; life of, 41n4; letters, 11, 40–64; literary humanism, 44; modern criticism of, 44; scribal hands of, 42, 52–54
Chester cycle, 20, 34–35, 39
Christ. *See* Jesus
Christianity: doctrinal knowledge, 22, 74, 76–78, 83, 87; education, 69–87, 121–

22; intellectualized, 69, 77, 82; natural reason, 85–87; religious practices, 121–22. *See also* orthodoxy; preaching; teaching; typology
Cicero, 43–44, 56n60, 63, 137, 162
  De Inventione, Rhetorica ad Herennium, 63
  De Oratore, 63
codicology. *See* form: material; manuscripts: codicology
confession, 125, 167, 168
Counter Reformation, 147
Cromwell, Thomas, 158

Dante (Alighieri), 93
David (biblical poet-king), 118, 152, 175–76
De Beauvoir, Simone
  Les bouches inutiles, 159
Demosthenes, 56n60
Derrida, Jacques, 123n28, 124n29, 184
devotional works, 8, 10–12, 28n21; inclusion of images, 27–28, 36; for meditation, 25, 28; readers influence on, 113n11; reading of, 28; reformist, 11; sanctioned, 140; for women, 12. *See also* hagiography; Marian devotion
de Worde, Wynkyn
  Bowge of Courte, 180, 182–83
  Fifteen Oes reprint, 113
  Margarey Kempe's Book extract, 111, 125, 128
dialogue, 166, 174, 191–92; Bakhtin on, 113n11; literary form, 110–11. *See also* Jesus (Christ): dialogues with
drama, 7, 108; in Book of Brome, 19–39; typological reading, 37–38. *See also* performance
dream vision: *Bowge of Courte,* 180–96; Chaucer, 179; *Life of Saint Katherine,* 12, 92–3, 98–100; *Mary Magdalene,* 72; *Piers Plowman,* 97n38

Edward III, 63n84
Elizabeth of York, 112n8, 113
eloquence: female, 69–70, 72, 75–84, 92,
103; rhetorical, 105, 108, 136, 139; Tully (Cicero), 162
Erasmus, 57, 174, 176
Eucharist, 82, 106–7, 117–22, 163–64, 167–69. *See also* Jesus (Christ): body of
Eugene IV (Pope), 44, 52
Everyman, 7

Fifteen Oes, The, 7, 10, 12, 110–18, 128–29
Fifteen Signs of Doomsday, 22, 31
fifteenth century: dullness, 5, 40, 63, 108; English poetic development, 177; recuperation of, 5–6, 40, 89, 134, 160–61
Fish, Stanley, 152, 163, 187n17, 196n29
form, 1–15; literary, 5, 10, 14, 20–21, 51, 62, 90–91, 100, 108; material, 9–11, 20–21, 23n14, 31, 33, 38, 41–48, 50, 51, 94, 97–99, 107, 164; medieval conception of, 1–2, 4, 21n6, 109n72; poetic, 1–2, 7, 10, 12, 31, 33, 88–91, 93, 100, 105–8, 113, 142, 151–52, 161, 164, 179, 190; templates (formulary), 22–23, 49, 55n51, 63
formalism, 2–3, 4n12, 5, 20, 21n7, 22, 178
Foucault, Michel, 124n29, 184
Foxe, John
  Acts and Monuments, 147–48

Gascoigne, Thomas, 48n26, 165n19
Gillespie, Vincent, 90, 150–54, 175–76
Gilte Legende, 82
Glossa ordinaria, 151
goliardic verse, 161, 164
Gower, John, 85n42
  Carmen super multiplici viciorum pestilencia, 141n26
Greenblatt, Stephen, 133–34

hagiography: politics of, 11; reformist, 69n6; rubrication of, 31; mixing of genres, 108. *See also* Capgrave, John; Bokenham, Osbern; Book of Brome
Hawes, Stephen, 7, 88, 142

217

Henry V: English language advocacy, 139, 155n52; Lydgate, relations with, 140–42, 157
Henry VI, 6, 44
Henry VIII: conflict with church, 158; Skelton, relations with, 154–55, 158
Henryson, Robert
Moral Fables, 188
heresy: accusation of, 85, 140; anti-Marian, 134–35, 141, 143, 146–49; attacks on, 174; education as remedial, 69; juxtaposed with orthodoxy, 87, 89, 141, 164; literary consequences of, 158, 160–61; rebellion linked with, 141; vatic response to, 148–49, 154. *See also* Arthur, Thomas; Bilney Thomas; Lollardy; Lutherans; Pecock, Reginald; preaching: women; satire; Wycliffism
Hoccleve, Thomas: critical recuperation, 40, 88; begging poems, 55; self-reflection, 88
Regiment of Princes, 6n17
Humanism, 40–41, 43–44, 48, 64; defense of poetry, 154; description of, 40, 61–62; in England, 10–11, 40n28, 41–45, 53, 56–57, 59n71, 61–62; individual fame, 57; language, 59–60, 63; literature, 40–41; neo-Latin, 62; periodization, 59–60, 62; scribal hands, 43–54; in Skelton, 150; view on logic, 175
Humphrey, Duke of Gloucester; 42; contemporary praise of, 57; donations by, 49, 59; epistolary and petitionary correspondence, 42, 50n34, 55–56, 58, 61–62; proponent of humanism, 56, 58–59

idolatry: in *A Replycacion,* 146; in *Life of Saint Catherine,* 98
images: devotional, 27, 28, 36; performative, 28, 36
Imitation of Christ, The, 12, 110–11, 116–23, 128–29
Imola, Benvenuto da, 93
inscription. *See* authority: by inscription
Ipomedon (Hue de Rotelande), 7

Jacobus de Voraigine
Legenda Aurea, 11, 68, 71, 74, 76, 78–79, 81
Jerome: authority figure, 81, 165, 174; book-eating, 96, 107; concern for poetics, 152; Paulinus, letter to, 151–52; praise of King David, 175–76
Jesus (Christ), 78, 80, 137–40; birth of, 73, 137, 141, 147; body of, 107, 114, 117–19, 138, 148, 164; conception of, 137–51, 146 148; death of, 34, 36, 71, 113, 128; dialogues with, 116–23, 125, 127–29; harrowing of hell, 152; imitation of, 116–18, 120–22; as lover/husband, 101, 106, 120; passion of, 28, 34–37, 76, 112–16; resurrection of, 38, 70, 128; voice of, 9, 12, 110–29; wounds of, 114–16. *See also* "Seven Words" of Christ

Katherine of Alexandria. *See* Bokenham: *Katherine of Alexandria;* Capgrave: *Life of Saint Katherine*
Kempe, Margery, 78–81, 97, 169; as aural reader, 112n6; hearing the divine, 125–29; married chastity, 126; pilgrimage, 126
Book, 12, 108, 110–11, 123–29

laity: clerical relations with, 161, 167, 169; deeds, 168; infantilization of, 90, 95n27; piety, 96; poets, 158; readers, 9, 12, 69, 91–92, 122; religious instruction, 12, 85–87, 89; women, 69, 81
Langland, William: diminished ecclesiastical authority, 160; influence, 13–14; Langlandianism, 161, 166, 170
Piers Plowman, 14, 21n6, 31, 33, 38, 97n38, 170, 186, 193
Latimer, Hugh, 158
laureate. *See* Skelton, John: laureate
Lerer, Seth, 2n4, 6n17, 88, 136n12
letter-writing: Anglo-Latin petitions at Oxford, 40–64; humanist hybrid scripts in, 40–45, 49–53; rhetoric in,

54–63; vernacular, 64; vernacular verse, relation to, 64
Life of St. Margaret (in Book of Brome), 22, 31
Lollardy: anti-Lollardy texts, 13, 139–42; as heresy, 13; ill-defined, 167; influence on literature, 160–61, 167; mediation of saints rejected, 141, 148; religious vernacular, 92n16, 139–40; reputed practices, 80; eucharist, 164
Love, Nicholas, 90, 95n27
  Mirror of the Blessed Life of Jesus Christ, 140–41
Luther, Martin, 147
Lutherans, 147–48
Lydgate, John: aureation, 88, 105, 136, 142, 151–52, 154, 172; relation to Chaucer, 9, 154; begging poems, 55; contemporary praise of, 85n42; critical denigration of, 2n3, 5, 40; critical recuperation of, 5–6, 40; death, 85; defense of poetry, 1; eloquence, 108; hagiographer, 69, 86, 93n20, 107–8; heresy threat, 134; as historical boundary, 7, 13, 158; laureate, 154; manuscripts, 33; Mariology, 13, 134, 136, 148–51; poetic form, 1–4; poetic legacy, 142n28; religious order, 134; Skelton, relation to, 151–52, 155, 157–58; vernacular theologies, 134
  Churl and the Bird, 196n28
  A Defence of Holy Church, 140
  Fall of Princes, 1–2
  verse translation of *Fifteen Oes,* 113
  Life of Our Lady, 13, 134–42
  Pageant of Knowledge, 22, 28–29
  Troy Book, 106n62, 140.
  See also Mary (Virgin): as analogy for poet; Henry V
lyric poetry, 7, 22, 28, 129, 161

Malory, Thomas, 7; Winchester MS, 33
Mandeville, John
  Travels, 33
Mankind, 7, 173
manuscripts: annotation of, 38; codicolgy of, 10, 21–25, 29, 42, 45–48; paleography in, 42, 44–45, 48–54; rubrication of, 21, 25–39. *See also* images; scripts
Abbottsford, Abbotsford House, Walter Scott Collection, Abbotsford MS (Bokenham legendary), 10–11, 68–69, 78–87
Cambridge, Jesus College MS, 63, 63
Cambridge, Trinity College MS R.3.2 (Trinity Gower MS), 48
Cambridge, Trinity College MS R.14.5, 53n43
Cambridge University Library MS Dd.i.17 (*Piers Plowman*), 31n26, 33, 38n46
Dublin, Trinity College MS 432, 19n2
London, British Library, MS Additional 37049, 28n21
London, British Library, MS Arundel 327 (Bokenham legendary), 11, 67–78, 80, 85–87
London, British Library, MS Cotton Cleopatra C.iv (a letterbook of William Swan), 48n27
London, British Library, MS Cotton Tiberius B.VI, 63
London, British Library, MS Cotton Titus A.xxiv, 52n42
London, British Library, MS Harley 43 (Walton's English *Boethius*), 52n42, 53n42
New Haven, CT, Yale University, Beinecke Library MS 365 (Book of Brome), 19, *24, 26–27, 30, 32*
Oxford, Bodleian Library, MS Arch. Selden B. 23 (a letterbook of William Swan), 48
Oxford, Bodleian Library MS Ashmole 789, 63
Oxford, Bodleian Library MS Douce 302 (Audelay's anthology), 166
Oxford, Bodleian Library, MS Lat. theo.e.33, 48n26
Oxford, Bodleian Library MS Tanner 407 (Robert Reynes commonplace book), 28n21, 114–15n13
Oxford, Corpus Christi College, MS 201 (*Piers Plowman*), 31n26, 33
Oxford, Lincoln College MS Lat. 43

219

Index

(Cicero's *De Officiis*), 53n43
Oxford, Lincoln College MS Lat. 54, 48n26
Oxford, Lincoln College MS Lat. 84, 53n43
Oxford, New College MS 288, 51n36, 52n42, 53n43
Oxford, St. John's College MS 17, 48n26
Oxford University Archives, NEP/supra/Reg.Aa, 53n43
Oxford University Archives, NEP/supra/Reg F (Registrum F/*Episolae academicae Oxon*), 10–11, 40–45, *45*, 46–64
San Marino, Huntington Library MS HM 1 (Towneley Plays), 29n22
Marcella (Mary Magdalene's handmaiden), 79
Marian devotion, 13, 146. *See also* Lydgate, John: Mariology; Skelton, John: Marian devotion; heresy: anti-Marian
Martha. *See* Bokenham, Osbern
Mary Magdalene. *See* Bokenham, Osbern
Mary (the Virgin): birth of Christ, 137; conception of Christ, 137–38, 140; as analogy for poet, 137–39, 150–51, 154, 158, 176; grace, 138; mediator, 139, 141; orthodox positions on, 13, 140–43, 161; rejection of Marian agency, 141, 146–49
Medwall, Henry, 7
Melton, Robert, 21–23
More, Thomas, 53
    Dialogue Concerning Heresies, 174
    Letter to Dorp, 175
Mum and Sothsegger, 101–2, 186–87, 193

Netter, Thomas
    Doctrinale, 166
new formalism, 2–4
new historicism, 3n6, 4, 135
Nolan, Maura, 3, 4n11, 5, 6n17, 43

orality, 111, 123

Orchard of Syon, 97
Origen of Alexandria, 82–83
orthodoxy, 87, 164; broad-minded, 178; dissonant, 178; dissent to, 11, 89; ecclesiastical, 9; enforcers of, 147; hagiography as a defense of, 69; reforming, 10; vatic defender of, 148, 163, 177; vernacular reclaimation, 90. *See also* Lollardy
Ovid, 106
    Ars amatoria, 150n44
    Fasti, 150n44
Oxford, University of: fifteenth-century descriptions of, 54–56, 58–60, 61; history, 54–62; humanist letters, 40–66; intellectual currents, 10; translation debate, 55n52. *See also* manuscripts

Pearl, 36
Pearsall, Derek, 5, 108n67, 139–40, 134n6, 166n21
Pecock, Reginald, 7, 69, 85–87, 165
performance, 11, 21, 23, 25, 28–29, 31, 34, 38–39. *See also* reading
periodization, 8, 10, 14–15, 43–44, 59–60
Peter of Celle, 102
Peter (Saint), 72–73
petitionary genres, 10–11, letters, 41–43, 54–64; rhetoric in, 55, 61, 63; vernacular language, 63–64; verse, 11, 55, 137–38
Petrarch, Francesco, 53n44, 57, 137
Pierce the Plowman's Crede, 102n53
plain style. *See* Capgrave, John: literary form
Plato, 43, 58n70, 133
Poeta theologus. See Skelton, John: as poet priest
political verse, 7, 10, 14, 88, 108, 134, 142, 150n42, 157–58; satire, 182
prayer, 118, 120, 168; as dialogue, 112–16; by Mary, 72; miracles through, 77, 84; neglect of, 172; written, 110. *See also* Lollardy: mediation of saints rejected
preaching, 69, 85–86; female saints, 12, 69–73, 76–81, 84; heretical, 146; Pauline restriction against women, 70,

220

80–81. *See also* Pecock, Reginald
prophecy: anti-clerical, 167; biblical, 95; eating as prerequisite for, 95; of King David, 176; of vatic poets, 158; reformist poem, 171
pseudo-Bonaventura
Meditationes Vitae Christi, 140–41
Pynson, Richard, (printer) 13, 143, *144, 145,* 147, 152, *153, 155–56,* 158

Rastell, John, 7
Reader-response Criticism, 114n12, 184, 196n29
reading, 101: consolation through, 122–25; contemplative, 96; as imaginative performance, 123; as mode of production, 9; praelection, 12, 23, 25, 28–29, 31, 34, 39; practices, 21; performative, 28, 39; in private, 39; women, 112n6, 112n8. *See also* Capgrave, John; devotional works
reception, 105
reform: historical modes, 5–6, 160; poetic, 159–61; religious, 8, 10–11, 13, 48, 69, 89–91, 105, 107, 140–41, 159–61, 163, 166–67, 169–71, 178; satire, object of, 182, 190; vernacular, 55n52, 69, 90, 134, 140, 167
Reformation, 7–8, 13, 158, 174n42
Registrum F/*Epistolae academicae Oxon. See* manuscripts; Oxford University Archives, NEP/supra/Reg F
rhyme royal: alliterative verse combined with, 93, 100; aureate, 142, 151–52; Chaucerian and Lydgatian legacy, 93, 107, 108, 151–52; Englishness, 108; Skeltonics combined with, 176
rhetoric: masters of, 75, 136–37; texts in England, 63. *See also* Augustine; aureation; Capgrave, John; Cicero; eloquence; letter-writing; Lydgate; petitionary genres
Richard III (King), 6
Robin Hood cycles, 7
Rolle, Richard
Meditations on the Passion, 102
romance, 7, 108

satire; court, 182, 187–89, 196n29; reformist, 171; Skelton, attack on heresy using, 13, 142–43, 163; tradition of, 178; Tutivillus as metaphor for, 173. *See also* Skelton, John; Lollardy; anti-clerical satire; political verse; reform
scholasticism, 43–44, 61, 174
scripts. *See* Chaundler: scribal hands; letter-writing: humanist hybrid scripts; manuscript: paleography in
scripture. *See* Bible
Scotus, 58, 174
Seneca, 102, 104, 189
"Seven Words" of Christ, 113–16
Sever, Henry (Chancellor of Oxford), 44, 46, 50, 61
Shakespeare, William
Henry V, 102
Simpson, James: 5–6, 9–10, 13–14, 158n58, 160, 161n9, 162, 167, 180–96
Skelton, John, 7–10, 13–15, 88, 160–67; attack on heresy, 13, 134, 142–43, 147–49, 163, 174–75, 178; Audelay, relation to, 159–79; aureation, 142, 151–52, 172–73; banishment from court, 157; *bricolage,* 162; defense of poetry, 13, 135, 142, 149–55, 175–76; diminished ecclesiastical authority, 162–65, 177, dream poem, 193–94; Langland, relation to, 161, 170, 186; laureateship, 152, 154–55, 157, 175, 177; Lydgate, relation to, 13, 134–35, 142, 151–58; Marian devotion, 13, 134, 136–58; narrator-poet, 181–82, 187–89, 192–96; paratext, 143, 182–83; periodization of, 13; poet priest (*poeta theologus*), 13, 14, 152, 159–61, 176; poetic authority undermined, 189–96; polyvocality, 178, 191; reformism, 171, 182; satire, 14, 142–43, 146, 157, 162–63, 170–71, 182, 186–89, 192, 196n29; vatic, 142n29, 148–49, 171, 17
Agenst Garnesche, 161–62
Bowge of Courte, 9, 13–14, 162, 180–96
Collyn Clout, 154n48, 167, 172–73, 187, 192

221

Garlande or Chapelet of Laurell, 151, 154, 179
A Replycacion, 13–14, 133–37, 142–43, *144–45*, 145–52, *153*, 154–58
Speke Parott, 170–71, 173, 176, 192
Upon the Dolorous Dethe, 142
Ware the Hauke, 10, 162–166, 171, 174, 176–78
See also Skeltonic verse; rhyme royal; Henry VIII; Wolsey (Cardinal)
Skeltonic verse, 135, 154, 162, 164–65, 175–76, 179
Smith, D. Vance, 3–4, 21n6, 109n72
Spenser, Edmund, 179
Swan, William (papal secretary): letter-book, 48–49. *See also* manuscripts: Oxford, Bodleian Library, Arch. Selden B. 23

teaching: Christian 69, 84, 87, 102, 122; humanists, 61; women, 12, 76–77
Towneley Plays, 29n22
translation, 68, 90–93, 151–52; connection to discovery, 99–101, 103; as degradation, 173; of learning, 58–59; reformist, 91; vernacular, 68, 90, 110, 112–13, 141, 151–52, 173. *See also*
Oxford University: translation debate; Capgrave, John: translation practices
Tully. *See* Cicero
Tutivillus, 162, 172–74
typological interpretation, 10, 35, 39; of Abraham and Isaac, 35–39

vates, vatic poet; Mary as, 139n18. *See also* Skelton, John: vatic

Watson, Nicholas, 55n52, 91n13, 93, 95n27, 100nn47–49, 123–24n29
Weiss, Roberto, 40–44, 51n38, 54–55, 62
Wolfson, Susan, 3, 9, 21n7
Wolsey, Thomas (Cardinal), 155, 157–58, 174
Woolf, Rosemary, 25n19, 34, 36
Worcester, William, 7
Wyatt, Thomas
  "*Stand whoso list, upon the slipper toppe*," 189
Wycliffism. *See* Lollardy

Ymaginatif (in *Piers Plowman*), 159–61

www.ingramcontent.com/pod-product-compliance
Lightning Source LLC
Chambersburg PA
CBHW020946230426
43666CB00005B/190